KILLING
HITLER

Also by Roger Moorhouse

Microcosm:

Portrait of a Central European City

KILLING HITLER

The Plots, the Assassins, and the Dictator Who Cheated Death

Roger Moorhouse

Bantam Books

KILLING HITLER
A Bantam Book / April 2006

Published by Bantam Dell
A Division of Random House, Inc.
New York, New York

Library of Congress Cataloging-in-Publication Data
Moorhouse, Roger.
Killing Hitler / Roger Moorhouse.
p.   cm.
ISBN-10: 0-553-80369-7
ISBN-13: 978-0-553-80369-3
1. Hitler, Adolf, 1889–1945—Assassination attempts. 2. Germany—History—
1933–1945. 3. Assassins—Germany—History—20th century. 4. Anti-Nazi
movement—Germany—History. 5. Opposition (Political science)—Germany.
6. World War, 1939–1945—Underground movements—Germany.

DD256.35.M66 2006   2005053653
943.086 22

Printed in the United States of America
Published simultaneously in Canada

www.bantamdell.com

10   9   8   7   6   5   4   3   2   1
BVG

For
Melissa,
without whom . . .

Acknowledgments

Writing is a strangely solitary existence. Yet any writer would concede that though the words on the page may be his, numerous personal debts are accrued in their preparation.

A number of individuals deserve special mention, therefore. At the research stage, Kate Gilbert provided great assistance. Krzysztof Bożejewicz handled all Polish-language research, in both the UK and Poland, aided by Andrzej Koroński. In Germany, Angelica von Hase and Peter Steinkamp gave vital archival support, as did Dr. Luba Vinogradova in Russia. In addition, a number of specialists read and commented on chapters of draft text. These include Antony Beevor, Professor M. R. D. Foot, Dr. Ted Harrison, Gitta Sereny, and Dr. Jacek Tebinka. Others who provided assistance, responded to queries, and are otherwise deserving of mention include Dr. Andreas von Breitenbuch, Dr. Bogdan Chrzanowski, Ewa Huggins, Ute Krebs, David List,

Eugenia Maresch, Dr. Iwona Sakowicz, Roy Seaton, Dr. Andrzej Suchcitz, Dr. Hilary Willard, and Dr. Wanda Wyporska.

A number of institutions should also be mentioned, including the British Library Newspaper Archive, the Gedenkstätte Deutscher Widerstand, the Bundesarchiv in Berlin, the Bundesarchiv (Militärarchiv) in Freiburg, the German Historical Institute in London, the Imperial War Museum Archive, the Polish Underground Movement Study Trust, and the Wiener Library.

Particular praise is reserved for the British Library and the National Archives in London. Having worked for many years as a researcher, I have extensive experience of working in archives and libraries across Europe and have come to the conclusion that these two institutions are without equal. There are, regrettably, few areas in which Britain can still claim to be world-class, but the British Library and the National Archives set a new benchmark in their efficiency, the competence and expertise of their staff, and the excellence of their working environment.

Three special debts must be acknowledged. Will Sulkin and Jörg Hensgen of Jonathan Cape were unflagging in their enthusiasm for the project, and my agent, Peter Robinson, was consistently supportive and negotiated the publishing deal that made it all possible. I would also like to thank Professor Norman Davies, who inspired me to embark on this path in the first place.

Lastly, I would like to thank my wife, Melissa. Hitler has been a part of our lives—the mustachioed elephant in our living room—for a long time now, and by way of apology for this intrusion, I feel it appropriate that I dedicate this book to her.

Contents

Introduction

I might be killed by a criminal, or by an idiot, at any time.
—*Adolf Hitler*

A SSASSINATION, IT WAS ONCE SAID, "HAS NEVER CHANGED the history of the world."[1] This benign sentiment, often repeated in times of crisis, is wishful nonsense, however. In response, one might point most obviously to the killing of Archduke Franz Ferdinand in Sarajevo, which unleashed the First World War, or to the murder of Sergei Kirov in 1934, which sparked the murderous purges in Stalin's Soviet Union. Assassination clearly has the capacity to affect world events.

More recently, the question of the utility of assassination as a political weapon has been subjected to closer examination. An analysis of eighteen famous assassinations through the ages concluded that not one of them achieved their wider political aims.[2] Indeed, in many cases, the results were the exact opposite of those intended. The murder of President Lincoln in 1865, for example, by a southern sympathizer proved disastrous for the

American South, while the assassination of Lord Cavendish by Irish nationalists in 1882 set the cause of Irish independence back by a generation. Assassinations, therefore, have certainly changed history; they have just never changed it in the way foreseen by the assassin.

Yet the possibility that Hitler could have been assassinated is one that has tantalized historians and fiction writers alike. It is tempting to speculate not only on the number of lives that could have been saved, the conflict that might have been avoided, and the suffering that perhaps would have been spared, but also on how differently European, and especially German, history might have played out in the twentieth century had Hitler been successfully felled by an assassin's bullet. Surely here, if nowhere else, is a case where an assassination might actually have brought the benefits intended by the assassin.

The majority of modern readers would probably agree, instinctively at least, with that statement. But it is interesting to note that unanimity on this issue was much harder to find during Hitler's lifetime. Then, discussions raged over the propriety of "playing God," the setting of dangerous precedents, the thorny concepts of "principled treachery" and "state-sanctioned terrorism," and the question of what further horrors might have followed Hitler's premature demise. Surprisingly, perhaps, the proposal to assassinate Hitler was never anything less than highly controversial.

Yet, for all these concerns, Hitler's would-be assassins were not dissuaded. Few leaders, of any century, can have been the target of so many assassination attempts: no fewer than forty-two separate plots on Hitler's life have been identified by German historians, and even that list is far from complete.[3] Of these, around twenty can be considered serious enough to warrant the attention given to them here.

Hitler was probably the most influential individual of the twentieth century. His name has become synonymous with brutality, intolerance, and racial hatred. His face, perhaps the most instantly recognizable and iconic image of the modern era, is one that few—even those blessed with living in peaceful times—will ever forget. Yet what of his would-be assassins?

In some cases, the assassin and his victim are bound together in perpetuity by their moment of shared history. Thus John F. Kennedy has his Lee Harvey Oswald, Abraham Lincoln has his John Wilkes Booth, and Franz Ferdinand has his Gavrilo Princip. The assassins of history are sometimes lauded as heroes and are often vilified as the most bestial of criminals, but they are rarely forgotten.

Yet Hitler's would-be assassins are, for the most part, unknown. Of them, only the name Claus von Stauffenberg might expect to register any reaction from the reading public. For all of them, of course, their greatest failing was that they were unable to carry out their allotted task—that of ridding the world of Adolf Hitler—but they nonetheless deserve greater recognition. They deserve better than to exist only in the footnotes of history, better than the obscurity to which they have been condemned by time and fashion, and in many cases by their Nazi executioners.

Hitler's assassins ranged from simple craftsmen to high-ranking soldiers, from the apolitical to the ideologically obsessed, and from enemy agents to his closest associates. Inexplicably, few of these men are known beyond the narrow confines of academic history. Their deeds would elicit scarcely a flicker of recognition from the general reader. This is their story. It is the story of their plans, their motives, and—inevitably—their failures. But it is also an account of the remarkable survival of a tyrant.

Prologue

Munich, Thursday, 8 November 1923, 8:30 p.m.

Few of the guests would have noticed the sallow-faced young man who entered the beer hall that evening. All of the great and the good of Munich were there: bankers, businessmen, newspaper editors, and politicians. They had gathered to hear an address commemorating the fifth anniversary of the November Revolution, given by the newly appointed state commissioner for Bavaria. They had expected a forceful denunciation of Marxism, an explanation of the administration's policies, perhaps even the advocacy of a restoration of the Bavarian monarchy. What they got was an attempted revolution.

The hall, the Bürgerbräukeller, was one of the largest in Munich. Located on the east side of the river Isar, which bisected the city, it was a cavernous room that belied the cozy image of the traditional beer hall. With a high ceiling, ornate chandeliers, and a wide balcony running down one side, it could accommodate around three thousand people seated on either side of long wooden trestle tables. As such, it was one of the primary venues in Munich for public lectures and political meetings. This evening, it was packed to the rafters. The doors had been closed already at 7:15 p.m. to prevent overcrowding, and the disappointed milled in the drizzle on the street outside.

The man loitering at the rear of the hall would have been known to many of the guests present that night. A pale individual in his mid-thirties, with sharp cheekbones, a toothbrush mustache, and striking blue eyes, Adolf Hitler was the leader of a local extreme nationalist group that called itself the National Socialist German Workers Party—or Nazis for short. He was renowned as a talented and inspirational public speaker, captivating his audiences with his impassioned and intemperate lectures on German politics. He had already spoken at the Bürgerbräukeller numerous times. This evening, however, he had come as an unlikely revolutionary. Dressed in a poorly cut black morning suit with flowing tails, his hair slicked close to his scalp and falling in unruly strands across his forehead, he looked more like an overworked waiter or an undertaker.

Nonetheless, about half an hour into the keynote speech, he began to make his way forward at the head of a phalanx of fellow putschists. As a detachment of Nazi storm troopers appeared, dragging a machine gun into the hall entrance, the distinguished speaker on the podium tailed off into silence. Whispers spread around the cavernous hall, drinkers craned their necks to see what was going on, women fainted, and tables were upended. In the commotion, Hitler clambered onto a chair, fired a pistol shot into the ceiling, and called for silence. "The National Revolution," he announced, "has begun."[1]

After a brief speech, he posted his troops and bodyguards at the exits and persuaded three of the honored guests present—who, between them, effectively ruled Munich—to retire with him to an adjoining room. There, in wild excitement, Hitler harangued his captive audience, announcing the formation of a new government with himself at its head, and promising ministerial posts for those present if they agreed to cooperate. Waving his gun, he warned melodramatically: "I have four shots in my pistol. Three for my collaborators if they abandon me. The last is for myself." With that, he put the gun to his temple, declaring: "If I am not victorious by tomorrow afternoon, I shall be a dead man."[2]

Germany in 1923 had endured five years of chaos. Emerging from defeat in the maelstrom of World War One, its fledgling democracy was assailed from both left and right, and undermined by a disintegrating economy. Political radicalism was fueled by a spiral of debilitating hyperinflation. By 1920, the price index stood at nearly 15 times its value in 1913; two years later it was approaching 350. 1923 was to be a crisis year. In the west, the French occupied the Ruhr in response to the German nonpayment of reparations, sparking passive resistance, strikes, and hunger riots. Elsewhere, disgruntled army units mutinied at Küstrin, east of Berlin, and in the subsequent months, pro-communist governments were established in Saxony and Thuringia. For a time, the instability appeared to be terminal, and all the while, the economy was heading into free fall. Prices in January 1923 were more than 2,500 times higher than they had been in 1913. By December they were 1.25 billion times higher.[3] The hyperinflation had become a full-scale currency collapse. The humble loaf of bread could cost over 400 billion marks, and many households found it more economical to burn money than attempt to use it to buy kindling or coal. Most Germans faced financial ruin.

The situation in Bavaria was no less fraught. There, the upheaval of the previous few years had awakened thoughts of separatism. The regional government in Munich was already plowing its own furrow, ignoring Berlin's strictures when it chose to and tolerating the radical right. Indeed, the two power bases in the province, the monarchist "old right" of the government and the revolutionary "new right" of Hitler and his allies, existed in a curiously symbiotic relationship. Both held the government in Berlin in contempt and were keen to cooperate in their intrigues against it. Both, too, were impatient to raise the standard of revolt. However, their visions of the would-be revolution differed widely. Put simply, the "old right" wanted to create an independent Bavarian government, while the "new right" wanted to replace the Reich government. One wanted to defect from Berlin, and the other wanted to march on it.

In the Bürgerbräukeller that evening, Hitler appeared finally to have succeeded in persuading Munich's ruling triumvirate to join in *his* vision of a revolution. About an hour after he had entered the hall, he returned to the podium, accompanied by his new confederates and the freshly arrived former army quartermaster, General Ludendorff. All five shook hands repeatedly and made short speeches to the assembled throng, announcing their new roles and their earnest intentions to cooperate. As they finished, the crowd, enthused by what they had heard, broke into an impromptu rendition of *"Deutschland über Alles."* One eyewitness recalled that the crowd had been "turned inside-out" by Hitler's words and that "it had almost something of hocus-pocus about it."[4] Ominously, Rudolf Hess, Hitler's secretary, then began calling names from a list of those present who were to be detained for interrogation and trial. With that, the remainder of the audience was allowed to leave, while sympathizers began arriving from around the city. Hitler, it appeared, had succeeded.

Beyond the confines of the beer hall, however, the putsch was proceeding less well. Troops loyal to Hitler had scored some early victories. They had been bolstered by the defection of the cadets of the Infantry School and had succeeded in occupying the three main beer halls in Munich. Elsewhere, they had taken over the Bavarian War Ministry and the offices of the influential *Münchener Post* newspaper. But as the night progressed, they achieved no more significant successes. Their own incompetence and the stiffened resolve of their opponents combined to prevent them from seizing other key buildings and barracks.

Moreover, the authorities in Munich were preparing for a fight. The members of the ruling triumvirate, far from serving the putsch, had now repudiated it and were directing the resistance. The government, transferred to Regensburg for its own safety,

had banned the morning newspapers and drafted in military reinforcements from the provinces. Across the city, its forces were
now fully apprised of events and had specific orders on how the
revolt was to be countered. As the would-be revolutionaries in
the beer hall settled down for a long night, succored by a generous supply of beer and bread rolls, they were still optimistic. In
truth, they had already lost the initiative and now faced a precarious stalemate.

The following day, as a cold dawn broke, the putschists finally
recognized that their initial attempt to storm the bastions of
power had failed. A British correspondent from the *Times* found
his way to the Bürgerbräukeller that morning, where he discovered Ludendorff and Hitler in a small upstairs room. Hitler, he
wrote, was "dead-tired" and barely seemed to fill the part of the
revolutionary: "this little man in an old waterproof coat with a revolver at his hip, unshaven and with disordered hair, and so
hoarse that he could scarcely speak." Ludendorff, in turn, was
"anxious and preoccupied."[5]

The putschists were considering their options. One suggested
that the Bavarian crown prince could be induced to lend the revolt his support. Another proposed a tactical withdrawal to continue their resistance from the town of Rosenheim near the
Austrian border. In the confusion, meanwhile, orders were delayed, and further troops drifted away from their positions, considering their cause to be lost. By midmorning, however, the idea
of a demonstration march through the city was mooted. That
way, the putschists besieged at the War Ministry could be relieved
and the enthusiasm of the local population could be harnessed.
The stalemate could be broken. After all, it was thought, the
army would surely not turn its machine guns on Ludendorff, one
of the most prominent generals of the First World War. The hotheads even considered that a march on Berlin could be attempted, in imitation of Mussolini. "We would go into the city,"
Hitler later recalled, "to win the people to our side."[6]

Shortly before noon that morning, a column of around two
thousand men, armed and defiant, stepped out of the Bürgerbräukeller and headed for the center of the city. In the front rank,

beneath the swastika banner and the flag of imperial Germany, Hitler marched with Ludendorff on one side and his fellow conspirator Erwin von Scheubner-Richter on the other. Alongside them were Hitler's bodyguard, Ulrich Graf, a bull-necked apprentice butcher and amateur wrestler; the Nazi "philosopher" Gottfried Feder; and the leader of the storm troopers, Hermann Göring, resplendent in a full-length leather coat, with his *Pour le Mérite*—Germany's highest military award—visible at his throat. Behind them, the ranks of Hitler's security force, the Munich storm troopers and the paramilitary *Bund Oberland* marched four abreast, followed by a car bristling with weaponry. Bringing up the rear was a ragtag collection of students, tradesmen, and fellow travelers, many inspired by the events of the previous night, many long-term disciples. Some marched smartly in uniform, some donned their medals from the Great War, and others shuffled along wearing work overalls.

Jeered and cheered by a curious Munich public, the putschists moved steadily on, sustaining themselves by singing nationalist songs. Close to the river, they encountered their first serious obstacle when they confronted a police cordon on the Ludwigsbrücke. With bayonets leveled and exhortations to the policemen not to fire on their comrades, they swept the picket aside and continued unhindered across the bridge and into the heart of Munich. Proceeding through the Isartor, they came to the Marienplatz, where large crowds had gathered to watch events unfold. From there, they turned north in the direction of the Odeonsplatz, beyond which the War Ministry was located. As they approached the Feldherrnhalle, however, barely fifty meters from their target, they were confronted by a second, larger police presence. Linking arms, they advanced, some singing, some with bayonets at the ready, down the Residenzstrasse.

This time, the police would not be brushed aside. As the two forces met, a shot rang out and the police opened fire. In the chaos, as a brief firefight ensued, the front rank of putschists fell to the ground, while the remainder fled. After a couple of minutes, only the dead and wounded remained. Göring had been shot in the groin. Scheubner-Richter, to Hitler's left, fell mortally wounded with a bullet in the chest. Graf, who had shielded Hitler from the onslaught, took numerous bullets and was gravely injured. Four Munich policemen had been killed as well as a further thirteen of Hitler's followers. The youngest of them, Karl Laforce, was barely nineteen.

Hitler, meanwhile, had fallen in the melee, believing himself to have been shot. In fact, though wild rumors quickly circulated that he had been killed, he had merely suffered a dislocated shoulder from being violently pulled to the ground by the dying Scheubner-Richter.[7] In the aftermath, he struggled to his feet and found his way to a nearby square, where supporters spirited him to a waiting car and south toward Austria. Later that day, after an eventful escape from Munich, he arrived at the house of his fellow putschist Ernst "Putzi" Hanfstaengl, in Uffing, where he was tended by a sympathetic doctor. Two days later, in the early evening of 11 November, the police finally tracked him down. According to one account, Hitler broke down when he heard of the police's arrival. With a cry of "Now all is lost!" he reached for his pistol.[8] Yet, rather than turn the gun on himself, as he had promised to do at the Bürgerbräukeller, Hitler submitted meekly. The arresting officer found him in a bedroom, dressed in pajamas, waiting calmly in sullen silence.[9]

Hitler had escaped death but had nonetheless failed. His "National Revolution" had been crushed, his party outlawed, and his loyal henchmen killed, arrested, or in exile. Tried for high treason the following spring, he was sentenced to five years' detention in the fortress at Landsberg. Contemporary opinion concluded that the name of Adolf Hitler had been a footnote in history, a chimera, soon to rank alongside countless other crackpots, radicals, and failed revolutionaries. He was haughtily dismissed by the *Times* as a "house decorator and demagogue."[10] Many took to speaking of him only in the past tense. The author Stefan Zweig, for example, considered that Hitler had fallen back "into oblivion."[11]

Hitler himself was immune to such prophecies, for he considered himself to be subject to another, higher calling. "You may pronounce us guilty a thousand times over," he railed to the state prosecutor at his trial, "but the goddess of the eternal court of history will smile and tear to tatters...the sentence of this court."[12] The bullets of the Bavarian police that had routed his forces in Munich had also given him his first brush with providence. He emerged from that experience, and from his imprisonment at Landsberg, with the unshakable belief that his life had been preserved so that he might fulfill a "historic destiny" to save Germany. He emerged as a man with a mission.

CHAPTER 1

Maurice Bavaud:
God's Assassin

One day a completely harmless man will establish himself in an attic flat along the Wilhelmstrasse. He will be taken for a retired schoolmaster. A solid citizen, with horn-rimmed spectacles, poorly shaven, bearded. He will not allow anyone into his modest room. Here he will install a gun, quietly and without undue haste, and with uncanny patience he will aim it at the Reich Chancellery balcony, hour after hour, day after day. And then, one day, he will fire.

—ADOLF HITLER[1]

SHORTLY BEFORE NOON ON THE WINTRY MORNING OF 30 JAN-uary 1933, the leader of the Nazi Party, Adolf Hitler, was ushered into a meeting with the German president, Field Marshal Paul von Hindenburg. Accompanied by the members of his new cabinet, he was received frostily by the president, who was irritated at being kept waiting and was dubious about Hitler's appointment. Hindenburg grunted a perfunctory welcome and expressed his pleasure that the nationalist right had finally overcome its differences. He then proceeded to the matter in hand: Hitler was to be sworn in as chancellor of the German Republic.

Dressed in a sober dark suit and tie, Hitler solemnly swore to uphold the constitution, to carry out his obligations without party bias, and to serve for the good of the entire German nation. In a short, unscheduled speech, he then promised to defend the rights of the president and to return to parliamentary rule after the next election. Hindenburg was less than loquacious in response: "And now, gentlemen," he intoned, "forward with God."[2]

That afternoon, the new cabinet sat for the German press in the Reich Chancellery. Hitler, seated in a generously upholstered chair, was surrounded by his new cabinet colleagues, with Göring seated to his right and von Papen, the kingmaker and vice chancellor, to his left. The remainder stood behind the trio, looking distinctly uncomfortable. Little of the expected camaraderie was on show. Though they knew one another well, few of them made eye contact. Ministers stared sternly ahead or off to either side. Only Hitler allowed himself a broad smile. In his first public proclamation as chancellor, he congratulated his followers on their "great political triumph."[3]

In truth, Hitler's ascent to power was less glorious than his propagandists would later proclaim. Though the head of the party with the largest share of the popular vote, he was not appointed as a result of due democratic process. Rather, he was levered into power by the political élites in a grubby backstairs intrigue. Power had not been seized; it had been handed to Hitler like a poisoned chalice. Hitler, it was thought, would swiftly embarrass himself and discredit his movement. And if by some miracle, he did not, he would lend the establishment his popularity in the country, while they, in turn, would endeavor to control him and rein in his wilder ambitions.

To this end, Hitler was appointed the head of a government containing only a minority of Nazis. Of eleven posts, just three were held by his men: the chancellorship, the Ministry of the Interior, and a ministry without portfolio. Beyond these, all the most important government positions had gone to the conservatives, thereby strengthening their belief that they could, between them, hold the rabble-rouser Hitler in check. Despite these restraints on Hitler's freedom of action, his appointment was still deeply unpopular among his new colleagues, and a number of additional concessions had been wrung out of him. For one thing, he had sworn to leave the cabinet unaltered regardless of the result of the elections he planned to hold. For another, he had made an empty promise to broaden the basis of his new government by approaching the centrist parties. It looked very much as though the conservative ruse had succeeded. Hitler appeared to have been laced into a political straitjacket. He would serve, it was hoped, as a popular figurehead but wield little in the way of genuine power.

For all these caveats, Hitler's victory was nonetheless substantial. The former corporal, beer-hall agitator, and self-confessed "drummer" for the nationalist cause had reached the pinnacle of political power. His followers, quite naturally, celebrated the success. Coordinated by Goebbels, the *Sturmabteilung* and *Schutzstaffel* of the capital congregated at the *Tiergarten* in preparation for an impromptu victory parade. Armed with torches, they set off in the evening gloom at 7 p.m., heading for the government quarter. Marching sixteen abreast to the thunderous acclaim of drums and military bands, they passed beneath the Brandenburg Gate and on into the Wilhelmstrasse, where they stopped to salute the aged president. Proceeding to Hitler's new residence at the Reich Chancellery, they broke into a chorus of *"Sieg heil"* as they were greeted by the new chancellor from a first-floor window. Goebbels confided to his diary that it was "just like a fairy-tale."[4]

Hitler's newly exalted status brought with it new requirements for his security regime. For one thing, his appointment was a profound shock to all those who had considered him and his movement to be a passing phase, or even faintly ridiculous. It caused his opponents, passive and active alike, to sit up and take notice of him, and to consider what action might be taken in response. Hitler's moment of triumph was arguably his moment of greatest vulnerability.

As chancellor, Hitler became heir to a surprisingly violent tradition of assassination plots. The famous nineteenth-century chancellor Otto von Bismarck had escaped two such attempts, and the volatile years after World War One had seen a spate of political murders, culminating in the assassination of the foreign minister, Walther Rathenau, in Berlin in the summer of 1922.

In the aftermath of that attack, security for the chancellor and his ministers was placed on an entirely new footing. Whereas previously, leading politicians would have been subject to only the most cursory of security measures—consisting of no more than a driver, an assistant, and perhaps a few policemen—they were now to be guarded much more closely. Barely five days after Rathenau's murder, new measures were being suggested and implemented. A second escort car was to accompany the chancellor, for example, while security at the Reich Chancellery was thoroughly reorganized. All those who sent threatening or defamatory letters to ministers could expect to be investigated by the police. Any threats made were to be taken very seriously.[5]

Thanks to these measures, a number of plots were discovered in the years prior to Hitler's appointment. In the winter of 1922, for example, a Dresden merchant called Willi Schulze was found in possession of two pistols, with which, he confessed, he intended to murder Chancellor Wirth. Some years later, in 1931, a crude explosive device addressed to Chancellor Brüning was intercepted by security staff. The following year, a female assailant was caught inside the Chancellery building armed with a 28-centimeter dagger. In spite of the improved security regime, she had succeeded in gaining entry through a side door and had reached the second floor of the building before being apprehended.[6] The revised security apparatus clearly functioned. But with Hitler's appointment as chancellor in 1933, it was to face its toughest challenge.

For one so steeped in violence, it is perhaps no surprise that Hitler had a heightened sense of his own vulnerability to attack. Right from the outset of his political career, Hitler realized that he needed a bodyguard, a unit of unquestioned loyalty, a group of "men who would . . . even march against their own brothers."[7] To this end, he employed a small coterie of toughs to serve as drivers, guards, and general factotums. This group was formed into the *Saalschutz* (Assembly-hall Protection) in 1920, which expanded to become the *Sturmabteilung* (SA, or "Storm Detachment") the following year. Yet while the SA was responsible for security in the broadest sense of the term, the more finessed requirements of Hitler's personal safety were still handled by a small group of trusted men. These included the former wrestler Ulrich Graf, who served as Hitler's bodyguard; Emil Maurice, a former watchmaker and *Freikorps* veteran, who was his driver; Christian Weber, a horse dealer and part-time pimp, who was his secretary; his valet, Julius Schaub; and his adjutant, Wilhelm Brückner. Between them, these men were initially responsible for Hitler's safety at public events and speaking engagements. They formed the Führer's innermost circle.

In the crisis year of 1923, it was decided to reorganize Hitler's security. An élite guard was established, the *Stabswache* (Staff Guard), which was recruited from the ranks of the SA and was sworn to protect Hitler from both internal and external threats. When the *Stabswache* fell victim to internal SA squabbling, however, a new bodyguard was formed. The *Stosstrupp* (Assault Squad) numbered about a hundred individuals, but its core was still made up of Hitler's old, informal bodyguards. Graf, Maurice, Weber, Brückner, and Schaub were all members. They would receive their baptism of fire in the Munich Putsch of November that year, when five of their number would be killed.[8]

In 1925, following Hitler's early release from prison, the Nazi Party and SA were refounded. The bodyguard was revived, too. It was initially given its original title of *Stabswache* but was then renamed the *Schutzstaffel,* the SS or "Protection Squad." In contrast to the deliberate proletarianism of the SA, the SS was to be unashamedly elitist. Originally numbering only eight men, it grew slowly, as each party cell was obliged to provide an SS unit of no more than ten men to provide for security. By the late 1920s it numbered only around 280, in stark contrast to the 60,000-strong SA. SS applicants were strictly vetted and discipline was tight. Only "the best and most reliable Party members" would be considered.[9] They were to be efficient, resourceful, trustworthy, and above all "blindly devoted" to Adolf Hitler.[10] They would not participate in political discussions but would attend meetings intended for political instruction. They would not smoke at party events, and would not leave the room until commanded to do so. Their motto was *"Meine Ehre heisst Treue,"* my honor is loyalty.

The SS would remain a relatively small, even insignificant organization until the advent of Heinrich Himmler. In January 1928, Himmler assumed responsibility for the everyday running of the SS; a year later he became its leader, the *Reichsführer-SS*. Under his stewardship, the SS was expanded, its discipline was tightened even further, and its unquestioning loyalty to Hitler was trumpeted once again. Himmler wanted to inculcate into the SS the same extreme ethos that he claimed of himself: "If Hitler were to say I should shoot my mother," he once boasted, "I would do it and be proud of his confidence."[11]

Thankfully, most of the tasks set for the SS were much more mundane, consisting of guarding the "Brown House," the Nazi Party headquarters in Munich, and providing routine security. One veteran of the period described the unit's remit:

> The SS...was still a very small group, sifted from the SA with the purpose of protecting the party, especially the party leadership, in public....I was at several of the larger rallies in Hamburg. It was our job to shield the podium, accompany the speakers to and from their cars, guard their hotel and so on...things would often get pretty lively.[12]

In stark contrast to the growing confidence of the SS, the SA was entering a period of crisis. By the late 1920s, the "brown ranks" of the SA had marched and fought, and had propelled the Nazi Party into the front rank of German politics. But Hitler, who was now increasingly playing the respectable bourgeois politician, had become faintly embarrassed by his mob. The vanguard of his revolution, he believed, had become a "dubious mass"—politically unreliable and totally unpredictable. Moreover, given that the SA contained a majority of unemployed members in many districts—some units could not even raise enough money for the requisite swastikas—he feared that it was becoming far too interested in the socialist element of National Socialism. The party leadership, meanwhile, with its expensive cars and plush apartments, was widely seen by the SA as betraying its proletarian power base.[13] The crunch came in 1931, when much of the SA was drawn into a revolt under their deputy leader, Walther Stennes. Though they were soon brought back into the fold, the event sounded the movement's death knell. Tellingly, the SS had remained scrupulously loyal to Hitler throughout.

Thereafter, as the SA waned, the SS was ideally placed to take over sole responsibility for Hitler's security, and accordingly, Hitler's new personal bodyguard would be drawn exclusively from its ranks. Its first commander, Sepp Dietrich, was a blunt Bavarian, a veteran of the *Freikorps* and the Munich Putsch, who would become one of the most decorated SS generals of the Second World War. Dietrich, who had joined the SS in 1928, rose quickly within the Munich cadre and within a year was a part of Hitler's inner circle and one of his unofficial bodyguards. As the political temperature rose in Germany, however, and the violence reached unprecedented levels, it soon became necessary to put Hitler's security on a more formal footing. In February 1932, Dietrich was requested to organize a permanent protection unit for the Führer. The result was the *SS-Begleit-Kommando "Der Führer"* (SS Escort Detachment). A contemporary described its men in vivid terms as

> fine, athletic German types. They had zipped motor-car overalls over their black coated uniforms...and wore close-fitting aviators' helmets. Armed with revolvers and sjamboks [hippopotamus whips]...they looked like men from Mars.[14]

Another eyewitness was less flattering, describing the Führer's bodyguards as "strangely delicate...almost effeminate." Though he went on to wonder whether they might have been selected by the senior Nazi and notorious homosexual Ernst Röhm, he did at least concede, after spending an evening in their company, that "they were tough all right."[15]

Initially numbering only twelve men under the command of
Dietrich, the bodyguard detachment was to accompany Hitler on
the turbulent election campaigns of that year. An account by a
British journalist described their modus operandi. In the spring
of 1932, Hitler was campaigning in the East Prussian town of El-
bing when his entourage was ambushed by communist protes-
tors. As his driver swerved to avoid the mob,

> Hitler's leathercoated bodyguards had already leaped out
> of their car and were lashing out...with rubber trun-
> cheons and black jacks. Stones started to fly and pistol
> shots rang out. Then the...men were back in their cars
> and on we went.[16]

When he was resident in Munich, Hitler's security measures were
more formal. His residence there, from 1931, was the so-called
Brown House, an elegant three-story palace that had once served
as the residence of the Italian emissary to the Bavarian royal
court. The guard detail consisted of three shifts, each of seven-
teen men, drawn from the SS. Of these, at least ten were stationed inside the building, while a further six guarded the
entrance, the grounds, and the perimeter. Access to the building
was permitted only upon production of a valid pass.[17]

It is, however, doubtful that the security in Munich was particularly effective. For one thing, prior to 1933, the guards on
duty were forbidden to carry weapons. In addition, it does not
appear that the measures instituted were always strictly followed.
One British visitor to the Brown House, for example, recalled
being barked at by the sentries not to walk on the pavement outside the building, but made no mention of encountering any security procedures once inside.[18] The security methods employed
by Hitler in 1932 were, in truth, much as they had been in 1923.
He had a dedicated and fiercely loyal bodyguard at his disposal,
but its efficacy was open to serious doubt.

Part of the problem facing anyone attempting to create a
credible security regime for Hitler was Hitler himself. The
Führer's attitude to his own security was shot through with con-

tradictions and inconsistencies. On one hand, he was almost obsessed with his own mortality. He viewed himself as the "man of destiny," the man to lead Germany out of slavery. Yet his fragile constitution caused him to believe that his time was short. Hitler, in truth, was not a well man. It has long been conjectured that he may have suffered the effects of syphilis.[19] But in addition to that phantom, he clearly felt the very real strains of political life. By 1936, he was complaining of a whole catalogue of ailments, including tinnitus, migraines, insomnia, eczema, stomach cramps, flatulence, and bleeding gums.[20] To this list one might add acute hypochondria. Hitler's concern for his own health peaked in May 1935, when he convinced himself that a polyp removed from his larynx would prove cancerous. From that point, he became a man in a hurry, politically speaking. As he confessed to an intimate: "I shall never become the Old Man of the Obersalzberg. I have so little time."[21]

In addition to all that, Hitler was preoccupied with the idea that he might fall victim to an assassin. Consequently, as he persistently impressed upon his bodyguards, his own survival was of paramount importance. He took an extraordinarily detailed interest in security measures and demanded that they be constantly updated and intensified. He regularly carried a pistol in public, and his personal bodyguards and adjutants were also invariably armed.

Of course, Hitler's political activities inevitably exposed him to some considerable danger. As head of the most violent and aggressive movement in German political life, he naturally aroused the personal enmity of his opponents. But in campaigning, whether speaking before hostile audiences or merely traveling to political events, he was regularly obliged to confront his detractors. He was ambushed a number of times. Once, a train he was traveling on was attacked. Communists also took potshots at his car. On another occasion, in 1920, he escaped detection by a menacing mob only by posing as the batman of one of his entourage.[22] Only his (then) relative anonymity saved his skin.

Yet, beyond what one might call necessary exposure to danger, Hitler also regularly and willfully undermined the efforts of his protectors. For one thing, he could be astonishingly reckless. Once, in the Black Forest city of Freiburg, when his car was pelted with stones, he jumped down from the vehicle waving his whip, forcing his astonished attackers to scatter.[23] On another occasion, Albert Speer described how Hitler's motorcade drove through hostile crowds in Berlin:

> The temper of the crowd grew ugly. When Hitler with his entourage arrived a few minutes later, the demonstrators overflowed into the street. Hitler's car had to force its way through at a snail's pace. Hitler stood erect beside the driver. At that time I felt respect for his courage, and still do.[24]

Years later, Hitler would explain his actions. If an idealist assassin wanted to shoot him or blow him up, he opined, it would make little difference if he was sitting or standing.[25] "In the heroic days," he said, "I shrank from nothing."[26]

Hitler was also utterly and deliberately unpredictable. Speer called him "royally unreliable."[27] His routine, insofar as it is worthy of the name, consisted of rising late and "working" long into the night, usually ranting to his minions. He was incapable of any systematic work, preferring to indulge his own whims or to submit to indolence.[28] In addition, he would often disappear to spend the weekend with associates in Berlin or Munich, but would accept little in the way of forward planning. Though this pattern served as an effective hindrance to any potential assassin, it also did little to facilitate the work of his bodyguards.

Indeed, for all his attention to security details, Hitler was fundamentally unconvinced that his bodyguards would actually serve any practical purpose. His belief in "fate" and "destiny" caused him to ascribe his continued survival "not to the police, but to pure chance."[29] Thus, though he paid painstaking attention to the details of his security regime, it is tempting to think that, in this case at least, he really was just playing at soldiers—reveling in his own supernatural importance, yet knowing in his heart that all such efforts would ultimately prove futile.

On one level, Hitler's apparent nonchalance would appear to have been justified. In the early months of 1933, numerous accounts were received in Berlin of the wildest plots and conspiracies to kill the new chancellor. They arrived from all parts: Switzerland, Holland, Morocco, Spain, Czechoslovakia, and the United States.[30] Some overheard Jews plotting in Basle, others had wind of anarchists conspiring in Barcelona, still others heard of communists scheming in the Saarland. Most of the reports were flimsy, based on hearsay or a flippant comment such as "someone should bump that Hitler off." But some defied credibility entirely. One informant from Augsburg, for example, wrote to inform Hitler of the possibility that the Chancellery building itself might be undermined and that "subversives" might plant explosives there. Though the correspondent confessed to having no knowledge of such a plot, he exhorted his Führer to guard his "precious life" most carefully.[31] As a result of such enthusiastic and imaginative informants, the Berlin police were alerted almost every week that a new plot was afoot. Most of the threats were investigated, but of the hundreds received, only about ten were considered to warrant serious attention, and even these amounted to very little.[32]

One might have assumed that the greatest threat to the life of the new chancellor came from the left. Certainly, Germany's socialists and communists were well aware that the new regime was likely to declare open season on them, and some were perhaps minded to prepare a preemptive strike. However, the German left was almost congenitally unable to rouse itself to target Hitler. The socialists were wedded to the democratic process and found such extreme measures hard to stomach, while the communists were being exhorted by their masters in Moscow to direct their efforts against the socialists. Beyond sheer myopia, much of their common problem was ideological. Marxist theory viewed fascism as the last gasp of the capitalist bourgeoisie, the bloody prelude to an inevitable socialist utopia. History, it was thought, was driven by grand social and economic forces, not by individuals. So, to many on the left, the elimination of Hitler made little sense.

Nonetheless, a brave few were willing to give history a helping hand. One was Beppo Römer, a communist and former *Freikorps* leader, who gained access to the Chancellery in the spring of 1933 but was discovered by the SS. He would spend the next six years in Dachau and would cease conspiring against Hitler only when he was executed, in 1942. Another was Kurt Lutter, a communist shipwright from Königsberg, who plotted a bomb attack on Hitler in the spring of 1933. Arrested and interrogated, Lutter was released without charge due to a lack of evidence. Later, in 1935, an ambitious communist conspiracy was uncovered in Vienna, which planned to assassinate Hitler as well as the minister of war, General Blomberg, along with Göring, Goebbels, and Hess.[33] Interestingly, the conspirators intended to give the impression that their plot had been hatched by the SA.

In contrast to the largely latent threat from the left, that emanating from the disgruntled on the right appeared to be more serious. First, there were many within the SA who still viewed Hitler as a traitor to their principles. Some of the more prominent among them could be bought off after January 1933, but much of the rank and file was barely reconciled to the new constellation of power or to the apparent success of "their" Führer. Indeed, in 1933, a would-be assassin in SA uniform was arrested carrying a loaded weapon into Hitler's residence at Berchtesgaden.[34]

The SA crisis culminated in the Röhm Purge in the summer of 1934. Yet, even while the SA was being purged, and its supposed threat to the "peace of the nation" was being widely touted by Hitler, it momentarily found an opportunity to avenge itself. As Hitler and his SS entourage were preparing to leave the Bavarian guesthouse where many of the SA leadership had been arrested, an SA bodyguard detachment arrived. Clearly confused and increasingly aggressive, they were ordered to return to barracks in Munich. However, they drove only a short distance before setting up a roadblock, with machine guns on either side of the road, to wait for Hitler. The Führer, meanwhile, had thought it wise to depart the area by another route.[35]

Another source of opposition to Hitler was the so-called Black Front, headed by the former Nazi Otto Strasser. Always on the fringe of the Nazi Party because of his eclectic ideology—a

curious amalgam of extreme nationalism, anti-capitalism, socialism, and anarchism—Strasser was forced out of the party in the
summer of 1930. He conceived the Black Front as an umbrella
organization for all those on the right who were disaffected with
Hitler, and by the time of the movement's prohibition in January
1933, it had attracted some five thousand members. Thereafter,
based in Vienna and then Prague, Strasser fought a propaganda
campaign against Hitler and maintained a small underground
network within Germany itself.

His most audacious move came in 1936, when he planned to
assassinate Hitler. His chosen assassin was a Jewish student from
Stuttgart, Helmut Hirsch, who was studying architecture in
Prague and was persuaded to carry out a "heroic act" to inspire
the Jews of Germany. Hirsch was to take a suitcase bomb to the
Nazi Party headquarters in Nuremberg but was arrested on crossing the German frontier in December 1936, and executed the
following spring. Two theories might explain his failure: either
the Gestapo had an informant within the Black Front, or else the
Black Front had cynically betrayed Hirsch itself, so as to benefit
from the attendant publicity.

Yet Hirsch was symbolic of another growing source of resistance to Hitler. Organized Jewish opposition to Nazism only
really sparked into life with the Warsaw ghetto uprising of 1943.
Until that point, the growing persecution of Jews within Germany and elsewhere was met with an almost stereotypically
phlegmatic response. Some individuals, however, were goaded
into action. Hirsch, for example, had been frustrated by his family's vain efforts to secure American citizenship.

He may also have been spurred by the actions of a young
Yugoslav Jew, David Frankfurter, who in February 1936 had
successfully carried out a near-perfect assassination. Frankfurter
was a failed medical student who had fled to Switzerland after
briefly attending Frankfurt University. In exile, he read reports of
the concentration camps and anti-Jewish propaganda and was
spurred to act.[36] He had initially wanted to target Hitler but had
settled on the German-born Swiss Nazi leader Wilhelm Gustloff.
Frankfurter did his homework. He studied Gustloff's routine,

memorized his movements, and carried his photograph to aid identification. He also bought himself a revolver and practiced on a shooting range in Berne. On 3 February, he purchased a one-way ticket to Davos, where he rented a room. The following day, he went to Gustloff's house, calmly rang the doorbell, and asked to see his target. He was ushered into a study, seated beneath a picture of Adolf Hitler, and asked to wait. When Gustloff entered the room, Frankfurter shot him five times in the chest and head before fleeing the scene and telephoning the police. He surrendered himself with the words "I fired the shots because I am a Jew. I am fully aware of what I have done and have no regrets."[37]

Like Hirsch, Frankfurter was seeking to spur his tormented people to resistance against the Nazis. Like Hirsch, he failed in this wider aim. While organized Jewish resistance was still absent, however, Hirsch and Frankfurter demonstrated that individuals could be provoked into action by their repeated humiliations and privations. And in such circumstances, they required few means beyond the humble accoutrements of the lone assassin. Their example would be followed once again, with horrific results, in 1938. That November, the secretary of the German legation in Paris was murdered by a seventeen-year-old Polish Jew, Herschel Grynszpan, whose family had been expelled from the Reich. Grynszpan was caught and subsequently killed by the Nazis.[38] But his crime would provide the cue for the murderous pogrom of *Kristallnacht*. Jewish resistance appeared to have scored a spectacular own goal, but it had at least demonstrated what was possible.

Following Hitler's accession to power in January 1933, and in view of the increased threat that the new chancellor was considered to be under, yet another revision of his personal security was carried out. For the first time, the Führer's protection could command state funding, and those surrounding Hitler wasted little time in exploiting the new situation for their own ends, creating power bases and seeking to exert influence. The foremost among them was Heinrich Himmler.

In March 1933, soon after the Nazi "seizure of power," Himmler established a new security body to operate in parallel to those already existing. He envisaged the new unit—christened the *Führerschutzkommando* (Führer Protection Group)—as a small group of "tried and trusted National Socialists, and [...] excellent criminal-police officers" that would guarantee Hitler's "unconditional safety," exercise conscientiousness, and show exemplary manners.[39]

This move would naturally serve to expand Himmler's growing influence and bring him closer to the epicenter of power. But it was also seriously flawed. First, officially at least, Himmler's own writ, and by extension that of his pet organizations, did not yet carry Germany-wide. His Führer Protection Group, therefore, could initially protect the Führer only in Bavaria. Moreover, the unit was made up almost exclusively of Bavarian policemen, the very officers who had put down Hitler's abortive putsch a decade before. Perhaps unsurprisingly, Hitler initially refused to be guarded by anyone other than the trusted *Leibstandarte Adolf Hitler* (Adolf Hitler Bodyguard), which had been established by Sepp Dietrich a few months before.[40]

The *Leibstandarte* had, in turn, been developed in parallel to Dietrich's previous bodyguard unit, the *SS-Begleit-Kommando "Der Führer,"* which had been set up the previous year. It was to serve as a model SS unit and would absorb all previous security organs. Initially numbering only 120 individuals, it was composed solely of the German "élite": those with proven Aryan ancestry, Nordic in appearance, possessing no criminal record, and having a minimum height of 1.80 meters (5 feet 11 inches). (One is tempted here to recall the contemporary Polish line: "as tall as Hitler, lean as Göring, blond as Himmler, and athletic as Goebbels.") The first detachment of the *Leibstandarte* to assume its post was a detail of twelve men assigned to guard the Reich Chancellery in April 1933. A second unit was sent to Berchtesgaden that July. By November, the entire *Leibstandarte,* now over eight hundred strong, swore an oath of allegiance to Hitler before the memorial to the fallen of the Beer Hall Putsch. Their oath was a personal one, which made no mention of the constitution, or even of the German people: "I swear to you, Adolf Hitler, as Führer and chancellor of the German Reich, loyalty and bravery. I vow to you and to my superiors appointed by you obedience unto death. So help me God." One witness recalled the scene with no little emotion:

> The midnight oath-taking ceremony before the Feldherrnhalle in Munich. Splendid young men, serious of face, exemplary in bearing and turnout. An élite. Tears came to my eyes when, by the light of the torches, their voices repeated the oath in chorus. It was like a prayer.[41]

Already by this point, the *Leibstandarte* was engaged guarding the Reich Chancellery, Berlin's three airports, numerous ministries, Berchtesgaden, and Himmler's home.

It was, of course, primarily a corps of bodyguards. As such it excelled, not least in its very obvious manner. Its giant sentries, in their immaculate black uniforms with white belts and white gloves, were a gift to the propagandists. They inspired fear, respect, and envy in equal measure. One eyewitness recalled their impressive appearance in Breslau in 1938, where they remained unperturbed as a march threatened to descend into hysterical chaos:

> There was, however, one group that remained immune to the excitement spreading around them, and stood fast in their positions with stoical ease. These were the Führer's bodyguards from the *SS Adolf Hitler*, gigantic men over two meters tall wearing black uniforms and black steel helmets. They surrounded the rostrum, and, at a sign from an officer, closed ranks.[42]

The *Leibstandarte* was, however, not *just* a corps of bodyguards. It was the élite troop of the élite SS: Hitler's "Household Cavalry." Its men provided the guard of honor for visiting dignitaries. They paraded for Hitler's birthday and for the numerous other anniversaries in the Nazi calendar, with their famed marching band leading the chorus. But they also fulfilled a much more sinister function. They served as chief executioners during the Röhm Purge and would attend every ceremonial entry as the Reich expanded: the Saar in 1935, the Rhineland in 1936, Vienna in 1938, Prague and Warsaw in 1939, Paris in 1940. As their oath demonstrated, they were the beginnings of Hitler's private army.

Despite the *Leibstandarte*'s apparent position of strength, a new rival was to emerge in 1935. By that time, Himmler had expanded his own power base and had succeeded in pushing for a further review of Hitler's security apparatus. After much wrangling, he persuaded Hitler to appoint him chief of the newly formed *Reichssicherheitsdienst* (RSD, Reich Security Service), which would supersede the earlier *Führerschutzkommando* and would be responsible for the protection of Hitler and other prominent government figures.

The RSD initially consisted of only forty-five officers, divided into a number of "bureaus," the first of which was assigned to protect the Führer. Its tasks included the routine surveillance of salient buildings, pre-event spot checks at venues, travel security, and the investigation of suspects. Wherever Hitler traveled within Germany, the RSD was granted authority over all local police forces for the duration of the visit. By the outbreak of war, the unit numbered over two hundred officers.

The fourth player in the prewar security regime was the *SS-Begleit-Kommando* (SS Escort Detachment), established by Sepp Dietrich in 1932. With the seizure of power, the clique of "old fighters" who had previously made up Hitler's entourage were rewarded with various administrative postings, honorary positions, and sinecures. The SS Escort Detachment, therefore, effectively had to be refounded, and its new members, drawn from elsewhere in the SS, were strictly vetted. Initially numbering only about eight, it was charged with accompanying Hitler on all domestic and foreign trips. Those not on duty with the escort served as valets, drivers, and orderlies.

Meanwhile, the tug-of-war for control of Hitler's security continued at the highest level. After Himmler's Führer Protection

Group fell by the wayside, absorbed into the regular police and sub-ordinated to the Ministry of the Interior, the remaining players—the RSD, the SS Escort Detachment, and the *Leibstandarte*—were forced to divide their labor sensibly. Where their remits over-lapped, they had to establish discrete areas of competence. The solution was that the escort duties were undertaken by the SS Es-cort Detachment; bodyguards, ceremonial guards, and sentry de-tails would be provided by the *Leibstandarte;* and the RSD would supply the professional police support, including surveillance and investigation. Between them the three formed a formidable bar-rier to anyone who wished Adolf Hitler harm.

An impression of the security surrounding the Führer can be gleaned from an examination of the procedures instituted in the Reich Chancellery in 1938. Any visitor to the building would have to pass through two SS sentry posts prior to entry. Then the visitor would be referred to a receptionist and issued an identifi-cation pass before receiving an SS escort to the relevant office. Thereafter, the visitor would pass the various sentries of the thirty-nine-strong permanent SS guard. On accessing the first floor, where the Führer's suite was located, the visitor would en-counter a visibly stricter security presence with meticulous iden-tity checks. Anyone without a valid pass was liable to arrest. Upon departure, the visitor would be escorted back to the reception area, where the pass would be surrendered. In addition to all this, Hitler was also widely rumored to have employed a double, al-though no documentary evidence supports this supposition.[43]

Hitler's transport arrangements were another obvious source of security concern. Hitler was an early enthusiast of the motor-car. He had owned one as early as 1923: a red Mercedes, which was confiscated by the Munich police following the Beer Hall Putsch.[44] Thereafter, he acquired a string of vehicles, mainly Mer-cedes or Maybach, for his personal and political use. Following the seizure of power, he began to assemble a fleet of specially modified Mercedes, some of which were armor-plated, with bullet-proof tires and 5-centimeter-thick glass, and were supposedly im-pervious to bomb blasts and small-arms fire. Despite its obvious shortcomings, however, Hitler's favored vehicle was an open-top tourer. Being seen was evidently more important to him than being safe.

On public appearances Hitler's car would usually form part of a convoy of at least four vehicles. A pilot car would lead the way, followed by Hitler's vehicle, with at least two more behind that: one carrying the SS Escort Detachment detail and another containing officers from the RSD. Elaborate routines were planned whereby the Führer's arrival could be effected while a security cordon was simultaneously thrown across the street. Any vehicle attempting to disrupt or infiltrate the convoy was to be rammed off the road. Occasionally even star-struck pedestrians were run down.

One pedestrian who was less than star-struck was the British military attaché, Sir Noel Mason-Macfarlane, who witnessed Hitler's convoy en route to Vienna in 1938. Near Linz, he pulled into a garage at a spot he heard that the Führer was due to pass. He recalled:

> I decided to wait and see the Arch-Thug pass. Only a few minutes later a couple of Mercedes [*sic*], filled with S.S. bristling with tommy-guns and other lethal weapons, came by; they were closely followed by half a dozen super-cars containing Hitler and his immediate entourage and bodyguard.... There was something terribly sinister about that string of shining black Mercedes, rolling along inexorably towards Vienna.[45]

In addition to his fleet of Mercedes, the "Arch-Thug" also kept a small fleet of airplanes. In the early 1930s, he had already made novel and extensive use of air travel in his political campaigning. This trend continued after 1933, when he appointed his pilot, Hans Baur, to supervise the creation of a "flying group." As well as using the ubiquitous workhorse, the Junker-52, Hitler also employed a modified Focke-Wulf Condor, bearing the registration D-2600, as his private plane. Security measures were especially tight. Only Baur was permitted to pilot the plane, and he would never reveal the destination of a flight, even to airport officials. D-2600 was kept in a secure hangar at Tempelhof airport in Berlin, where it was guarded by a joint detail of RSD and *Leibstandarte* and maintained by a strictly vetted team of engineers. Before every departure it made a fifteen-minute test flight, and the carriage of parcels, mail, and unauthorized luggage was expressly forbidden.

From 1937 Hitler also operated a personal train: the *Führersonderzug,* or "Führer Special." Constructed almost entirely of reinforced steel, it consisted of a locomotive pulling a succession of as many as fifteen cars and conference coaches. It had a permanent staff of over sixty, including guards, adjutants, valets, and maintenance personnel. When on the move, the Führer Special was often preceded by a dummy train to attract any malicious intent. It was to be given priority at all times, and scheduled services were forbidden to overtake, while any following locomotive had to proceed after a five-minute interval.

Despite these measures, it was, of course, extremely difficult for the RSD to keep Hitler's train movements out of the public domain. Given the constraints of timetabling, any departure required a minimum of two hours' advance notice to the rail authorities, to adjust timetables and minimize confusion. And in every case, word would inevitably be swiftly passed down the line to railwaymen, stationmasters, and beyond.

For all its apparent effort and expense, Hitler's security regime suffered a number of fundamental flaws. Most important, there was a surprisingly lax attitude toward the vetting of staff in potentially sensitive positions. Few of the RSD members, for example, were initially Nazi Party supporters, and even the unit's commander, the rotund Bavarian Johann (Hans) Rattenhuber, only joined the party *after* his appointment.[46] Among the *Leibstandarte,* too, Nazi Party membership was apparently not a precondition, and over a quarter of the personnel were not paid-up members.[47]

Even among Hitler's inner circle, the same apparent laxity prevailed. One of Hitler's secretaries, Traudl Junge, owed her position not only to her stenographic skills but also to her sister's relationship with Bormann's brother.[48] Similarly, Hitler's cook,

Marlene von Exner, was engaged solely on the strength of a personal recommendation from the Romanian dictator Marshall Antonescu and did not undergo any vetting procedure. Had she been of a mind to do so, Frau von Exner would have been ideally placed to poison Hitler. She was later dismissed when it was discovered that she had a Jewish grandmother.[49]

Albert Speer, who was to become one of Hitler's closest confidants, noted the almost complete lack of security checks for his first meeting with the Führer in the summer of 1933. Though an acquaintance of Goebbels and Rudolf Hess, Speer was still a virtual unknown. Yet when admitted to an interview with Hitler in his Nuremberg apartment, he was ushered in by an adjutant and stood, alone, before "the mighty Chancellor of the German Reich."[50] Security measures, if there were any, were not mentioned.

In addition, it appears that some of Hitler's guards did not treat their positions with the conscientiousness that one might have expected. In one instance, a formal complaint was forwarded to Sepp Dietrich after *Leibstandarte* men were caught riding in the Reich Chancellery lift. Another of Dietrich's men was reprimanded for pressing his nose against the ground-floor windows when on duty. More seriously, weapons were inadvertently discharged within the complex on a number of occasions.

The bodyguards themselves described their efforts as insufficient, even amateurish.[51] One veteran of the *Leibstandarte* recalled that they were given no special training in their task and were merely told not to be rude to the public when protecting Hitler at speaking events. He also claimed that when on guard duty at Hitler's residences, the bodyguards often had little to do and so doubled as messengers or errand boys.[52]

Perhaps because of these shortcomings, a number of uninvited visitors managed to penetrate the Reich Chancellery. All of them were intercepted, but their presence made it clear that the Chancellery was not as hermetically sealed as Hitler would have wished. Operations in the field were often just as flawed. When Hitler entered Vienna in 1938, for example, his bodyguards attempted to merge into the crowd dressed in what he described as

an "astonishing collection of clothes—rough woollen mackin-
toshes, ostler's capes and so forth." The urbane and sartorially so-
phisticated Viennese viewed them with amusement. Hitler was
furious. "Any moron," he raged, "could recognise them for what
they were at a glance."[53]

Perhaps for this reason, Hitler considered his bodyguards to
be of only limited utility and felt that his continued survival was
due to the benign attentions of providence. Indeed, he was notori-
ously impatient with his closest defenders. He had an almost visceral
aversion to policemen, perhaps as a result of "years of struggle,"
and could not bear to feel himself being watched. He would often
shout at his SS patrols: *"Go and guard yourselves!"*[54]

In the circumstances, the overlapping spheres of competence
of Hitler's numerous security organs must have proved a constant
irritation. Yet this curious state of affairs was entirely of the
Führer's own making. Being congenitally suspicious, he was unwilling to allow one individual to take charge of his security apparatus. And he was also keen to utilize the principle that guided
many of his political machinations—that of "administrative
chaos." Under this system, numerous organizations and individuals would be encouraged to compete in fulfilling a single task.
This competition, it was thought, bred efficiency; but it also appealed to Hitler's "Darwinian" ideal of the survival of the fittest.
As one Nazi memoirist recalled, Hitler also liked to play his paladins off against each other:

> It pleased Hitler immensely to see organisations which
> dealt with similar issues engage in feuds with one another.
> For only in such circumstances, so he believed, would he
> be able to maintain his independence from the specialised
> ministries.... Those who became too powerful he gladly
> cut down to size; to those who were stranded out on a
> limb he extended a hand and helped them back onto their
> feet.[55]

This practice may have been beneficial in politics, but in the security sphere it did little but sow confusion and, of course, violate the

golden rule: that of making one authority solely responsible. In one instance, Hitler ordered his driver to accelerate to escape a strange car that had attached itself to his motorcade. He was unwittingly escaping from yet another set of his own bodyguards.[56]

The result of all this was that despite huge advances in personal safety, surveillance, and what in modern parlance one might call counterterrorism, Hitler's security regime of the late 1930s still offered tantalizing opportunities to a would-be assassin. The regime was certainly not as refined and practiced as it would later become. And until 1938, the threats to Hitler's person remained largely theoretical. His bodyguards—larking in the lifts and making faces in the windows—were probably bored of chasing phantoms and will-o'-the-wisps.

In addition, Hitler was reveling in his overwhelming popularity. The year was studded with numerous public appearances that had become enshrined in the Nazi calendar, including the "Day of the Seizure of Power" in January, Hitler's birthday in April, the Bayreuth Wagner Festival in July, the Nuremberg Rally in September, and, of course, the commemoration of the Beer Hall Putsch in Munich every November. Moreover, Hitler busied himself in the early years with speaking tours, election campaigns, and military reviews, shuttling up and down the country between highly publicized events. In short, he was far from being the recluse that he would become in his later years. He was a regular at numerous cafés and restaurants in Berlin and Munich, with a table perpetually reserved should he choose to stop by.[57] And in 1936, he attended almost every day of the Berlin Olympics, much to the frustration of his security personnel.

For the determined assassin possessed of a modicum of ingenuity, Hitler must have offered a number of possibilities. He would have recognized that, despite its perpetual revisions and reorganizations, his target's security apparatus was still feeling its way to genuine effectiveness. He would have seen how his target's routine included a wealth of public appearances, where the throngs of believers could create confusion and facilitate an escape. His chances of success, he might have concluded, looked promising.

Maurice Bavaud was born in Neuchâtel, Switzerland, in January 1916. The eldest of seven children from a middle-class, devoutly Catholic family, he underwent a conventional education, leaving school at the age of sixteen to be apprenticed as a draftsman. The young Bavaud inherited the strict Catholicism of his parents and was briefly active in a church youth group before deciding, in the spring of 1935, to become a missionary. That autumn, he en-rolled in a four-year course at a French seminary, the École Saint-Ilan Langueux at St. Brieuc in Brittany.

Fellow students from Saint-Ilan remembered Bavaud as a calm, sensitive young man of average intelligence with a tendency toward mysticism. He read philosophy and was a keen singer, joining the Gregorian chant in the church and often reciting tra-ditional Swiss songs. He enjoyed his classes and relished the re-laxed atmosphere of the seminary. But one colleague was to exert a decisive, even fateful influence on him. Marcel Gerbohay was highly intelligent and charismatic. But he was also a fantasist, and possibly a schizophrenic. Despite being born in the most modest of surroundings, he convinced himself that his mysterious father, who had died in his infancy, was related to the Romanovs.[58] (He would later claim to be the illegitimate son of Charles de Gaulle.) While studying at Saint-Ilan, he suffered hallucinations, delu-sions, and disorientation, and was held back a year following what appears to have been a minor nervous breakdown. Returning to the seminary in the autumn of 1935, he met Maurice Bavaud.

The relationship that developed between the two has invited much speculation. It may, for example, have had homosexual overtones.[59] Certainly Bavaud's later prison correspondence indi-cated that, at the very least, he had an extremely intimate friend-ship, if not an infatuation, with Gerbohay.[60] It has also been shown that the developing friendship coincided with a renewed crisis in Gerbohay's mental condition.[61]

Bavaud and Gerbohay formed a student group, the *Compa-gnie du Mystère,* where current affairs, among them the merits and demerits of communism and Nazism, were keenly discussed.

As the *soi-disant* son of émigré Russians, Gerbohay was a passionate anti-communist. Bavaud, for his part, had flirted in his youth with the Swiss fascist movement, the *Nationale Front*.[62] Yet, peculiarly perhaps, the result of their discussions was that not Stalin but Adolf Hitler was the primary danger to mankind, even an "incarnation of Satan."[63] Within the group, a number of opinions were represented. Bavaud, for example, appears to have been concerned about Hitler's persecution of the Catholic Church and the neo-paganism then fashionable in the Nazi movement. Gerbohay, meanwhile, considered Hitler to be too soft on the atheist Soviet Union and longed for him to declare war on Stalin. On one thing they both agreed, however: Hitler had to be removed.

It is unclear at which point the plot graduated from mere student pontificating to become a genuine conspiracy to murder Hitler. But in the summer of 1938, Bavaud left Saint-Ilan for the vacation. He traveled to his family in Neuchâtel and informed them that he would not be returning to Brittany at the end of the summer. He then sought work as a draftsman, read *Mein Kampf,* and began learning German. His plan was to gain access to the Führer by posing as an enthusiastic National Socialist. Later that year, he began to put it into effect.

On 9 October 1938, Maurice Bavaud caught the early morning train out of Neuchâtel. At the family home, he left a short and somewhat Delphic note for his parents, which read: "Do not worry on my account. I am going to make a life for myself."[64] Armed with his copy of *Mein Kampf* and 600 Swiss francs stolen from his mother, he was heading for Baden-Baden and the home of distant relatives, the Gutterer family.

He found a cautious but welcoming reception. After looking, in vain, for work, he would go for walks in the neighborhood and write postcards to Gerbohay. Though he posed as an ardent admirer of Hitler, his presence had nonetheless raised eyebrows. His cousin Leopold Gutterer was a senior official in the Propaganda Ministry, and he had told the family to keep clear of the new arrival and had warned that Bavaud was under no circumstances to use him as a reference in his search for work. He also informed the local Gestapo of Bavaud's arrival.

Whether Bavaud had indeed planned to use cousin Leopold as his entrée to Berlin society—and to Hitler—is unclear, but the latter's frosty attitude toward him would have convinced him that it was time to move on. So, after only ten days with the Gutterers, Bavaud left Baden-Baden, sending his luggage on to Berlin before taking a train to Basle, where he bought himself a 6.35 mm pistol and ammunition. He then proceeded to Berlin, arriving on the twenty-first.

After finding lodgings, he began his surveillance of the government district, but soon learned that Hitler was at his residence at Berchtesgaden at the time, more than 550 kilometers distant. He then hurried to Upper Bavaria, only to discover that his quarry was now in Munich. Nonetheless, Bavaud spent a couple of days in the region of Hitler's Berghof, making subtle inquiries about the security of the area and practicing his marksmanship in the woods. By chance, he met a senior policeman, Karl Deckert, who suggested (in all innocence) that, though a personal interview was out of the question, the best opportunity to get close to Hitler would be at the Commemoration of the Beer Hall Putsch in Munich on 8 and 9 November.[65]

Bavaud's plan was taking shape. On 31 October he traveled north again to Munich, found lodgings, and went about trying to secure himself a seat in one of the temporary grandstands overlooking the procession route. After numerous requests, he finally obtained a complimentary ticket by posing as a Swiss journalist. In the remaining days before the celebrations, he walked the procession route and considered his options. He toyed with the idea of choosing a vantage point and rushing directly into the street to shoot Hitler at close range, but finally opted to remain in the grandstand. Thereafter, he purchased more ammunition and traveled to the Ammersee, west of Munich, to practice his gun skills again.

On the morning of 9 November, he arrived at the grandstand early and found himself a seat in the front row. In his overcoat, he would have felt the cold steel of the loaded pistol. The parade was just hours away.

The parade was a commemoration of the failed Beer Hall

Putsch of 1923. The festivities had begun the previous night with a Hitler address to his veteran comrades at the Bürgerbräu Beer Hall, where the putsch attempt had started. The following morning, just after midday, a procession retraced the steps of the putschists. At its head marched the *Gauleiter* of Nuremberg, Julius Streicher, followed by the *Blutfahne* or "Blood Standard," a swastika flag from 1923 that had been soaked with the blood of the fallen. Then followed two ranks of the most senior Nazi leaders, with Hitler among them, marching ten abreast. Behind them were arranged thousands of uniformed marchers: groups of "Old Fighters" (*Alte Kämpfer*) and honor guards from the SS, SA, and Hitler Youth. The procession made its way slowly along the prescribed route from the Bürgerbräu Beer Hall to the Feldherrnhalle, where the putsch had been bloodily halted. As it progressed, it passed numerous pillars, specially erected along the route, bearing the names of the Nazi fallen and topped with an eternal flame. At each one, the procession halted. Heads were bowed, shots rang out, and the names of the movement's martyrs were solemnly invoked.[66] At its climax, the procession reached the Feldherrnhalle, where an honor guard fired sixteen shots. There, Hitler laid a wreath, consoled the widows, and observed a minute's silence. Then the procession moved on to its final act of homage, at the nearby Königsplatz, where the bronze sarcophagi of the sixteen dead of 1923 were displayed in two classical pantheons. There, Hitler would walk alone among the tombs.

The crowd that gathered to witness this spectacle would have known the exact course and program of the procession from their experience of previous years. They would have gathered many deep at salient points along the route and would have jostled for the best positions. They would have been moved by the military band of the *Leibstandarte,* playing all the Nazi favorites: the "Horst Wessel Song," *"Das Deutschlandlied,"* and *"Ich hatt' einen Kamaraden."* They would have seen the flags fluttering, observed the uniforms and medals gleaming, and heard the incessant drumming of the Hitler Youth. Separating them from the procession was a rank of SA men lining the route and teams of security men flanking the procession itself.

Bavaud had chosen his position well. He was located close to the Holy Ghost Church, at a juncture on the route where the procession slowed to pass through an archway and then turned north toward the Feldherrnhalle. He would have heard the funereal drumming and the blare of the military band, all relayed across the city by loudspeaker. The cacophony would have increased as the head of the procession approached. A ripple of excitement would have passed through the crowd, followed by a hush of expectation.

Bavaud watched as the front rank drew near. He saw Hitler and reached for the weapon in his pocket, poised to fire. But as the crowd around him grew more animated, a forest of right arms was raised, briefly obscuring the target. He tried to pick his moment, but Hitler was closely flanked by Göring and Himmler, and he was denied a clear shot.[67] The crowd, the SA guard, and the shifting group of marchers presented him with no opportunity to fire. He thought briefly of rushing the parade, but he doubted that he would get clear of the grandstand before being intercepted. He watched, in pained impotence, as the procession continued past the tribune and turned the corner into the Marienplatz. The chance was gone. Hitler, like history, was turning his back on Maurice Bavaud.

Though thwarted, Bavaud continued to look for an opportunity. That afternoon, he returned to his hotel and forged himself a handwritten letter of introduction from a former French prime minister, addressed to the *Reichskanzler*. The following morning, he set off again for Berchtesgaden armed with his letter and a loaded pistol. Arriving in the early evening, he was stopped at the outermost security picket, at the foot of the Obersalzberg, and asked his business. He duly produced the letter and announced that he had to deliver it personally to the Führer. The guard explained that he would not be permitted to pass, and that in any case Hitler was not in residence. Bavaud returned to Munich the same evening.

The next day he tried again, this time forging a letter from the French nationalist leader Pierre Taittinger on a hired typewriter. On the morning of 12 November, he took the letter to the Nazi

Party headquarters in Munich, the Brown House, where he again asked to see Hitler. He was then accompanied into the building to the office of a party official, who politely but firmly informed him that a personal meeting with Hitler was out of the question, and suggested that he leave the letter with him or send it through the post.

By this time, Bavaud was growing desperate. He was running out of money and had, as yet, failed to confront his target. That same afternoon, he caught a train to Bischofswiesen, close to Berchtesgaden, and began walking the ten or so kilometers to Hitler's residence. By the time he arrived, however, it was already dark and he realized that he would certainly not be admitted that evening. Circumstances, he believed, were forcing him to abandon his "holy" mission. He opted to return home.

After returning to Bischofswiesen on foot, Bavaud spent the last of his money on a ticket to Freilassing, en route to Munich. Despite lacking the funds to reach the French border, he hoped to make it to Munich and then to France by stealing onto a Paris-bound train. Initially the plan worked well, but outside Augsburg he was challenged by a ticket inspector. Without the funds to pay the necessary fare, he was handed over to the railway police, who in turn passed him on to the Gestapo.[68]

Under interrogation, Bavaud initially maintained the pretense of his enthusiasm for National Socialism. His gun aroused suspicions, but he calmed them by claiming that it was his hobby. At first, then, he managed to keep his attempt to kill Hitler secret, and he stood trial in early December 1938 only for illegal possession of a weapon and ticket fraud. When his baggage was retrieved from Berlin, however, the Gestapo was given more to work with. A map of Munich was found, as well as one of Berchtesgaden, along with additional ammunition.[69] Further interrogation followed and soon revealed Bavaud's true purpose. In February 1939, he was transferred to Berlin and formally charged with attempting to assassinate the Führer.

Bavaud's testimony was puzzling. He initially claimed to have been acting on the orders of a person of considerable influence within Germany, who acted as his "protector." But as his interrogation progressed, he steadfastly refused to name the individual or to give details of his motives. He was assessed by a psychologist, who testified that he was of sound mind and was fit to stand trial. The opinion was also given that he was a "religious fanatic," who had acted alone out of a mistaken sense of mysticism and in the desire to become a martyr.[70]

On 18 December 1939, Bavaud stood trial in the People's Court in Berlin. Witnesses recalled him looking exhausted and pale-faced, seated between two police officers.[71] Facing a panel of five judges, he was accused under paragraph 5 of the Law for the Protection of the German People and State of 1933, which concerned the attempted murder of a member of the government and carried the death penalty.[72] His defense lawyer bravely stressed Bavaud's previous good conduct and argued in vain that his client had only planned a murder and not attempted to commit one. He would pay for his temerity with a lengthy interrogation of his own.

That morning, witnesses were called and expert testimony was heard. Bavaud himself was asked to account for his actions. He informed the court that he had acted alone, for the benefit of humanity and all Christendom. He made no attempt to plead diminished responsibility or to beg for leniency but, in a closing statement, confessed to having exaggerated his role and expressed his regret for his actions. It would help him little. Found guilty, he was described as an assassin of "exemplary circumspection, shrewdness, intelligence and skill" and sentenced to death.[73] The Swiss authorities chose not to intervene. They submitted no plea for clemency and made no request that the sentence be commuted. They failed even to keep Bavaud's family informed of his fate. Bavaud, meanwhile, was transferred to the *Todeshaus* (death row) of Plötzensee prison in Berlin.

The routine at Plötzensee was bestial. Prisoners were woken at 5 a.m. to slop out their cells and receive a breakfast of watery ersatz coffee and a piece of bread. Those on death row, such as Bavaud, were kept in strict isolation, shackled hand and foot, their meals pushed through a small metal hatch in the door. Above their heads, an electric light burned constantly, illuminating every corner of their tiny cell. They were permitted no visitors, no exercise, and no work. The food was predictably awful, consisting most often of a thin, watery broth containing potato peelings or fatty meat scraps.

Prisoners scheduled for execution were informed the afternoon of the day before that they should tidy their things. They all knew what this meant. The guards usually came for them at dawn. In silence, they would be taken for "preparation." Their necks would be shaved, their hands shackled behind their backs, and their torsos bared. In the distance, a single bell would toll. The condemned would then be led to the execution room, where the guillotine was concealed behind a heavy black curtain. On a signal from the commanding officer, the curtain would be drawn back. The condemned would be strapped to a wooden board beneath the polished blade of the guillotine. Execution followed almost instantaneously.[74]

Bavaud had originally been scheduled for execution in January 1940, but, unlike most condemned men, he was kept alive while the mysterious background to his plot was investigated again and again. Germany, by this time, was at war, and the possibility of enemy involvement in the conspiracy could not be ruled out. Bavaud was interrogated by the Gestapo in February 1940 and in May 1941, but little more information of substance was gleaned.

Bavaud's extended stay in Plötzensee must have been unbearable. Every day, for nearly eighteen months, he had to prepare himself anew for his turn: the click of heels in the corridor, the key in the door, his appointment with death. His letters home, mostly confiscated by the authorities to aid their investigations, expressed his homesickness and fear, as well as his strengthened faith and renewed optimism. They also demonstrated regret for his involvement with Gerbohay, who emerged as the shadowy "protector" and instigator of the assassination plot. Writing on 5 April 1940, Bavaud cursed his fate, saying:

> If only I had stayed at Saint-Ilan, in the service of God. If only I hadn't abandoned the creator for that creature; the

eternal for the worldly; light for darkness, I would not be here.[75]

His final letter, written on the night of 12 May 1941, relayed to his parents the news that his turn had finally come:

> Dear Father, Dear Mother,
> ... this is the last night that I will spend down here. I almost didn't think this day would come, but I have kept a cool head, which gives me hope for the morning, for the moment when my head will roll.
> ... I beg the Lord to forgive my enemies. I beg forgiveness from those against whom I have trespassed.
> ... I embrace you all ... for the last time. I want to cry, but I can't. I feel my heart would explode ... Thank you for everything that you have done for me ... I entrust my soul into the hands of God.
> Your son.[76]

As it turned out, Maurice Bavaud was forced to maintain his "cool head" for one more day, while his last words were translated, analyzed, and censored. He was guillotined at dawn on 14 May 1941.

What light does Maurice Bavaud's attempt shed on the effectiveness of Hitler's security regime? After the event, investigations into Bavaud's background, motivations, and possible accomplices were predictably thorough. Convinced that Bavaud was part of a wider conspiracy, the Gestapo made tireless inquiries, retracing the assassin's steps and interviewing all those with whom he had come into contact. Following the fall of France in 1940, Bavaud's former classmates at Saint-Ilan were questioned. Marcel Gerbohay—implicated in Bavaud's prison correspondence—was arrested, interrogated, and, like his former friend, guillotined.

Yet the security forces had been much less thorough in detecting or preventing Bavaud's attack. Certainly Bavaud could not get close enough in Munich to risk a shot, and his subsequent attempts to secure an interview with his target also failed. But beyond that, he does not appear to have been hindered in any way at all. He was never stopped, frisked, questioned, or checked, despite speaking little German. He purchased ammunition freely in Berlin and in Munich, and repeatedly practiced his marksmanship in rural Bavaria and close to the Berghof.[77] His identity was not checked when he requested a ticket for the parade in Munich. And he was not searched when he took his seat in the grandstand. Even his repeated demands to see Hitler aroused no suspicions. In fact, he twice received advice from Germans on how he might get close to the Führer—from a policeman at the Berghof and from Karl Deckert, who was an officer of the Reich Chancellery staff. Apart from his final arrest, which owed everything to chance, he never once came to the attention of the police, in spite of the fact that the Gestapo had received two tip-offs about him, from Leopold Gutterer and from his Berlin landlady.[78] In dealing with Bavaud (or rather in failing to deal with him), the Nazi security organizations had demonstrated some grievous failings.

It should be added at this point that Bavaud was almost certainly *not* the criminal mastermind described by the People's Court. That backhanded compliment was probably paid to cover up the ineptitude of the authorities. Though charming and persuasive, Bavaud made a very amateur assassin. As a convinced pacifist, he was hardly cut out for the task, and his actions do not suggest a razor-sharp intellect or indeed a killer instinct. Even his choice of weapon betrayed his lack of proficiency. The Schmeisser 6.35 mm pistol was certainly small and easy to conceal, but it lacked the firepower and accuracy of larger-caliber weapons. To be genuinely effective for an assassin, therefore, it would have to be fired a number of times at very close range—below 5 meters, or better yet point-blank. If Bavaud had succeeded in securing an audience with Hitler, it would have been ideal, but it was entirely ill-suited for his master plan: the task of picking Hitler out of a crowded procession at 15 or 20 meters.[79] Even if Bavaud *had* fired during the parade, it is extremely unlikely that he would have hit his target at all.

Yet if one starts from the recognition that he *was* an amateur, Bavaud's achievement is nonetheless impressive. Only twenty-two, he single-handedly tracked Hitler across Germany, armed and trained himself, and came within a few feet of his target. Only fear, inexperience, or his own scruples prevented him from firing a shot. Most important, he demonstrated the courage and strength of conviction to act, when many millions of others across Europe were content to criticize, wring their hands, and do nothing.

For this reason perhaps, news of Bavaud's case was conspicuously absent in the German press when it came to trial in the winter of 1939. Hitler, of course, was well apprised of the case and certainly took the matter seriously. Perhaps predictably, in the Führer's mind it assumed more ominous and monumental proportions. He inflated and embellished Bavaud's three-week pursuit of him to three months, during which the "Swiss sniper," as he called his assailant,[80] had been armed with two pistols and had "hunted" him during his walks around Berchtesgaden.[81] But, beyond the hyperbole, Hitler undoubtedly thought Bavaud to have been a genuine threat to his life. Typically, he considered Bavaud's relative success to be proof positive both of the shortcomings of his bodyguards and of the protection he enjoyed from providence. Bavaud had "confirmed his belief that there is nothing one can do to stop an idealistic assassin, who is prepared to die for his mission."[82]

The Führer's security regime did indeed change in the year after Maurice Bavaud's arrest, but it is hard to ascertain the extent to which those changes were in response to Bavaud or merely a response to the rising international tensions of the time. The new Reich Chancellery, for example, completed in January 1939, had revamped security arrangements, with double sentries and an alarm system. Arrangements for Hitler's tours were also tightened, with a sentry of *Leibstandarte* men to be posted outside the Führer's chosen residence, and an anti-aircraft battery added to his train.

There were, however, two clear consequences of Bavaud's attempt. The first was that, from 1939, the rules regarding foreign nationals wishing to participate at party events were tightened.

An application had to be made in writing and a strict vetting procedure was to be followed, including an interview with the Gestapo. Staff were reminded to be especially vigilant of dubious letters of recommendation.[83]

The second consequence was that the annual commemorative parade in Munich was scrapped after 1938.[84] The "Swiss sniper" had evidently convinced Hitler that it was too risky to concentrate the Reich leadership in one narrow street for such a widely publicized event. Indeed, in time of war, such willful exposure to risk was unthinkable, even for Hitler. In later years, therefore, he would usually merely drive to the Feldherrnhalle, lay his wreaths, and depart again for Berlin.

What Hitler's security men didn't know, however, was that just as Bavaud was agonizing at seeing the Führer march away from him that day in Munich, another assassin was watching the spectacle, looking for opportunities and plotting an attack of his own.

CHAPTER 2

Georg Elser: The Lone Bomber

I considered that the situation in Germany could only be changed by the elimination of the current leadership.

—GEORG ELSER[1]

O N THE EVENING OF 27 FEBRUARY 1933, LESS THAN A MONTH after Hitler's appointment as chancellor, an intimate soiree was in progress at Joseph Goebbels's Berlin apartment. With an election campaign in full swing and due to culminate in a week, Hitler had been engaged in a frantic electioneering tour, criss-crossing the country speaking to huge audiences and giving radio broadcasts. He had intended to strengthen the position of his new government by giving it the democratic mandate that most previous governments had so grievously lacked. The indications were that he would succeed in his task. The new state-sponsored terror apparatus had cowed his political enemies, while his propaganda machine had managed to persuade the undecided to give him the benefit of the doubt.

That evening, however, Hitler was enjoying a break from the hectic political schedule and was a guest with the Goebbels family.

At around 10:00, after a fine dinner of braised trout, the guests were relaxing and reminiscing when the telephone rang. Goebbels answered and was informed by a colleague that the Reichstag building was on fire. He was incredulous. "Is this meant to be a joke?" he demanded.[2] After phoning around for confirmation of the report, he passed the news on to Hitler. Together they gazed across the Berlin skyline at the spreading orange glow. Hitler was in no doubt as to the perpetrators. "It's the communists," he raged.[3]

Within minutes, the two were hurtling to the scene in one of Hitler's limousines. The Reichstag was already well ablaze. Fire crews and police were doing what they could, but the debating chamber—oak-paneled and generously upholstered—was already an inferno, and flames licked up at the night sky through the cracks in the great glass cupola. In the foyer, Goebbels and Hitler encountered Göring, who informed them that a suspect, a Dutch communist, had been arrested at the scene. Together, the group ascended to a viewing gallery overlooking the chamber. There Hitler stood staring silently at the blaze below. After a time, he turned to the assembled group, his face red with the heat and his own fury. As one witness recalled: "He shouted uncontrollably, as I had never seen him do before, as if he was going to burst: 'There will be no mercy now. Anyone who stands in our way will be cut down.'"[4]

That very evening, Hitler began to translate those words into deeds. Along with Goebbels, he hurried to the editorial offices of the Nazi newspaper, the *Völkischer Beobachter* (National Observer), where he spent much of the night composing articles and dictating proclamations for the morning edition. The following day, emergency legislation—the Decree for the Protection of People and State—was passed by the president. In it, many of the fundamental human rights previously enshrined in the German constitution were formally suspended, including the right of association, freedom of the press, and freedom of expression. Violations could be punishable by death. The first foundation stone of the Nazi dictatorship had been laid.

One of the first to feel the full force of the new legislation was the suspect captured at the scene. Marinus van der Lubbe was a twenty-four-year-old former bricklayer from Leiden in Holland. Invalided in an industrial accident, he had become a militant communist and was in almost constant trouble with the authorities. After several attempts to reach the Soviet Union, he finally traveled to Berlin in 1933, as he claimed, to help foment proletarian revolution against Nazi rule. Though suggestions were made at the time that the Nazis had torched the Reichstag themselves to provide a pretext for suppressing their political opponents, little evidence has emerged to support this theory, and the most plausible conclusion is that van der Lubbe had indeed set the fire himself. Arrested and tortured into a confession, he claimed to have worked alone. He was tried, found guilty, and duly beheaded. The venerable institution that he was supposed to have torched was itself abolished a little over a month later.

Within weeks of his appointment, therefore, Hitler began the "coordination" of German political life. By a series of measures combining the quasi-constitutional with the downright illegal, he contrived to eliminate his political rivals. Within a month, playing on the fear of a communist uprising, the Nazis forced the so-called Enabling Act on the Reichstag, now meeting in a cramped Berlin opera house and easily cowed by Hitler's storm troopers. The act's clauses provided for the formal suspension of the constitution and for rule by decree. The communists were then outlawed and the socialists were terrorized into exile and dissolution. The formidable trade unions were forcibly absorbed into the Nazi-led Labor Front. The parties on the right were similarly "persuaded" to dissolve. Those who resisted were taken care of by the burgeoning network of concentration camps. By the spring, the Weimar constitution, which Hitler had solemnly sworn to uphold less than two months before, was already a dead letter. Within only a few months of the Reichstag fire, Hitler's political dictatorship would be all but complete.

German society took somewhat longer to "coordinate." Just as in the political sphere, rival social organizations were forcibly amalgamated, while opposition groups were outlawed. Social divisions, meanwhile, were smoothed by stressing the existence of a

Volksgemeinschaft, a "national community" that would embrace all Germans and transcend class and creed. This was not an entirely spurious concept. Many Germans had tired of the rancor of politics and longed for a return to the sense of community and patriotism that they had witnessed during the First World War. Coercion, then, was not always necessary, but it was nevertheless ever-present.

The first degree of coercion under Nazism was the omnipresence of the party. Though much less influential than the Communist Party had become in the Soviet Union, the Nazi Party was still the driving force behind the transformation of German society. Pressure to join the party was relentless, and after 1933, opportunism, cowardice, and an instinct toward subservience conspired to sap the public's fragile will to resist. Party membership brought with it privileged status, preferential treatment, and in some cases even legal immunity. It was the key to political and social advancement and could also aid progress in the professions. In 1935, for example, it was decreed that 10 percent of civil service vacancies should be filled by party members.[5] Already by that point, over 60 percent of senior state employees were card-carrying Nazis.

Whether one became a member or not, the party's influence penetrated every aspect of life. At the lowest level was the *Block-wart,* or block warden, whose job was to keep the residents of each block under close surveillance. The block warden circulated the party collecting tin, ensured that the swastika was flown on red-letter days, and was authorized to snoop into all aspects of an individual's affairs.[6] He was a lowly, often despised figure, but he was a part of a system that had the power to deprive a recalcitrant of his livelihood, his status, and even his life. Noncompliance could be fraught with danger.

Those who failed to comply faced the wrath of the SS and Gestapo. In theory, the Gestapo, or state police, defended the state, while the SS protected the party. Yet in truth, as the state and party merged, the Gestapo and the SS became ever more closely related; all Gestapo men, for example, were obliged to be members of the SS.[7] Their task was not only the purely defensive one of rooting out dissent and checking opposition activity but also the preemptive one of inspiring conformity. The Gestapo and SS, with their network of agents and informers, operated as a state within a state. Their task was secretly to penetrate every aspect of German public and private life. Their power was vast. They could arrest a man and consign him to a concentration camp without recourse to the formal legal process. There was no appeal. As Hitler himself explained, apparently without any hint of irony: "[E]very means...is considered legal, even though it may conflict with existing statutes and precedents."[8] Many Germans lived in fear of the knock at the door. The experience of one was typical of those who dared to resist:

> One morning, the Gestapo knocked at our door.... They searched our apartment, confiscated our diaries and took us away.... They left me sitting in a cell for eight days before coming to question me. I heard footsteps above me and footsteps in the courtyard. Once I heard a woman's voice, which I thought could be my mother's. Perhaps they had picked her up too.... I wondered if they had already shot my father. Heaven only knew.... I was afraid. I was afraid of anything that might lead to my being taken to prison again, and that was exactly what they wanted.... [That] fear made me very timid and passive, just completely inactive.[9]

One of the most important targets for the Nazi Party and its agencies was to win over the working class. It was one of the largest and most influential social groups, and working-class support was essential for the Third Reich to function as it did. Accordingly, a masterly seduction was planned. Widespread acceptance of the new regime was initially ensured by the fact that Hitler's government provided work. After the long years of the Depression, that commodity was too valuable for many to allow political or ideological objections to intercede. Thus pacified, the workers reacted with a combination of rage and resignation when their political and trade union organizations were subsequently abolished. Yet the new regime did much to court the working class and ensure their continued support. May Day, for example, was transformed into a national paid holiday, when the German worker (or "plant follower," as he was officially known) was feted. As the economy boomed and labor became increasingly scarce, the employers had to battle to keep staff. Some introduced initiatives such as subsidies for house purchases, and elsewhere holiday entitlement was doubled. Wages, meanwhile, were subjected to a statewide freeze.

Even the field of welfare provision was taken over by the party. The Nazi People's Welfare organization, known by its German initials NSV, was established as an umbrella for a huge number of independent charities, which were then forcibly absorbed. It practiced an especially involuntary form of voluntary donation. Not only did it circulate the ubiquitous collecting tins and make deductions from workers' wages, it would also admonish those who failed to contribute, even threatening "protective custody" for persistent nondonors, to "pre-empt popular outrage."[10] The NSV was little more than a vehicle for licensed extortion. But its collection campaigns did have the ulterior motive of inculcating in donors a heightened sense of community. The distribution of its funds, through programs such as the annual Winter Aid drive, was also ruthlessly exploited, predictably, for propaganda purposes.

Leisure time, too, was regulated and exploited. The German worker could avail himself of cut-price opera tickets, buy a subsidized wireless, or even go on a package holiday. In 1938, one German worker in three enjoyed a vacation[11] hosted by the Nazi organization Strength Through Joy, often at purpose-built complexes, such as the enormous Prora resort on the island of Rügen in the Baltic, which was to house twenty thousand holiday makers and employ over two thousand staff.[12] Other destinations included Lake Constance, the Black Forest, or the Harz Mountains. The fortunate few could even enjoy a cruise to Madeira or the Norwegian fjords aboard a purpose-built liner such as the *Wilhelm Gustloff*. Whatever destination the worker chose, he could rest assured that all the necessary measures were in hand to continue his effective indoctrination. The *Wilhelm Gustloff*, for example, had 156 loudspeakers for the relaying of propaganda.[13]

Nazi influence reached even the most apparently apolitical of groups. All commercial, industrial, and professional bodies were "coordinated" in the summer of 1933.[14] The following year, the majority of youth organizations, from the Scouts to sports societies to chess clubs, were incorporated into the Hitler Youth. One recruit, the young Helmut Schmidt, for example, later chancellor of West Germany, automatically became a Hitler Youth member when his rowing club was absorbed.[15] Hitler Youth membership increased 3,500 percent as a result of this expansion, to over three million.[16] Few German boys could resist its heady mixture of uniforms, war games, and small-arms drill. The girls of the associated German Girls' League, meanwhile, were instructed in physical culture, eurythmy, and domestic science. They were all obliged to swear loyalty to the "Supreme Father"—Adolf Hitler.[17]

The force that prepared and underpinned the "coordination" of German life in the Third Reich was propaganda. Described as the "genius" of the regime, propaganda in many ways made up for the ideological shortcomings of Nazism.[18] With its pyrotechnics, fanfares, and screeching editorials, it could be relied upon to induce compliance, even when the eclectic mishmash of ideas behind Hitler might have failed to inspire. Its power became legendary. As Hitler once asserted: "By the clever and continuous use of propaganda, a people can even be made to mistake heaven for hell, and vice versa."[19]

The genius behind the Nazi propaganda machine was Joseph Goebbels. Born in Rheydt on the Lower Rhine in 1897, Goebbels was an archetypal misanthrope. Highly gifted intellectually, he was tormented by feelings of physical inadequacy as a result of his weak constitution and clubfoot. After gaining a doctorate in literature in 1921, he was frustrated as a writer and drifted toward the socialist wing of the Nazi Party. He was to become one of its most impassioned and eloquent spokesmen. Despite ideological disagreements with Hitler, he eventually came under the latter's spell and was rewarded with the post of

Gauleiter of Berlin in 1926. There, his energy, organizational talents, and demagoguery began the transformation of the capital from a bastion of the left into a stronghold of the right.

Goebbels's methods were deceptively simple. Backed by the ever-present threat of violence, he used every means at his disposal to browbeat, taunt, and humiliate his opponents. He never allowed the truth to cloud his judgment. The essential aspect of propaganda, he asserted, was that it "achieved its purpose"; whether it was true or not was immaterial.[20] Defamation, therefore, was a specialty, and at one point Goebbels was defending five separate libel actions.[21] He would ridicule his enemies as simpletons, nincompoops, or philanderers, start scurrilous rumors, and make outrageous accusations. His words, honed with consummate skill, would almost drip with malice and cynicism. When the German chancellor Gustav Stresemann died after a long illness in 1929, for example, he was accorded little respect by Goebbels. Despite being a Nobel laureate and the architect of Weimar Germany's brief flirtation with stability, Stresemann was described by Goebbels as having been "executed" by heart failure.[22]

Commensurate with his skills, Goebbels enjoyed a rapid political rise. Elected a Reichstag deputy in 1928, he was appointed national head of party propaganda two years later. In 1933, he was awarded the top prize—leadership of the newly created Ministry for Popular Enlightenment and Propaganda, with the entire German media under his control. At his first press conference, he was remarkably candid about the new ministry's purpose. It was, he said, to make people "think uniformly, react uniformly, and place themselves at the disposal of the government, body and soul."[23] Thereafter, his position was unassailable. Through the editorials of the Nazi press, especially the breathtakingly mendacious *Völkischer Beobachter* and the ever-burgeoning radio sector, he was free to propagate the Nazi worldview to an audience that was increasingly unable to discern the truth from lies.

But Goebbels's talent was not confined to the printed and spoken word. He was also a gifted stage manager. His marches, rallies, and torchlight parades provided the model for Nazi ceremonials, utilizing every means available—flags, fanfares, ban-

ners—to induce near-ecstasy in the watching public. His vision of
National Socialism was as an "experience," encompassing every
aspect of the follower's life: a fusion of politics with religion.[24] It
was not enough, he thought, for the German public to simply accept National Socialism; they had to participate in it, celebrate it,
and believe in it.

Everyday life under the Third Reich required every individual
to make his or her own compromise with the regime. The experience of the majority, admittedly, was not that of SS terror, concentration camps, and extrajudicial murder. Many would reminisce
with some fondness about the peacetime years, stressing the economic boom, "the guaranteed pay packet... adequate nourish-
ment... and the absence of disarray in political life."[25] It has been
argued, for example, that unless one had the misfortune to belong to a specific risk group—Jews, communists, Gypsies, homo-
sexuals, and so on—and unless one actively conspired against or
resisted the regime, one could live comparatively free from fear.
This is probably accurate. After all, the Gestapo did not resort to
the randomized terror then employed in the USSR. Their victims
were usually identified via denunciations and were usually guilty
of at least a minor transgression or misdemeanor.

Yet everyone, regardless of their enthusiasm for the regime,
was expected to conform. They were expected to contribute to
the People's Welfare, to hang out the swastika when required,
and to listen to Hitler's speeches on the radio. At work, they were
expected to be members of the required state and party bodies.
When they married, they would receive a complimentary copy of
Mein Kampf. Their children would be expected to join the Hitler
Youth, attend schools purged of "unreliable" teachers, and learn
from "revised" textbooks.

The Nazi state, therefore, was almost omnipresent and virtually omnipotent. Those who refused to conform and resisted its
threats and blandishments did so at great personal risk. They were
taking on a network of agencies that demanded unquestioning
obedience and which could exercise the power of life and death
over their opponents. In these circumstances, it took a great deal
of integrity, courage, and downright bloody-mindedness to resist

the Nazi onslaught. Some chose what was called "internal emi-
gration"—a form of moral and intellectual self-sufficiency that
did not openly challenge the regime but rather sought to avoid its
attentions by effecting a withdrawal from all public and political
participation.

A few opted actively to resist the strictures and seductions of
the Third Reich. Some did so by attending illegal dance clubs,
tuning in to foreign radio broadcasts, or hosting political discussion groups. Fewer still set out to confront the regime by the use
of violence. One of the latter was Georg Elser.

Georg Elser was born in the village of Hermaringen, in eastern
Württemberg, in January 1903.[26] The eldest of five children,
with a pious mother and a violent father, he grew up in modest
surroundings. His family worked on the land, trading in lumber,
tending a mill, and managing their smallholding.

The young Georg was very much the product of his child-
hood environment. Small in stature, with unruly dark wavy hair,
he often bore a pinched, slightly troubled expression. He was not
unintelligent, but he was an average pupil, distracted from his
studies by the burdens of being an oldest child, working for his
father, and looking after his siblings. He was also somewhat of a
loner. He made few friends and was content with his own company. But, perhaps most importantly, Georg developed one particular character trait in response to the nightly violence visited
on the family by his father: a profound sense of justice.

After finishing secondary school in the summer of 1917,
Georg briefly worked for his father before finding an apprentice-
ship in a local foundry. Health problems then forced a change of
career, and he was apprenticed as a cabinetmaker. He was conscientious and hardworking, and he demonstrated a genuine talent
for woodworking. He had found his métier. His patience and per-
fectionism meant that he left the technical school in Heidenheim
at the top of his class. At age twenty-two, a qualified cabinetmaker, he left home, with all its unhappy memories, to make his
living as a journeyman.

Elser found employment in a succession of jobs. He worked as a simple carpenter, building furniture, clock housings, and even wooden propellers. But when the economic crisis of 1929 broke, his modest existence became unsustainable. He regularly found himself unemployed, and was eventually forced to return to his family.

While little had changed at home, Georg had matured. He was still largely uninterested in politics per se, but he had developed a clear political standpoint: a visceral and uncompromising opposition to the Nazis. This was in part due to his background. Hitler's slogans perhaps reminded him of the loudmouthed bombast of his drunken father. But he also believed that only the Communist Party could deliver improved wages and conditions for workers and craftsmen such as himself. Consequently, he voted for the German Communist Party and was briefly a member of its affiliated paramilitary "defense force," the *Rote Front-kämpferbund.*

Elser was no ideological communist, however. He was a practical man at heart and was not interested in political discussions. He had no desire to change other people's minds, but he steadfastly refused to make any accommodation with the new regime. When Hitler's speeches were broadcast, he would silently leave the room. One incident illustrates his attitude very clearly. In May 1938, a Nazi parade threaded its way through his hometown of Königsbronn. Elser, like many others, turned out to watch, but as those around him gave the Hitler salute, he refused to do likewise. When a colleague reminded him that it might be sensible to conform, he replied curtly: "You can kiss my ass."[27] He then ostentatiously turned about and started whistling to himself.

How Elser metamorphosed from a small-time nonconformist to an assassin is unclear. He certainly held a deep and personal hatred for Hitler, but that was not so unusual. He gave a clue to his motives when he later claimed that he had made his decision to assassinate Hitler in the autumn of 1938.[28] At that time, war with Czechoslovakia appeared imminent, and indeed was averted only by the licensed treachery of the Munich Conference. But Elser, like many others, was convinced that Munich would not spell the end of Germany's aggressive designs. He believed war, with all its attendant miseries, to be inevitable.[29]

However, there were many in Germany who felt the same hatred and the same fear, yet did nothing. Other factors, therefore, must have contributed to Elser's radicalization. For one thing, his home life was as unbearable in 1938 as it had been in 1922. His father's business had finally failed and the family unit had begun to disintegrate in acrimony. His own circumstances were little better: he was chasing a married woman and paying support for a child he had never wanted.[30] He was also struggling for work. After cutting ties with his parents, he once again scratched out a living as a jobbing carpenter but was shocked at how the hourly rate had sunk as a result of the Depression; it was barely possible to make even a modest living. By 1938, he simply had nothing left to lose.

So in the autumn of 1938, Georg Elser began to plot. By his own admission he had no idea of how he might carry out his attack. But the perfectionist went to work with a will. That November, he traveled to Munich to observe the commemoration of the Beer Hall Putsch of 1923. After Hitler's evening speech in the Bürgerbräukeller—the traditional curtain-raiser of the celebrations—he entered the hall posing as a regular customer. Unnoticed by the lingering group of Nazi bigwigs and bodyguards, he noted the layout of the room, the position of the lectern, and the patent lack of effective security measures. The following morning, he returned to observe the start of the parade—the very same parade that Maurice Bavaud had hoped to disrupt so spectacularly. He then caught the train home.

As a result of his reconnaissance in Munich, Elser now had a clearer idea of a possible way to hit his target. The following year, he decided, he would plant a bomb in the Bürgerbräukeller to kill Hitler and as many of the leading cadre of Nazis as possible. He gave himself twelve months to collect the necessary hardware and to design and build his bomb.

First, he stole a fuse and a quantity of gunpowder from his employer, an armaments manufacturer in Königsbronn. He then found another job in a nearby quarry, where he was able to acquire explosives and a detonator with comparative ease. Working evenings and weekends in his workshop, he drew up plans and experimented. Having no experience of explosives, he tested prototype bombs in the fields around his home before satisfying himself on the amount required for the task. In the spring, he returned to Munich to take measurements and make more detailed sketches of the hall of the Bürgerbräukeller.[31] He also saw the ideal location for his bomb: behind the dais and lectern was a thick stone pillar supporting an upper gallery that ran the length of the hall. An explosion there, he reckoned, not only would kill those in its immediate vicinity but also could bring down the heavy balcony above.

Throughout more than eight months of plotting, Elser betrayed nothing of his activities to his family, his work colleagues, or his few friends. The only time he risked discovery was when, during his short stay in Munich in the spring of 1939, he tried in vain to get a job in the Bürgerbräukeller.[32] Beyond that, he kept the entire operation secret. If asked what he was making, he would reply simply: "An invention."[33] When pressed by an intrigued colleague if his invention was an alarm clock that would ring and simultaneously activate a light, he answered evasively: "Yes, something like that."[34]

In early August 1939, Elser finally left his home and traveled to Munich. With him, he took a wooden chest containing his tools: planes, hammers, saws, files, and, hidden in a special compartment, his bomb, with a further 50 kilograms of explosives, six clock movements, detonators, wire, and a battery.[35] After registering under his own name with the authorities and finding accommodation, he set to work.

His modus operandi was shockingly simple. He would visit the Bürgerbräukeller every night at around 9:00 to take his evening meal. An hour or so later, he would sneak up to the gallery of the function room, where he would hide in a storeroom until the bar closed and the building was locked. Thereafter, he was free to work by flashlight until the bar staff returned at around 7:30 a.m., when he would sneak out of a back entrance.

His first priority was to chip out a cavity in the stone pillar to hold the bomb. But, finding that the pillar was now dressed with wooden cladding, Elser was forced to spend three nights sawing a hole in the wooden surround. Every sound had to be muffled, every speck of sawdust collected and disposed of. He could afford to leave no evidence of his presence. Even the sawn wooden panel was fashioned into a flush-fitting secret door.

Having accessed the pillar, he could now begin to dig out a recess for the bomb. Using a hand drill and a hammer and chisel, he spent most of the following month loosening mortar and prising out bricks—all of which, of course, had to be meticulously tidied and removed from the scene in a cloth sack. Progress was painfully slow. In the cavernous hall, every hammer blow he struck echoed like a gunshot, and to escape detection he had to time his blows to coincide with external sounds, such as the passing of a tram or the automatic flush of the toilets.[36] Working by night preparing the pillar in the Bürgerbräukeller, he labored by day putting the finishing touches to his bomb and, of course, the elaborate timing mechanism.

Elser had planned to be safely in Switzerland by the time his bomb exploded, so he needed to build a timer, linked to a detonator, that could be set several days in advance. His solution was ingenious. By modifying a clock movement with extra cogs and levers, he created a timer that could run for a maximum of 144 hours before activating a lever. That lever then triggered a system of springs and weights to launch a steel-tipped shuttle, which struck the percussion cap of a live rifle round (with the bullet removed) embedded in the explosive.[37] For good measure, Elser then added a second clock mechanism to act as a fail-safe.

For the finishing touches, Elser enclosed the timing mechanism in a wooden case lined with cork to muffle its telltale ticking. He then attached a sheet of tinplate to the inside of the outer wooden door so that the area would not ring hollow if knocked. On the night of 2 November, two months after he had started work in earnest, he finally installed his bomb in the pillar. Three nights later he added the timer. It was set to explode at 9:20 p.m. on 8 November—right in the middle of Hitler's speech.

Hitler arrived in Munich in the afternoon of 8 November. He had flown down from Berlin, accompanied by Joseph Goebbels and a secretary. He was a man in a hurry. His war was barely two months old: Poland had been overrun, and the British and French were entering the so-called Phony War, dropping leaflets instead of bombs, imploring Germany to desist. His planning for a western offensive, meanwhile, was well advanced. Three days earlier, on 5 November, the order for the attack on France had been given, detailing the twelfth of that month as "X-Day."[38] On the seventh, that order was then rescinded due to an unfavorable weather forecast, and a final decision had been postponed until the ninth—the day after Hitler's scheduled visit to Munich.

For this reason, Hitler had initially wanted to cancel his Bürgerbräukeller speech on the evening of the eighth. Though this was unrealistic—commemoration of the Beer Hall Putsch was one of the highlights of the Nazi calendar—he had stressed that he certainly wanted to be back in Berlin that same night to attend to business. However, his personal pilot feared that fog might prevent a return flight, so it was decided to return by train, thereby necessitating a shortening of the traditional program of events. The address to the "old fighters," therefore, would begin earlier than usual—at 8:00 p.m.

Inside the hall of the Bürgerbräukeller, military music set the mood. An audience of around three thousand was seated at long wooden tables laden with beer jugs. Most wore the field gray of the Wehrmacht, though a few sported the black of the SS or the brown of the SA. They chatted and laughed, reminiscing about past struggles and looking forward to new successes. As their leader approached, a momentary hush descended. In the gallery, some stood on the tables to get a better view.

The first of Hitler's party to enter the hall was a standard-bearer holding aloft the holiest relic of Nazi Germany, the *Blutfahne* from the failed putsch of 1923. Behind him followed Hitler, accompanied by Goebbels, Heydrich, Hess, and a number of other prominent Nazis. They were welcomed by Christian Weber, a former confidant of Hitler and a veteran of 1923, who presented the hall for a mock inspection and, after a short but incoherent speech, gave a triple *"Heil!"*[39]

Against a backdrop of huge swastika flags, Hitler took his place on the podium in front of the pillar in which Elser's bomb silently ticked. For a moment he paused, surveyed the room, glanced down at his notes, and drew breath. He began in customary fashion, paying tribute to the veterans of 1923. His tone was subdued, his delivery halting. As he warmed to his task, he turned his vicious and sarcastic rhetoric on the new enemy, the English:

> Today, an English minister steps up, tears in his eyes, and says: "Oh, how we would love to come to an understanding with Germany. If we could only trust the word of the German leadership!" The same is on the tip of my tongue! How we would love to come to an understanding with England. If only we could trust the word of its leadership! When has there ever been a people more vilely lied to and tricked than the German *Volk* by English statesmen in the past two decades?
>
> What happened to the promised freedom of the peoples? What happened to justice? What happened to the peace without victors and vanquished? What happened to the right of all peoples to self-determination? What happened to the renunciation of reparations? . . .
>
> All lies. Broken promises.

He went on, his delivery growing more animated, his volume steadily increasing. He gleefully compared English and German cultural achievements:

> The English cannot tell us Germans anything about culture: our music, our poetry, our architecture, our paintings, our sculptures, can more than stand a comparison to the English arts. I believe that a single German, let us say,

Beethoven, achieved more in the realm of music than all Englishmen of the past and present together!

Hitler spoke for around an hour, giving an outline of the achievements of the Nazis and the perfidy of their enemies. As he neared his conclusion, Hitler the actor took over. He rolled his eyes skyward and gesticulated wildly, clenching his fists, clutching at his chest. His words poured out, some spat with passion, some rolled for emphasis. He concluded on a typically defiant note:

> This is a great time. And in it, we shall prove ourselves all the more as fighters.
>
> In so doing, we shall best honour the memory of this first sacrifice made by our Movement. I cannot end this evening without, as always, thanking you for your loyal following throughout those long years, or without promising you to hold up high our old ideals in the future. We shall stand up for them and we shall not shrink from putting our own lives on the line to realise the programme of our Movement, that programme which demands nothing but to secure our *Volk*'s life and existence in this world.
>
> This is the first commandment of our National Socialist profession of faith and it also is the last one which hangs over every National Socialist when, after the fulfilment of his duties, he departs this life.
>
> *Sieg Heil!*—to our Party Comrades of the National Socialist Movement, to our German *Volk,* and above all to our victorious *Wehrmacht*! [40]

To tumultuous applause, Hitler brought the evening to a close. He then left almost immediately for the train station, accompanied by the party hierarchy. It was 9:07 p.m.

Some minutes later, as the dying tones of *"Das Deutschland-lied"* rang through the hall, the "old fighters" were collecting their possessions, saying their goodbyes, and preparing to file out into the cold November air. Of the three thousand who had packed the hall, only around one hundred now remained, mainly musicians and bar staff clearing the glasses. Then, at 9:20 exactly, Elser's bomb exploded.

The bomb had the desired effect. It smashed the central pillar in which it had been planted, and brought both the gallery and the hall ceiling crashing down into the room. In a flash, the hall filled with smoke and dust, briefly obscuring the falling masonry. A blast wave raced through the building, shattering windows and blowing out doors. The tables and stools closest to the pillar were splintered to matchwood. The dais and lectern were crushed.

One eyewitness was Emil Wipfel, an SA man who was busy dismantling the sound system when the bomb went off. "Suddenly," he recalled,

> there was a bright light, and in the same instant we heard a terrible blast. I was thrown back two meters, falling into the rubble, while all hell broke loose above me. When I came to my senses, I was lying on my stomach with my right arm over the foot of my comrade, Schachta. I did not know at the time that he was already dead. I couldn't move my left arm, and my feet were stuck fast. . . . I realised later that a section of the roof, that had fallen across the Führer's podium, was on me. I suspect that it was only held up and prevented from crushing me by a broken table nearby, and perhaps by the body of my comrade.[41]

In the aftermath, three lay dead and sixty-seven more were injured, five of them fatally. Those who were able sought to free themselves from the rubble. Cries for help mingled with groans and coughing. The survivors emerged, covered in dust, bloodied and bruised, many of them assuming that they had fallen victim to an air raid. One of their number was more perceptive, however, and quickly concluded that it had been a bomb intended to kill their Führer. "My God," he gasped, "what bestial brain could have conceived and carried out such an atrocity?"[42]

Once the dust had settled, and the dead and injured had been removed, the detectives of the Munich *Kriminalpolizei* began their painstaking investigation of the crime scene. The heap of rubble in the hall was methodically sifted and searched. Splinters were collected, photographs taken. By the early hours of the following morning, they were already feeling their way toward the correct interpretation of events: the bomb had been substantial and had been placed at the base of the pillar behind the dais.

Hitler, meanwhile, was already en route to Berlin. His train had left Munich at 9:31 p.m. and would not arrive in the capital until the following morning. He learned of the attack only when the train stopped at Nuremberg. At first he thought the news was a joke. He blanched when he realized that no one was laughing. While pondering this latest brush with death, he drew the conclusion that providence was once more sparing him for great things. Himmler, meanwhile, was drawing conclusions of his own. That night he wired his minions with news of the attack. He concluded, "There's no doubt that the British Secret Service is behind it."[43]

Like his target, Elser was many miles away from the scene of the attack. He had left Munich on the morning of 6 November and traveled to his sister in Stuttgart. Strangely, having exhausted his savings, he borrowed 30 Reichsmarks and actually returned to Munich on the seventh, to check that his bomb was still ticking. Around 10:00 that night, he once again stole into the Bürgerbräukeller, hid in his usual spot, and made sure that the timer was still running true. At dawn the next morning, he crept out again and headed for the railway station. At 10 a.m. he caught a train, via Ulm, to Friedrichshafen, where he took a ferry across the lake to Constance, arriving a little after 9:00 on the evening of the eighth—the evening of the speech.

He reached the Swiss frontier around forty minutes later. As part of his meticulous preparation, Elser had reconnoitered this stretch of the border the previous year and had found it unmanned. Now, however, in the autumn of 1939, with Europe once again at war, it was closely controlled. His only option would be to make a run for it and hope to avoid attracting attention. Loitering close to the frontier fence, however, he was challenged by two German border guards. He told them lamely that he was looking for someone. When they offered to help, he reluctantly agreed to accompany them into their guard post. On entering the building, it was said, Elser turned and cast a last longing glance at the fence, and Switzerland beyond.[44]

The questioning initially was routine, and Elser remained calm and composed, sticking to his story that he was looking for an old friend. When he was asked to empty his pockets, however, he began to arouse serious suspicions. His possessions that night read like a confession. As well as a pair of pliers to cut the fence, he was carrying a postcard of the Bürgerbräukeller, a fuse, a Communist Party badge, and sketches detailing the design of his bomb. Perhaps they *were* a sort of confession. Perhaps he was hoping to impress the Swiss authorities with proof of his author-ship of the attack that was taking place almost at that very mo-ment. Elser's problem, however, was that the contents of his pockets were confessing to the wrong set of border guards. He was handed over to the Gestapo for further questioning. And when news filtered through later that night of the bomb attack in the Bürgerbräukeller, his fate was sealed. The following morning, he was driven back to Munich.

On 13 November, five days after his arrest, Elser finally confessed. He had been caught out when his interrogator asked to see his knees. Though he had worn protective pads, weeks of working at ground level had left his knees badly bruised and suppurating. And when he failed to explain the injuries convincingly, he aban-doned his resistance and conceded that he had indeed planted the bomb.

The following day, Himmler took Elser's interrogation file, along with the signed confession, to show Hitler. The Führer was fascinated. He studied the file and asked to see photographs of his would-be killer. He commented favorably on his appearance: his intelligent eyes, high forehead, and determined expression. But when presented with a preliminary Gestapo report concluding that Elser had worked alone, he was incredulous. "What idiot conducted this investigation?" he demanded.[45] It was just not possible, he thought, to imagine that Elser was a lone wolf.

To many Nazis, Elser was simply an enigma. He was an ordinary German. He exhibited none of the typical signs of "degeneracy" that they claimed to be combating: apart from his brief flirtation with communism, he was a virtual teetotaler, was not promiscuous, did not consort with Jews, and was not close to the Church. In fact, he was exactly the sort of solid, upstanding, working-class German that they thought they had won over— and, indeed, that had become the backbone of the Nazi Party.

Perhaps for this reason, they simply could not believe that he had worked alone. They initially arrested over a hundred suspects in connection with the Munich bombing, but they realized fairly swiftly that Elser was their man. Yet as the investigators at the scene pieced together his plot, coming to see its thorough planning and high standards of workmanship, foreign complicity was assumed almost as a precondition. Elser, the ordinary German, they thought, must have been led astray; he must have been aided and abetted by the nefarious agents of Germany's enemies.

That assumption fitted neatly with the requirements of the German propaganda machine. In the winter of 1939, the "perfidious English" were portrayed as being behind every kitten stuck up a tree. Thus, officially at least, a bizarre conglomerate of domestic communists, the exiled Black Front, and British intelligence was blamed for Elser's attack. Elser, meanwhile, though most forthcoming and cooperative under interrogation, was little help in uncovering any wider conspiracy. Despite repeated beatings, torture, and hypnosis, he stuck doggedly to his implausible tale: he had had no accomplices and had received no foreign assistance. And when told to build a second example of his complex bomb, timing mechanism, and detonator, to prove that he had acted alone, he complied, skillfully re-creating his invention, to the astonishment of his interrogators.

Himmler even took it upon himself to torture Elser personally. A witness noted:

With wild curses [he] drove his boots hard into the body
of the handcuffed Elser. He then had him removed by a
Gestapo official . . . and taken to the lavatory . . . where he
was beaten with a whip or some similar instrument until
he howled with pain. He was then brought back at the
double to Himmler, who once more kicked him and
cursed him.[46]

Elser, by this point, was said to be "beside himself," but he stuck
to his story.

So if Elser would not name his accomplices, then the Nazi
Sicherheitsdienst (SD) would name some for him. On the day
after the Munich attack, at Venlo, on the Dutch border, SS-
Sturmbannführer Alfred Naujocks was preparing an exercise in
unorthodox warfare. Fresh from his adventure in Gleiwitz (see
pages 115–117), he headed a kidnap squad aiming to snatch two
British agents from neutral Holland. On the German side of the
frontier, he had twelve burly SD men arranged on the running
boards of two Mercedes cars. At the agreed signal, he was to lead
them in a dash across the frontier to a café, where the British had
been lured by a German officer posing as a member of the resistance.

The British agents had thought they were on the verge of
masterminding a coup that would remove Hitler and restore
peace in Europe. They were an odd pair. Major Richard Stevens
had worked in intelligence for some years before being appointed
head of the British intelligence office in The Hague. His brief
there was to oversee espionage activities in Germany. His colleague, Captain Sigismund Payne Best, had worked in military
intelligence during the First World War but had resigned his com-
mission and settled into a comfortable life as a businessman in
Holland. He had then been reassigned to the service on the outbreak of war in September 1939. The two had contacts with the
deputy chief of MI6, Stewart Menzies, and their plan had been
approved at the highest level.[47]

They were, however, being lured into a trap. Their German
contact, a Wehrmacht officer going by the name of Captain

Schaemmel, was in fact Walter Schellenberg, a major in the SS and Reinhard Heydrich's chief of counterintelligence. He had been wooing the British agents for some weeks, promising negotiations with high-ranking anti-Nazis seeking to overthrow Hitler.[48] But, following Elser's attack, Schellenberg was ordered to seize his contacts and bring them to Germany for questioning. He offered a meeting with a senior anti-Nazi as bait. Naujocks was to provide the muscle.

Soon after 3:00 that afternoon, the British arrived at the rendezvous. Almost immediately, they were accosted by Naujocks and his SD squad, who had crashed through the barrier at the border. After a brief tussle and exchange of fire, they were bundled into the cars and whisked to Berlin for interrogation.[49] In time, they would furnish the SD with a great deal of information, including the names of numerous agents and details of all MI6 operations on the Continent. British intelligence would be fatally compromised and exposed as plodding and amateurish, but a bona fide link to Elser would not be established.

Despite this failure, Elser's bombing would prove a boon for the Nazi regime. Goebbels's propaganda machine swung into action, accusing the British of all manner of things, from the Munich bombing to the assassination of Franz Ferdinand. Goebbels forbade his newspaper editors from printing anything that might incriminate any other opposition groups within Germany, such as the Jews, the monarchists, or the clergy. The popular wrath had to be targeted specifically against the British. Accordingly, the news report about the Bürgerbräukeller bomb was given to the German press direct, with the instruction that it was to be quoted on the front page of every newspaper with every sentence in the same order.[50] The banner headline left little room for doubt: "Miraculous Escape for the Führer—Chamberlain's Fervent Hopes Are Not Fulfilled."[51]

The propaganda campaign was necessary to inflame passions in a public that was in danger of growing tired of the Phony War. With the euphoria of victory over the Poles already fading, it sought to prepare the ground for new enemies and new offensives. It was also notable in signaling Hitler's new obsession with defeating the British. It had the desired effect: popular support for the war strengthened markedly.[52]

Aside from inciting hatred for the British, Elser's attack was also exploited to boost Hitler's popularity. The German press went into overdrive, lauding Hitler's survival as a sign of divine intervention. Messages of congratulation poured in. The lead was taken by Pope Pius XII, who sent a telegram expressing his congratulations on the Führer's survival. The German churches swiftly followed suit: a *Te Deum* was sung in Munich Cathedral, while the Protestants held a special thanksgiving service.[53] Many foreign heads of state also expressed their best wishes. Mussolini sent his congratulations but was criticized by some for giving the impression of insincerity.[54]

Ordinary Germans, too, sent countless letters and telegrams. Some expressed their anger and dismay over the attack; others gave thanks to God for Hitler's survival. Many sent donations as a reward for the capture of the culprits or to aid the families of the victims.[55] A few ventured to express their feelings in verse. One poetess eloquently gave voice to the adoration that many Germans felt for "their" Führer:

> *He lives! The enemy's plans were thwarted!*
> *He lives! Our thanks to the Almighty,*
> *That the death of our Führer does not leave*
> *A sorrowful Germany—a people to grieve.*[56]

The aftermath of the attack also provoked much more sinister events. Tip-offs from the public about potential assassins multiplied, as did the list of suspects and conspiracies uncovered (or imagined) by Nazi agents and informants abroad. The German legation in Berne, for example, received a report of two suspicious individuals meeting conspiratorially in a café in the city shortly before the attack; tellingly, it was noted, one of them spoke with an English accent.[57] The consulate in Zürich, meanwhile, was informed of an Austrian Jew who was considered to be a suspect because she had allegedly cursed her misfortune that Hitler had not been killed in the attempt.[58] Another suspect had apparently bet a colleague that Hitler would not survive until 1940. Other reports came from farther afield. One, from Venezuela, linked Elser to the dissident Nazi Otto Strasser,[59] while another, this time from Connecticut, suggested that the authors of the Bürgerbräukeller attack were in fact "highly emotional fanatics," who frequented a pool hall in the city of Hartford.[60]

Countless innocent Germans also fell victim to anonymous denunciations, many of them for merely expressing a lack of enthusiasm for Hitler, in some cases many years before.[61] In such instances, arrest, interrogation, and a sentence of imprisonment almost inevitably followed. Barely six days after the attack, a lengthy new directive ordered that all such reports from the public were to be given the closest scrutiny.[62] Hints were even included for those investigators unclear of their task: Did the suspect display a special interest in Hitler's Munich speech? Did the suspect express surprise that the speech had concluded without incident? And had the suspect remarked recently that the Nazi government's days were numbered?

The regime naturally also exploited the attack as an excuse to deal with dissidents and perceived opponents of all shades. In Düsseldorf alone, more than seventy arrests were made. Forty Bavarian monarchists were also taken into custody.[63] And in Buchenwald, an unknown number of Jews were simply taken out and shot.

For Hitler, the attack seems to have been an almost mystical experience. While Goebbels cynically pushed the divine intervention angle for all he was worth, Hitler appears to have actually believed it. When he first heard of the attack, he took it as a sign. "Now I am completely content!" he exclaimed. "The fact that I left the Bürgerbräukeller earlier than usual is a corroboration of Providence's intention to let me reach my goal."[64] Each time the story was told and retold, it was embellished and gilded a little more. Hitler would later recall that during the Bürgerbräukeller speech, a "little voice" had repeatedly told him, "Get out! Get out!"[65] He gave a more dramatic version to his photographer, Heinrich Hoffmann: "I had the most extraordinary feeling and I don't know myself how or why—but I felt compelled to leave the cellar just as quickly as I could."[66] A later concoction claimed that he had changed his plans that very morning after a seemingly insignificant conversation about his security arrangements.[67]

It is probable that Hitler really did believe these imagined and post hoc justifications for his fortuitous survival. But what is most telling is that he now felt that he had empirical proof of his status as Germany's anointed savior. From this point on, he would only become more trenchant in his beliefs, more convinced of his own opinions, and more contemptuous of the advice of others. He was slipping into megalomania.

On one point at least, however, Hitler was perhaps right to ascribe his survival to the intercession of a higher power. It certainly had nothing to do with his security regime. One of the most astounding aspects of the attack is the incredible ease with which the assassin was able to work. Elser routinely stole explosives and detonators and purchased ammunition without hindrance. Once in Munich, he worked undetected in the Bürgerbräukeller for some thirty-five nights, allowing himself to be locked in, and escaping through a back door at daybreak. Until his arrest, he was never challenged by security guards, SS sentries, or policemen. He even returned one last time to check his bomb the day before it was scheduled to explode. Again he spent the night undetected. Hitler was due to appear the very next day and the country was at war—yet no security checks were carried out and no searches were undertaken.

For some, this apparent laxity was taken as proof of the complicity of the German authorities in the attack. The truth is probably more prosaic. The lack of any systematic security measures in the Bürgerbräukeller was the result of an administrative squabble and of Nazi nepotism. In 1936, a dispute had arisen between the chief of the Munich police and Christian Weber about who was to be responsible for security at the beer hall event. Hitler had decided in favor of his crony Weber, presumably on the logic that he had run the party meetings in the early years, and the Bürgerbräukeller speech was essentially a repeat performance with many of the same faces present. What he didn't realize, however, was that Weber had graduated from a pimp and bruiser to a notorious sybarite, grown fat on the corruption and hedonism available to him under the Nazi state. Weber had won the turf war over the beer hall meeting, but he had done nothing to discharge his new responsibility. The other security organs, the *Leibstandarte* and the RSD, had been passed over in favor of the party and one of Hitler's clique—with fatal consequences. Elser's ingenuity and Weber's laxity made a general overhaul of security inevitable.

That process was completed by the spring of 1940. In a sixty-page directive, Reinhard Heydrich aimed at a thorough review of all security procedures, to sharpen awareness and root out complacency. "The protection of the Führer," he wrote, "must take priority over all other tasks."[68] To this end he argued for closer cooperation between the existing agencies, but he could not resist establishing yet another body under his own supervision. Heydrich's new player was the "special protection service," organized within his power base, the *Reichssicherheitshauptamt* (Reich Security Head Office). It was to serve as a central agency in the assessment of risks, the investigation of tip-offs, and the coordination of activities. Though it contained little that was new, and was still technically subordinated to the RSD, it gave a welcome boost to a network that had become jaded and inefficient. Security for all events was reviewed, with revised, more proactive procedures. Surveillance was revamped: spot checks and precautionary arrests were authorized, and the purchase of explosives and firearms was tightly controlled.[69]

Other innovations included another new body: the *Sicherheits-Kontrolldienst,* or Security Control Service, to oversee security in the New Reich Chancellery, and yet another, the *Führer-Begleitbattalion,* or Führer Escort Battalion, to accompany Hitler into military theaters and defend his military headquarters. Both domestic and travel arrangements were altered. All mail and gifts for Hitler were to be handled by trained SS personnel, while all luggage carried by the Führer's party was to be kept under constant guard. The supreme irony was that the author of this raft of reforms, Reinhard Heydrich, would himself fall victim to an assassin.

It would appear that many postwar historians shared the per-
plexity of the Nazis in their interpretations of Georg Elser. Like
Hitler, they found it difficult to square the sophistication of his
attack with the simplicity of his motives. As a result, a number of
myths developed, some of which have tenaciously clung to the
story almost until the present day.

The first of these was the account that was given at the time—
that Elser was in league with the British and that Payne Best and
Stevens, who had been seized at Venlo, were his controllers. It
was widely trumpeted that all three would be tried for espionage
and exposed to the full penalty of German law. But in reality,
given the complete lack of evidence, no trial could be convened,
so all three men were quietly consigned to a concentration camp.
Tellingly, even senior German intelligence personnel and those
responsible for the interrogations denied the link.[70] Nonetheless,
the official story stuck and the unhappy trio were kept incarcer-
ated pending the expected German victory, whereupon they
would probably have featured as star witnesses in a show trial of
prominent British politicians.

The second, more persuasive interpretation was that Elser was
a Nazi stooge. Almost from the outset, opposition elements, such
as Otto Strasser, viewed the Munich attack as a "provocation."
The earlier Reichstag fire, they claimed, had been engineered by
the Nazis so as to give an excuse to clamp down on the political
left. The Munich bomb plot, they suggested, was a "second
Reichstag fire," a ruse to generate enthusiasm for an unpopular
war. Elser, therefore, was described as "Lubbe Number 2," in reference to the ill-fated Dutch arsonist of 1933.[71] He was portrayed
as a simple patsy, plucked from a concentration camp and sent to
create a diversion, an "incident" that the authorities could then
exploit for their own ends.

Given the Nazis' proven fondness for such ruses, this idea also
took root with a generation of postwar historians.[72] Despite a
complete lack of documentary proof, it appeared to be confirmed
by circumstantial evidence and rumor: Hitler had left the Bürger-

bräukeller early that night, missing the explosion by a matter of minutes, and no security personnel were ever reprimanded over the incident. This theory was supported by the erroneous assumption, common at the time, that Hitler's speech at the Bürgerbräukeller had been shorter than on previous occasions and that he had even spoken more hurriedly than was customary.[73] Unreliable memoirs also lent it credibility. Payne Best, interned with Elser in Sachsenhausen, claimed to have been told that the latter had been hauled from Dachau to plant the bomb. In 1946, the theologian and anti-Nazi Martin Niemoller went further, relating that he had heard on the concentration camp grapevine that Elser had been a sergeant in the SS and that the attack had been personally ordered by Hitler.[74]

These myths were finally put to rest by two German historians in the 1970s.[75] Elser, it appeared, had indeed worked alone. He was not the tool of others, neither the creature of British intelligence nor a Gestapo stooge. Unaided and undetected, he had built a bomb and planted it, coming within a whisker of killing Hitler. He could finally be cleared of all the accusations of complicity and was at last free to take his place among the ranks of the German resistance. In 1998, sixty years after his murderous deed, a memorial to Georg Elser was finally unveiled in his hometown of Königsbronn.[76]

By way of a coda, it is fitting to bring Elser's story to its conclusion. After his confession, Elser was sent to Sachsenhausen concentration camp outside Berlin. However, given his importance to the regime as a fraudulent witness against the British, his life could not be put at risk, and he was kept as a *Sonderhäftling,* a "special prisoner." He was afforded some creature comforts. He was given two rooms and was permitted to turn one into a small workshop. He was also granted a generous ration of cigarettes and was allowed to play a homemade zither. But he was kept in isolation for five years, with an SS guard permanently posted outside his door. Elser is usually described, perhaps unfairly, as a loner. But even he must have felt the chilling lack of human contact.

As the end of the war loomed and a German victory slipped from improbable to implausible, Elser became surplus to requirements. He would never take the stand in a show trial against Churchill and his "clique of warmongers and criminals." He would never utter the damning lines that had been scripted for him. He had outlived his usefulness. In early February 1945, he was transferred to Dachau, on the outskirts of Munich.

A couple of months later, on 9 April—barely a few weeks before the German surrender—Elser was called once more for interrogation. A doleful glance shared with a fellow prisoner showed that he knew what was coming.[77] On the direct orders of Himmler, all "special prisoners" were being put out of the way, where they could not embarrass the dying regime. The commandant of Dachau was curtly informed that Elser was to meet with a fatal accident during one of the next air raids on Munich.[78] That very evening, Elser was taken out by a young SS man and shot in the back of the neck. His body was burned. A week later, his death was reported in the press as the result of an Allied bombing raid. In the frantic last days of the Third Reich, few would have noticed the report. Even fewer would have remembered Elser's name.

CHAPTER 3

The Abwehr: The Enemy Within

There are those who will say that I am a traitor, but I truly am not. I consider myself a better German than all those who run after Hitler. My plan and my duty is to free Germany, and with it the world, of this pestilence.

—HANS OSTER[1]

IN OCTOBER 1919, LESS THAN A YEAR AFTER THE END OF THE First World War, a Committee of Enquiry was established in Berlin to investigate the circumstances surrounding the German military collapse of the previous summer. One of its star witnesses was Field Marshal Paul von Hindenburg, former commander in chief and the new darling of the nationalist right. His appearance before the committee was remarkable. Outside, the crowds cheered his every move, while the newly republican army fell over itself to pander to its erstwhile commander. Inside, Hindenburg contemptuously ignored the questions put to him and embarked instead on a tirade against the new rulers of Germany. His statement ended with words that would threaten the very basis of the new German Republic: "No blame" for the defeat, he said, "was to be attached to the sound core of the army."[2] Rather, he claimed that "civilian demoralization and disunion"[3] had so permeated the military cadres that "our will to victory was undermined. I looked for energy and co-operation, but found pusillanimity and weakness."[4] In his memoirs, he gave his spurious analysis a more lyrical, heroic bent: "Like Siegfried," he wrote, "stricken down by the treacherous spear of savage Hagen, our weary front collapsed."[5] Behind the rhetoric, the message was the same—the German army had been betrayed.

The myth of the *Dolchstosslegende,* the "stab in the back," was born. It held that the German military had *not* been defeated in the field and that the ambitious and unscrupulous politicians of the left and center had shamefully asked for an armistice without the army's knowledge. The politicians, it claimed, had seized defeat from the jaws of victory solely to be able to usher in their own revolution.

This interpretation of events was so far removed from the truth that it took some considerable feats of amnesia for it to be even vaguely credible. It was quietly forgotten, for instance, that it had been the German General Staff that had panicked in the summer of 1918 and had asked the politicians to sue for peace. It was forgotten that the German grand "victory" offensive of the previous spring had failed, to be followed by a long retreat into Belgium. It was forgotten that a brave few staff officers had predicted that Germany would be unable to defeat its enemies in the west, especially after the entry into the war of the United States in 1917. Such inconvenient facts were ignored, even at the highest level. After all, it naturally appealed to the German generals to shift the blame for the lost war. Revolution or no revolution, the prestige of the army was still paramount. Its position and privileges had to be defended, if necessary by distortions and untruths. So the myth of betrayal was deliberately propagated and allowed to develop.

This implausible theory found a ready audience in German society, which had been ill prepared for the prospect of defeat. For four years the people had been fed tales of heroism and adventure with the subtext that advances were being made on all fronts. The soldiers, too, found defeat hard to comprehend. Though they had not been fed the same propaganda and knew the truth of their military predicament, they had difficulty accepting that their sacrifices and the wanton slaughter that they had witnessed had been for nothing.

The defeat, therefore, came as a profound shock and the automatic response of many was to assume that dark forces must have been at work. The reaction of one corporal was typical. He was recuperating following a gas attack when word reached him that the German government had sued for peace:

> And so it had all been in vain. In vain all the sacrifices and privations; in vain the hunger and thirst... in vain the death of two millions.... Was it for this that... the volunteer regiments marched after their old comrades? Was it for this that these boys of seventeen sank into the earth of Flanders?... Did all this happen only so that a gang of wretched criminals could lay hands on the fatherland?[6]

One day, the author of these words would become a household name and a byword for political extremism. But Corporal Hitler's reaction on that day was shared by the vast majority of his countrymen.

In these circumstances, the idea that the political left had betrayed Germany, undermined civilian morale, and hamstrung the army rapidly gained credence, and it soon became one of the totems of the German right. It would not only cripple the democratic left but also fatally weaken any sense of independent thought within the army itself. It would become the cancer at the heart of German politics.

It has been noted, with some justification, that the German army (Reichswehr) dominated the political life of the German Republic after 1918.[7] This might appear surprising. After all, Germany was, in theory at least, a model democracy. It had been largely successful in expunging the worst aspects of Prussian militarism. No longer did military personnel appear ubiquitous in public life. No longer could a university professor consider his rank of captain in the reserves to be his most important title.[8] Moreover, the Reichswehr itself had been emasculated by the Versailles Treaty. Restricted to a mere hundred thousand men, stripped of its heavy weapons, tanks, and offensive capability, it had become little more than a glorified police force.

Yet the German Republic, though perfect on paper, was operating in very imperfect times. Besieged in its early years by enemies on the left and right, it was forced to rely for its very survival on the halfhearted and often grudging support of the military. The nascent republic, therefore, owed its life to the beneficence of its enemy, the army, and as a result, the influence and status of the latter were allowed to grow far beyond what the German politicians or the Western Allies would have wished. The army and the republic were bound together in a marriage of political convenience, which neither side had entered with any genuine conviction. The republic had never been enamored with its partner and had agreed to the union out of fear of the possible alternatives. The army, for its part, was merely going through the motions and waiting for a more appealing suitor to emerge.

Thus, many within the military welcomed the advent of Adolf Hitler to the German Chancellery in January 1933. Hitler—who had been appointed, of course, by the *Reichspräsident* and former commander in chief of the army, Hindenburg—promised a return of Germany's preeminent position in Europe, a revision of the Treaty of Versailles, and a restoration of Germany's military might and martial dash. In him, the army thought it had found an ideal cat's-paw. Here was a politician, the generals thought, who could guarantee a compliant parliamentary majority and through whom they could perpetuate their domination of politics and pursue their own agenda. All they had to do, in turn, was to rein in Hitler's wilder ambitions. They firmly believed that Corporal Hitler would be their man: someone who would heed their orders, someone whom they could control.

Hitler's attitude toward the army, meanwhile, was profoundly contradictory. While he had a deep respect for the military as a whole, and admired its values and way of life, he held the General Staff and officer corps in barely disguised contempt. This had much to do with his earlier political career, in which "the generals," as he described them, had by turns patronized, encouraged, and then betrayed him. He knew very well that his appointment as chancellor was but another stage in this process. But this time, he was determined to gain the upper hand. Revenge would have to be postponed, of course. In the meantime, the military was to be courted, seduced, and controlled.

That seduction began almost immediately upon Hitler's appointment as chancellor. The very next day, Hitler visited the barracks of the Berlin garrison to address the troops on the spirit of the "new Germany." Some days later, when invited to dine with the chiefs of staff, he did the same for the generals, treating them to a two-hour *tour d'horizon* of his policies, principles, and ambitions. His audience, though initially skeptical, was evidently pleasantly surprised. One guest even left the dinner thoroughly enthused, stating that "no Chancellor has ever expressed himself so warmly in favour of defence."[9]

The courtship between Hitler and the Reichswehr continued into 1934, surviving the death of Hindenburg and rumors of a monarchist restoration. It was succored throughout by the ongoing clandestine rearmament program and by Hitler's gentle but persistent wooing of his generals. A test of the new relationship came with the Röhm Purge of June 1934. Hitler sided firmly with the army against the rebellious SA, but he could not resist settling a few old scores in the process. The murder of his old enemies Generals Schleicher and Bredow that summer by the SS sowed misgivings, even anger, among the military. But most regular soldiers were pleased to see Röhm's militant rabble humbled and their own status as the nation's sole bearers of arms reconfirmed. Eighty-three individuals had been murdered, but the minister of war, General Blomberg, saw fit only to praise the "soldierly courage" of the Führer in crushing the "mutineers."[10] The relationship had certainly been strained, but the General Staff still believed that Hitler was their man.

That autumn, the association was cemented a little more. Following Hindenburg's death, Hitler decreed the amalgamation of the functions of the president of the Reich with those of the chancellor. As Führer and chancellor, he then received the revised oath of allegiance of the army. Across Germany all officers and men of the Reichswehr paraded in the presence of their superiors and recited the new oath:

> I swear by almighty God...I will render unconditional obedience to the Führer of the German Reich and people, Adolf Hitler, Supreme Commander of the Armed Forces, and, as a brave soldier, I will be ready at any time to stake my life for this oath.[11]

Whether the soldiers realized it or not, a seismic shift had taken place. They had previously been required to swear allegiance to their "people and country." Their new oath, however, called for them to swear allegiance not to the Republic, the flag, the constitution, or even the office of the head of state. Rather, they were to swear obedience to Adolf Hitler personally. From that moment on, the Reichswehr became, in effect, Hitler's private army.

Yet the removal of its rival and the revision of its oath did little to secure the military's position. Its generals were still blinded to political realities. They still believed that they pulled the strings and that they could unmake "their" chancellor, just as (they believed) they had made him. But another rival was already on the scene. The primary beneficiary of the removal of the SA had not been the Reichswehr; rather, it had been Himmler's SS. Having eliminated the SA, Himmler was already in charge of the burgeoning concentration camp empire and was strengthening his grip on the German police network. He would soon be turning his porcine gaze on the Reichswehr. Spies were dispatched, and damaging rumors were spread. In time, another crisis was in the offing.

Hitler opted to nip this new controversy in the bud. On 3 January 1935, he delivered a speech at the Prussian State Opera House in Berlin before the massed ranks of the party, the SS, and the military. In it, he denied all rumors of dissension and declared the Reichswehr to be an integral part of his vision for Germany. He stressed his "absolute and unshakeable faith" in its loyalty.[12]

Despite his misgivings and his natural preference for the SS, Hitler realized that if his foreign policy goals were to be achieved, he needed an army that was well trained, well armed, and above all compliant. He could not allow his seduction to falter.

Hitler's overarching aim throughout the 1930s was the piecemeal revision of the Treaty of Versailles. That "shameful document," forced on a defeated Germany in the aftermath of World War One, was designed to serve as a punishment for Germany's past aggressions and an effective emasculation to prevent aggression in the future. Versailles became the symbol of Germany's humiliation. Most interwar German governments, of whatever hue, agreed on the desirability of its revision. Many secretly circumvented its proscriptions. Some surreptitiously plotted its dismantling.

But Hitler was more blatant. Right from the outset, he proclaimed his fundamental opposition to Versailles. His "25 Point Program," formulated for the nascent Nazi Party in 1920, stated unequivocally: "[W]e demand . . . the revocation of the peace treaty of Versailles."[13] In his speeches and electioneering, he was no less strident. A tirade from 1939 was typical. In it, he stated that every one of the 440 articles of the treaty was "an insult and a violation of a great nation."[14] In spite of the numerous accommodations and concessions that he made in the transition from a rabble-rouser of the radical right to a would-be chancellor, on one point Hitler never wavered. He wanted to smash Versailles, remove its stipulations, and expunge its memory.

Prior to 1938, Hitler sought to reverse only those parts of the treaty that applied to domestic German affairs. Thus, in 1935, he reintroduced conscription to the German army, forbidden under article 173 of Versailles. The following year, he ordered the remilitarization of the Rhineland, forbidden under article 43. Hitler was achieving what no previous Weimar chancellor had managed. Gradually, and most important peacefully, he was removing the most onerous clauses of Versailles. The army was being restored to its rightful place as the defender of the nation. Its writ now ran unhindered throughout the land; its right to conscript troops had been restored; its size was no longer limited by foreign powers. For this reason, its ranks were slow to develop opposition to the Nazi regime. The army was once again being raised to its former exalted status. It was being supplied with generous funding, able personnel, and up-to-date equipment. Revolt was simply inconceivable.

Nonetheless, 1938 would prove to be a critical year. The previous autumn, Hitler had gathered his most senior generals for a secret discussion, whose minutes were recorded in the famous Hossbach Memorandum.[15] He had given forth, at some length, on Germany's strategic and economic position and had discussed the circumstances under which Germany might go to war in the coming three or four years. His generals were alarmed—not by the ultimate goal of expansion, but by the prospect that Germany might again be embroiled in a conflict with France and Britain. They raised objections and criticized the analysis; some even demanded reassurances that there were no immediate plans for war.[16] But they failed to realize that Hitler was testing them, watching their reactions to his radical ideas. It would soon become apparent that their timidity had singularly failed to impress.

By the early spring of 1938, therefore, Hitler's long-feigned affection for his General Staff was turning to contempt. He was tiring of having to force his generals to plan for war, tiring of having, as he put it, to "goad the butcher's dog."[17] No longer did he flatter and cajole, as he once had. Rather, he blustered and threatened. One outburst from the spring of that year was typical. During an inspection visit to a barracks, he was asked his opinion of the purges then raging in the Soviet Union, which had cost the lives of numerous prominent generals. He replied bluntly: "I, too, would not recoil from destroying ten thousand officers, if they opposed themselves to my will. What is that in a nation of eighty millions? I do not want men of intelligence," he concluded, "I want men of brutality."[18] In the event, no show trials or public purges would be necessary. Hitler's uncanny ability to exploit events as they developed would ensure the army's seamless subjugation.

The first crisis to develop was that surrounding the war minister, Field Marshal von Blomberg. Blomberg, who had initially been installed as a brake on Hitler's ambitions, had in fact become an early enthusiast for the Nazi program.[19] In 1938, however, he made the mistake not only of marrying a former prostitute but also of inviting Hitler to be a witness at the wedding. With the integrity of the army and Hitler's own especially prudish sense of honor so spectacularly sullied, Blomberg had no alternative but to resign.

Thus forced to divest himself of his war minister, Hitler was less than enthusiastic about the designated successor, the supreme commander of the army, General von Fritsch. Fritsch was a rather different character from Blomberg. An instinctive anti-Nazi, he had often made unflattering remarks about Hitler and his followers, yet was still in line to succeed Blomberg as war minister in the spring of 1938.[20] When spurious allegations of homosexuality against him had crossed Hitler's desk that winter, they had initially been dismissed out of hand. However, following a theatrical intrigue engineered by Göring, involving a notorious con man and former rent boy, the Führer's confidence in his general was severely dented. Ultimately, though exonerated by a court of honor, Fritsch was forced into retirement. He would die an infantryman's death the following year during the Polish campaign.

Though the Blomberg and Fritsch crises had not been of his own making, Hitler was determined to benefit from the serendipitous departure of two of his perceived opponents. He decided to take over the leadership of the military himself. "From henceforth," went the decree, "I exercise personally the immediate command over the whole armed forces."[21] His first act was to relieve sixteen senior generals of their posts; a further forty-four high-ranking officers were transferred to other duties. Not only would his new deputies be subservient to his orders, but they would also be men who thought very much as he did.

Hitler had outwitted, outmaneuvered, and humiliated his generals. In 1933, he had inherited an institution that was intended to serve as a check on his more ambitious designs. In five short years, he had seduced it, suborned it, and finally bent it to his will. By 1938, he was in immediate command of a powerful military machine that had sworn allegiance to his very person.

The German army had sustained a grievous defeat. Its independence, long guarded and for some time illusory, had now finally been destroyed. Its role as the "state within the state," the final arbiter of German politics, had been brought to an ignominious end. At best, the army was now but one pillar of the Nazi state, alongside the party and the government, but, like the other two, totally subordinate to the will of the Führer. For those in the German military who still had eyes to see, the developments of the spring of 1938 were to prove a watershed.

One of those whose "vision" was unimpaired was the chief of the Abwehr, Wilhelm Canaris. The Abwehr (the name means "defense") was the military intelligence department of the Ministry of Defense. Its remit was the collection, evaluation, and presentation of intelligence material for its military and political masters. Directly responsible to the chief of staff, it had officers in each branch of the military as well as a network of agents and informants in other fields. By the time of Canaris's appointment in 1935, however, the Abwehr had spent a number of years in the doldrums, underfunded, understaffed, and largely ignored.[22]

Canaris was widely thought to be the man who would change all that. Already involved in supervising the clandestine submarine building program, he also possessed numerous foreign contacts and a glorious war record. These qualities, allied to a reputation as a pro-Nazi, made Canaris the ideal man to forge the Abwehr into the foremost intelligence agency of the Third Reich. Under his command, the Abwehr did indeed grow in stature and influence. This was, of course, partly due to the resumption of conscription and the expansion of the military, which was announced in the spring of 1935. But it was also undoubtedly a result of Canaris's ability to placate his rivals, the Gestapo and SD.[23] Though the SD and SS continued to spy on the Abwehr and often worked to undermine its operations, a form of modus vivendi was eventually reached, and a number of successes were scored.[24] Besides establishing an extensive network of agents in the Soviet Union and the United States, the Abwehr also secured blueprints of the top-secret American Norden bombsight—reputedly the most accurate then available.[25]

Canaris himself cut a peculiar figure. A little over 152 centimeters (5 feet) in height, white-haired, and soft-spoken, with a distinctly unmilitary bearing, he initially failed to impress his new subordinates. He was indeed an enigmatic character. Born near Dortmund in 1887, the son of an industrialist, he had opted for a career as a sailor. After service in World War One, predominantly as an intelligence officer and U-boat commander, he had enjoyed a swift rise in the postwar navy, culminating in a posting as captain of the aged battleship *Schlesien* in 1932.

Yet for all his success in that most demanding of professions, Canaris had a number of peculiar traits. First, he was deeply superstitious, with a pronounced aversion to tall people and those who were garrulous, energetic, or talkative. In other words, he had a dislike for all those who were not like himself. Second, he was an incurable hypochondriac. An inveterate pill popper who suffered from neuralgia, insomnia, and a host of other, more or less imaginary ailments, he had a pathological fear of infection. This had evidently even been the case during his time at sea. In 1924, the ship's doctor on the cruiser *Berlin* had described First Officer Canaris as having a "condition aggravated by a tendency to interpret all kinds of minor symptoms as signs of severe illness."[26]

Canaris was also a natural spy. Even at school he had been dubbed "the peeper," because of his insatiable curiosity.[27] In later life, this trait was allied to inscrutability and a talent for deception. In his Abwehr office, Canaris gave pride of place to a statuette of three monkeys, which demonstrated the cardinal virtues for a successful agent—see all, hear all, say nothing.[28] It was a mantra that he was to follow most assiduously. Many believed that he spied for fun or for its own sake. It has even been suggested that he had agents engaged within his own household to spy on his guests.[29]

In his political affiliations Canaris was no less enigmatic. He was a military man who abhorred violence.[30] He was an impassioned nationalist and anti-communist who had initially welcomed the advent of the Nazis, though he never joined the party.

Indeed, his relationship to the Nazi Party would perplex both his contemporaries and a later generation of historians. The dilemma at its heart was typical of the entire German officer class—Canaris had welcomed Hitler's anti-communism and his plans for expansion, rearmament, and a return to greatness, but at the same time he loathed the lawlessness and amorality of the SS and the degradation of the military. Upon his arrival at the Abwehr in 1935, therefore, Canaris gave a very good impression of being a Nazi sympathizer. He began parroting Nazi slogans and stressing the desirability of close cooperation with the Gestapo. His very appointment was thought to have been facilitated by Reinhard Heydrich, his archrival and head of the SS espionage agency, the SD. He was certainly close to Heydrich. The two shared their memories of service in the navy and were neighbors in the Berlin district of Schlachtensee, where they frequently rode together and where Heydrich was a regular visitor to Frau Canaris's soirees.[31] It may well have been that this closeness was, for both of them, a matter of professional necessity. However, following Heydrich's assassination in 1942, Canaris openly wept at his funeral and claimed to have lost "a true friend."[32]

Despite all this, it has been suggested that Canaris had been a convinced opponent of the Nazis from the outset and, indeed, that he had taken the appointment at the Abwehr only to be able to frustrate Hitler's aggressive plans. Though the opinion is contested, one of his colleagues claimed after the war that Canaris had started conspiring against the Nazis immediately after assuming command of the Abwehr. "The Canaris group," he recalled, "...was the first united military clique working against Hitler with any semblance of a planned programme.... This rebellion," he added, "began when Admiral Canaris was put in charge of the Abwehr."[33]

Whatever the truth of that assertion, it is clear that by 1938, Canaris had undergone some sort of conversion to the anti-Nazi cause. He had been deeply shaken by the Fritsch affair, which was widely considered to have severely dented the independence and integrity of the military.[34] The purges then under way in the USSR, meanwhile, had served to awaken in him a realization that generals were destined merely to be exploited by politicians and scapegoated when necessary.[35] Numerous firsthand accounts from the period point to his increasing hatred for the SS in particular, and his growing propensity to refer to them simply as "criminals."[36] By the time he recruited the former chief of the Austrian counterespionage office, Erwin von Lahousen, to the Abwehr in March 1938, his conversion appears to have been complete. Canaris laid down the following ground rule for his new section chief: "[Y]ou may not, under any pretext, admit to this section ... or take on your staff any member of the NSDAP, the Storm Troopers or the SS, or even an officer who sympathises with the Party."[37] For a senior serving officer of the German Reich, these were brave words.

Yet, for Canaris, doubts and obstacles clearly remained. For one thing, he may have been hamstrung by his belief in the sanctity of the oath of allegiance.[38] But, much more importantly, he faced an awkward yet fundamental dilemma. His sense of duty and honor dictated that, in the face of his profound misgivings about the regime, he should resign his post. Yet he knew that if he did, he would be succeeded by one of the new breed from the SS, who would destroy the network that he had established. This was the predicament shared by many others. "How could we hope to bring about change," they would argue, "if every important position was voluntarily abandoned to the Nazis?"[39]

Canaris's solution was to remain in office and to serve as a facilitator to the opposition circles that he had fostered, while playing no perceptible role himself. After all, what better vehicle was there for a conspiracy than an intelligence service, where secrecy was paramount and clandestine operation was the norm? Thus Canaris remade the upper echelons of his department in his own image, surrounding himself with men of a mind similar to his own. The senior staff that he recruited almost all shared his unashamedly independent view of German politics. They would become the core of what might be called the Abwehr opposition. These included Helmuth Groscurth, head of Section II (sabotage); his Austrian-born successor, Erwin von Lahousen; Hans von Dohnanyi, deputy head of Central Section; and Hans Gisevius, later head of "special projects" and one of the primary chroniclers of the German resistance movement. But foremost among them was Hans Oster.

A career soldier, Oster had served in the First World War and in the Reichswehr before a romantic scandal brought about his resignation in 1932. The following year he was employed in the Abwehr in a civilian capacity and so was already active there prior to the appointment of Canaris. Contemporaries described him as "an absolutely sound and decent fellow," and all were agreed on his mental ability and intelligence.[40] A Christian, patriot, and monarchist, he had a profound sense of justice, which the "new morality" of the Nazis could not corrupt. But beyond that, his character was in many ways the antithesis to that of Canaris. Oster had something of the show-off about him. Tall and elegant, he liked to dress well and occasionally sported a monocle. In stark contrast to his mentor and master, he could be audacious, impatient, and sometimes unwisely vocal in his opinions.

Oster would become the "soul" of the German resistance movement.[41] His conversion to the cause came earlier than most. From the outset, he viewed the lawlessness of the SA with outright contempt. But it was the execution of his former colleague and superior General Kurt von Schleicher in the summer of 1934 that began his transformation into an active opponent of the Nazis.[42] From that time, he developed a fanatical hatred of the SS. And from his position within the Abwehr he had the ideal vantage point from which to watch its gradual penetration of German society and to collect documentary evidence of its crimes. By 1937, it was said, Oster had already decided that Hitler—whom he customarily referred to as "the pig"[43]—had to be killed.[44] By 1938, therefore, when many other future resisters were barely opening their eyes to the grim realities of the Nazi regime, Oster was already a veteran. The events of that year would suffice to push him from passive opposition into active resistance.

Like Canaris, Oster gathered to him would-be resisters and others critical of the regime. His office, a colleague later confided, was "a port of call for all those members or associates of the Ab-

wehr who were self-acknowledged opponents of National Socialism."[45] Another contemporary described it as "a pigeon coop,
filled as it was with mysterious persons."[46] But Oster's network of
contacts spread much farther than that. For all their apparent determination, the disparate opposition groups of the 1930s could
barely be described as "the resistance." They were not one body
of men. They did not speak with one voice. In fact, they barely
spoke at all. Those who conspired even to express criticism of the
regime did so only in small groups of trusted friends and confidants. Concerns would be aired during a walk in the park or at a
private dinner party. The presence of a stranger or a supposed
"new recruit" would be cause for profound alarm. Some went to
great lengths to avoid detection. A series of code words was developed to disguise sensitive discussions: Oster was code-named
"Uncle Whitsun"; Hitler was "Emil"; his headquarters was
"Mount Olympus."[47] Two resisters met regularly in a Berlin
swimming pool, where they found they could catch up on events
without fear of eavesdroppers.[48] Another, fearing being caught in
possession of incriminating documents, learned the wording of
memoranda and telegrams by heart before passing them on ver-
batim to his superiors.[49]

Yet for all the precautions employed by some, there was also
some shocking laxity. Hans von Dohnanyi, for example, rightly
insisted on keeping documentary evidence both of the crimes of
the Nazis and of the resistance's discussions and plans. However,
his files were kept not in a locked safe but in a simple filing cabinet in the corner of his office. According to one contemporary,
the security failings went further:

> The lack of caution exercised by Dohnanyi and Oster was
> truly devastating. They used to like meeting their friends
> and other like-minded people in the kind of upmarket
> bars where anybody with a grain of sense would suspect
> that the various intelligence services had long ago in-
> stalled listening devices. Furthermore, had the Gestapo or
> the SD bothered to install a couple of agents equipped . . .
> to monitor the coming and going at Abwehr headquarters,

then they would surely have grasped sooner rather than later what was afoot.[50]

Nonetheless, it took tremendous courage to attempt to bring the groups together, to forge contacts between them, and to seek to do more than merely air grievances and share horror stories. This was to be the role taken on by Hans Oster. Through countless phone calls and meetings in Berlin apartments, restaurants, and parks, Oster forged the basis of the German resistance movement. Standing in his office beside a bank of telephones, he once outlined to a colleague his own perception of the position that he held. "This is what I am," he said, "I facilitate communications for everyone everywhere."[51]

Oster really did speak to just about everyone. He courted the politicians, sounded out the generals, kept in touch with the monarchists, and even entertained disgruntled former Nazis. Like a spider at the center of its web, he was the liaison man, linking the various parties who wanted Hitler removed. But he also played a more active role, cajoling, persuading, and stiffening the resolve of the waverers. Without Hans Oster, many of the resisters of 1938 would simply have been unaware of one another's existence.

Shortly after 4:00 on the afternoon of 12 March 1938, Adolf Hitler entered Austria. In a cavalcade of gray, open-topped Mercedes vehicles "bristling with weapons," he crossed the border at his birthplace, Braunau am Inn.[52] He was returning not as a tourist but as a self-proclaimed "liberator." Yet for all the swagger, the Führer was nervous. His "invasion" of Austria would be a test of his boldness and of his theory of the quiescence of the Western powers.

The "invasion" had begun that morning. The previous day the Austrian chancellor had caved in to German pressure and resigned, to be replaced by a prominent Nazi. German troops and tanks then moved off at dawn. They were greeted by enthusiastic crowds, peals of church bells, and a carpet of flowers. Their advance soon slowed to a crawl. Following in their wake, Hitler proceeded to Linz and thence to Vienna, where he was greeted by crowds "delirious with joy."[53] Two days later, he addressed a quarter of a million people gathered in the city's Heldenplatz. "This land," he said, "is German; it has understood its mission, it will fulfil this mission, and it shall never be outdone in its loyalty to the great German national community." "As the Führer and Chancellor of the German nation and the Reich," he concluded, "I now report to history that my homeland has joined the German Reich."[54] Once again, the enthusiasm of the Viennese was undeniable. They endorsed Hitler's "invasion" en masse; their republic would become a province of the greater German Reich, their army would be absorbed into the Wehrmacht, and their new Führer would return to Berlin a conquering hero. Hitler had carried out a classic bloodless coup. By his bluster and guile, he had removed one of the most hated clauses of the Treaty of Versailles—that forbidding the *Anschluss*, the union of Austria and Germany—at one stroke. And yet war had not been declared. The Western powers had not intervened and not a drop of blood had been shed. Hitler was at the peak of his powers.

Despite the general euphoria that the *Anschluss* with Austria had engendered, some were troubled by the events of that spring. Following the Blomberg and Fritsch affairs and the subordination of the army, those still unseduced by the Nazis saw the Austrian adventure as a dangerous escalation. Whereas Hitler had previously confined his actions to domestic affairs, now they saw him embarking on foreign adventures. Whereas Hitler had previously reacted to events, now they saw him forcing the pace. What was more, they saw that the bloodless victory against Austria had reinforced his contempt for all those who had advocated a more cautious policy. They saw him become impervious to all those who counseled moderation. When, soon after his triumphant return from Vienna, he set his sights on Czechoslovakia, they saw that it was time to act.[55]

Throughout that spring and summer, a number of emissaries from the resistance embarked on clandestine missions to Western capitals. Their brief was to warn the British and French that

Hitler was bent on war and to convince them that only a resolute and unyielding stand from Paris and London could deter him. The messengers, most of whom were sent by Oster, came from widely differing backgrounds. They included a Pomeranian landowner, an industrialist, a diplomat, and an eminent historian. All of them had high-level contacts in London. All of them delivered their message in the starkest terms. All of them failed.

The fundamental problem was that the British were committed to a policy that was diametrically opposed to what the German resistance demanded of them. They were of a mind to yield to Hitler's demands rather than stand firm. Their policy of appeasement, synonymous with Prime Minister Neville Chamberlain, was predicated on the widespread feeling that Germany had been harshly treated at Versailles and was entitled to a position in the world commensurate with her population and resources. Moreover, Nazi Germany was anti-communist, and communism was widely viewed as a greater threat to the established order than fascism. At the root of appeasement, however, lay the understandable desire to avoid another war. The British Empire had barely survived the First World War and another large-scale conflict would surely spell its end.

Yet appeasement was more than mere woolly-headed pacifism. Chamberlain's policy, though subsequently vilified, was more hardheaded and realistic than is often appreciated. A series of negotiated territorial concessions, it was thought, would leave Hitler's Germany "sated, indolent and quiescent."[56] War would be avoided, Hitler would be pacified, and the established order—and the Empire—could be maintained. The British, therefore, viewed the emissaries of the German resistance with barely disguised incomprehension, if not distaste. They offered sympathy and kind words, but little more. They were, after all, looking to avoid confrontation rather than provoke it.

Nonetheless, Oster was undaunted and continued with his planning. In this, he was aided by a number of prominent soldiers and politicians, who met repeatedly that summer to finesse their plot. The network of conspirators included two successive chiefs of the General Staff, Ludwig Beck and Franz Halder; the head of the Reichsbank, Hjalmar Schacht; and the commander of the Berlin Military District, Erwin von Witzleben. It consisted of two distinct groups. The first, represented by Beck and Halder, was what one might call the anti-war party. They were mostly military men who were desperate to avert the disastrous military confrontation toward which Hitler appeared to be headed. The second, the coup party, represented by Schacht and Witzleben, aimed to remove Hitler and replace him with a more cautious, conservative leader. In many ways, therefore, the conspiracy was an uneasy marriage of disparate allies driven by political convenience and desperation. Not all of its members were enthusiastic traitors or even convinced resisters.

One of its key players was the head of the Berlin police, Wolf von Helldorf. Helldorf made a most peculiar resister. A notorious anti-Semite, playboy, and former leader of the Berlin SA, he had become disillusioned by Nazism and had apparently been appalled by the treatment meted out to General von Fritsch.[57] According to Schacht, he may also have been moved by a sense of guilt for his previous enthusiasm for the Nazi cause and was seeking to rehabilitate himself by making contact with the opposition. Whatever his motivations, Helldorf provided the plotters with vital inside knowledge and even supplied Oster with documentary evidence of Nazi misdeeds. His exposition of the callous and underhanded treatment of Fritsch and Blomberg, meanwhile, won many converts to the cause, including Schacht.[58]

So, armed with moral indignation, the plotters devised a plan in the summer of 1938. Once a mobilization against Czechoslovakia had been ordered—thereby giving proof of Hitler's recklessness—they would engineer a coup. It was a bold plan. Troops of the crack 23rd Infantry Division, based in Potsdam, would occupy all key ministries, radio stations, and police, Gestapo, and SS installations in Berlin. The 1st Light Division would block the return to the city of Hitler's bodyguard division, the SS-Leibstandarte, then stationed in Saxony near the Czech border. A third force would then take the Reich Chancellery, capture Hitler, and spirit him away to a secret location.

It was at this point, however, that the plotters' plans appeared to diverge. The military men among them were content for Hitler to be formally tried or declared insane, while a new government would take charge. Others were less optimistic. Chief among the latter was Friedrich Heinz, an Abwehr colleague of Oster's.[59] Heinz was a typical example of the "lost generation" that had flocked to the Nazi ranks. He had served in the First World War and the postwar *Freikorps* and had participated in the right-wing Kapp Putsch of 1920. He then featured in almost every right-wing terrorist and conspiratorial organization of the interwar years, including the Organization Consul, the Ehrhardt Brigade, and the Viking League, before joining the Nazi Party in 1928. However, as a follower of the "national-bolshevik" wing of the party, under Otto Strasser, he soon found himself increasingly at odds with the leadership. Expelled from the party in 1930, he became, in effect, an anti-Hitler Nazi.

In 1935 Heinz joined the Abwehr, where he was responsible for monitoring the German press. By 1938, he was one of the key figures in the Oster plot. His initial task was the recruitment of the *Stosstrupp*, or raiding party, that was to take the Reich Chancellery and arrest Hitler. He recruited mainly from the Abwehr but also included friends and acquaintances that he considered politically sound and ruthless enough to carry out the action.[60] By mid-September, he had a commando unit of around twenty individuals armed and installed in safe houses around Berlin. All that was needed now was the trigger.

For much of the summer of 1938, Europe stood on the brink of war. Hitler's relentless saber rattling against Czechoslovakia, ostensibly in support of the Sudeten German minority in the country, had spurred a round of shuttle diplomacy in an attempt to defuse the crisis. So, just as the German resistance was sending its emissaries to London demanding firmness, so London was sending its own emissaries to the Czechs demanding submission. Though every concession was made, it was all in vain. As Hitler had told the Sudeten German leader that summer: "We must always demand so much that we can never be satisfied."[61] In this way the crisis continued to worsen, with the British increasingly

determined to placate Hitler, while Hitler was increasingly determined not to be placated.

By 12 September, matters appeared to be coming to a head.
On that day, as Hitler stepped up to the microphone at the Nuremberg rally, many expected him to declare war on the Czechs.
He resisted, but his speech was a masterpiece of defiance and
veiled menace:

> The...abnormal Czechoslovakian state...[was pursu-
> ing] a mission to ravage and rape a mass of millions of
> other nationalities....The misery of the Sudeten Ger-
> mans defies description. [But they] are neither defenceless
> nor have they been abandoned....If these tortured crea-
> tures can find neither justice nor help by themselves, then
> they will receive both from us....It is the duty of all of us
> never again to bow our heads to any alien will.[62]

The following day, right on cue, the Sudeten German leader demanded the secession of the Sudetenland from Czechoslovakia.

Oster's plans, meanwhile, were in a high state of readiness.
Meetings had been convened and procedures agreed upon. The
day before Hitler's Nuremberg speech, Oster and Gisevius had
made a tour of Berlin by car, reconnoitering the government
quarter and discreetly inspecting the target buildings. Escape
routes had been identified and copious notes taken. Heinz's men
were already in place, and the cooperation of the key military
units had been ensured. The coup was set to take place following
Hitler's order for a mobilization, which was expected on 15 September. Oster told a colleague that the action would be launched
within the following forty-eight hours.[63] Everything was ready.
Confidence was high. On the evening of the fourteenth, one of
the plotters, Helmuth Groscurth, confided to his brother,
"Hitler will be arrested tomorrow!"[64]

The tension was broken by news that Chamberlain was flying
to Germany to speak to Hitler. Chamberlain believed himself to be
playing his masterstroke. The sixty-nine-year-old prime minister,

who was in failing health and had never flown before, was to meet Hitler for face-to-face talks, having convinced himself that he could achieve success where others had failed. At Berchtesgaden, he was subjected to Hitler's well-rehearsed rant about perfidious Czechs and terrorized Germans. He left to discuss matters with his cabinet, promising to return. He had succeeded only in gaining a paltry agreement from Hitler not to begin military action in the meantime, but he deluded himself into believing that he had made progress. As he later confided to his sister: "In spite of the harshness and ruthlessness I thought I saw in his face, I got the impression that here was a man who could be relied upon when he had given his word."[65] He could not have been more wrong. Hitler, for his part, viewed Chamberlain with outright contempt and among his intimates referred to the British prime minister simply as "the arsehole."[66]

The plotters were initially devastated by the news of Chamberlain's visit. What they wanted was a declaration of war, not international mediation. Further negotiations, they thought, did nothing to defuse the tension, while playing into Hitler's hands and making all those who had counseled caution look distinctly foolish. Severely shaken by this turn of events, some of them now vowed to launch their coup only if the British declared war on Germany. Others were inclined to give up their efforts entirely. As Gisevius noted grimly: "We bowed our heads in despair. To all appearances, it was all up with our revolt."[67]

Nonetheless, once their nerves had been restored, the plotters resumed their planning. On the evening of 20 September, a meeting was held at Oster's Berlin apartment, where the plan for the coup was to be finalized. Proclamations were drafted, a constitution was discussed, and the restoration of the monarchy was even mooted. The role assigned to Heinz's *Stosstrupp* was outlined once again, along with those allocated to the other units involved in securing the wider Berlin area. When the other conspirators left, Heinz remained behind to speak to Oster. He had long been unhappy with the plan merely to arrest Hitler and put him on trial. Even from a prison cell, he argued, Hitler was stronger than all the conspirators combined. The Führer, he said, should be killed. This would have been wholly unacceptable to many of the senior members of the conspiracy, who would have been appalled by the cold-blooded murder of the head of state. As Beck had warned, "assassination is still murder."[68] Oster, however, was certainly not averse to the proposal; indeed, it is highly likely that he had already arrived at the same conclusion himself. After a brief discussion, he concurred with Heinz and the two agreed that during the action, regardless of the degree of resistance offered, a scuffle would be engineered and Hitler would be shot.[69] The other plotters would not be informed of the change of plan. The September Conspiracy had grown a conspiracy of its own.

Meanwhile, Chamberlain's shuttle diplomacy continued. His second meeting with Hitler was scheduled for 22 September at the Rhine resort of Bad Godesberg. He arrived in a triumphant mood, having secured Anglo-French agreement to the demands raised a week before at Berchtesgaden. But he was to be given a rude awakening. When he outlined his "good news," Hitler was unimpressed. He then sat in fury as Hitler again raised the stakes: "I'm sorry Herr Chamberlain ... this solution no longer applies."[70] The following day, exasperated and exhausted, he was presented with a fresh ultimatum—the withdrawal of Czech troops from the Sudetenland was required within four days. Chamberlain meekly replied that Hitler had "not supported in the slightest [his] efforts to maintain peace," and flew back to London to discuss matters with his cabinet.[71]

The conspirators were now once again in high spirits, believing that Hitler's fresh demands must not only cause an irrevocable breakdown in negotiations but also give unequivocal evidence of his malicious intent. When Oster heard details of the Bad Godesberg meeting, his enthusiasm returned. "Thank God," he said, "finally we have clear proof that Hitler wants war, no matter what. Now there can be no going back."[72] In these circumstances, his primary concern was to ensure that Hitler remained in Berlin, where he had been a rare visitor for most of the previous month. He knew only too well that the putsch depended entirely on Hitler's presence in the capital. So he asked his Foreign Office contact, Erich Kordt, for assistance: "Do everything you can," he instructed, "to get Hitler back to Berlin. The bird must return to the cage."[73]

At this point, the conspirators received the news that they had been hoping for. The British were finally making a stand and would not be attempting to persuade the Czechs to accept the new German demands. Some days later, they sent Chamberlain's advisor, Sir Horace Wilson, to Berlin formally to reject the terms that Hitler had set out at Bad Godesberg. After a heated discussion, Wilson delivered his message: "If, in pursuit of her treaty obligations, France became actively engaged in hostilities against Germany, the United Kingdom would feel obliged to support her."[74] That evening, in a speech at the Berlin Sportpalast, Wilson heard Hitler's response. In a "masterpiece of invective"[75] the Führer focused his wrath on the Czech president, Edvard Beneš:

> We shall not wait.... I demand that Herr Beneš be forced
> to honesty.... He will have to hand over the territories on
> October 1.... He can either accept my offer and give the
> Germans their freedom, or we Germans will go and get
> it for ourselves. The decision is his now! Be it war or
> peace![76]

The conspirators finally appeared to have what they wanted. Hitler's mask had fallen. Rather than playing the reasonable statesman, he was issuing ultimatums and making immoderate demands. Moreover, the British had finally made a stand. Though certainly an improvement, their statement was still too equivocal for some. It still tied any British action to a French response and noted only that Britain would only "feel obliged" to support France, not that she would automatically do so. Nonetheless, Britain and Germany were now on the brink of war, and once again the plotters prepared for imminent action. Kordt expressed the feelings of many of them after a month or more of secret meetings and heightening tension. "For the first time in weeks," he wrote, "a feeling of relief washed over me. The deliberations and discussions appeared to be over."[77]

The mobilization order for the invasion of Czechoslovakia

was expected at 2 p.m. on 28 September. That morning, the plotters made their final preparations. In the Reich Chancellery, Kordt checked that no special security measures had been instituted. He also offered to ease the entry of the *Stosstrupp* by opening the Chancellery doors from the inside. He implored a colleague: "Don't wait until this afternoon, or tomorrow. We must move now before we are discovered."[78] At army headquarters, Witzleben declared excitedly that "the time has come," while Halder pleaded with the commander in chief, General Brauchitsch, to issue the order authorizing the coup.[79] At the Abwehr, meanwhile, Oster remained at his desk, ready to give the order to Heinz to move. Gisevius noted that "the minutes passed into hours of unutterable suspense."[80]

The tension was broken, this time, by news from Mussolini. The Italian dictator had sent his ambassador to urge Hitler to accept a final attempt to settle the Sudeten issue peacefully—a four-power conference between Germany, Italy, Britain, and France. Hitler initially reacted with fury. He had already rejected similar requests from Chamberlain, Roosevelt, and even Göring, but the pressure to pull back from the brink of war was now coming from all sides. He quietly informed the ambassador: "Tell the Duce that I accept his proposal."[81]

The following day, Chamberlain again flew to Germany. At the Munich Conference, he was browbeaten into colluding in the bloodless dismemberment of Czechoslovakia. The border regions were ceded to Germany, leaving the remainder dangerously exposed and denuded of its fortifications. Chamberlain had helped Hitler to achieve his maximum objectives. Though he would publicly laud the Munich Agreement as "peace for our time," he privately described the meeting as a "nightmare." Munich was a humiliation for the Western powers. It was an abject surrender dressed as a negotiated peace. Gisevius noted bitterly that Hitler had "pocketed one of the neatest victories in diplomatic history."[82] For Churchill it was "the first foretaste of a bitter cup."[83] As one historian has pithily summarized: "Under pressure from the ruthless, the clueless combined with the spineless to achieve the worthless."[84]

The plotters had been thwarted. They had been denied their trigger. The mobilization had been stayed and war had not been declared. Gisevius thought they might carry out the plan anyway, but he was shouted down. Witzleben explained that the troops would never revolt against Hitler in the hour of his greatest triumph. The plot, they conceded, was done for. Gisevius considered emigrating. Kordt took a holiday. Some days later, a small group of conspirators gathered around the fireplace at Witzleben's home. Musing on their failure and "the calamity that had befallen Europe," they "tossed [their] lovely plans and projects into the fire."[85]

In the aftermath of the failure of the September Conspiracy, the circle of conspirators, disparate at best, soon began to disintegrate. Those from the military had largely lost their nerve, been transferred to new commands, or else been seduced by Hitler's obvious successes. Beck, having resigned in protest in 1938, maintained contact with resistance circles but, as one historian put it, "retire[d] into an impenetrable cloud of glacial aloofness."[86] Witzleben continued to approach like-minded officers who were prepared to support a coup, but he had been transferred to the provinces and was out of touch. Halder was more typical. Torn between his moral responsibility and his military duty, he preferred to fulfill neither. He continued to believe that Hitler was evil and he knew that war had to be avoided, but he would never be able to bring himself to act again. Nervous and skittish at the best of times, he would later suffer a nervous collapse and confess to a colleague, with tears in his eyes, that "for weeks on end, he had been going to see Hitler with a pistol in his pocket in order to gun him down."[87] He prevaricated, as Gisevius noted, with "a hundred ifs and buts . . . [but] he simply lacked the will."[88]

Some were driven in the opposite direction. The opposition circle within the Foreign Office around Ernst von Weizsäcker and Erich Kordt, for example, felt themselves drawn deeper into the growing resistance movement and became increasingly willing

conspirators. To facilitate their efforts, they engaged in a deliberate dispersal of like-minded personnel with the goal of creating a
functioning resistance network within Germany's foreign service.[89] Some members of that network would become players in
subsequent assassination attempts.

The Abwehr, meanwhile, carried on much as it had before. It
continued officially to undermine Hitler's enemies, while some
of its senior personnel were unofficially undermining Hitler.
Though perhaps 99 percent of its operatives were unaware of
Oster's "moonlighting," a select few under his leadership remained wholly committed to treasonable activities.

When war loomed again in the autumn of 1939, Oster sought
to resurrect his coup plan from the previous year. He sounded
out the Vatican, recalled Heinz's *Stosstrupp* to Berlin, and again
approached the generals to secure their cooperation. This time,
however, though war did indeed come, the order for the coup
was not given. The generals were halfhearted, cowed by Hitler's
rage against them and fearing that their earlier conspiracy had
been uncovered.[90] Oster, too, was insufficiently prepared to cap-
italize on events. To his dismay, he found that the September
Conspiracy could not simply be brought to life once again—too
many pieces of the puzzle were missing, too many participants
were unwilling or absent entirely.

Yet the opposition refused to give up. On the morning of the
British declaration of war, 3 September 1939, Erich Kordt visited
his Foreign Office colleague Ernst von Weizsäcker. They discussed the news. Weizsäcker then posed the rhetorical question:
"Is there no way to prevent this war?" Kordt was gripped by the
sense that he had to act. Two months later, as the proposed offensive against the West was imminent, he was given his chance
when Oster asked him bluntly: "We have no-one who will throw
a bomb to free our generals from their scruples. I've come to ask
you to do it."[91]

Kordt thought about the proposal for a while:

> My conscience told me it was my duty. I considered the
> chances of success and concluded that mine were better

than anyone else's from our group. Entry into the Reich Chancellery was no problem for me. I could get to the ante-room of Hitler's quarters with ease, unchecked. I couldn't hope for a private meeting with him, of course, but didn't he often come out into the ante-room to call visitors in or to give orders to his adjutants? Wouldn't that present a possibility?[92]

Kordt agreed and was promised the necessary explosives by 11 November. He prepared the ground well, making more frequent, often unnecessary visits to the Reich Chancellery, partly as reconnaissance and partly to make the guards used to his presence. However, due to new restrictions introduced with the outbreak of war, Oster's contacts were unable to supply the explosives. Kordt was enraged. As he complained to a colleague:

> Along comes a civilian, such as myself, who is prepared to run the kind of risk that our gallant Prussian generals should themselves have run long ago, and these bloody professional heroes . . . are not even in a position to supply an uncompromising diplomat with something as simple as a small bomb.[93]

Kordt then suggested shooting Hitler, but Oster deterred him, commenting despairingly: "You would not have a chance."[94]

Oster continued to resist but opted to change his tack. He appreciated that while Hitler and his military were all-conquering, he had little chance of motivating sufficient anti-Nazi sentiment to make an attempted coup feasible. Therefore, he adopted the so-called "setback theory" that had once been in vogue among the military conspirators.[95] If German armies could suffer an unexpected defeat, he reasoned, then the shock on the home front might be sufficient to topple Hitler's government.

In the autumn of 1939, therefore, with much trepidation, Oster began passing German military secrets to the Dutch military attaché in Berlin. He did not do so lightly. He confessed to his driver: "It is much simpler to take a pistol and shoot someone down, or to run into a machine-gun burst...than to do what I have done."[96] He went on to give detailed information about the Norwegian and Danish campaigns, as well as the Western Offensive of 1940. Indeed, he was so confident that Hitler's armies would suffer a setback during the French campaign that he made a bet with two of his colleagues. When Paris subsequently fell, he was obliged to treat them to a lunch of oysters and champagne in the Berlin Cavalry Guards Club.[97] Though he accepted his own loss with good grace, he was devastated.

Oster knew that he had crossed a line. He knew that he was committing high treason and was risking innocent German lives. But he believed his actions could prevent a greater catastrophe. Most importantly, he made it abundantly clear that he had irrevocably broken with the spurious ties of honor and duty that still bound so many of his colleagues.

With over sixty years of hindsight, what conclusions can be drawn about the September Conspiracy? First, the respective roles of Oster and Canaris deserve closer inspection. Though Generals Ludwig Beck and Franz Halder are often correctly identified as the "kingpins" of the conspiracy[98]—after all, the coup required their cooperation if it was to function at all—the godfather of the plot was undoubtedly Hans Oster. Oster served in a number of capacities. He was the virtual chief of staff of the resistance—the rock around which all of its disparate groupings moved—and he was the liaison man and go-between, setting up meetings, forging contacts, and sounding out potential recruits. But he also supplied the wellspring of impassioned and principled anti-Nazism that succored the waverers. His radicalism, like that of Gisevius, shocked some but was inspirational to others. He was, as one eminent historian has put it, the resistance's "indefatigable driving force."[99]

The role of his immediate superior, Wilhelm Canaris, is much more difficult to define. By 1938 at the latest, he had clearly become an opponent of the regime, but he could not or would not assume the active role that Oster had assumed for himself. He supplied documentary evidence to the plotters, was on intimate terms with many of them, and was in broad agreement with their plan, but he took no active part in it himself.

Some have speculated on the reasons behind this apparent ambivalence. Canaris's critics would refer to his deliberately enigmatic nature. He was a typical spymaster: mysterious, duplicitous, and dissembling to the last. His equivocal attitude toward the plotters, they would argue, was but one manifestation of this character. As one contemporary recalled:

> Canaris played a double game; in the existing situation he could not help doing that. Nevertheless, I can scarcely say where the limits of that game lay. In general, in all that Canaris did or, as the case may be, omitted to do, it was very difficult . . . to recognize a clear and undeviating line. The role he played was conditioned, in this respect as in all others, by his peculiar personality.[100]

Canaris may also have been fundamentally unconvinced that the plot would succeed.[101] He had confided his pessimism to one contemporary, stating bleakly: "What you fellows are up to will not do you much good . . . one cannot prevent history from taking its course." Then he added, "But carry on . . . It's just that I don't believe that you will achieve anything."[102] In addition, he was known to have been against an assassination and had privately expressed concerns about the plot's feasibility. Yet on the very eve of the Munich Conference, he promoted Oster to be his second-in-command, thereby appearing to give tacit support for his subordinate's clandestine plans.[103] His role, therefore, was what one might call passive leadership. Though he would play no active role himself, he would serve as the spiritual leader of the resistance. As one historian has written, "His contribution was to provide cover for [conspirators] . . . who utilised the *Abwehr* as a means of movement and underground communication, and to close his eyes to [their] more energetically dissident activities."[104]

What, then, of Canaris's concerns? What can be concluded about the feasibility of Oster's September Conspiracy? The first thing to note is that most historians tend to give it short shrift. Though the plans were finally made public in a handful of post-war memoirs, they rarely feature in the primary chronicles of the Third Reich or biographies of Hitler. One of the standard works, for example, devotes only a paragraph to Oster's plan,[105] while the most recent synthesis dismisses it in one sentence as a "nascent conspiracy" hatched by "ill-coordinated groups."[106]

The participants themselves, in contrast, were in no doubt as to their chances. Those that survived to pen their memoirs expressed the clear opinion that the coup would have been carried out had Chamberlain's last gasp of appeasement not interceded. Halder would later rage to a British interviewer that "it was your Prime Minister, your Prime Minister, who ruined our hopes by giving in to Hitler."[107] The most famous of the conspirators, Hans Gisevius, was blunt: "Chamberlain saved Hitler," he wrote.[108] Only Erich Kordt was more circumspect in seeking a deeper truth: "Conscience," he complained, "makes cowards out of all of us."[109]

Later historians who have studied the events of that autumn in more detail are generally more divided in their assessments. Some are quite positive. They stress the plan's attention to detail, and the favorable set of circumstances that accompanied it.[110] Others note that the plot marked the first emergence of a "concrete, organized resistance."[111] The veteran German historian Joachim Fest, for example, has concluded that "no other attempt to strike Hitler down...would come close to having as good a chance of success."[112]

Others are less convinced, however. They point to the lack of popular support, the minimal military participation, and the absence of any coherent political program to replace Nazism. In 1938, they would argue, the plotters were swimming very much against the tide. Most Germans were alarmed at the prospect of another war, but they were not yet ready to turn against the regime. For this reason, one of the authorities on the German resistance movement has dismissed the September Conspiracy as having only "minimal chances."[113] One contemporary plotter went further, refuting the theory that Chamberlain "saved

Hitler" by suggesting that the reasons for the failure of the coup must be sought in Berlin rather than London. "Dissension and indecision at home," he wrote, "not timidity abroad, doomed the plan."[114]

Yet a number of additional factors should also be considered. First, there must be a fundamental question mark about whether the coup would ever have been launched in the first place. Despite Oster's energy and planning, that decision had been left in the hands of generals who, for all their good intentions and positive words, were fundamentally unable to think in the radical terms that Oster, Gisevius, and others did. As one contemporary observed of General Beck, for example: "[He] was a brilliant theoretician and a staunch moralist, but he lacked the revolutionary spirit which is the essential quality for anyone who aspires to lead a coup d'état."[115] Though supportive, the generals still instinctively viewed the conspiracy as treasonous and were bound by their code of honor and oath of loyalty to disavow it. In the event, when their conscience came into conflict with their sense of duty, the latter would invariably win out. As the events of that autumn would show, they were the first weak link in the chain.

Second, the conspirators had predicated their plot on two factors over which they had no control: British support and Hitler's declaration of war. The final decision, therefore, was completely out of their hands. This attitude was symptomatic of the caution exhibited by the German resistance in the early years, and it was most likely influenced by the "stab in the back" myth from the end of the First World War. If the alleged betrayal of a dying regime in 1918 could so poison public life in peacetime, the resisters reasoned, the effect of their betrayal (and indeed murder) of a successful leader at the height of his power would be catastrophic. As Witzleben had sarcastically mused: "History would have nothing else to report about us than that we refused to serve the greatest German when he was at his greatest."[116]

This "proxy syndrome" would become one of the defining features of the German resistance. They wanted to be rid of Hitler but lacked the popular support, will, or wherewithal to do the deed themselves, and were instead reduced to naively hoping for a third party to act in their stead. Thus, Canaris privately berated the Austrians for not resisting the *Anschluss,* while Oster and many others were content to blame the failure of the September coup on British appeasement.[117] The most telling example, however, was the chief of the army General Staff, Halder, who often expressed the wish that Hitler should meet with an "accident" or be assassinated, yet balked at doing the job himself, although he was frequently in Hitler's presence armed.[118]

The uncomfortable truth of the matter was that for all its moral indignation, determination, and ingenuity, the German resistance was effectively hamstrung by Hitler's diplomatic and military successes. Only when the tide of war had turned, in 1943, were they freed from this grievous affliction. Only then could they begin to plot with a reasonable expectation of success.

After the failure of the conspiracies of 1938 and 1939, the plotters of the Abwehr went back to their day jobs serving the German military machine. They procured intelligence, planned "diversions," and plotted sabotage, but this time in support of Hitler's war—the war they had sought to prevent. Many of them received promotions and awards from the regime; Canaris was promoted to full admiral and awarded the German Cross in Silver for "exceptional contributions to the military conduct of the war."[119] Oster was made a major general. Heinz was appointed to command a regiment of the élite Brandenburg commando division.

And yet, despite their outward conformity, many of them continued in their efforts to undermine the Nazi regime. Chief among them, as before, was Hans Oster. After passing military secrets to Germany's opponents in 1940, Oster later hatched an aborted plot to assassinate Ribbentrop.[120] He then developed a scheme, with his colleague Hans von Dohnanyi, that aimed to save a number of German Jews by posting them abroad as supposed Abwehr agents. In 1943, he procured explosives for an attempted assassination of Hitler, carried out by disgruntled officers of Army Group Center (see Chapter 7). In them, Oster had finally found some truly vigorous and determined allies.

Canaris, too, continued his shadowy double game, providing tacit support for Oster while outwardly maintaining the martial integrity of the Abwehr. His balancing act began to falter during the war, however. Abwehr operations in the West had been allowed to drift and had long degenerated into a state of endemic corruption and inefficiency. Its foreign networks had been penetrated by Western intelligence services to such an extent that it was becoming a liability. Indeed, the SS and SD had long been monitoring Abwehr activities, and Reinhard Heydrich had established a "Canaris file" to record the admiral's failings. According to Walter Schellenberg, Canaris's fate was sealed as early as the spring of 1942, when he failed to gain foreknowledge of a British raid on the German radar installation at Bruneval.[121]

From that point on, the SS placed Canaris and the Abwehr under constant surveillance. In time, they found at least some of the proof they required. In the spring of 1943, Oster was implicated in an investigation into the activities of his colleague Dohnanyi. He was dismissed from the Abwehr and placed under house arrest while the investigations continued. The net was closing. The following February, after a number of defections of its agents, and having failed to anticipate the Allied landings at Anzio, the Abwehr itself was disbanded. As Schellenberg put it: "Canaris's personal and professional failings had so incriminated him in Hitler's eyes that he had him relieved of his post."[122] Canaris, too, was placed under house arrest, albeit in a medieval castle. The Abwehr was amalgamated into the party intelligence organization, the Reich Security Head Office (RSHA), and Schellenberg became its nominal head.

The spring and early summer of 1944 passed with both Canaris and Oster under arrest and investigation. Canaris appeared to have escaped serious censure when, in late June, he was appointed to a sinecure within the army high command and returned to Berlin. However, a month later, the fragile peace was shattered by news of a renewed plot to kill Hitler. Oster was brought in for interrogation the following day, Canaris two days later. His arresting officer was none other than his successor as head of the Abwehr, Walter

Schellenberg. Schellenberg described the scene in his memoirs: "I went to Canaris's house in Berlin-Schlachtensee and he himself answered the door. . . . [He] was very calm. His first words to me were, 'Somehow I felt that it would be you.'" Schellenberg claimed to have gallantly suggested that he would allow his prisoner to abscond, saying: "I shall wait in this room for an hour, and during that time you may do whatever you wish. My report will say you went to your bedroom in order to change." But Canaris demurred:

> "My dear Schellenberg," he said, "flight is out of the question for me." . . . He returned after about half an hour, having washed, changed and packed a bag. . . . He embraced me with tears in his eyes, and said, "Well then, let us go."[123]

That autumn, Canaris and Oster joined the thousands of others caught in the SS dragnet. However, as archsuspects, they were subjected to an especially harsh regime. Imprisoned in the cellars of the Gestapo headquarters on Prinz Albrechtstrasse in Berlin, they were constantly manacled and placed on one-third of normal rations.[124] Yet neither appeared to be fazed. Canaris, in particular, seemed to relish the opportunity to lead his interrogators on a wild-goose chase, admitting nothing, leading them off the scent, and swamping them with contradictory information. It was a virtuoso performance, which a former colleague described as "an artistic deformation of the truth."[125]

The composure of the former Abwehr men was shaken only by the discovery that September of a cache of documents—the so-called Oster file—recording both the nefarious activities of the SS and the plans of the September conspirators. Now their carefully crafted covers and alibis were shot through, and a new group of conspirators was implicated. In the face of this apparently conclusive and incontrovertible evidence, Oster evidently broke down, giving vent to a "quasi-suicidal spate of admissions."[126] But Canaris continued doggedly to fight his corner, parrying every accusation and supplying plausible reasons for his actions.

This was the situation in early February 1945, when intensified Allied bombing on Berlin caused the prisoners held by the
Gestapo to be dispersed throughout what remained of the Reich.
Oster and Canaris were sent to the concentration camp at Flossenbürg in northern Bavaria. There they were once again held under
a harsh regime—manacled day and night and subjected to what
was euphemistically called "vigorous" interrogation.

This continued until April, when the discovery of Canaris's
own diaries brought matters to an abrupt conclusion. A show
trial was convened for the afternoon of 8 April, and Canaris and
Oster were to appear together. Both were charged with high treason. In this, their darkest hour, the differences between the two
men once again became clearly manifest. Canaris refused to give
up. He disputed every count and claimed only to have humored
the conspirators for the sake of surveillance. Oster then bitterly
contradicted his former superior, claiming that Canaris had been
involved in everything that his circle had undertaken. After a
heated exchange, the prosecutor finally asked Canaris point-blank
whether Oster was falsely incriminating him. Canaris paused and
then quietly replied: "No."[127] The courtroom drama was instructive but legally superfluous. The sentence had been passed some
days before, and it had come from the very top. Both Oster and
Canaris had been condemned to death.

That night, Canaris resumed his correspondence with his
neighboring prisoner, a Danish intelligence officer. The two had
communicated by tapping an improvised Morse code through
the wall of the cell. Soon after ten o'clock, Canaris tapped out
what would be his final message—his epitaph: "Nose broken...
Time is up. Was not a traitor. Did my duty as a German."[128]

The following morning, 9 April 1945, Oster and Canaris
were hauled from their cells at 6:00. They were ordered to undress and were herded across the cell-block yard to the gallows.
There, with the camp commandant and SS doctor acting as witnesses, they mounted a small pair of wooden steps and a noose
was placed around their necks. The steps were then kicked away.

CHAPTER 4

"The Nest of Vipers": The Polish Underground

An attempt on Hitler's life was of the primary importance.
—JAN SZALEWSKI, POLISH HOME ARMY[1]

ON THE EVENING OF 31 AUGUST 1939, IN THE GERMAN TOWN of Gleiwitz, close to the Polish border in Upper Silesia, a small SS force was preparing for action. Their mission was simple: they were to provide the world with unlikely proof of a Polish attack on Germany and thus give Hitler the excuse he required to declare war on Poland.

Their leader was an SS *Sturmbannführer* (major) by the name of Alfred Naujocks. Naujocks is often and somewhat bizarrely described as an "intellectual gangster."[2] He was born in 1908 in Kiel, the son of an engineer. In the turbulent 1920s, he joined the Nazi Party, briefly studied at university, developed a talent for brawling, and had his nose flattened by a communist wielding an iron bar. In 1931 he joined the SS, and three years later he was appointed as aide to the high-flying Reinhard Heydrich, head of the SS security service, the *Sicherheitsdienst* (SD).

In this capacity, Naujocks was given license to indulge his twin passions for violence and subversion. The "Gleiwitz incident," as it came to be known, was to be his greatest and most infamous mission. He had been sent to the town in mid-August, two weeks previously. There he had scouted the radio station and had been briefed by the Gestapo chief, Heinrich Müller, who was billeted nearby. He was told that his mission would involve a consignment of a dozen concentration camp inmates, referred to cryptically as "canned goods."

At midday on 31 August, Naujocks received a telephone call from Heydrich. The password was given: "Grandmother has died." The mission was on. Naujocks contacted Müller to arrange delivery of the "canned goods," put the finishing touches to his plan, and gave a final briefing to his team. At 8:00 that evening, he and five SS men stormed into the Gleiwitz radio station. They fired a few shots and handcuffed the bemused station personnel before locking them in the cellar. Naujocks then found the microphone. A stirring speech was broadcast in Polish, full of anti-German rhetoric, and calling on the Poles to rise against their historic enemy. "The hour of freedom has arrived," it concluded. "Long live Poland!"[3] Outside, meanwhile, the "canned goods" had been delivered. Drugged but alive, they were strategically arranged around the site and then machine-gunned.[4] Their bodies were to add bloody veracity to an unlikely scene.

This somewhat bizarre performance was all part of Hitler's master plan. Despite his later reputation as a reckless gambler, in 1939 Hitler could scarcely afford to unleash a world war. His expansion thus far had been piecemeal, and he had stressed his good intentions at every turn, hoping to avoid an all-out conflict with France and Great Britain. What he intended in the autumn of 1939, therefore, was a limited war, a swift, surgical strike to knock out Poland while avoiding any wider conflagration. Hence his rather clumsy attempt at Gleiwitz to cast Poland as the aggressor. A week earlier, in conference with his generals at Berchtesgaden, he had foreshadowed the ruse, saying: "I will provide a propaganda pretext for beginning the war, however implausible," before adding darkly that "the victor will not be asked afterwards whether he told the truth or not."[5] Gleiwitz, therefore, was intended as a fig leaf to cover Hitler's naked aggression.

At first sight, the ruse appeared to have been successful. An astonished world awoke on 1 September to the news that Poland had launched an unprovoked attack on Hitler's Germany and that German forces were responding in kind. All along the border, German troops moved off from their forward positions. In the north, in the free city of Danzig, the German heavy battleship *Schleswig-Holstein,* moored on a courtesy visit, opened its murderous fire on the Polish fort on the Westerplatte, barely 300 meters away.[6] Hitler, addressing the Reichstag later that day, did his best to pose as the injured party:

> This night, for the first time, Polish regular soldiers fired on our own territory. We have now been returning fire since 5:45 a.m.! Henceforth, bomb will be met with bomb. He who fights with poison gas shall be fought with poison gas. He who distances himself from the rules for a humane conduct of warfare can only expect us to take like steps. I will lead this struggle, whoever may be the adversary, until the security of the Reich and its rights have been assured.[7]

It was a vintage performance. But, for all his righteous rage, Hitler may have inadvertently betrayed his guilt in one tiny detail. In accordance with his orders, the *Schleswig-Holstein* had opened fire an hour earlier than he had admitted: at 4:45 a.m.

The September Campaign, as it came to be known, was brutal and mercifully short. As German forces, vastly superior in numbers and equipment, swept over the frontier that morning, they quickly overran Polish defensive positions and threatened the disintegration of the entire front. Within days, the Poles were in desperate straits. Their successes, such as the counteroffensive at

Kutno, were few and short-lived. Their air force was outgunned and outmaneuvered. Their General Staff was overwhelmed by the deadly new military doctrine of the *Blitzkrieg*.

The Poles were also shocked by other innovations. The September Campaign, the first serious military adventure undertaken by Hitler, gave ample proof of the sheer murderous brutality of the Nazi regime. The tone was set by the SS Death's Head Division, which, while making no tactical contribution to the campaign, concentrated instead on terrorizing the civilian population and hunting down Jews and "suspicious elements." In the town of Bydgoszcz, for example, it arrested and shot some eight hundred individuals whose names had been recorded on a "death list."[8] Few of those killed would conventionally be considered to be the mortal enemies of the advancing forces. As one eyewitness recalled:

> The first victims . . . were a number of Boy Scouts, from twelve to sixteen years of age, who were set up in the marketplace against a wall and shot. No reason was given. A devoted priest who rushed to administer the Last Sacrament was shot too. . . . Among the [others] was a man whom I knew was too ill to take any part in politics or public affairs. When the execution took place he was too weak to stand and fell down; they beat him and dragged him again to his feet.[9]

Such actions, coupled with the widespread strafing of refugee columns and aerial bombing of residential areas, demonstrated that Hitler's forces considered themselves not simply to be fighting the Polish army. They were at war with the entire Polish nation.

The central plank of the Polish defense plan was to hold out until the promised Western offensive against Germany materialized, whereupon, it was thought, the pressure on Poland would be eased.[10] However, when the British and French failed to make an appearance in the west, and after the Soviets invaded eastern Poland on 17 September, Polish resistance began to crumble.

Thereafter, only the capital and a handful of other isolated pockets continued the fight. The night after the Soviet advance, the Polish government fled to Romania. The majority of Polish troops then surrendered and marched into German or Soviet captivity, but a few followed their government into exile, beginning an odyssey that, in some cases, would last a lifetime.[11] Others followed a third course: they hid their weapons, shed their uniforms, and went into hiding. They would form the nucleus of the Polish underground.

After Warsaw finally fell, on 28 September, it took the Germans another week to subdue the remaining resisters. As the campaign drew to a close, on 5 October, Polish casualties stood at an estimated two hundred thousand; German losses totaled less than a quarter of that figure. The Poles had certainly been comprehensively defeated on the field of battle, but whether they would meekly succumb to occupation was another matter entirely. On this point, the Nazi leadership would have been wise to remember the words of the Polish national anthem:

Poland has not perished yet
So long as we still live
That which alien force has seized
We, at swordpoint, shall retrieve.[12]

Poland, in fact, had a rich tradition of resistance to foreign occupation. The Polish Republic, established in 1918, had emerged out of the ruins of a three-way occupation of the Polish lands—between Austria, Russia, and Germany—that had lasted more than 120 years. As one might expect, the popular responses to those occupations spanned the spectrum. While only a few opted to collaborate wholeheartedly, many more chose conciliation, seeking to find a modus vivendi with the occupier rather than confront him. But one of the most persistent reactions was that of principled and determined opposition—the route to conspiracy and, ultimately, military resistance. That tradition, as a prominent historian of Poland has written, was eminently successful . . . [Its] strength bore no relation to the numbers of its adherents, or to the outcome of its political programme. It reflected not the support of the masses, but the intense dedication of its devotees whose obstinate temper, conspiratorial habits and romantic approach . . . [were] effectively transmitted from generation to generation.[13]

Thus resistance to foreign occupation was not only an integral part of the Polish self-image but also an experience of which many Poles in 1939 still had firsthand knowledge. They found little hardship in switching to the conspiratorial lifestyle, little difficulty establishing the organs of a functioning underground, and little trouble finding recruits. It is highly doubtful that the Nazis fully comprehended what they were up against.

German policy in 1939, however, was vastly different from what it had been in 1915. Poland occupied a peculiar position in the Nazi worldview. In the interwar years, it had served as a universal hate figure for the German right: the territorial cessions made after World War One still rankled, as did the perceived maltreatment of the German minority in Poland. Yet, initially at least, Hitler appears to have been less concerned about the Poles than about the Czechs, who earned many more critical references, for example, in *Mein Kampf*.

As Nazi ideology matured, however, Poland soon assumed a more prominent position. Occupying, as it did, much of Germany's desired *Lebensraum* and with a population made up almost entirely of Slavs and Jews, this was perhaps inevitable. The new tone was set by the brutal murder of a Polish laborer by Nazi thugs at Potempa in Silesia in 1932, an act that was later defended by Hitler.[14] But, for all the official opprobrium that followed, Berlin and Warsaw were not yet irrevocably set on a collision course: high-level discussions were still held, diplomatic niceties were maintained, and treaties were signed. Germany's "rough wooing" aimed ultimately at chivvying Poland into a bloodless suicide, similar to that achieved in Czechoslovakia, except the Poles refused to play along. Polish resistance to German offers, blandishments, and threats sowed such frustration in Berlin that war was soon viewed as the only way out of the impasse. By having the temerity to resist, Poland had earned itself a special place in Hitler's demonology.[15]

The Nazis, therefore, had nothing but contempt for the conquered Poles. Joseph Goebbels spoke for Hitler when he wrote in his diary:

> The Führer's verdict on the Poles is damning. More like animals than human beings, completely primitive, stupid and amorphous...[Their] dirtiness is unimaginable. Their capacity for intelligent judgement is absolutely nil.[16]

Thus, while imperial Germany had been content during the First World War with a Polish client state, Nazi Germany intended to erase Poland from the map entirely. Territories were hived off and annexed to the Reich, and eastern Poland was taken by the Soviets. The rump was then designated as the "General Government"—a supposedly autonomous state run by a German administrator in Kraków.

The Polish population, meanwhile, was subjected to a crude racial sorting. Individuals were examined and categorized— Germans and non-Germans, Aryans and non-Aryans, humans and subhumans. One's designation decided one's fate. Those in the higher categories were considered eligible for Germanization, with all the benefits that it implied, while the lowest category qualified only for a starvation diet of 184 calories per day and could expect little but expropriation, expulsion, and forced labor.[17]

Poland's sizeable Jewish community, consigned to the lowest category, was separated from the Aryan population and herded into ghettos. There, they were terrorized, starved, and worked to death. By the time the Warsaw ghetto finally closed its gates in November 1940, it contained around four hundred thousand inhabitants, living from hand to mouth and slowly wasting away. As an eyewitness recalled:

One well-known case involved a family from Łódź, which at first numbered eight people. Their entire belongings consisted of two baby strollers: the father pushed three children in one, while the mother kept two others in the top of the second. They rolled the strollers along the curb and sang old Yiddish songs. They had beautiful voices. He sang and she sang, accompanied by six children's descants. After a while there were only four voices; then there were three, then one stroller disappeared, along with the family's shoes and what was left of their outer garments. Finally only two people remained. The father pushed while the mother lay in the stroller, singing to accompany her husband. She was thirty-nine years old but looked one hundred.[18]

The Warsaw ghetto was, in effect, a highly efficient killing machine. Containing over 30 percent of the city's population crammed into barely 2 percent of the city's area, it soon descended into indescribable squalor. Within a year, it was claiming more than five thousand lives every month through starvation and disease. Yet the Nazis would soon devise even more efficient methods of killing.

In addition to the racial categorization, Polish society was effectively decapitated. Its natural leadership—priests, intellectuals, military officers, and politicians—was to be murdered regardless of racial status. The head of the General Government, Hans Frank, stipulated that Polish intellectuals were to be dealt with "on the spot and . . . in the simplest way possible."[19] Those in any doubt as to the true meaning of his words would soon have had their worst fears confirmed. That November, the entire academic staff of the ancient Jagiellonian University in Kraków was sent en masse to Sachsenhausen concentration camp. The following spring, the so-called extraordinary pacification campaign (or *AB Aktion*) accounted for a further six thousand people, including numerous professors, doctors, lawyers, and teachers. Countless more would be sent to Auschwitz or to the notorious Pawiak prison in Warsaw.

The attempt to destroy Polish society was complemented by

a destruction of the Polish economy. Most industrial concerns, shops, restaurants, and hotels were simply confiscated, and the looting of personal and public property became commonplace. To pay for the disruption, meanwhile, taxes were raised and the Polish currency was devalued, thereby setting all Poles at a profound economic disadvantage compared to their German occupiers. Polish manpower was also exploited. The majority was consigned to the labor camps that were quickly established to service the larger industrial centers. There, only the fit and determined could hope to survive any length of time; the sick and the old could hope for little but a swift death. Many thousands were also deported to forced-labor camps in Germany, where they were treated with outright contempt. As one notice admonished: "Germans! The Poles can never be your equals. Poles are beneath all Germans. . . . Be just, as all Germans must be, but never forget that you belong to the Master Race."[20]

Alongside all of these official measures—the racial selection, the ghettoization of the Jews, the murder of the élites, and the laming of the economy—Poland was also exposed to an astonishing level of casual, everyday brutality. Death was ever-present. As one fifteen-year-old Pole would recall:

> I was a veteran. I had seen sudden death at work many times. I had seen . . . SS Special Forces smash my mother's skull with a pistol butt. . . . I had seen people shot like dolls, prisoners murdered with clubs and pitchforks, desperate men throw themselves on high-tension wires. Sudden death was the chequerboard on which we inhabited a few temporary squares. Stunned by it at first, you soon came to regard it as routine.[21]

Poles could be shot on almost any pretext—black-marketeering, defying the curfew, making anti-German comments, or simply failing to make way for a German soldier on the pavement.[22] In addition, the principle of collective responsibility was liberally applied. If German soldiers were killed, Polish civilians paid the price. In December 1939, for example, after two German NCOs had been murdered in Warsaw, 170 innocent civilians were dragged from their homes and shot in reprisal.[23] Officially, the German authorities stated that one hundred Poles were to be killed for each dead German; however, in some cases, as many as four hundred Poles paid for a single German life.[24]

Hostage taking was another German specialty. Roundups of civilians were commonplace, and church congregations and other similar gatherings were frequently targeted. No warning was given, and the victims were selected at random. They would then either be deported as forced laborers or held as hostages to ensure the good behavior of their fellow countrymen. In the event of further transgressions, the hostages would be stripped, handcuffed, and shot. Their bodies would then be loaded onto trucks and taken to the ghetto to be burned. The names of the deceased would then be broadcast in the streets.[25] For many, it was the first news of a missing loved one.

The German governor, Hans Frank, gave a flavor of the sheer brutality endured in occupied Poland when he was asked by a German newspaper correspondent to outline the differences between the occupation regime in Poland and that in the neighboring Czech lands. In reply, he boasted:

> I can tell you a graphic difference. In Prague, for example, big red posters were put up on which could be read that seven Czechs had been shot today. I said to myself: "If I put up a poster for every seven Poles shot, the forests of Poland would not be sufficient to manufacture the paper for such posters."[26]

In private, Frank was more prosaic. He confided to a colleague that his mission was to "finish off the Poles at all costs."[27]

But perhaps the best summary of life in occupied Poland was given by one of those who experienced it at first hand:

> Under German occupation, a Pole had no right to own property, no right to participate in any sort of cultural ac-

tivity, no right to study. He was only to sweat and labour under the supervision of German slave-drivers. Even so he could never feel safe or be sure to survive. . . . There is no family in Poland that did not suffer, not one that did not mourn somebody dear. . . . We in Poland never met the so-called "good Germans." Towards us they were always ruthless tyrants and murderers.[28]

The Polish response to all this was to organize the largest and most effective underground network in occupied Europe. In the immediate aftermath of the Polish defeat in the September Campaign, underground resistance groups mushroomed in every sphere. Every Polish political party—from the communists to the Peasant Party—sprouted a paramilitary wing, as did the Scouting movement. In addition, wildcat military units formed to continue the fight against the Germans by guerrilla means. One of the most spectacular such units was that established by Major Henryk Dobrzański. Dobrzański, a cavalry officer and former member of the Polish equestrian Olympic team, recruited a three-hundred-strong partisan force to harry supply lines and ambush troops. By the time he was finally killed in battle in the summer of 1940, he had succeeded in tying down eight police battalions and a regiment of SS cavalry.[29] He had also provided a shining example to his fellow Poles and even earned the grudging admiration of his German opponents.[30]

In such circumstances, the priority for the Polish government, in exile in France and later Britain, was to bring this plethora of underground groupings under its exclusive command. The task was considerable. As the later commander of the underground recalled:

Every day officers, civilians—once even a monk from a remote monastery—turned up, reporting to me the numbers and other details of their local organisations. Often they had sworn in a few hundred people, mostly youths determined to fight to the last. They were all coming for instructions and orders.[31]

The integration of the various underground bodies was achieved only slowly, but the groundwork had been laid prior to the defeat in 1939. Immediately upon the fall of Warsaw, the command and legitimacy of the regular Polish army was transferred to the newly formed Polish Victory Service (PVS), a clandestine organization that pledged to carry the fight "into whichever field of activity the enemy might engage."[32] After a series of further mergers, the PVS then became the core of the Polish Home Army, known in Polish as the *Armia Krajowa* or AK.*

The AK was no partisan rabble. As the underground arm of the Polish military establishment, it was an integral part of the Polish armed forces. Its commander in chief was directly subordinate to the Polish commander in chief in exile, and its writ ran throughout occupied Poland. Its high command was organized like any other, with seven departments dealing with everything from logistics and supply to finance, propaganda, and counterintelligence. Its forces numbered approximately two hundred thousand men, spread throughout the country, and its motto, "Poland fights," was daubed on countless walls.

Despite the bellicosity of the original statute of the PVS, the later AK demonstrated a more circumspect approach to underground warfare. In the face of merciless and vastly superior opposition, it sensibly shrank from declaring outright war against the occupying forces. Rather, it set itself two goals. The first was the construction of a viable underground army with the long-term aim of fighting to regain independence once the Germans were weakened and in retreat.[33] The second was the preservation of the "biological substance of the nation." With the Polish people facing the very real threat of extermination, the underground sought to provide whatever vital civic amenities it could. In this regard, it became a "secret state."[34]

*The title *"Armia Krajowa"* was only used from the spring of 1942 onward, but for the sake of simplicity the term will be used here throughout.

Its most immediate priority, however, was secrecy. Pitted against the Gestapo and SS, the underground was under constant threat of infiltration and destruction. As a result, it soon became a maze of safe houses, passwords, and pseudonyms. Every member had a nom de guerre, ranging from the mundane (Daniel) to the fanciful (Tony Flamethrower).[35] Family names were not used, and no one was supposed to know the precise identity of their superior. An absolute minimum of information was written down: orders were transmitted verbally, messages were memorized. The results could be disconcerting:

> I approached a fair girl whose appearance corresponded with [the] description.
> "I have come about a drawing..." I began.
> "Do you want a water colour or a pastel?"
> "No, I have come about drawing lessons."
> After this exchange of passwords, she led us to a room behind the shop, where a liaison girl turned up to fetch us. She took us to our lodging for the night....
> Next morning, the same liaison girl came back and took me to a private flat. I had again to wait, all the time without the least idea whom I was actually waiting to see.[36]

Once established, the underground quickly found its feet. In the civilian sphere, it provided educational facilities, and through concerts, poetry readings, and drama circles it enabled an unlikely blooming of Polish culture. A thriving underground press was also formed. Every political party and every branch of the "state" soon produced a newspaper of some sort. The very first, titled *Poland Lives,* appeared just five days after the surrender.[37] A precious few titles would even boast an unbroken publication run throughout the occupation.

The continued functioning of the underground depended on sound intelligence and effective communications. The first of these was supplied by a network of informants and by the professional intelligence officers of the underground's Second Bureau— described by the British as "the best source of information among the Allies."[38] It was Polish intelligence, for example, that in 1939 had presented the British with two working replicas of the German Enigma encryption machine, thereby rendering an incalculable service to the Allied war effort. They were also instrumental in locating the top-secret research facility for German V-weapons at Peenemünde on the Baltic coast.[39] Their most famous intelligence coup, however, was the theft of an intact V-2 rocket from a crash site in eastern Poland in May 1944. Their booty was dismantled, photographed, and meticulously examined, long before the German investigators had pinpointed the location of the crash. It was then loaded into crates to be flown to Britain.[40] Germany's secret weapon was no longer a secret.

The provision of an effective communications and supply network was the responsibility of two remarkable groups of people. The first of these was the British Special Operations Executive, or SOE, formed by Churchill in 1940 with the remit to "set Europe ablaze" through subversion and sabotage.[41] Though established to aid all European resisters, SOE had especially close contacts with the Poles. Its first parachute drop was into Poland, and its chief, Major Colin Gubbins, was a fluent Polish-speaker who had been head of the prewar British military mission to Warsaw. Over the course of the war, SOE would fly over three hundred agents into occupied Poland and successfully carry out 485 airdrops delivering 600 tons of vital matériel.[42] In many cases, SOE supplied the hardware, weaponry, and training, and the Polish underground supplied the naked courage and determination. It was to be a most fruitful relationship.

The second was the élite group of AK couriers, who secretly traveled across Europe entirely dependent on their wits and their immaculately forged papers, and seemingly oblivious to the war raging around them. They helped to maintain the link between the Polish government in exile and military command in London and the underground at home. Their feats quickly passed into legend. One Polish courier shuttled between Warsaw and Paris, traveling first-class dressed as a German general. He would bring the first grim news of the Holocaust to the outside world.[43]

One vital aspect of any self-respecting resistance organization was sabotage and diversionary activity. Right from the very beginning of the occupation, possible targets for sabotage were listed, including "railway transports, supplies of fuel and cereals, any arms and food factories, arms and fuel dumps."[44] By the spring of 1940 a dedicated unit had been formed to mastermind such attacks: the *Związek Odwetu,* or Retribution Union, under the command of Major Franciszek Niepokólczycki, code-named "Theodore." It, and its successors, would prove remarkably effective. While some units specialized in freeing prisoners from jails and labor camps, robbing banks, stealing official documents, and raiding stores, most concerned themselves with the simple destruction of the German infrastructure. A later summary of their activities listed nearly twenty thousand damaged locomotives, more than four thousand disabled army vehicles, and twenty-five thousand sundry sabotage actions.[45] One attack was particularly impressive. During the night of 7–8 October 1942, all rail links around Warsaw were simultaneously cut.[46] Not only was rail traffic seriously disrupted, but the underground had demonstrated itself to be more than just a nuisance.

The Poles even established a number of cells to carry out diversionary attacks abroad. The most successful, code-named *"Zagralin,"* operated on German territory and in the spring of 1943 successfully bombed targets in Breslau and Berlin, including the Friedrichstrasse and Schlesischer railway stations in the capital.[47] At the same time, the underground in Warsaw was preparing an audacious "diversion" of its own. That spring, a number of suspicious parcels were intercepted in Berlin, addressed to numerous German government agencies including the Reich Chancellery. The packages measured around 20 by 10 by 10 centimeters and had been posted as registered deliveries in Warsaw. Each contained explosives set to detonate by electronic ignition when opened.[48] The bombs were successfully dealt with and safely defused, but they provoked alarm throughout the German security network.

With Polish forced laborers making up a large proportion of the German workforce, industrial sabotage was another favorite.

Alongside the time-honored tactics of passive resistance, other, more active measures could be undertaken: machinery could be tampered with, sensitive settings could be changed. In this way, countless relatively minor (but nonetheless courageous) actions could bring impressive results. It was later claimed, perhaps optimistically, that such activity resulted in the production of 92,000 unusable artillery shells, 4,710 defective aircraft engines, and 570,000 faulty condensers.[49]

But, though successful, sabotage was only a part of the underground's activity. In early 1943, a new organization, the Directorate of Diversion (or *Kedyw*), was established to supervise the sabotage campaign, absorbing the Retribution Union in the process. But the *Kedyw* also widened its remit to include the elimination of traitors to the Polish cause and the targeted assassination of selected German functionaries.

The campaign against traitors and collaborators had already begun prior to 1943. Two years earlier, for example, a Warsaw actor and director, Igo Sym, had been assassinated after betraying Polish artistes at the Warsaw City Theater to the Germans.[50] But, under the *Kedyw,* the process was formalized. Legal procedures were strictly adhered to, and collaborators were usually given ample warning that their misdeeds had been noticed. The underground court would intimidate its defendant by keeping him fully apprised of the progress of his case. First, he would receive a warning, giving his number on the "Index of Suspect Persons" and informing him that he was under observation. Then, assuming that the defendant did not desist from his activities, he would receive notice that his case would be brought before the Special Court. Next, he would be informed of the verdict and the sentence imposed (usually death), and warned that the principle of collective responsibility would be applied should he choose to flee. Finally, the convict would receive a reminder of his verdict and a final notice that the sentence was soon to be carried out.[51]

Not all such cases ended with an execution, however. In some instances, the pressure of being under sentence of death from an unseen enemy was sufficient to force a miscreant to improve his behavior. As a senior AK commander recalled:

This method turned out to be the most effective we had yet tried. Poles noticed a marked change in the behaviour of many German officials. For instance, a certain German county-lieutenant . . . after receiving his indictment at once retired to bed and called in the local Polish doctor. He proposed to arrange for the immediate release of all Polish political prisoners in the county and offered to moderate greatly his policy towards Poles if the findings of the court investigation were quashed.[52]

Despite these minor successes, many German personnel proved more resistant to change, and so the targeting of individuals for assassination also gathered speed. In the first four months of 1943, for example, more than five hundred separate attacks were carried out on the German administration and its terror apparatus.[53] The German police were especially targeted. In 1943, one policeman was killed in Warsaw, on average, every day. By the following year, that figure had risen tenfold.[54] In addition, more than 750 Gestapo agents were murdered in the first half of 1944,[55] while occupation forces as a whole lost over a thousand killed and injured every month.[56] Soon, a number of prominent Germans were also targeted for assassination. One by one, senior German officials, prison staff, and SS men were faced with teams of well-organized and well-armed attackers. In all, more than five thousand such assassinations were planned.[57]

The AK assassins, for their part, had a well-rehearsed procedure. Each target was methodically researched. He would be watched day and night, to build up details of his routine and his personal profile. His addresses, guards, drivers, and vehicles would all be logged and often photographed.[58] Finally, armed with this information, a plan of attack would be devised. Most often, the attacks took place in broad daylight, usually in the early morning, with vehicles providing both an element of surprise and a swift escape. The assassination team would generally consist of around ten individuals, including perhaps three or four lookouts and two groups of three gunmen, each in a car, armed with Sten guns, pistols, and grenades. One group would aim to eliminate the target, while the other would provide support and engage the bodyguards and police. If they were to escape with their lives, they had to hit their target and flee within no more than a couple of minutes.

With the Polish underground increasing its attacks and scoring such public successes, the Germans were in desperate need of an enforcer to restore order and bring the Poles to heel once and for all. That man was to be SS *Brigadeführer* Franz Kutschera, an Austrian and one of the rising stars of the SS. A Nazi Party member since 1930, Kutschera had already been appointed *Gauleiter* of Carinthia and become a member of the Reichstag at the tender age of thirty-four. After active service in the French campaign, he had then held a number of prominent positions in the administration of occupied Russia, prior to his appointment as SS and police chief of Warsaw in September 1943. Especially close to Himmler (whose sister was his mistress), he was considered to have the connections, ruthlessness, and brutal determination necessary to tackle the Polish underground head-on.

He began his term in Warsaw in impressive style. His security regime was formidable. He was driven everywhere with a large corps of bodyguards—even the 150 meters or so from his residence to SS headquarters. He also opted not to be named, signing himself merely as "SS and Police Chief—Warsaw." Undoubtedly, this was partly out of concern for his own safety, but it was also to lend his office an increased air of mystery and menace. With the permission of Governor Frank, he then introduced public executions. Every few days, a dozen or so Poles would be rounded up and shot for any misdemeanor or for no reason at all. In two weeks of October 1943, for example, 177 Poles were publicly executed in Warsaw alone.[59] The lists of those killed would be printed on bright purple posters and distributed around the city. One, from December 1943, was typical:

> On 2.12.1943 . . . in Warsaw, another surprise attack was carried out on a *Schutzpolizei* unit, in which 5 policemen and 1 member of the *Waffen-SS* were killed and numerous other officers injured. . . . It is clear that the attack was executed by a terror group of the resistance.

In retribution for this, I have had the following 100
criminals . . . publicly executed.

The SS and Police Chief—Warsaw District[60]

Rather than allow themselves to be intimidated, however, the AK
responded in kind. They did not shrink from targeting the highest Nazis in the land, and drew up a so-called head list of potential victims. In addition, a blanket order was given that effectively
declared open season on all servants of the occupation.[61] Thereafter, unsuccessful or aborted assassinations were attempted on a
host of senior German officials, including the governor of Warsaw, Ludwig Fischer; the *Gauleiter* of Danzig, Albert Forster;[62]
and SS General Wilhelm Koppe, who was one of those responsible for the establishment of the extermination camp at Chełmno.

One attempt demonstrated the assassins' technique especially
well. SS General Friedrich-Wilhelm Krüger was in charge of security in the entire General Government. In February 1943, after
publishing a list of seventy civilians executed in Warsaw, he was
sentenced to death (in absentia, of course) by the Polish underground. Two months later, on the morning of Hitler's birthday,
20 April, he was ambushed on the street in Kraków and two hand
grenades were detonated beneath his car. Though one AK memoir recalls that Krüger thereafter "disappeared from the scene and
was never heard of again," he did in fact survive the attack with
only minor injuries.[63] In response, Himmler wrote to Bormann
the day after the attempt to request that an armored limousine be
placed at Krüger's disposal.[64] According to a Polish report,
Krüger was then targeted again in May, when he was shot at by
four assailants brandishing machine guns.[65] That report concluded that the target had been killed, but Krüger appears to have
survived and is thought to have committed suicide at the end of
the war.

Many more high-profile targets were successfully eliminated,
however. Eight were assassinated in Warsaw alone, including
Franz Bürckl, the deputy commandant of the Pawiak prison, and
August Kretschmann, the commandant of the city's Gęsiówka
concentration camp. The functionaries of the city's civilian

administration were also liquidated, including Emil Braun, the head of the Warsaw housing department; Kurt Hoffmann, head of the Labor Office; and the latter's deputy, Hugo Dietz.[66] The underground's communiqués to London were short and to the point: "October 11, 1943...On October 1, 12.05 hours, in Warsaw, killed by shooting, SS-Sturmmann, Ernst Weffels, the cruel oppressor and executioner in the Women's Prison in Pawiak."[67]

In December 1943 Kutschera was himself slated for elimination. As was customary, he was first sent a warning that he would be killed if he did not cease the atrocities. Then a second note was sent, reminding him that though he had escaped retribution at his previous postings, he would not do so in Poland.[68] Soon an AK team began watching his residence and his office, recording his movements, noting the strength of his bodyguards and the various vehicles that he used. The assassination was entrusted to a team of twelve from the Parasol battalion, under the command of a twenty-year-old former scoutmaster, Bronisław Pietraszkiewicz, code-named "Flight." The team was divided into three cars, with three lookouts to signal the target's arrival. They planned to carry out their attack on Kutschera's own doorstep—outside Warsaw SS headquarters.

After an aborted attempt two days before, the assassins struck just after 9:00 on the morning of 1 February 1944.[69] As Kutschera's gray Opel limousine proceeded down a wide Warsaw boulevard, flanked and followed by SS guards, a car careened out of a side street and screeched to a halt, blocking its path. In the confusion, Flight hurled a Molotov cocktail and then ran alongside the Opel, firing his machine gun into the open window, killing the driver and mortally wounding his target. As a fierce firefight with the bodyguards ensued, he and an accomplice then dragged Kutschera from his vehicle and shot him in the head. After checking his body for vital documents, they made their escape in two waiting cars. Their attack had lasted less than two minutes.

Three days later, Kutschera's funeral cortege was carried through the deserted streets of Warsaw, en route to the main station and a transfer to Berlin. That same day, Flight was fighting for his life. Shot in the stomach during the attack, he had been taken to numerous hospitals in the vain search for a surgeon who would dare to treat a wanted man. Hunted by the Gestapo, he was finally operated on, but died on the afternoon of Kutschera's departure. His action had cost him his life, but he had pulled off one of the most spectacular and high-profile assassinations of the war. He had demonstrated the truth of his target's grim prediction: "There is no certain defence against people who are eager to sacrifice their own lives."[70]

What defense, then, did the Germans attempt to mount against the Polish underground? The first thing to note is that they did not expect to face such determined opposition. Their occupation of Poland had a number of priorities, foremost among them the political emasculation of the Polish nation and the exploitation of Polish industry and agriculture. Any resistance to the realization of those aims was to be ruthlessly crushed, of course, but the creation of a functioning, integrated underground state, with military and civilian sectors, was simply beyond the Nazi imagination. After all, weren't the Poles supposed to be subhuman Slavs?

Yet while the usual German reflex was to escalate the terror, a few officials recognized that their repressive and brutal methods were proving almost entirely counterproductive. They saw that just as their brutality intensified, so did the response of the underground. They were not motivated by concern for the well-being of the Poles; rather, they noted with alarm that the occupation of Poland was not bringing the economic benefits for Germany that had been foreseen at the outset. Despite his deserved reputation for cruelty, Governor Hans Frank was an early convert to the policy of ameliorating living conditions in occupied Poland. Already in 1940, less than six months into the job, he proclaimed that his primary task of destroying and exploiting the country had changed to the subtly different one of utilizing all of Poland's "productive possibilities."[71] He would later warn that "you should not slaughter a cow you want to milk."[72] Frank soon began to advocate a softer line of concessions, toleration, and détente, and won many highly placed supporters, including

Goebbels.[73] Himmler, however, was violently opposed to any change of course that might interrupt his plans for a racial reorganization of Central Europe. Where Frank sought to use a careful combination of carrot and stick, Himmler knew only stick. All plans for reform of the occupation regime were subsequently dropped.

So, by dint of their own ideologically driven myopia and the stubborn will of the Poles to resist, the Nazis had stumbled into a morass of their own making. By 1943, their security apparatus was already buckling under the strain. In Warsaw alone, it was investigating more than ten thousand Poles, and fewer than 20 percent of those had even been identified.[74] For their own safety, its operatives lived in tightly controlled quarters, barricaded into the German colony behind sentries and barbed wire. Rarely did they venture unaccompanied into the city beyond. Alcoholism and stress-related illness were rife. Even the governor, Hans Frank, rarely left the comparative safety of Kraków. He visited Warsaw—the main bastion of the resistance—only four times after 1941, the last occasion being in September 1943.[75] The posting to occupied Poland was dreaded by every official of the Third Reich. Many regarded it as an appointment from which they could scarcely expect to return alive.[76] Poland, which was statistically the most dangerous part of occupied territory for the Germans, was regarded as "bandit country." It was "the nest of vipers."[77]

In the face of this perpetual threat, Hitler's time in Poland was potentially fraught with danger. His first visits were made during the September Campaign of 1939. A fortified Führer headquarters was initially established on the German side of the frontier at Bad Polzin in Pomerania, where Hitler himself arrived by train in the early hours of 4 September. For the following month, he shifted his train headquarters numerous times and made no fewer than nine tours of the front. When he was stationary, security was tight, presumably against the remote threat of a surprise Polish attack. An outer perimeter was provided by infantry of the élite *Grossdeutschland* Division, who barricaded access roads and established strongpoints. An inner perimeter was held by Hitler's own security force, the RSD. The troops involved resembled a miniature army, with units of reconnaissance, signals, motorized infantry, anti-tank troops, anti-aircraft troops, and a supply section.[78]

When Hitler traveled to the front, security was no less tight. A bystander in rural Pomerania would have been stunned by his Führer's stupendous cavalcade of vehicles. First, he would have seen motorcycle outriders, followed by two reconnaissance cars. Next came Hitler's convoy, which consisted of two groups of convertible, six-wheeled Mercedes limousines, painted beige and riding on all-terrain tires. In the first group, Hitler sat in the back of one car, accompanied by his driver and a handful of aides and bodyguards. This was followed by two further cars of bodyguards, a car of the SS Escort, a car of RSD bodyguards, an adjutants' car, and a car of military liaison staff. The second group of Mercedes vehicles consisted of cars containing perhaps Ribbentrop and Himmler (each with their staff and bodyguards), another with invited guests, a reserve vehicle, a luggage car, a field kitchen car, and a gasoline tanker. Bringing up the rear was a further group of motorcycle outriders, a platoon of signals, a platoon of anti-aircraft personnel (with guns), and an anti-tank unit.[79] It was not unusual for this traveling circus to cover more than 250 kilometers in a day, and though clearly laden with weaponry, it would have been hard for a potential assassin to overlook.[80]

The security risk was greatest when Hitler approached his destination, however. His convoy would trundle past trucks of troops, groups of civilians, and lines of POWs with little apparent concern. Overexcited soldiers occasionally even had to be shooed off the running boards of Hitler's car.[81] Once at the local headquarters, Hitler was evidently considered to be at his most secure. Meetings with local commanders and even military briefings were often conducted in the open, surrounded by a mass of curious soldiers. There was no cordon of police or SS, and Hitler's bodyguards, though present, did little to intervene. They would generally idle around, watch the proceedings, and talk among themselves.

On one occasion, Hitler was even mobbed by admirers, and it took some minutes before his aides could reach him.[82] The strict security regime that was habitually instituted during Hitler's public appearances in Germany was almost entirely absent.

But this was not to suggest that the only threat that Hitler faced was from disgruntled members of his own military. The Polish army, though in retreat, was still capable of springing a nasty surprise. On 4 September, near Topolno on the Vistula, Hitler's convoy was halted by evidence of a very recent Polish ambush. Later that same day, the Polish air force bombed a target only 3 kilometers away. It was not known whether the Poles were even aware of Hitler's presence in the region, but that night, his train was moved to a new location to escape their attentions. Another incident occurred near Koronowo, north of Bydgoszcz, when a German supply lorry crashed into the tail end of Hitler's convoy. Its driver had been shot in the chest by a Polish sniper.[83]

In the following weeks, Hitler made numerous visits to the front, crisscrossing Poland in the process. Sometimes he traveled ahead by plane and then had to wait for his convoy to catch up to take him to the action. Often, plans were changed at short notice due to the weather or the situation in theater. This naturally placed tremendous strain on the security apparatus, which many considered had proved itself insufficient for the task.

But Hitler was also at least partly to blame for any shortcomings. He appears to have been so enthused by the Polish campaign that he was willing to forget or circumvent all the established security procedures. Convoys departed half formed, bodyguards were ignored, and crowds were not restrained. As the subject's most renowned historian has concluded: "Almost every day during his visits to the Polish Front . . . Hitler got himself into situations in which his life was in great danger."[84]

At the end of the Polish campaign, Hitler made his only visit to Warsaw, where a lavish victory parade was planned. Arriving by plane at the main Okęcie airport, he was greeted on the runway by his victorious generals before being taken into the city center in an armed convoy. As he was driven through the streets, only recently cleared of rubble, he was enthusiastically cheered by his soldiers. In response, he stood in the front seat of the Mercedes, acknowledging the adulation with his arm outstretched.

Unsurprisingly, the Warsaw visit was carried out under tight security. The center of the city had been effectively cleared. Its Polish population had been either forcibly evacuated or subjected to a strict lockdown, and only German military personnel were permitted into the immediate area of the parade. Hundreds of police patrols prowled the streets, and many roofs were adorned with machine-gun nests. In addition to all that, the Germans had demanded a number of prominent Polish hostages as security against any possible attack. In response, twelve senior municipal politicians, including the city's former mayor, Stanisław Starzyński, were taken prisoner.[85] They would be held in the basement of the city hall for the duration of Hitler's visit, unaware that a further four hundred ordinary civilians were being held hostage for the same purpose.

The parade was to take place on one of the main boulevards through the administrative district, Aleje Ujazdowskie. There, among the opulent villas and elegant former embassies, a low dais had been built, bedecked with swastikas, and a huge German war flag had been strung between the yellowing trees behind. As a military band blared out martial music, Hitler stood flanked by his generals and took the salute of the victorious 8th Army. For over two hours, he stood at attention in the bright autumn sunlight—an easy target for even the most amateur of snipers—as the massed ranks of infantry, cavalry, and artillery filed past.

Barely a kilometer to the north, meanwhile, a small group of Polish soldiers had established a stronghold deep within a ruined building. During the cleanup that had followed Warsaw's surrender, a group of Polish sappers had been ordered to remove a barricade from the junction between New World Street (Nowy Świat) and Jerusalem Avenue (Aleje Jerosolimskie). In the process, they had succeeded in surreptitiously hiding 500 kilograms of TNT and assorted munitions beneath the road.[86] The order for the operation had come from Theodore, who had met the commander of the nascent underground immediately after the Polish capitulation to plan diversionary attacks. Theodore had rightly anticipated that Hitler would visit the defeated capital and had initially planned to bomb the victory parade itself, but heightened security presumably put paid to such an ambitious plan. Instead, he had chosen a busy junction between the administrative district and the Old Town as the site of his first "diversion." The day before the parade, he had reported to his superiors that everything was ready—his men were in place and the detonators had been set.

At around 3 p.m., as the victory parade finally drew to a close, Hitler once again climbed into his six-wheeled Mercedes. After spurning the offer of lunching al fresco with his generals, he opted for a brief tour of the defeated city. He began with the Belvedere Palace, where he cast a scornful eye over the former residence of the Polish president. He then returned to his car and headed north toward the Old Town, passing the abandoned British embassy and finally entering New World Street. As his cavalcade pressed on, it often slowed to walking pace as it negotiated streets still strewn with the detritus of war and thronged with soldiers, many of whom had just attended the victory parade. Throughout, Hitler stood impassively in the passenger seat, arm outstretched. With the acclamation of his soldiers ringing in his ears, he passed over the junction with Jerusalem Avenue—over the spot where the explosives had been placed—and on to the Old Town. Later that afternoon, he returned by air to Berlin to prepare an important Reichstag speech for the following day.

It is unclear precisely why the explosives failed to detonate. It may be that the lookout was moved on by the army or police and that this prevented the signal being given to the detonator team. Perhaps the final order was not given because of fears about the hostages held by the Germans, or perhaps the wiring was defective.[87] One commentator considered that human error was to blame. The officer in charge of the detonator, it was claimed, had been ordered to act upon his own initiative, but only if he was sure that Hitler himself was there. Given the high stakes and the confusion, however, he hesitated, and the moment for action was lost.[88] Whatever the cause, Theodore's first foray into diversionary tactics had failed; Hitler had escaped once again.

Though that was to be Hitler's only visit to Warsaw, he would also be an infrequent visitor to Polish territory beyond the former capital. He established two makeshift field headquarters on Polish soil, for example, prior to the attack on the Soviet Union: one near Tomaszów Mazowiecki (100 kilometers southeast of Warsaw), code-named "Installation Centre," and the other near Strzyzów (130 kilometers east of Kraków), code-named "Installation South." Both consisted merely of reinforced tunnels to accommodate Hitler's train, with some hastily built platforms and wooden buildings.[89]

By far his most famous field headquarters, however, was Wolfschanze, or Wolf's Lair, near Rastenburg in East Prussia, barely 70 kilometers from the prewar Polish border. Begun late in 1940, under the guise of a chemical works, Wolfschanze consisted initially of a small group of bunkers with associated outbuildings, all disguised with camouflage netting and elaborate landscaping. By the time Hitler moved in—on 24 June 1941, two days after the attack on the Soviet Union—it was already a substantial installation, with its own airfield, barracks, weather station, and sauna. It would become his home away from home. In the twenty months that followed, Hitler left Wolfschanze only four times, and was absent for only fifty-seven days.[90] In total, he would spend more than eight hundred days—more than two years—inside the complex.[91]

The location had been well chosen strategically. The district of Masuria, a charming landscape of gently rolling hills, was sparsely populated and well forested. It was also fairly easily accessible, with good local roads and a nearby railway line providing a simple connection to the main line to Berlin. Wolfschanze itself was located immediately to the west and south of a network of lakes and waterways, which effectively defended the site from land-based attack, while from the air it was practically invisible, with netting, trees, and landscaping providing near-perfect camouflage.

For all these advantages, however, Wolfschanze failed to impress its intended resident. Hitler protested that he felt "like a prisoner" in its bunkers and complained that his "spirit" could not escape.[92] Worse still, the nearby lakes caused an infestation of mosquitoes, which terrorized everyone from the Führer to the lowliest laborer or guard. Hitler was evidently driven to distraction and even threatened to call in the Luftwaffe to deal with the problem. He concluded angrily that his planners had chosen for him "the most swampy, midge-infested and climatically unfavourable area possible."[93]

Naturally, security at Wolfschanze was tight. The entire site, measuring 2.5 by 2 kilometers, was divided into three concentric security zones, each with its own checkpoints, fences, and patrols. The outer perimeter consisted of minefields and a 5-meter-wide barbed-wire fence, with machine-gun nests located approximately every 150 meters. The second zone contained additional flak batteries, watchtowers, and anti-tank gun emplacements.[94] In all, approximately two thousand personnel were employed at Wolfschanze. Of these, the vast majority provided security, yet few of them would ever catch a glimpse of the man whom they were charged to guard. Barely a hundred individuals, all strictly vetted and cleared, had access to the inner security zone.[95]

Any legitimate visitor, therefore, whether arriving by road, rail, or on foot, would have to pass through a minimum of three security checks before even approaching the inner compound, where further checks could be expected. Access to the entire complex was controlled by a system of passes, which could be issued solely by the headquarters commandant after consultation with senior security staff. Only those with the correct pass would be permitted into the inner security zone.

Officially at least, those found inside Wolfschanze without a pass would be liable to arrest and interrogation. The reality could be more brutal. In the summer of 1942, a Polish laborer inadvertently strayed inside the outer perimeter while seeking a shortcut home. He was unceremoniously shot.[96] On another occasion, a German guard was shot and seriously injured when he gave the wrong password approaching a checkpoint at night.[97]

At the center of it all stood a complex of bunkers and barracks blocks including Hitler's private quarters. The barracks and workrooms, often erroneously described in postwar literature as wooden huts, were solid brick structures often measuring over 30 meters in length. The bunkers, too, were enormous, especially after being revamped in 1943. Constructed of reinforced concrete, they were up to 12 meters in height, with a further 7 meters of foundation below ground.[98] Some boasted additional features: Hitler's had a single-story kitchen appended to its western side, while Göring's sported an anti-aircraft gun on its roof. Inside, they generally consisted simply of a corridor with a number of small rooms accessed from it. Albert Speer described Hitler's bunker in Wolfschanze in the following accurate but unflattering terms:

> From the outside it looked like an ancient Egyptian tomb. It was actually nothing but a great windowless block of concrete, without direct ventilation, in cross section a building whose masses of concrete far exceeded the usable cubic feet of space. It seemed as if the concrete walls sixteen and a half feet thick that surrounded Hitler separated him from the outside world in a figurative as well as a literal sense, and locked him up inside his delusions.[99]

Yet, despite being probably the best-guarded facility in the German Reich, even Wolfschanze was not immune to the attentions of the Polish underground. One memoir claims that the Poles considered using a Russian colonel from the renegade Vlassov army as their informant within Wolfschanze, but rejected the idea out of concern that their activities might be compromised.[100] Whatever the truth of that suggestion, a more promising source soon emerged. In 1942, a glamorous Warsaw socialite by the name of Sława Mirowska was involved in an affair with a Waffen-SS general, Wilhelm Bittrich. Subsequently "persuaded" to inform for the AK, she became in effect a latter-day Mata Hari. That summer, she accompanied Bittrich to his own headquarters on the eastern front and stopped at Wolfschanze en route. During the visit, she surreptitiously noted everything she saw, from the layout of the site to the security procedures then in force.[101] In due course, the details would be forwarded to her superiors in Warsaw.

Despite this knowledge, the Poles do not appear to have planned any attacks or "diversions" on the site of Wolfschanze. It may be that they thought better of targeting the complex, where the prospects for an assassin were decidedly bleak, or else simply lacked the local manpower to do so. Wolfschanze, after all, was situated in the heart of the then German province of East Prussia, beyond the official remit of the AK, and little in the way of an infrastructure existed there for the maintenance of an underground cell. One more promising possibility, however, was to try to target Hitler during his infrequent trips to and from his headquarters. Though he sometimes traveled by air, he usually shuttled between Wolfschanze and Berlin by rail, using his personal train. His route, along the old main line from Königsberg via Konitz and Küstrin to Berlin, took him straight across the territory of the prewar Polish Republic.

With the outbreak of war, Hitler's train, the peacetime Führer Special, was given the code name "Amerika." It was also substantially upgraded. An extra locomotive was added, as well as a communications carriage and two anti-aircraft cars.[102] According to those who traveled in it, the train offered every luxury: silk bedspreads, polished wooden paneling, and hot and cold running water.[103] More important, perhaps, it was built entirely of high-grade welded steel panels and was sufficiently robust to withstand all but the most determined attacks.

As has been shown, the Polish underground was adept at sabotage operations, and train derailment was one of its specialties. Right at the outset of the occupation, a special unit had been formed for that purpose, and quotas were even issued by the high command, stipulating the number of German trains to be derailed each month. In total, over seven hundred such operations were carried out.[104] Tactics were largely left to the discretion of the saboteurs involved, but they could involve blowing the rail with explosive charges or simply dismantling the tracks. Either method, of course, would prove devastatingly effective against a speeding train.

The problems were encountered when saboteurs attempted to target a specific train, such as Hitler's. As would be expected, Amerika was placed under guard when in a station, or in the sidings at Wolfschanze, and security was no less tight when on the move. It could not be passed by scheduled or freight services, and a dummy locomotive often preceded it down the line. The problem for a would-be saboteur, therefore, was to have advance knowledge of exactly when Amerika would be passing a particular point. For that, he would need inside information.

It would appear that on one occasion, at least, this vital precondition was met. On the evening of 8 June 1942, Hitler left Rastenburg aboard his train en route for Berlin, where he was to attend the state funeral of Reinhard Heydrich, assassinated by Czech agents some days previously. However, news of Hitler's travel arrangements seems to have reached a local AK commander, Captain Stanisław Lesikowski, code-named "Forest," whose area of operations included a section of the main rail line between Königsberg and Berlin. A former optician and a veteran of the defense of Warsaw in 1939, Forest was already a hardened resister, having organized numerous underground groups in Pomerania.[105] He would devise the operational plan for the derailment of Hitler's train, which he code-named *"Wiener Blut"* (Viennese blood) in reference to the Führer's Austrian origins.

Forest entrusted the mission to a local resistance organization called *Gryf Pomorski,* or Pomeranian Griffin, under the command of Lieutenant Jan Szalewski, code-named "Sable." Another veteran of the battle for Warsaw, Sable had escaped German captivity and found his way to the underground. After a briefing from Forest, he assembled his men—all dressed in stolen Waffen-SS uniforms and speaking only German—into two teams: one group of saboteurs to cut the line and a second to secure the target area. For the location of the attack, he chose a site close to the village of Strych, just west of Preussisch Stargard, where the rail line ran through woodland.[106]

According to Sable's deposition, at around 2:45 that morning, his sappers allowed the dummy locomotive to pass before hurriedly dismantling the track and retreating to a fortified area in nearby woods.[107] In the ensuing chaos, as the train crashed off the rails and slewed down an embankment, they reemerged to machine-gun the survivors, whom they identified as members of the *Leibstandarte,* Hitler's bodyguard.[108] Eventually forced to flee by superior numbers, they withdrew without sustaining any losses and disappeared back into the underground. They were firmly convinced that they had succeeded in their task. As Sable recalled: "When I met with my unit after the action, we were all radiant with joy: [we] were saying 'Hitler has gone to hell!'"[109]

In the aftermath, it was claimed, two hundred German soldiers lay dead, including two generals.[110] Hitler, however, was not among them. He had apparently opted to break his journey at Marienburg, to confer with the *Gauleiter* of Danzig, Albert Forster. Nonetheless, the German response was typically brutal. Reprisals were carried out in the villages surrounding the crash site, and 150 suspects were arrested, of whom some fifty unfortunates were sent to the concentration camp at Stutthof, near Danzig. Some weeks later a bounty was offered for information leading to an arrest—the figure on offer was the princely sum of 250,000 Reichsmarks.[111]

One might conclude, therefore, that Hitler had pulled off yet another lucky escape. However, little in this story is as it seems. German sources, though confirming that a derailment took place on the night in question, do not consider it to be an attempt on Hitler's life and state merely that a Berlin-bound scheduled passenger service was attacked at the cost of three lives.[112] Indeed, the German authorities appear to have learned about the assassination attempt only two years later, following the capture and interrogation of one of Sable's team.[113] The available Polish accounts, even those of participants and eyewitnesses, are also contradictory. The source of the information about Hitler's movements varies between rail employees, the German resistance, the Wehrmacht, and even the SS. Some accounts place the attack at Rytel,

40 kilometers down the line, while others have the train traveling in the opposite direction, *away* from Berlin.[114]

The resultant confusion was not helped by a curious report, released from the British archives in 1998, that formed part of SOE's planning for their own proposed assassination of Hitler. That account, apparently supplied by Polish intelligence, gave a date of autumn 1941 and cited a *third* nearby location, Czarna Woda.[115] It claimed that while Hitler's train was inexplicably delayed at a neighboring station, a scheduled passenger train passed it and was then derailed at the cost of 430 lives. Despite arousing some considerable interest in the British press at the time of its release, the document appeared to be little more than an amalgam of other events, half-truths, and embellishments. German sources, for example, make no mention of such a spectacular derailment, and (as is now known) Hitler was safely ensconced at Rastenburg at the time and did not leave until early October. Most implausibly, the document claims that the rails were detonated by short-wave remote control. Given that the AK often struggled to arm itself with even the most basic weaponry, this seems improbable in the extreme. One can only conclude that the SOE officer charged with drawing up the report either was fed spurious intelligence or allowed his imagination to run away with him.

So, what *can* be salvaged from the wreckage of Sable's operation? It is at least incontrovertible that a derailment occurred on the stretch of track between Dirschau and Konitz on the night of 8 June 1942. It is also known that Hitler *was* intending to travel to Berlin that night.[116] Barring a most fortuitous coincidence, this would suggest that the Pomeranian underground *had* been furnished with details of Hitler's itinerary by an inside source, most probably a railway employee. Sable's team, therefore, staged their attack in the sincere belief that their target was Amerika, and it was therefore logical that their own subsequent accounts of the event should conform to that preconception. Thus, an earlier scheduled service was assumed to be the dummy train, and regular German soldiers stumbling from the wreckage were considered to be the *Leibstandarte*.

But this is not to denigrate the efforts of Sable and his men; it is merely to acknowledge that there is much work still to be done before a definitive version of the events of that night emerges from the gloom of unreliable memoirs and speculation after the fact. Sable, for his part, was not discouraged. He continued to lead his men, and by 1944 had the confidence to harass and ambush German forces in his district. Wounded three times, he ended the war in a Soviet field hospital.[117]

Neither did Forest cease his subversive activities. Indeed, he masterminded a second derailment—this time of a goods train—on the same stretch of track barely two weeks later. Appointed an AK regional commander at Kościerzyna, he was arrested by the Gestapo in April 1944. Following sustained torture and interrogation, he attempted to poison himself by eating soap, but succeeded only in securing a transfer to the Stutthof concentration camp, where he was finally executed in July 1944.[118]

The Polish underground has, until very recently, been strangely absent from the pantheon of would-be assassins of Adolf Hitler. This absence may, in part, have something to do with language. Though the events outlined here have been openly discussed in Poland, especially in the last decade, they have not yet found an echo in German- or English-language works on the subject.

It should also be conceded that the savagery of the German occupation was such that comparatively few of the participants involved in such risky operations survived the war to put pen to paper. Many, such as Forest, found only death in the concentration camps or in the torture cells of the Gestapo. Others were slaughtered in the Dantean hell of the Warsaw rising. Of the élite Parasol battalion, for example, which carried out many of the "liquidations" of German officials, only around three hundred soldiers survived the war, barely one in three of their former number.[119]

But there is another, darker reason for this absence. After the defeat of Nazi Germany, Poland was occupied by another totalitarian power, the Soviet Union, which was just as inimical to the activities of the wartime Polish underground as the Nazis had been. The Soviets could not tolerate any rival power base in their new satellite, so they began their reign by hunting down the leaders of the underground, denouncing them as spies, "crypto-fascists," and collaborators and putting them on trial.[120] In a string of high-profile court cases, the surviving members of the wartime underground were slandered, humiliated, and in many cases judicially murdered. Few escaped the maelstrom. In such circumstances, the historian should not be too surprised by the relative dearth of memoir accounts from veterans of the actions against Hitler. Those who were fortunate enough to survive the war also had to survive the peace, and the latter was best achieved by keeping one's mouth firmly closed.

Sable, for instance, who would become the primary source for the attack on Hitler's train, was handled in a less than heroic fashion by the Soviets. Arrested by the communist secret police in 1946 and again in 1950, he was sentenced to eighteen months of imprisonment for his role in the Polish underground. Thereafter, he suffered a nervous breakdown.[121]

Another example was Theodore, the mastermind of the failed bomb attack on Hitler's convoy in 1939. After returning to Poland from a German POW camp at the end of the war, Theodore was arrested by the communist secret police in Kraków the following year and was charged with membership of an illegal organization. Though condemned to death in 1947, his sentence was commuted to life imprisonment, of which he served ten years before being freed in the amnesty of 1956.[122] Thereafter, to his death in 1974, he understandably refused to speak of his wartime activities and denied all knowledge of the attempt on Hitler's life, even claiming not to have been in Warsaw at the time. One tiny clue suggests that his amnesia may have been tactical, however. As his wife later recounted, he would always refuse to travel along the stretch of New World Street where his bomb had been placed.[123]

In retrospect, it might appear surprising that the Polish underground—rightly hailed as the most active and effective resistance organization of the Second World War—should have failed to target Hitler more often, or indeed more successfully. This conclusion is understandable, but only from the comfortable, peaceful perspective of the early twenty-first century. During the war, Poland was being crushed under the heel of the Nazi occupation, and the very survival of the Polish people was at stake. For all their ingenuity, daring, and skill, the agents of the Polish underground had much more immediate concerns. Their failure to assassinate Hitler was doubtless a tribute to the security arrangements surrounding their target, but it should also be seen as evidence of the diabolical conditions under which they were forced to operate. One should therefore not bemoan the fact that they tried and failed; one should applaud the fact that they tried at all.

CHAPTER 5

The Implacable Foe:
The Soviet Union

I am extremely anxious to see Hitler dead.
—JOSEF VISSARIONOVICH STALIN[1]

IN THE HOUR BEFORE DAWN ON THE LONGEST DAY OF 1941, the code word "Dortmund" crackled through countless field telephones and radio receivers on the eastern frontier of the greater German Reich. On that signal, forward German assault troops advanced, while 7,000 artillery pieces opened a withering barrage on the Soviet lines. They were embarking on the largest military operation in European history: 3.5 million men, supported by nearly 4,000 tanks and more than 2,500 aircraft, advancing along a front stretching 2,000 kilometers from the Baltic to the Black Sea.[2] Their Führer, in a message to the soldiers, described the coming conflict as a "war for . . . Europe's destiny, for the future of the German Reich and the existence of our people."[3] Operation Barbarossa had begun.

The Soviet response was initially one of surprise, confusion, and outright panic. Front-line soldiers, shaken from their sleep by the crash of incoming artillery rounds and the rattle of advancing German armor, often fled. Baffled unit commanders radioed their superiors in vain to request instructions. Meanwhile, Soviet forces were being decimated where they stood. As the German columns advanced, prisoners were taken by the tens of thousands. Communications collapsed and entire Soviet armies ceased to exist. On that first day alone, twelve hundred aircraft—fully 20 percent of the Red Air Force—were destroyed.[4] The vast majority of them had failed even to get into the air. When Göring received the figures, he ordered a recount, convinced that they were exaggerated. A revised report increased the total by a quarter.[5]

Yet for all the shock at the front, the only real surprise of Barbarossa was that the Soviets could have been surprised by the attack at all. British intelligence pinpointing the likely date, gleaned via the decryption of German Enigma signals, had been duly passed to the Soviet ambassador. Churchill himself had sent telegrams to Moscow. Soviet intelligence, too, primarily via the virtuoso spy Richard Sorge in Tokyo, had long been warning of an "initiation of hostilities" with Nazi Germany.[6] For weeks, Wehrmacht forces had been massing on the Soviet western frontier; the Luftwaffe had flown countless reconnaissance missions over Soviet territory. All of this had been noted and reported to Stalin.

Shortly before the attack, German deserters even braved crossing the front line to inform the Soviets of the impending assault. One, a former communist by the name of Alfred Liskow, swam the river Pruth to announce to the Red Army that the order to advance had been given. Yet all such reports were dismissed in Moscow as the work of "disinformers" and agents provocateurs—Sorge was ridiculed, Liskow was ordered shot. Stalin, terrified of offending the Germans, preferred to prevaricate and refused to believe the mounting evidence. Even as the most catastrophic reports began to arrive from the front, he refrained from ordering his forces to resist.[7]

In the ensuing confusion, the Germans made rapid gains. Within the first week, the front had advanced by an average of around 200 kilometers. The cities of Riga, Minsk, and L'vov had already fallen. Within a month, German armies had made further enormous advances in the north and center, and in the south they were approaching the Ukrainian capital, Kiev. Moscow was already under air attack.[8] In places, the front line fractured as huge encirclement battles yielded whole armies of Soviet prisoners; at Białystok over 300,000 were captured, at Smolensk nearly 350,000. Hitler's optimistic assessment of the parlous state of Stalin's army appeared to have been borne out. Though the Soviets' will to fight remained unbroken, they were poorly led and ill-supplied, with little answer to the now well-rehearsed tactics of the *Blitzkrieg*.

The near collapse at the front was mirrored by a near collapse at the heart of the Soviet state. When Stalin learned of the size of the catastrophe he was facing and realized his own error in ignoring the imminent German attack, he suffered an apparent emotional and nervous breakdown, alternating between bleak depression and impotent rage. Briefly, the "Man of Steel" was broken, sulking unshaven and unwashed at his dacha for two days, receiving no one and refusing to answer his telephone. One colleague admitted that she had never seen him "so crushed." Stalin himself was brutal in his assessment of the situation that he faced: "Lenin left us a great heritage," he cursed, ". . . and we have fucked it up."[9]

Aside from the more immediate fears of military defeat and political collapse, Stalin doubtless felt that he had been personally humiliated. His earlier flirtation and alliance with Hitler had been, in part, the result of his fearful realization that the Western democracies would do little to halt German expansion. But that fear had been married to a wary admiration of the Führer. Despite their ideological differences, Stalin had instinctively felt that he could do business with Hitler, perhaps better than he could with the leaders of the Western democracies. He had admired his rival's rise, his evident popularity and his brutal, uncompromising way with his opponents. In 1934, for example, when Hitler engineered the Röhm Purge against his own former allies in the SA, Stalin was said to have heartily approved, exclaiming "Hitler, what a lad!"[10]

In alliance with Hitler from 1939, Stalin had also prospered politically. His own profile had been raised worldwide and, of course, he had succeeded in expanding the Soviet Union to the west, annexing new territories and restoring an approximation of the old Russian Imperial frontier. Yet, for all this, Stalin cannot have been under any illusions. He would have suspected that Hitler intended ultimately to attack him, and for this reason he had half-formed offensive plans of his own.[11] Nonetheless, when he was beaten to the draw in the summer of 1941 and fell victim to a German attack, he would have viewed it as a stab in the back and a betrayal. And Stalin did not take betrayal at all well. He nurtured his hatreds and delighted in harboring grudges. He was, as a colleague recalled, a man for whom the very sweetest of victories was the perfectly executed revenge on an enemy.[12]

When Stalin pulled out of his crisis of confidence, he threw himself into a flurry of activity. He began with a radio address to the Soviet people, the first time he had been heard from since the German invasion, now almost two weeks old. He opened in uncharacteristic style, addressing his listeners as "Comrades, citizens, brothers and sisters . . . my friends," before launching into a tirade on the perfidy of "Fascist Germany" and the grim sacrifices required to secure a Soviet victory. His delivery was slow and quiet, almost monotone, with the thick drawl of his Georgian accent. Every inch of soil and every drop of blood must be fought for, he said. All Soviet production was to be placed on a war footing, every enterprise was to intensify its production. No quarter would be given to deserters, panic-mongers, spies, and diversionists. Where the Red Army was forced to retreat, it would leave nothing of use in its wake; anything that could not be evacuated was to be destroyed. This was not an ordinary war between two armies, he warned; "it was a war of the entire Soviet people against the German-Fascist troops."[13] Every means was to be utilized, every advantage exploited to drive the invader from the motherland. If the assassination of Hitler was not already on the agenda, it very soon would be.

·   ·   ·

In fact, assassination, alongside judicial murder and kidnapping, was already an integral part of the Soviet political landscape. Stalin himself had a brutally simple attitude toward human life. As one recent biographer has observed, he talked about the lives of men as one would old clothes: "some we keep, some we throw away."[14] Thus, for all its "scientific" guiding principles, his regime demonstrated a remarkable degree of casual brutality. In the Ukraine in the early 1930s, some five million or so peasants were starved to death in the course of a forced collectivization campaign. Soon after, the first of the great purges began, devouring numerous prominent politicians and senior military personnel on the basis of personal grudges, rumors, and forced confessions.

The network that was developed to deal with such supposed miscreants was a simple expansion of the existing system of punitive camps, or gulag, dotted around the more inhospitable parts of the Soviet Union. From the bleak Arctic coast to the forests of the Far East, new camps mushroomed and the older ones were packed to bursting point with a total of some 1.8 million unfortunates.[15] Their names—Vorkuta, Solovetsky, Kolyma—are largely unknown in the West, yet they deserve the same shudder of recognition as Auschwitz, Dachau, and Belsen. Labor and punishment were their primary functions, though with primitive conditions, lack of food and medical care, death was ever-present and, indeed, was viewed by the authorities as a happy by-product.

Many never reached the gulag at all. In the generalized slaughter that followed the purges, those slated for death were often dealt with in the local NKVD (secret police) headquarters or merely spirited away. Across the road from the notorious Lubyanka prison in Moscow, for example, there was even a specially constructed abattoir for the execution of prisoners, with a sloping concrete floor, hoses to wash away the blood, and a wooden wall to absorb stray bullets.[16] The victims were transferred into steel coffins and taken for cremation. Their ashes would be dumped in a mass grave.

The executioners, and their political masters, went about their task with alacrity and a nefarious attention to detail. Killings were organized by quota, and many enthusiastic and ambitious paladins sought to exceed their prescribed limit. A young Nikita Khrushchev, for instance, ordered the murder of 55,741 individuals in Moscow—5,741 over quota. Sixty-eight thousand more were arrested in Leningrad.[17] Every city and town of the Soviet Union was affected. Almost every family would have told a similar tale: the dreaded knock at the door, arrest, torture, confession, and execution. The majority of cases crossed Stalin's own desk. On one day, for example, he is reported to have personally signed 3,167 death warrants.[18] On another occasion, he signed an order authorizing 48,000 executions.[19] Stalin possessed the power of life and death over every Soviet citizen, and it was a power that he did not shrink from using.

Even the Soviet élite was not immune from the whirlwind of bloodletting. Early victims included Stalin's former comrades Zinoviev and Kamenev, and the hero of the civil war, Marshal Tukhachevsky. Of the 139 members of the Soviet Central Committee in 1934, more than 100 had been arrested by 1938; most of them were shot.[20] Later, the onetime head of the NKVD, Nikolai Yezhov, fell victim to his own murderous machinery. Yezhov, who had reached the pinnacle of power as a member of the Kremlin inner circle and died with Stalin's name on his lips, was disposed of in a common grave. Some cases highlight not only the Stalinist contempt for human life but also its all-pervading perversity. The wife of Stalin's secretary, Bronka Poskrebysheva, for example, was arrested by the NKVD in 1939 after spurning the advances of its priapic and sadistic leader, Lavrenti Beria. She was held for two years before being executed in the autumn of 1941. Her husband, meanwhile, made numerous pleas for clemency on her behalf, only to be comforted by Stalin with the words "Don't worry, we'll find you another wife."[21] He never remarried, yet remained in his post until 1952.

Foreign citizens were also caught up in the maelstrom. In 1939, a large number of Poles were deported to the USSR from the area of eastern Poland annexed by Stalin. This included a sizeable contingent of Polish soldiers and around twenty thousand former Polish officers. While the civilians and ordinary soldiers fed the gulag, the debate raged within the Kremlin as to what should be done with the Polish officers—most of whom were doubly if not trebly damned as aristocrats, intellectuals, and landowners. The solution finally arrived at was as simple as it was brutal. In April 1940, Stalin's favorite executioner, Blokhin, was dispatched to Byelorussia, where the officers were being held. There, in a soundproofed room, he donned a leather butcher's apron and proceeded to execute 250 Poles every night for the following month.[22] Of the final death toll of around twenty-eight thousand, Blokhin supplied at least seven thousand corpses.

Ultimately, the number of those who fell victim to the executioner's bullet is unknown, and perhaps unknowable. The total number of victims of the Great Terror is still disputed, though some reliable authorities on the issue estimate that a total of around twenty million individuals were imprisoned, of whom some seven million perished.[23] There should be no dispute, however, about the sanctity of human life in the Soviet Union. In the drive toward the communist ideal, human beings were simply expendable. As Stalin's maxim ran: "Death is the solution to all problems—no man, no problem."

This attitude extended to the NKVD's foreign operations, where enemies, real or imagined, were assured of a grisly end. Just as the purges and the Great Terror were rooting out "Trotskyists" and "deviationists" at home, so the NKVD foreign section carried that same fight beyond the Soviet frontier. Their primary targets were the "Whites" (the anti-Soviet Russian exile community) and the followers of the communist heretic Leon Trotsky. And while the majority of their activities consisted simply of observation, infiltration, and intelligence gathering, a small unit, the Administration for Special Tasks, was established in Paris to handle "wet affairs"—the messy business of kidnapping and assassination.[24]

The Special Tasks section soon grew to become one of the largest divisions of the Soviet foreign intelligence service, boasting some 212 operatives across Europe by 1938. Its agents were trained as linguists, socialites, spies, and saboteurs. Many learned their trade at an NKVD facility outside Moscow, where they were made accustomed to life in luxurious "capitalist" surroundings.[25]

Thus prepared, they were sent to infiltrate "enemy" organizations, businesses, and even households, where they would observe and report. On a signal from "Center," infiltration agents
could then become assassins, or a specialist "mobile group" could
be brought in, thus leaving the infiltration agents in situ, undercover. Their most notable victims included the discredited head
of NKVD foreign intelligence, Abram Slutsky, the exiled former
White general Yevgeni Miller, and the defectors Ignace Poretsky
and Walter Krivitsky. Their methods varied with time and opportunity, though they did specialize in the use of poisons.[26] In most
cases, they worked with such skill that there was little evidence
that any crime had been committed. Miller, for instance, was kidnapped on a Paris street and secretly shipped to Moscow for interrogation before being murdered. Slutsky was poisoned with
cyanide, though the death was made to look like a heart attack.[27]
And Krivitsky's murder in a Washington hotel room was faked as
a suicide.[28] Only rarely did the slick killing operation falter. One
such example was that of Poretsky, an NKVD agent in Paris who
had chosen to side with Trotsky. After failing to be lured to his
death by an "old friend" bearing a box of chocolates laced with
strychnine, Poretsky was simply machine-gunned in a Lausanne
side road. Even then, he evidently did not go quietly. When his
body was found, he was discovered to be clutching a clump of his
assassin's hair.[29]

The most famous victim of the NKVD's assassins, however,
was Trotsky himself, the hero of the Russian revolution and civil
war who had fallen foul of Stalin in the late 1920s. Living in exile
in France and later Mexico, Trotsky headed a small movement
of followers, propagating his heretical brand of communism.
Though he exerted negligible influence politically and ideologically, he became an obsession for Stalin. Inevitably, his small
network was infiltrated by NKVD agents, who succeeded in murdering his son during an apparently routine appendectomy and
beheading his Paris secretary. One of those agents, the Spaniard
Ramón Mercader, had been trained in Moscow. In Mexico, living
under the pseudonym of Frank Jacson, he posed as the lover of
Trotsky's courier, and soon became a frequent visitor to Trotsky's

fortified villa outside Mexico City. He worked patiently to gain his target's trust, bringing gifts, playing with the grandchildren, and earnestly discussing politics.

On the morning of 20 August 1940, he arrived with an article that he had written, which Trotsky had agreed to read. He was also carrying a dagger, a revolver, and an ice pick. While Trotsky sat in his study reading the article, Mercader smashed the ice pick into the back of his skull. As he later told the police:

> [He] screamed in such a way that I will never forget it as long as I live. His scream was *Aaaaa*...very long, infinitely long and it still seems to me as if that scream were piercing my brain. I saw Trotsky get up like a madman. He threw himself at me and bit my hand.[30]

After a short struggle, Mercader was arrested. Trotsky, meanwhile, died of his injuries the following day. In many ways, the assassination was a far from perfect "wet" operation. The target's body had not been disposed of, and the scene had not been made to look like a suicide or a medical emergency. Worst of all, the assassin had been caught and had confessed to his crime. Nonetheless, when he was finally released from prison in Mexico in 1960, Mercader traveled to Moscow and was awarded the title of Hero of the Soviet Union.[31]

Trotsky's assassination was certainly a botched job, but Stalin had at least succeeded in eliminating his rival and had demonstrated that his agents were capable of liquidating high-level, well-protected targets outside the Soviet Union. After the removal of Trotsky, of course, the next perceived threat to Stalin came from European fascism, which had evolved in many ways in opposition to Bolshevism. Thus, while Hitler's government was clamping down on the activities of domestic communists, so Stalin's agents were also beginning to target the Nazi élite.

As early as 1934, the then head of Special Tasks, Yakov Serebryanski, had received an instruction to assassinate the German *Reichspräsident*, Hermann Göring, during a visit to France. A sniper was recruited and infiltrated into Le Bourget airport to the east of Paris, where the target was expected to land. But when the visit was canceled, the assassin was told to stand down.[32]

Hitler, too, was beginning to attract the close attentions of Stalin's NKVD. By the summer of 1939, Alexander Foote, a British-born NKVD operative, had been based in Munich for some months.[33] A tall, bluff Yorkshireman and veteran of the Spanish civil war, Foote was being groomed by the Soviets as an infiltration agent. Posted to Munich to learn German and watch political developments, he became a regular visitor to a small restaurant in the city, the Osteria Bavaria, which, it turned out, was also one of Hitler's favorite haunts. As Foote later reminisced:

> Looking one day for a cheap place to lunch, I found by accident the Osteria Bavaria, and, having settled down to the good 1s.6d. set lunch, I noticed a flurry at the door and Hitler strode in accompanied by his adjutant Brueckner, his photographer and toady Hoffmann, and two A.D.C.s.[34]

After reporting the incident to Center, Foote was ordered to maintain surveillance, while a second agent, another Briton by the name of Len Brewer, was sent to assist him with what was now called the "Hitler scheme." Foote and Brewer watched the comings and goings of Hitler and his entourage, noting details of the times of the visits and the apparently lax security. On one occasion, they decided to try an experiment. While Foote sat at his regular table, Brewer stood on the other side of the restaurant as the Führer's party passed through to a function room in the rear. At a given signal, Brewer reached into his inside pocket (as though reaching for a pistol) and pulled out a cigarette case. To his amazement, he elicited no reaction from the bodyguards.[35]

As a number of sources would recall, security at the Osteria Bavaria was certainly not what it might have been. In 1935, for example, Unity Mitford was lunching there with a friend when one of them allegedly dropped a bag of explosive stink bombs, which "all went off together . . . with sensational effect." Hitler, who was at his regular table at the time, did not react. His bodyguards reached for their weapons, but no further action was taken.[36]

One of Hitler's secretaries would later confirm this apparent laxity. Invited to dine at the restaurant with the Führer and a small group of four other intimates in the spring of 1943, she was amazed to discern no special measures in force for Hitler's visit at all:

> Of course I looked to see if [the few other diners in the restaurant] were police officers, wondering what precautions were taken for Hitler's security in such cases. But, either they were particularly intelligent agents or genuine customers, because they acted entirely normally, looked with interest at the distinguished guest, and some of them left quite soon.[37]

Meeting his NKVD handler in the summer of 1939, Alexander Foote learned that his suggestion to target Hitler in the Osteria Bavaria had "burgeoned in the mind of the Kremlin into a full-blown scheme for assassination, with [Brewer] and myself apparently cast for the principal roles."[38] He agreed to pursue the matter in greater detail and make further inquiries. Hitler, it transpired, had known the proprietor of the restaurant since the First World War and visited as often as three times per week when he was in Munich. It was there that he had first been stalked by Unity Mitford, and it was there that he had wooed Eva Braun, who worked nearby. Most important, Foote and Brewer ascertained that the function room was separated from the main restaurant by only a thin partition wall, and that a bomb placed against the partition would cause a great deal of destruction within:

> As far as we could gather there was no special surveillance of the place, and no extra precautions were put into force when the *Führer* honoured it with his presence. What could be easier, we argued, than to put a time bomb in an attaché case along with our coats, and, having had an early

lunch, abandon the lot in the hope that our bomb would blow Hitler and his entourage, snugly lunching behind the ... boarding, into eternity?[39]

Hitler, they concluded, was vulnerable, and the option of a bomb attack would even afford them a safe escape. Yet, strangely, when they finally reported their plans to Center, they were met with a stony silence.

Foote had the misfortune to have presented his plan for an assassination at the exact time when Stalin was seeking to ally himself with Nazi Germany. Despite years of fulminating against the depredations of the "fascist beast," Stalin switched seamlessly to praising the achievements of the "German government." "Just think how we used to curse each other!" he quipped to Ribbentrop during the signing of the Nazi-Soviet Pact.[40] He now became a supplier of grain and oil to Hitler's Germany and an accomplice in the invasion of Poland. Naturally, any plot to assassinate his new ally, though viewed favorably only weeks before, was now out of the question. Back in Munich, Alexander Foote, who had become an enemy national with the outbreak of war, was obliged to make his escape before attracting the attentions of the Gestapo. With that, the "Hitler scheme" was shelved indefinitely.

Though Center had apparently, albeit briefly, considered Foote's plan to be a blueprint for an assassination attempt, Foote himself was curiously blasé about his activities in Munich. The planned murder of Hitler, he wrote, was one of the "innocent sports" with which he "whiled away the time."[41] In due course, he would turn his hand to more serious matters. As a key player in the famed Lucy Ring, he would become one of the most prolific spies of the war.[42]

With the outbreak of the German-Soviet war in 1941, such half-hearted dalliances appeared to belong to another, altogether more genteel age. At the beginning of the campaign, Hitler's armies scored an almost unbroken series of victories, which brought them to the gates of Moscow by early December. Yet, bogged down by winter weather and stiffened Soviet resistance, their advance stalled. Moscow was held; Stalin survived.

The following year, German armies drove to the south, hoping to secure the oil fields of the Caucasus and eliminate Stalin's military reserves. They made huge advances in the Ukraine and southern Russia, taking a succession of cities in the drive for Stalingrad, which was reached in mid-September. However, as some German forward units gazed on the Volga and the "immense steppe" beyond, they had little inkling that they were also witnessing the high-water mark of German military might.[43] The Soviet victory at Stalingrad, in the type of encirclement battle that had hitherto been a staple of the German advance, marked a very real turning point in the war on the Eastern Front. Hitler's troops were no longer seen as invincible. They had been halted this time not by the weather or by the desperate deployment of reserve armies but by superior tactical thinking and its practical application. Their war would now play itself out as a long and bloody fighting retreat back into the very heart of Germany.

The fighting on the Eastern Front bore no relation to that in North Africa or the later Western European campaign. It was brutal in the extreme. It was a clash of two regimes that were ideologically opposed and had trained their soldiers to view their opponents not as fellow human beings but as so many vermin to be exterminated. No quarter was asked or expected. German soldiers facing capture would invariably save their last bullet or grenade for themselves. Soviet captives, meanwhile, could expect little charity from the Germans and were even viewed by their own superiors as traitors. For both sides, therefore, fear, rather than ideology, was often the primary motivator. As one German veteran explained:

> We no longer fought for Hitler, or for National Socialism, or for the Third Reich—or even for our fiancées or mothers or families trapped in bomb-ravaged towns. We fought from simple fear, which was our motivating power. The idea of death, even when we accepted it, made us howl with powerless rage. We fought for reasons which are

perhaps shameful, but are, in the end, stronger than any
doctrine. We fought for ourselves, so that we wouldn't die
in holes filled with mud and snow; we fought like rats...
with teeth bared.[44]

One of the greatest fears for German soldiers was falling into the
hands of Soviet partisans. These irregular units had been formed,
in Stalin's words, "to spread the partisan war everywhere, blowing
up bridges, destroying roads...to create intolerable conditions
for the enemy and his accomplices."[45] Naturally, their creation
was officially credited to Stalin, but the reality was more mundane. They were often made up of civilians and ex-soldiers caught
behind the front by the rapid German advance. They came together and fought, in the first instance, only to survive and usually sought to avoid conflict rather than provoke it. Often their
martial spirit had to be stiffened by an influx of NKVD officers
and "interceptor battalions" deliberately left behind the lines.[46]

In time, however, the partisan movement grew into something much more fearsome. From the Baltic to the Black Sea, few
regions of the occupied Soviet Union did not see partisan activity. Some units emerged spontaneously; others were spirited
through German lines. Each one was approximately fifty to
eighty members strong. Within a month of Barbarossa, there
were already more than two hundred partisan detachments in the
Leningrad district alone. A further ten thousand guerrillas were
active in the Moscow sector.[47] By the end of the year, their total
numbers would exceed three hundred thousand.[48]

The German suppression of the partisans was grimly pre-
dictable. Hitler initially welcomed the guerrilla war, as it gave his
forces the opportunity to "eradicate" their enemies. Thereafter,
all captured partisans were assumed to be communists and would
be treated accordingly—that is, shot out of hand. Every German
death, meanwhile, was to be avenged by the execution of between fifty and one hundred "prisoners." Large-scale anti-partisan
sweeps of the rear areas were undertaken, invariably yielding hundreds of weapons and thousands of victims. In one instance, only
492 rifles were discovered on 4,500 dead "partisans."[49] Clearly

the Nazi definition of a partisan could be extremely elastic. The troops assigned to such grisly activities were usually the most brutal and brutalized of the German war machine. Among them were the notorious *Einsatzgruppen* murder squads and the so-called Dirlewanger Brigade, a ragtag collection of ex-poachers, turncoats, and criminals who delighted in their hideous work.[50]

Yet, under NKVD guidance and using stocks of "liberated" weapons, the partisans continued to flourish and soon developed into a genuine force, committing acts of sabotage and harassing German supply columns in the rear. As one SS officer admitted:

> The greatest difficulties were posed by the partisans. Militarily they were the biggest threat to be found behind a fighting army. Ruthless, brave up to the moment of annihilation, with Asiatic cruelty. This enemy forced our units to stay on constant alert on account of their broad-based organization and their excellent communications network. Their familiarity with the terrain, their continual blocking of roads by laying mines and destroying bridges, their ability to dig in quickly and build machine-gun nests at strategic points, and their display of calm during hand-fought battles in the marshlands are the hallmarks of their fighting skills.[51]

Derailing German trains was another specialty, as was the destruction of military hardware. Ambushes, too, claimed countless German lives. Some units were even given performance quotas; the Yalta Brigade, for example, stipulated that "each partisan must exterminate at least five fascists . . . per month."[52] Few prisoners were taken, and torture and mutilation were commonplace. In one instance, the heads of four captured German soldiers were returned to their unit commander in a leather box.[53] Countless others simply disappeared. In total, it is thought that more than fifty thousand German soldiers were killed by partisan forces in the occupied Soviet Union.

In the wide expanse of territory behind the Eastern Front, some partisan units were more ambitious still and organized

autonomous regions, such as the grandly named Partisan Republic of Lake Palik, a short-lived experiment in self-government established in rural Byelorussia. Indeed, a confidential German
report of July 1942 conceded that large tracts of the German rear
were "endangered." An appended list outlined the thirty-two regions considered most at risk.[54]

This expansion of partisan activity in 1942 coincided with a
growth in NKVD influence. Increasingly, the NKVD viewed the
partisan network as a useful ally for the infiltration, support, and
exfiltration of its agents into German-occupied areas.[55] In the
course of the war, more than ten thousand such agents were sent
behind enemy lines.[56] The majority fought, at least temporarily,
with the partisans, serving to bolster their military and ideological resolve in the process. Their primary purpose, however, was
often the targeting of senior German military and civilian personnel. In many cases, they were working from a list, which had been
prepared in Moscow, containing the names of those tried and
sentenced in absentia for crimes against the Soviet people.

In pursuing their quarry, a few Soviet agents posed as German
officers. One of those was Nikolai Kuznetsov. Code-named "Fluff,"
Kuznetsov was tall, blond, and handsome and, with his cold, reserved manner, could easily pass for a Nazi. Indeed, it was said
that he could speak seven German dialects, as well as Russian with
a German accent.[57] In the summer of 1942, he was parachuted
into Rovno in the Ukraine, where he adopted the identity of
Oberleutnant Paul Siebert, an officer from the Wehrmacht Transport Corps. Expertly trained in covert operations, he succeeded
in spending eighteen months behind German lines, where his primary task was the assassination of prominent functionaries of the
occupation. His methods were simple. He would approach his
targets in broad daylight, confirm their names, and announce
their death sentence before dispatching them from close quarters
with his service pistol.[58] Operating in Rovno, the German "capital" of occupied Ukraine, and later in L'vov, he had no shortage
of targets. He was credited with the murders of, among others,
the SS judge Alfred Funk and the vice governor of Galicia, Dr.
Eugen Bauer; the attempted murder of Paul Dargel, the deputy

Reichskommissar for Ukraine; and the kidnapping of General Max Ilgen, who was spirited to Moscow for interrogation and never heard of again.[59]

Despite these successes, however, his greatest scalps eluded him. The first, the German minister for the Occupied Eastern Territories, Alfred Rosenberg, descended on Rovno in the summer of 1943, but his attendant security regime left little opportunity for Kuznetsov to carry out an attack.[60] The second was the German governor-general of the Ukraine, Erich Koch. Though he succeeded in making the acquaintance of Koch's orderly and a member of his personal guard, Kuznetsov only once got close enough to Koch to make an attempt.[61] On that occasion, despite engaging in conversation with his target, he was unable to act, presumably due to the presence of security personnel. Legend has it, however, that during the exchange he learned crucial details of the forthcoming Kursk offensive, which, of course, he duly passed to Moscow.[62]

As the front neared in 1944, Kuznetsov went underground again and joined a local partisan group, the People's Avengers. On trying to cross the front line, however, he was captured by Ukrainian nationalists, and opted to commit suicide with a grenade. In a letter to be opened in the event of his death, he wrote of his love for his Russian motherland and concluded: "I will go into the mortal fight with the name of Stalin: my father, my friend and my teacher. Give him my greetings."[63] He was posthumously awarded the title of Hero of the Soviet Union.

One of Kuznetsov's fellow agents was Nikolai Khokhlov. Described by later historians as "one of the outstanding Soviet heroes of World War Two," Khokhlov was infiltrated into a POW camp to perfect his German, and became one of the first NKVD agents to operate behind enemy lines.[64] He apparently began his underground career as a member of a group of circus performers—a "theatrical combat team"—who, somewhat bizarrely, planned to throw grenades at visiting Nazis while juggling.[65]

In 1943, however, Khokhlov graduated to more serious matters. That autumn, he was flown into Minsk, behind the front line, where his target was the local Nazi commander, Wilhelm

Kube. A journalist and nationalist agitator from Silesia, Kube had joined the Nazi Party in 1927 and had advanced rapidly through the ranks, mainly due to his talent as a public speaker. After holding a number of administrative positions within the Nazi hierarchy, he was appointed *Generalkommissar* for Byelorussia three weeks after the attack on the Soviet Union. Though he would later gain a reputation as a moderate and even fall foul of the SS, he was nonetheless ultimately responsible for the barbaric occupation policy pursued in the region. To the Soviets, Kube was a war criminal to be slated for execution. As Khokhlov's handler put it: "The grave has been waiting for him for too long."[66]

Once established in Minsk, Khokhlov savored the frisson of life undercover. Smartly turned out in his German uniform, he and an accomplice would visit the officers' club or the casino, saluting their superiors, being saluted in turn, and falling easily into conversation with their neighbors. He had been given the identity of *Oberleutnant* Otto Witgenstein, an officer of the German *Feldpolizei,* or Military Police. He would explain that he was on leave from the front, and had immaculately forged orders to back up his story if required. He would later recall: "I began to feel almost exuberant. Here we were . . . with a bunch of Nazi soldiers, and they did not have the least suspicion who we were."[67]

In due course, and in cooperation with the local partisans, Khokhlov set about planning the assassination. A frontal attack was out of the question. Kube ran a tight security regime, which had been honed by a number of unsuccessful attacks.[68] He employed loyal bodyguards, traveled in a closed car, and was never seen out in public. Even his office hours were erratic, and a personal audience with him was unlikely. His only possible point of weakness, Khokhlov concluded, was his housemaid, a Byelorussian named Jelena Masanik. After engineering a meeting with Masanik, Khokhlov played on her patriotism and persuaded her to help him. At their next meeting, he brought with him an innocuous-looking bundle in garish pink wrapping paper, containing a British-made magnetic mine. He suggested that she might conceal it in Kube's quarters during her cleaning rounds.

She was alarmed at such a prospect, protesting that she wanted to keep away from "the terrors of war." Yet, after Khokhlov's expert persuasion, she left promising to think about his proposal. Three days later, on 23 September 1943, Khokhlov received the news that Kube had been killed. The previous evening, Masanik had placed the bomb beneath Kube's bed, set it to explode in the early hours, and then disappeared into the partisan underground. Khokhlov was stunned. He had expected that another meeting would be necessary to convince his reluctant assassin to act. Yet, he mused, "the mission was accomplished . . . the Butcher of Byelorussia had been assassinated."[69]

Khokhlov went on to fight with numerous partisan groups in Byelorussia and Lithuania before being recalled to Moscow. He was being groomed for covert activity abroad, and in the postwar years he would undertake missions in Romania, France, Austria, Italy, and Denmark. His last mission, in 1954, was the assassination of an exiled Russian émigré in Frankfurt, West Germany. Disillusioned, he confronted his target and told him that he intended to defect. He became the first major intelligence defector of the Cold War, and his astonishing testimony to the CIA seriously weakened KGB foreign actions for years to come.[70]

It has been claimed that Khokhlov, Kuznetsov, and their fellow agents assassinated as many as 137,000 German officers and soldiers during World War Two.[71] This figure is highly questionable and smacks somewhat of the fevered imaginings of a Soviet statistician. But one thing is incontrovertible: the assassins of the NKVD clearly had the skill, training, and sheer audacity to operate for long periods behind enemy lines and to carry out their missions quickly and without detection. As Stalin had demanded, they had made life for the occupier on the Eastern Front distinctly uncomfortable.

By 1941, Hitler no longer had the boyish enthusiasm for the front that had been in evidence in the Polish campaign. Nonetheless, at times of crisis, he felt the need to be closer to the action.

Soon after the start of Operation Barbarossa, therefore, he began looking for a suitable location for a new headquarters on the Eastern Front, and in September 1941, one was found near the town of Vinnitsa in western Ukraine. The site, surrounded by pine forests and farmland, was swiftly cordoned off and a complex of wooden huts and log cabins was erected using local forced labor and prisoners of war. By the time Hitler arrived in July 1942—descending with his traveling circus of advisors, stenographers, doctors, and secretaries in a fleet of sixteen aircraft—it already boasted two bunkers, a cinema, and a further dozen or so buildings.[72] It was given the code name "Wehrwolf."[73]

Contemporaries described Wehrwolf as comfortable rather than luxurious. Its paneled ceilings and pine-clad walls were faintly reminiscent of an Alpine ski lodge, while Albert Speer haughtily described the dining hall as "rather like a railroad station restaurant in a small town."[74] Hitler's secretary, Christa Schroeder, was even less complimentary, complaining about the mice and the all-pervasive damp.[75] The quarters were simply furnished, with plain wooden tables and chairs, and food, though plentiful, was monotonous, due to the requirements of Hitler's sensitive stomach. As at Rastenburg, mosquitoes were a constant plague, and all those present had to take a bitter-tasting antimalaria medicine every day. The greatest problem, however, was the climate. Unbearably hot and humid in the summer, Vinnitsa was also bitterly cold in winter.

Hitler hated Wehrwolf. He loathed both the daytime heat and the nightly invasions of mosquitoes. He endured interminable headaches and was invariably in a foul temper, frequently arguing with his generals. His Luftwaffe adjutant recalled Vinnitsa "plunged in gloom" after one such confrontation:

> Hitler had withdrawn into seclusion. The situation conferences were no longer being held in the *Wehrmacht* Command Staff house, but in the large study at Hitler's quarters. When one entered he would not offer his hand but acknowledge the caller's presence by merely extending his arm. He dined alone in his bunker.[76]

Some sources have suggested that the cause of Hitler's ill-temper and his headaches was radiation poisoning emanating from the granite used at the site.[77] There may be something in this. Many of Hitler's closest associates noticed a profound change in his behavior during his time at Vinnitsa; he would descend into uncontrollable rages and became worryingly unpredictable.[78] Nonetheless, he spent two extended stays in the complex: more than three months in the late summer and autumn of 1942, and a month in the spring of the following year.

Security was predictably tight. The Nazis had succeeded in removing the real and imagined threats to their rule in the region the previous autumn by a brutal program of ethnic cleansing. In Vinnitsa that September, around fifteen thousand Jews and other "undesirables" were murdered in a two-day killing spree.[79] The executions continued sporadically until the following summer. In January 1942, the Jews of the village of Strizhevka, close to Wehrwolf, were liquidated, as they were considered to pose a special risk to the site.[80] In all, only about one thousand of Vinnitsa's Jews were spared for use in the construction program, and once Wehrwolf was complete, they, too, were murdered. Those local inhabitants who were permitted to remain in the vicinity were strictly vetted. Everyone over the age of fourteen was issued with a personal pass to be carried at all times on pain of death. They were not permitted to plant crops within a hundred meters of the forest and were forbidden to enter the complex unless they had written authorization.

Wehrwolf itself was set in a secured rectangular enclosure of about 1 square kilometer. It was surrounded by a 2-meter mesh fence and an elaborate cat's cradle of barbed wire called the "Flanders hedge," which stood around a meter high and fully 3 meters wide.[81] The perimeter was also studded with machine-gun nests and patrolled by SS guards with dogs. A sign on the road entrance proclaimed the fiction that the site was a sanatorium. Inside that enclosure, a smaller security zone—barely 400 meters square—contained the complex of huts and barracks blocks that made up the headquarters. Within this zone, all food was strictly controlled and sampled by a taster, the water supply was checked daily, and oxygen tanks stood ready if required. Even the returning laundry was X-rayed.[82]

With Hitler encamped on its northern outskirts, Vinnitsa naturally became a hotbed of military activity and a virtual outpost of the German General Staff. In addition, the SS, Gestapo, and SD all established their own presence in the town. Numerous other residences were also created in the vicinity for Nazi paladins. Relations with the local Ukrainian population were apparently good, at least initially. Göring was chauffeured around in an open-top Mercedes,[83] and Speer felt safe enough to dispense with his guard detail.[84] Another regular visitor noted that "we used to walk unescorted through the woods and swam in the River Bug nearby . . . there were never any incidents."[85]

Such confidence, however, was misplaced. Though the Germans went to some lengths to conceal the installation and preserve its secrecy, it was difficult to hide a flight of sixteen transport aircraft and the influx of thousands of associated personnel. Stalin, meanwhile, was extremely keen to know of Hitler's whereabouts and pestered the British in the spring of 1942 with requests for the relevant intelligence.[86] The same urgent demands would have been transmitted to the partisans. And, though the Ukraine was generally unfavorable territory for the partisan movement, there was nonetheless a substantial underground network in and around Vinnitsa. One contemporary source noted the existence of five groups in the region, with the largest of them consisting of up to three hundred men.[87] They soon began to target the new arrivals. Attacks on German patrols in the region proliferated. Himmler's pilot, Karl Schnäbele, was murdered in broad daylight by partisans in Zhitomir, in October 1942.[88] Göring's car was ambushed and machine-gunned near Vinnitsa.[89] Farther west, the head of the SA, Viktor Lutze, was attacked in his car and fatally wounded.[90] Ominously, Hitler's arrival at Wehrwolf, in July 1942, had coincided with the transfer to the region of the Central Staff of the Ukrainian partisan movement.

The NKVD was also soon alerted to Hitler's new headquarters. One source states that its interest had initially been spurred by an announcement in a local Ukrainian newspaper of a performance in Vinnitsa of Wagner's *Tannhäuser*.[91] It may also be that a downed German fighter ace, Franz Josef Beerenbrock, betrayed the location while under interrogation in November 1942. (Beerenbrock had received the Oak Leaves to the Knight's Cross from Hitler in person at Wehrwolf only three months earlier.) Subsequent investigations in the Vinnitsa region revealed the comings and goings of numerous prominent Nazis. Soon, a detachment of partisans was sent to establish the exact location of the headquarters. And, following the capture of two German officers, maps and even detailed plans of the Wehrwolf complex were passed to Moscow.[92]

Once Hitler's presence in Vinnitsa had been definitively established, a special operation, code-named "Munich," was set up to investigate his routine there and examine the possibility of an assassination attempt. The plan was to use the experienced agent Dmitri Medvedev, one of Kuznetsov's former accomplices from Rovno, to mastermind an infiltration of Hitler's Vinnitsa headquarters.

Medvedev was a veteran NKVD officer who had long experience of life behind enemy lines. Since his infiltration in September 1941, he had headed a number of detachments operating in the German rear and had carried out numerous "special actions," including the kidnapping of Prince Lvov, who was foreseen by Germans as the post-Soviet governor of Moscow.[93] In the spring and summer of 1943, Medvedev began his observation of Wehrwolf. Yet, though his men on the ground claimed on one occasion to have spotted Hitler traveling through Vinnitsa in a black Maybach limousine, they had, in truth, missed their chance.[94] Hitler had last stayed in the complex in March, and he paid a final, fleeting visit on 27 August 1943.[95] When he left, he ordered that Wehrwolf was to be destroyed. "It is most important that there should be no furniture left," he insisted, "otherwise the Russians will send it to Moscow and put the whole lot on display."[96] Had he remained much longer, the fate of his furniture would have been the least of his worries.

·   ·   ·

Hitler naturally placed himself at risk every time he left Berlin and decamped to one of his field headquarters. His preferred mode of transport was flying, and he had a well-established staff, under the leadership of Captain Hans Baur, with whom he had first flown in 1932. By 1941, Baur's fleet consisted of over twenty aircraft, from the sleek Focke-Wulf Condor and the workhorse Junkers Ju-52 to the tiny Fieseler Stork spotter plane. Of these, it was the Fw-200 Condor that was to serve most regularly as Hitler's personal plane. Entering service in 1937, the four-engine Condor had originally been a commercial airliner and was renowned for its nonstop Atlantic crossings. In its military variant, it was armed with four machine guns and uprated engines, and it specialized in long-range naval reconnaissance. Hitler's aircraft boasted a number of additional modifications, including improved soundproofing, and, from 1942, a "Führer seat" with an armor-plated base, integral parachute, and emergency trapdoor.[97]

Yet, despite all these precautions, flying in the 1940s was still a most hazardous occupation, even away from the combat zone. In November 1941, for example, the German fighter ace Werner Mölders was killed while attempting to land in fog at Breslau. Three months later, the Reich armaments minister, Fritz Todt, was killed during an aborted takeoff from Hitler's headquarters at Rastenburg, and Field Marshal von Reichenau died of heart failure during a forced landing at Kraków. Even Hitler's fleet experienced a number of close shaves. In December 1941, the Führer's accompanying aircraft, another Focke-Wulf Condor, was destroyed on landing at Orel on the Eastern Front.[98] The following summer, Hitler's own plane narrowly avoided catastrophe when a wheel caught fire upon landing at Micheli in Finland.[99]

As well as the risk inherent in flying, it must be remembered that Hitler did most of his traveling during wartime, often shuttling to and from the front, at times facing attack from enemy fighters and anti-aircraft fire. On one occasion, on a flight to Poltava in the Ukraine, Hitler's Condor was attacked by Soviet planes while leaving an airfield outside the city of Nikolayev. Though Hitler was not on board at the time, his pilot reported the event with startling nonchalance:

As I taxied forward for the take-off there was a fountain of dirt where the man who had given me the signal had been. At the same time I became aware that my machine was being fired on. Russians were over the airfield, and my big four-engined plane—it was Hitler's own, the D-2600—must have looked a tempting morsel for them. When I had gained sufficient height, I flew straight at one of the Russians . . . he preferred not to wait for me. He turned away and disappeared into the clouds, and all we suffered was a few bullet holes.[100]

In another incident, Hitler was almost caught by a surprise Soviet attack on the ground. In February 1943, he paid an urgent visit to the field headquarters of Field Marshal von Manstein at Zaporozhye in the Ukraine, where Army Group South was taking a battering. While Hitler proceeded to a conference with von Manstein, his pilot, Baur, waited at the airfield to the east of the city, where they soon received the alarming news that a column of two dozen Soviet tanks had breached the German defenses and was approaching at speed. As Baur noted: "There was nothing between them and the airfield."[101] With Hitler still in conference with von Manstein, a defense force was hastily assembled, despite lacking artillery and anti-tank weaponry. When the column of twenty-two Soviet T-34s appeared at the airfield perimeter, Baur hurried to find Hitler and request a tactical withdrawal, but Hitler refused, replying that such measures would not be necessary. Soon after, the Führer duly returned, boarded his aircraft, and departed. As Baur later learned, the Soviet vanguard was running low on fuel and, expecting stiff resistance at the airfield, had opted not to press their attack. When informed of the seriousness of the situation, Hitler would describe their escape simply as "a bit of luck."[102]

The problem common to all Soviet forces wishing to target senior Nazis on Soviet territory was that of locating their quarry. Beyond the few months that Hitler and his henchmen spent near Vinnitsa, their visits to the Eastern Front were fleeting and surrounded by the tightest security. NKVD assassins operating behind German lines were rare enough, but it would have been a stroke of the most improbable good fortune if one of them had ever come face-to-face with Himmler, Göring, or even Adolf Hitler. If serendipity would not lend a hand, Soviet planners would be forced to rely on Allied intelligence to supply information on the whereabouts of prominent Nazis.

The problem with Allied intelligence, however, was that it was rarely trusted by the Soviets. The assumption in Moscow after 1941 was that their new Western Allies were merely reluctant partners in a marriage of political and military convenience, and that they would use every opportunity to induce the twin threats of Communism and Nazism to bleed each other white. This analysis was not entirely fanciful. After all, Churchill's quip on the occasion of the German attack on the USSR about making "at least a favourable reference to the Devil, if Hitler invaded Hell" would have done little to calm Soviet paranoia. Thus, though British policy was not nearly as Machiavellian as Stalin believed, its intelligence offerings were still treated with the utmost suspicion.

Whether he trusted it or not, Stalin's most accurate source of information in trying to find Hitler was still British intelligence, much of it gleaned from German Enigma decrypts. That information and its origins were top-secret, and there were discussions among the British about whether such high-grade, sensitive material should be handed to the Soviets at all.[103] In the end, it was considered prudent to pass on the information but to withhold its precise provenance. Yet for all that, it is highly probable that Stalin already knew a great deal about the Enigma decrypts via Kim Philby and his other agents within the British Secret Service.

In November 1941, British intelligence learned crucial information on Hitler's possible whereabouts. Accordingly, the British military mission to Moscow relayed the news to Stalin, saying:

Most reliable source reports conference to be held in special train at Orsha during daylight 13th November between High Command of Army and all Army Comman-

ders on Eastern Front. If daylight attack impracticable
suggest night attack on 12th or 13th.[104]

The conference in question was called to address the failing mo-
mentum of the German advance on Moscow. Its participants,
under the chairmanship of the chief of the General Staff, Franz
Halder, included the chiefs of staff of all the armies and army
groups on the Eastern Front. Its agenda was clear: should the
Wehrmacht press its advantage and push for the Soviet capital, in
spite of the worsening weather and strained lines of communication, or should it dig in for the winter and resume the advance on
the spring thaw? Given the crucial nature of these discussions, it
was assumed in London that Hitler himself would be present.

To aid the deliberations at the conference, Halder supplied a
number of maps. One—showing a line from Lake Ladoga near
Leningrad, stretching 250 kilometers east of Moscow and then
south to Stalingrad and the Black Sea—purported to show the
minimum targets for the offensive.[105] Though discussion was
lively, there could be only one outcome. After all, Operation Ty-
phoon—the attack on Moscow—was already in progress, and the
Red Army was widely considered to be on its last legs.[106] One
final push, it was thought, would bring the whole edifice of Soviet Communism crashing to the ground.

Stalin, however, had other plans. A few days earlier, on the
morning of 8 November, with snow swirling around Red Square,
he had presided over the traditional military procession celebrat-
ing the anniversary of the revolution. After seeing off a parade of
tanks and conscripts en route to the front, barely 80 kilometers
away, he had spoken briefly to the assembled crowd. Mother Russia was imperiled, he said, but she would prevail.[107] That night, as
the Russian winter began in earnest, reserve troops from Siberia
were thrown against the freezing German vanguard. The Nazi
Blitzkrieg had stalled.

Stalin's Red Air Force was also preparing a few surprises.
Though mauled in the opening phase of the Barbarossa campaign, and still unable to wrest battlefield air superiority from the

Germans, it had nonetheless recovered sufficiently by late summer to restart limited offensive operations of its own. In August,
for example, it was claimed that long-range bombing raids had
been launched against Berlin using the Ilyushin Il-4, a twin-
engine medium bomber with a crew of four and a laden range of
around 3,500 kilometers.[108] By November, with Berlin now effectively out of range, other targets had to be found. The conference at Orsha would be ideal.

As dusk fell on the evening of 12 November, a force of
around twenty Ilyushin Il-4 bombers from the newly formed
Long-Range Bombing Division prepared to leave their airfield,
probably at Pushkino, near Leningrad. Their target was the railyards at Orsha, where Halder's special train, code-named "Europa," was thought to be stationed. The ninety-minute approach
flight, almost all over enemy-held territory, would have been
made in V-formation at around 6,100 meters, beyond the range
of most anti-aircraft weaponry. According to established procedure, the engines would then have been cut on the final approach
and the bomb run would have been made in silence, the planes
gliding down to a height of around 2,000 meters before releasing
their payload of high explosives, restarting their engines, and
turning for home.[109]

This is a good story, but it is mostly supposition. There is a
great deal of confusion as to whether the Orsha raid ever took
place at all. The only known archival reference to the event came
from the British mission to Moscow. Working on information
supplied by the Soviets, they recorded:

> The Russians bombed Orsha...railway station heavily on
> the night of 13 Nov. They lost one aircraft. From infor-
> mation of Hitler's movements subsequently received,
> they think it unlikely that he was at Orsha on the day in
> question.[110]

On this last point, they were certainly correct. The Führer had, in
fact, spent the whole week comfortably installed at his headquarters in East Prussia. Yet beyond this observation, little else rings

true. The primary failing is the lack of any corroboration for the story. A search of the available Russian archives, for example, yields little. More tellingly, there is a similar lack of evidence on the German side. None of those who participated at the conference appear to have recorded that it was attacked. General Halder, for example, who hosted the meeting, made no mention of the raid in his diary,[111] while a photographic record of the conference contains no evidence of an attack.[112] The German military archive, meanwhile, which contains numerous relevant files, throws up nothing definitive beyond a vague reference to "lively air activity" on the night in question.[113] It could be, of course, that the Long-Range Bombing Division lost their way and bombed another hapless Byelorussian town, or that they found Orsha but were unable to target the railyards. Or it may be that they never took off at all. Some modern commentators clearly believe the story to have been a myth or a Soviet fabrication.[114]

Whether he ordered his planes to Orsha or not, Stalin appears to have pursued his enemy with some considerable determination. As the British ambassador in Moscow reported to London, the Soviet leader needed only the necessary information on Hitler's whereabouts and he would dispatch the bombers. He showed the same approach in pursuing the German General Staff. As London was informed:

> A week or so ago he heard of [the General Staff] at Minsk, and Minsk was heavily bombed. Then it had moved to Vilna, and three days ago Vilna had been bombed. It was now believed to be back at Minsk and, as we were talking, Minsk was being bombed again. Could we keep him constantly and quickly informed of any news we had on the whereabouts of Hitler?[115]

On this occasion, London regretted that it was unable to furnish Stalin with the necessary intelligence, though a promise was made to "pass on immediately any information . . . receive[d]."[116] Accordingly, two months later, when it was learned that Göring was due to visit the Ukrainian city of Poltava, Moscow was informed without delay.[117] On the night in question, Poltava sustained a heavy air raid, but Göring, who was never a willing visitor to the East, had changed his plans. Receipt of accurate intelligence, it appeared, was only one piece of the puzzle. And even if the target had deigned to show up, the blunt weapon of aerial bombing was clearly of only limited use in carrying out an assassination.

The other option available to Stalin, of course, was to target Hitler on German soil, where he was easier to locate and where his movements could be better predicted. Indeed, his agents already had some experience of wartime "wet" operations abroad—not all of it positive. In the spring of 1942, for example, the mastermind of Trotsky's murder, Leonid Eitingon, was ordered to plan the assassination of the German ambassador to Turkey (and former chancellor), Franz von Papen, who, it was rumored, was plotting a separate peace with the Western powers.[118] His chosen assassin, a Macedonian named Omar Tokat, did not share his employer's expertise, however, and, while following von Papen on an Ankara street, succeeded only in blowing himself up while standing behind his target. Lightly injured and covered in his assassin's blood, von Papen initially had no idea what had happened:

> I picked myself up . . . noting with some satisfaction that no bones seemed to be broken. "Don't go a step further!" I shouted. I could only assume that we had set off a mine. This was my first reaction, for when I looked round there was not a soul to be seen.[119]

In the aftermath, two Soviet consular officials were arrested and charged with organizing the attack, but the whereabouts and identity of the assailant were unknown. According to the official Turkish account, the would-be assassin had "completely disappeared."[120] Only the subsequent discovery of Tokat's foot, lodged in a nearby tree, enabled the macabre mystery to be solved. Though Moscow gamely sought to shift the blame onto unknown German agents, the two officials were sentenced to twenty years' imprisonment, contributing to an acrimonious diplomatic rift between Moscow and Ankara in the process.[121]

In the case of Hitler, the NKVD could be spared any such wider concerns, but they were under no illusions. They knew that security would be tight. Their agent could not expect to simply sidle up to Hitler in the street with a bomb, or walk into the Reich Chancellery and gun him down. The action would require meticulous planning, watertight cover stories, and, most important, a well-placed contact to engineer a meeting between the Führer and his would-be assassin.

The agent selected appears, at first sight, to be a peculiar choice. Lev Knipper was a former White émigré and the nephew of the playwright Anton Chekhov. Already over forty by the time war broke out in 1941, he had established himself as a composer, penning rousing patriotic works such as his Symphony No. 4, *Poem of the Komsomol Fighters,* which included the moving "Polyushko Pole," and Symphony No. 6, *The Red Cavalry.* However, he was also leading a double life as an NKVD agent.[122]

In the autumn of 1941, he was recalled to Moscow from the Caucasus, where he was training recruits. He was informed that an independent network of "battle groups" was to be established to remain behind enemy lines should Moscow fall into German hands. His group, he was told, was charged with the special mission of assassinating Hitler during the latter's expected victory visit to the cradle of communism.[123] This was a sound plan. Hitler had held a victory parade in Warsaw in 1939 and had paid a fleeting visit to Paris after its capitulation the following summer. It was perfectly reasonable to assume that Hitler would wish to see a defeated Moscow. As we now know, however, Hitler had no intention of visiting Moscow, even in the event of the defeat of the Soviet Union. As he confided to his intimates, he planned simply to turn the city into an enormous artificial lake.[124] In other comments, he was still more forceful: "Moscow," he said, "must disappear from the earth's surface."[125]

When Moscow failed to fall and Hitler failed to appear, Knipper was given a new mission. He was a willing agent. Though doubtless living in fear of his capricious NKVD masters, he also appeared to have become something of a Russian nationalist. As he wrote to his aunt in the winter of 1941, he felt that he had found a cause for which he was willing to give his life:

> It's not even so frightening to die. There are at last some powerful things in which I believe.... I am Russian, Russian to the marrow in my bones. I've realised that I love my ridiculous, idiotic, uncultured and dirty Motherland, love her with a tender... love, and it's a pain to me to see her big, beautiful body violated.[126]

His new mission was simple. With his privileged background, Aryan good looks, and fluent German, he was to pose as a defector, make his way to Berlin, and target Hitler there.

Knipper's contact in Berlin was to be his elder sister Olga Chekhova. Like him a Russian émigrée, Chekhova had remained in Berlin and had forged a successful career as an actress. By 1941, she was already an established star, having appeared in over a hundred films, regularly cast as the elegant and seductive "grande dame." She had also become part of the cultural élite of the Third Reich and was often seen entertaining the troops or dining with Goebbels. Indeed, when she was photographed having her hand kissed by Hitler, the rumor rapidly spread that the two were romantically attached. One fan even wrote to congratulate her, enthusing: "It is good to know that you will marry Adolf Hitler. At last he has found the right partner.... Make him happy—he has deserved it!"[127]

But Chekhova was also moving in circles of which the Führer would scarcely have approved. As a Russian émigrée, with family still in the Soviet Union, she was an easy target for the foreign agents of the NKVD, and contact had been made as early as 1923. In return for allowing her family to join her in Berlin, she could be persuaded to divulge low-level intelligence or simply promise to keep her eyes and ears open. Though she would certainly not have recognized herself as such, Moscow considered her to be a "sleeper."[128] Indeed, in 1939, the NKVD sought to activate her. With the Nazi-Soviet Pact only recently signed, Stalin was keen to maximize the positive aspects of his relations with Germany. To this end, he considered a clique of influential pro-Russian individuals in Berlin to be essential, and thought that Olga Chekhova might serve as the nucleus for just such a group.[129] In due course, she was visited by NKVD agents, who presumably briefed her on her new task. However, given that there are no records of any such clique ever being formed, it must be assumed that the plan failed. Though well connected, Chekhova was clearly either unwilling or unable to act in the capacity required of her. She went back to being a sleeper—at least as far as Moscow was concerned.

Lev Knipper, meanwhile, was in Iran, where he was plotting his defection. His cover story was that he was researching Iranian folk music, and later that year, his musical labors bore fruit with the completion of his "Two Preludes on Iranian Themes." His political labors were more complex, however. It was planned that he would defect to the Germans in Iran, or possibly Turkey, and then travel to Berlin, where he would make contact both with his famous sister and with one Igor Miklashevsky, a former boxer and fellow NKVD agent who was also posing as a defector.

Miklashevsky had been in Germany since late 1941. He had followed in the footsteps of his uncle, a genuine defector, who had become a Russian-language radio announcer for the Nazis. While living in his uncle's home, he also became the contact for two Soviet agents who had been sent to form an NKVD cell. He first met Chekhova in the summer of 1942, and subsequently reported to Moscow that an assassination of Göring was feasible.[130] Moscow was unimpressed, however, and new instructions were issued requesting that Miklashevsky wait for Knipper to arrive.

As far as Moscow was concerned, the plan was simple. Having probably seen photographs and newsreels of Olga Chekhova with Hitler, the NKVD had concluded that Chekhova's position was such that she would be able to bring the assassins and the target together. This was preposterously unrealistic, however. It would have been ambitious even prior to 1939, when Hitler still attended gala functions and was featured on the celebrity circuit.

But by 1943, he was barely seen in public and spent most of his time at Rastenburg or Vinnitsa, surrounded by his generals. Chekhova, in fact, had last seen the Führer in the summer of 1940. Nonetheless, the NKVD naively believed that she could still act as a facilitator and introduce Miklashevsky and Knipper to their target.

Then, in the summer of 1943, the entire project was suddenly canceled. Stalin no longer saw the logic of killing his rival. With the defeat at Stalingrad heralding a long German retreat, he had recognized that Hitler could no longer feasibly vanquish him. His own star was clearly in the ascendant, while Hitler's was inexorably on the wane. An assassination at this juncture, he considered, could even prove counterproductive, leading to a revitalization of the German military and, possibly, a separate peace with the Western Allies, leaving the USSR to fight on alone.

Thus, all the agents plotting to kill the Führer, from Miklashevsky in Berlin to Medvedev in Vinnitsa, were ordered to stay their hand. Knipper was recalled from Iran to resume his day job as a composer. Medvedev disappeared back into the partisan underground and dreamed of becoming a writer.[131] Miklashevsky murdered his uncle, but refrained from murdering anyone else, and escaped from Berlin in 1944. Olga Chekhova, meanwhile, was probably none the wiser. She was made aware of the role that Moscow had had in mind for her only during an interrogation in Moscow in the summer of 1945.[132] She doubtless would have been horrified that her life had been put at risk in such a madcap scheme. In later life, she would strenuously deny her involvement in any espionage activity. The postwar rumor mill, meanwhile, would claim that she had been awarded the Order of Lenin for her services.

Stalin's suspension of the plans to assassinate Hitler made good tactical sense. Having survived the second winter of the Great Patriotic War and scored a hugely significant victory at Stalingrad, he realized that Hitler had passed the zenith of his power and influence. Moreover, with the threat of defeat by Germany receding, Stalin's new priority was to ensure that Germany remained in the war and was prevented from making a separate peace with the British and Americans. Thus, he recognized that the primary targets for his assassins should now be those who were best placed to supplant Hitler in the event of a coup in Berlin.[133] Ironically, therefore, Stalin suddenly found that he had a vested interest in Hitler's continued survival.

There was also little ideological sense in assassinating Adolf Hitler. According to the dictates of Marxism-Leninism, fascism represented the last, violent death throes of the capitalist body politic. It was something that had to be defeated, certainly, but, like communism, it was also part of something much greater—it was a world-historical force. And just as communism was seen as inevitably, even scientifically destined to triumph, so fascism was just as inevitably destined to run its bloody course and ultimately destroy itself, dragging capitalism with it into the abyss.

Seen in this light, there was little ideological rationale for the devoted communist to murder the leaders of European fascism. One or two individuals might be eliminated, but the social and political conditions that had created and nurtured them would remain, and others would soon emerge to take their place. Like a latter-day Hydra, it was believed, fascism would not be defeated by the simple removal of its head.

And yet, aside from all these strategic and ideological concerns, it was perfectly natural for a politician to wish to eliminate his enemy. Rage, hatred, and betrayal have just as powerful a role to play in politics as the more sober considerations of doctrine or strategy. And, as we know, Stalin was a man of raging passions. As countless contemporaries and eyewitnesses observed, he was a man for whom the normal rules of engagement did not apply. He was motivated as much by petty spite as by grand theory.[134] He was a paranoiac, a megalomaniac, and a man of innate cruelty, who had brought the Georgian culture of the vendetta and the blood feud to Moscow.[135] As the Yugoslav communist Milovan Djilas summarized, Stalin was "the greatest criminal in history," an unlikely amalgam of "the senselessness of a Caligula...the refinement of a Borgia and the brutality of a Tsar Ivan the Terrible."[136]

But there may have been an element in Stalin's relationship with Hitler that went beyond mere criminality and pathological bloodthirstiness. Some have even conjectured that, although the two never met, the relationship had homoerotic undertones.[137] Whatever the truth of that suggestion, it is perhaps plausible to conclude that Stalin's targeting of Hitler was as much the result of fury as of ideology. Stalin had allied himself with Hitler in 1939 and had been betrayed. That betrayal alone was sufficient for Hitler to be slated for assassination. The only surprise, perhaps, is that Stalin had the circumspection to call his assassins off.

CHAPTER 6

The Dirty War: The British and the Special Operations Executive

If I were given a gun and told to take two shots, I would shoot Himmler, then Ribbentrop and brain Hitler with the butt of the rifle.

—NEVILLE HENDERSON, BRITISH AMBASSADOR IN BERLIN 1937–39[1]

THE TWENTIETH OF APRIL 1939 WAS ADOLF HITLER'S FIFTIETH birthday. A public holiday and one of the most important dates in the Nazi calendar, it was to be a day of grand celebrations the length and breadth of the German Reich. The streets were festooned with bunting, church bells tolled, and public buildings proudly displayed the swastika. Across the country, local party officials made last-minute preparations for their parades and veterans polished their medals. Thousands of nervous teenagers rehearsed the oath that they were to recite on their formal induction into the Hitler Youth: "I promise to do my duty at all times, in love and loyalty to our *Führer* and our flag."[2] In Munich, meanwhile, a new crop of entrants was ceremonially welcomed into the leadership cadre of the Nazi Party. Elsewhere, a fortunate few were amnestied and released from the concentration camps, after swearing not to breathe a word of their experiences.

In Berlin, the celebrations had begun the previous day. In the afternoon, Hitler had overseen the inauguration of the new East-West Axis, a redesigned and widened boulevard stretching for 7 kilometers west of the Brandenburg Gate, the first phase in his ambitious plans to create a new capital for the Nazi Reich: Germania. In a convoy of limousines, he had traveled the length of the Axis to rapturous applause, before alighting to declare the grand new avenue open to traffic.

That evening, he had repaired to the Reich Chancellery for a celebratory dinner and had watched the now customary torch-light parade thronging the streets beneath his balcony. As midnight struck, Hitler received the congratulations of his closest acolytes, as well as those of a succession of delegates from across the country. A display of gifts was prepared, and he perused the offerings—statues, paintings, and porcelain—with interest and occasional amusement. His most precious gift, however, had been prepared by his architect, Albert Speer. Set up in a side room was a 4-meter-tall model of the huge triumphal arch that would crown his rebuilt capital. Hitler contemplated the model "with visible emotion," returning to it several times that evening.[3]

The following day, Hitler spent the morning receiving congratulatory telegrams from around the world, among others from Henry Ford and Pope Pius XII. Despite such benedictions, the international situation was tense. Little over a month previously, Hitler's troops had occupied the rump of Czechoslovakia, thereby removing entirely from the map the mutilated remnant left by the Munich Agreement of the previous autumn. Soon after that, his next target had been lined up. Poland, it was thought, could be cajoled and threatened into an ominous-sounding "final settlement of the German-Polish relationship."[4] But, unlike Czechoslovakia, Poland had stubbornly refused to be bullied and had stood fast.

The Western powers, too, finally began to show some resolve in their dealings with Hitler. They recognized the true aggressive nature of the Nazi regime and realized that appeasement had failed. They had not succeeded in sating Hitler's territorial appetite; rather, it appeared, they had encouraged him to gorge himself. Now, though they possessed few means to counter the German threat, they were determined to stand firm. Barely three weeks before Hitler's birthday, they had offered a formal guarantee to the Poles, promising to "lend all the support in their power" in the event of any action that "clearly threatened Polish independence."[5] Hitler, it appeared, faced checkmate.

Shortly before 11 a.m. that spring morning, Hitler returned to the stage on the new East-West Axis for the traditional parade. He traveled in an open Mercedes at the head of a convoy of seven vehicles containing bodyguards, police, and SS. The surrounding streets had been cordoned off, and security personnel had manned the nearby vantage points. The crowds were enthusiastic and less than orderly. Trees, windowsills, and scaffolding were all used to get a better view.

At the reviewing stand, Hitler stood on a raised dais, backed by an enormous German eagle and six swastika banners. He was flanked by his bodyguards, chiefs of staff, aides, generals, field marshals, and admirals, while invited guests, foreign ambassadors, and countless other dignitaries were seated in a large overarching grandstand. Lesser notables and privileged members of the public crowded into a second stand on the opposite side of the avenue. Together, they were to witness a spectacular display of German military might. For almost five hours every branch of the armed forces paraded past the podium—column after column of Wehrmacht, cavalry, paratroopers, sailors, airmen, and SS-*Leibstandarte,* all marching in perfect order to the blare of a military band. All the latest machinery was on display: tanks, anti-aircraft guns, state-of-the-art artillery, even searchlights. Overhead, swarms of Messerschmitt fighters and Heinkel bombers droned past in formation. For the finale, the regimental colors were massed before the Führer and dipped in solemn salute. Hitler stood impassively throughout, acknowledging each unit with his trademark "German greeting." He was presiding over the greatest military spectacle ever staged in the Third Reich and was sending an unequivocal message to his enemies and those who sought to curb his ambitions.

One of those present was the British military attaché to Berlin, Colonel Noel Mason-Macfarlane. A career soldier, Mason-Macfarlane had been a cadet at the Royal Military Academy before joining the Royal Artillery in 1909. Service in France and Mesopotamia in World War One had earned him the Croix de Guerre and the prestigious Military Cross. He was soon being tapped for senior staff positions. A poet, eccentric, and first-class cricketer, Mason-Macfarlane was described by a contemporary as "a man who believed in direct action" and one with "an incurable and out-of-date yearning to take a personal hand in righting the affairs of the world."[6] Despite these distinctly undiplomatic traits, he was sent to Vienna as military attaché in 1931, moving to Berlin in the same capacity six years later. In that time, he developed an unrivaled knowledge of the German military machine and drew the conclusion that Hitler was not to be trusted. In consequence, he gained a reputation as a hawk, advocating a belligerent policy toward Germany and suggesting that Britain should not wait to be attacked.[7]

In the autumn of 1938, as the Czech crisis loomed, word of Mason-Macfarlane's unorthodox opinions had evidently reached the Gestapo. He was visited that August by a German by the name of von Koerber who, professing revulsion for the Nazis, attempted to enlist the colonel as a fellow conspirator. Unimpressed by what he considered to be an agent provocateur, Mason-Macfarlane responded with the standard diplomatic reply: "Any attempt to interfere with domestic German politics from without," he said, "would most assuredly lead to exactly what we wish to avoid."[8]

Despite such protestations of innocence, Mason-Macfarlane was indeed considering some interference in German politics. In fact, he was beginning to think the unthinkable. In a letter from the British embassy in Berlin to London in March 1939, he was described as being "in very warlike mood" and "anxious that we should declare war on Germany within the next three weeks."[9] Three weeks later, at Hitler's birthday parade, he was photographed for the official commemorative volume. While a French colleague next to him relaxed with a half-smile of Gallic hauteur,

Mason-Macfarlane wore what can only be described as a scowl of contempt.[10]

A few days before the parade, Mason-Macfarlane had been standing at his drawing-room window, overlooking the new Axis. He was watching the workmen prepare the decorations, hanging swastika banners and erecting the plywood columns that flanked the saluting base. While talking to a colleague his mind wandered to the scene unfolding below. After a short silence, he spoke. "Easy rifle shot," he said, adding, "I could pick the bastard off from here as easy as winking." He went on: "There'd be hell to pay, of course, and I'd be finished in every sense of the word. Still . . . with that lunatic out of the way we might be able to get some sense into things." When his colleague warily conceded that it was "an idea," he agreed: "Yes. Bloody awful one . . . but I'd be prepared to do it."[11]

It was, in fact, an idea that Mason-Macfarlane had been mulling over for some time. A few weeks earlier, in a memorandum to London, he had warned of the dire consequences for Britain if Hitler was not "unexpectedly wafted to Valhalla."[12] He then developed his thoughts further. His residence, he argued, was barely 100 meters from the saluting base used for the large military reviews. During a parade, a marksman with a high-velocity rifle could make an end of Hitler, while the noise of the crowd and the military band would suffice to drown out the rifle shot and afford the assassin a good chance of a getaway.[13]

Though Mason-Macfarlane had offered to pull the trigger himself, some sources claim that he had a rival for the role of assassin.[14] William Stephenson was a Canadian businessman and former Great War pilot who had apparently also suggested assassinating Hitler with a sniper's rifle at around the same time. Yet Stephenson's role in the drama, if any, is very difficult for the sober historian to divine. Though he went on to play an important role in promoting wartime intelligence cooperation between the United Kingdom and United States, no contemporary evidence supports his claim to have advocated Hitler's assassination in 1939. Indeed, to make matters worse, Stephenson later gained an unenviable reputation as somewhat of a fantasist, engaging numerous biographers to further embellish and exaggerate his already impressive life story.[15] In this way, he would unilaterally award himself the Legion d'Honneur, the Croix de Guerre, and two bars to his (genuine) Distinguished Flying Cross. He even claimed to have won the world amateur lightweight boxing championship while serving in the Royal Flying Corps in 1918.[16] One has to conclude that Stephenson's claim to have been a would-be assassin of the Führer most probably belongs in the same category.

Mason-Macfarlane, meanwhile, was deadly serious, and was motivated not by vainglory but by a genuine concern that Hitler was leading Germany once again into war. When Whitehall heard of his plan, however, it was aghast. The foreign secretary, Lord Halifax, commented sternly that "we have not reached that stage...when we have to use assassination as a substitute for diplomacy."[17] Mason-Macfarlane was informed, with masterly British understatement, that such an act would be "unsportsmanlike."[18] Two months later, he was transferred back to Aldershot. He had clearly hit a nerve. But it was not that he was treading on the toes of the intelligence service; rather, he was advocating something close to heresy.

Established just before the First World War, the British Secret Intelligence Service (SIS) consisted of two branches, responsible for domestic and foreign security and counterespionage. The foreign section (which became known as MI6) operated on a shoestring budget via the network of British embassies and consulates, where the passport control officer usually doubled as the resident intelligence agent.[19] Its primary objective, of course, was the gathering of information via a network of agents and informers. Any dabbling in the darker arts of assassination and sabotage was viewed with the utmost distaste. For one thing, MI6 agents were forbidden to operate against their host country.[20] For another, MI6 still clung to a quaint nineteenth-century ideal of the "gentleman spy" and had a profound aversion to all such nefarious activities. As MI6's founder, Mansfield Cumming, wrote, the secret agent should be a gentleman, and a capable one, absolutely honest with considerable tact and at the same time force of charac-ter...experience shows that any amount of brilliance or low cunning will not make up for a lack of scrupulous per-sonal honesty. In the long run it is only the honest man who can defeat the ruffian.[21]

Indeed, when Britain's most celebrated spy, Sidney Reilly, arrived in Moscow in 1918, he soon fell foul of the ruling "softly, softly" ethos. After marching to the Kremlin gates, posing as an emissary of Lloyd-George, and demanding to see Lenin (whom he al-legedly intended to assassinate), he was given a dressing-down by the MI6 station chief and threatened with expulsion.[22] In the opinion of one fellow agent, Reilly was considered "untrustwor-thy and unsuitable to work." According to another, he was "very clever [but] entirely unscrupulous."[23] Reilly, who would one day serve as the inspiration for James Bond, would clearly never qual-ify as a gentleman spy.

This attitude even extended to the unofficial British spy net-works. In the early 1930s the dramatically named Z-Organisation was established by a former SIS operative named Claude Dansey. It was to function as an independent intelligence agency, using Dansey's network of businessmen, informers, and journalists, and was intended to continue to operate even if the official network was compromised. Dansey himself was a controversial figure. A brilliant organizer, he was also vicious, intolerant, and tyrannical. One of his staff even described him as "an utter shit."[24] As the master of an extensive spy network, Dansey effectively possessed the power of life and death over his agents, and did not hesitate to have his contacts and informers liquidated if he suspected them of duplicity. Yet for all that, he considered sabotage and assassina-tion to be activities that were always counterproductive.[25] It was a view that he shared with the vast majority of his superiors.

Thus while German and Soviet agents abroad were as much interested in murdering their enemies as observing them, the British tended to cleave to a more genteel view of the role of the secret agent. They saw themselves as being in the business of clandestine intelligence-gathering, and considered that that complex task would not be aided by a descent into murder and mayhem. Not only was assassination frowned upon, therefore, but the targeting of a foreign head of state was considered to be completely beyond the pale. Yet as war loomed in 1939, that opinion was increasingly to come under review.

When Britain entered the Second World War in September 1939, she appeared, at first sight at least, to have re-created the successful alliance of the Great War two decades earlier. Once again, she had allies on both German flanks—Poland to the east and France to the west. Once again, she had secured American economic support, though not yet full-blown military assistance.

Any cautious optimism would soon prove illusory, however. In the east, Nazi Germany swiftly defeated Poland and shifted the bulk of its forces west to confront France. There, it was faced by a British Expeditionary Force that was far below strength and beset by shortages, disorganization, and complacency. As Churchill wrote to a colleague:

> The squandering of our strength proceeds in every direction.... Our Army is puny as far as the fighting force is concerned; our Air Force is hopelessly inferior to the Germans;...we maintain an attitude of complete passivity dispersing our forces ever more widely.... Do you realise that perhaps we are heading for defeat?[26]

By the spring of 1940, Churchill's grim prediction was fast becoming a reality. That April, German forces occupied Denmark and Norway, virtually unopposed save for the naval engagement at Narvik. A month later, they moved west with a feint through Belgium and the Netherlands before the main force swept through the Ardennes and raced for the Channel coast, leaving their opponents in disarray. The British humiliation was completed with the ignominious but brilliantly improvised evacuation from the beaches of Dunkirk. Two weeks after that, Paris fell.

Britain was suddenly alone, with only the English Channel separating her from the Nazi-occupied Continent. Winston Churchill—the Cassandra of appeasement—was raised to prime minister, at the head of a coalition national government and a nation in shock. Though he spoke inspiringly of "blood, sweat, and tears," the public mood was anxious, even somber. And when Britain herself came under attack that autumn, that mood deteriorated still further. George Orwell, who was writing *The Lion and the Unicorn* at the time, would record:

> I began this book to the tune of German bombs, and I begin this second chapter in the added racket of the barrage. The yellow gun-flashes are lighting the sky, the splinters are rattling on the house-tops, and London Bridge is falling down, falling down, falling down. Anyone able to read a map knows that we are in deadly danger. I do not mean that we are beaten or need be beaten. . . . But at this moment we are in the soup.[27]

In this perilous situation, Churchill recognized that he had to abandon the accepted norms of warfare. He knew that Britain was fighting for its very existence, awaiting the Nazi invasion and lacking the necessary military hardware to defeat it. If he was to win the war, he concluded, he would have to fight dirty. Thus, after he had vowed to "fight on the beaches . . . in the fields and in the streets," he also gave orders to take the fight behind enemy lines. On 16 July, the very day that Hitler ordered the invasion of Britain, Churchill established the Special Operations Executive (SOE), with the brief to "set Europe ablaze."[28] According to its founding statement, the SOE was to act as a "democratic international" to spread revolt in Germany's conquered territories by sabotage, propaganda, and labor unrest. Crucially, however, its remit also included "terrorist acts against traitors and German leaders."[29]

Despite the urgency of the hour, SOE's birth was not an easy one. First, the new organization was established from scratch and had to combine various offices from other government bodies. It incorporated (among others) D Section from MI6, which specialized in sabotage, as well as MI(R) from the War Office, which planned paramilitary warfare, and EH from the Foreign Office, which dabbled in subversive propaganda. Its personnel were similarly eclectic, combining bankers and lawyers with the most cunning and daring of the British military élite.

The second difficulty that SOE faced was disapproval and even outright hostility from many of its rivals in the military and intelligence communities.[30] SOE's raison d'être was to sow mayhem, confusion, and ultimately revolt, none of which was conducive to the covert gathering of sensitive information. Many in the intelligence establishment were extremely dubious about the wisdom or even the value of SOE operations, which they usually viewed as counterproductive. As a later fictionalized account would put it: "SIS walked in soft shoes, SOE walked in spats."[31] Tension between the two was inevitable. The SIS old guard tended to view SOE as "bungling amateurs."[32]

Many within the regular military also disapproved of SOE's unconventional methods. They considered that special operations exceeded the limits of civilized warfare and, by resorting in effect to state terrorism, set a dangerous and unconscionable precedent. In short, they preferred to continue to fight by the Queensberry Rules, even if their opponents did not, and even if it could spell their own defeat. Sir Charles Portal, chief of the Air Staff, was one of the critics. He was most unimpressed by SOE's first operational plan, Operation Savanna, which called for agents to be dropped in northwest France to ambush and murder the crews of a German Pathfinder bomber squadron. He wrote to SOE command to complain:

> I think that the dropping of men dressed in civilian clothes for the purpose of attempting to kill members of the opposing forces is not an operation with which the Royal Air Force should be associated. . . . There is a vast difference, in

ethics, between the time-honoured operation of the dropping of a spy from the air and this entirely new scheme for dropping what one can only call assassins.[33]

SOE clearly faced a battle of hearts and minds at home almost as fierce as the very real battles it hoped to join abroad. Operation Savanna was aborted.

Despite this setback, SOE soon swung into operation. Its primary training camps, at Beaulieu in Hampshire and Arisaig in the Scottish Highlands, were swiftly staffed and supplied. Prospective agents were recruited, mainly from the military and civilian exiles of occupied Europe. They were trained in all manner of ungentlemanly arts, from sabotage to unarmed combat and silent killing. As one trainee would recall:

> [Our] training officer was Major Sykes...[who] looked and spoke like a bishop, very quiet and mild. In his lectures he would say the most gruesome things in his soft bishop's voice...and after describing particularly vicious ways of crippling and disarming an enemy, he would often end with the remark, "and then kick him in the testicles."[34]

The Queensberry Rules clearly did not apply.

Agents were also supplied with a plethora of specialized military hardware, or "toys," all developed by SOE's brilliant technical department. They could choose from a range of ingenious devices, including exploding rats, barometric fuses, clam mines, and the famed Welrod: a silent, single-shot assassin's pistol. The usual weapon of choice, however, was the Sten gun, a light, three-piece submachine gun, which (though it had a nasty habit of jamming) was largely impervious to the elements, and accurate to around 200 meters. It would soon become the staple of the European resistance from the Atlantic to the Black Sea.

Once trained and equipped, all that remained for the agent was his or her infiltration into occupied Europe. The vast majority were to be dropped by parachute, so a brief training course was

organized, based at Ringway airport near Manchester. The first
SOE agents flew out on 15 February 1941, bound for Warsaw
and a successful rendezvous with the Polish Home Army. In time,
a further 300 or so would be dropped into occupied Poland,
while some 350 would be infiltrated into the Low Countries and
1,350 into occupied France.[35] Having landed, they could com-
municate with London by radio and could find succor with the
domestic resistance, but they were essentially on their own.

Once "in theater," the primary purpose of SOE agents was
the fostering and coordination of resistance to occupation. Infiltrated personnel were to provide the backbone of the native underground movements, where they were to train their fellow
resisters in all aspects of clandestine activity. Armed with SOE
supplies and captured weaponry, their role was to give the resistance teeth: plan sabotage, sow confusion, and tie down as many
enemy soldiers as possible.

One part of their remit, of course, was the assassination of
German occupation officials and their collaborators. And though
they played a comparatively minor role in overall operations, such
targeted executions were seen as a powerful demonstration of the
continued vitality of the underground. They sent the message
that the occupation was not unopposed and that collaboration
with the enemy would not be tolerated. In the vast majority of
cases, the selection of targets was considered a matter for the local
resistance. Though London might be informed, especially with
the targeting of high-profile individuals, no specific approval was
necessary. SOE provided the training, the skills, and the supplies,
while its agents on the ground were free to select their objectives
according to local conditions.

The results of this opening phase of SOE-inspired activity
were impressive. In Poland, the underground Home Army,
which enjoyed especially close ties with SOE, was resisting the
Germans with exemplary vigor (see Chapter 4). In France, meanwhile, a veritable "epidemic of assassination" was troubling
Goebbels.[36] One resistance group there even claimed to be killing
five hundred Germans every month.[37]

Yet the policy was still not without its critics. In August 1941,

the French communist underground assassinated a prominent
Gestapo informant in Paris, thereby provoking a gruesome wave
of reprisals. In response, de Gaulle publicly denounced the policy
of assassination, and the Foreign Office in London was forced to
canvass the exiled governments of Europe to establish their true
attitudes toward SOE's underhand activities.[38] Though few were
willing to actively discourage the incitement to violence in their
homelands, not one of them came out explicitly in favor of it. It
was hardly a ringing endorsement, but in the space between these
two positions, SOE could at least continue to function. Its directive for the coming year, however, would dilute its own founding
ethos: direct action by civilian forces was now to be discouraged
for fear of the reprisals that could be provoked.[39]

Undeterred by this crisis of conscience, the Czech government in exile devised a plan, in the winter of 1941, to assassinate
a high-profile German target. The name of the prospective victim
was not initially specified, but weapons, supplementary training,
and infiltration were requested. Two agents were then selected:
Josef Gabčík and Jan Kubiš, one Slovak, one Czech, both of
whom had already undergone SOE training. SOE staff knew better than to ask questions. Assassination was well within their
purview, and if the Czechs wanted to eliminate a senior Nazi,
then so much the better. The two agents underwent additional
training, mainly in parachuting and ambush techniques, and by
the time they left British shores, their SOE handlers boasted that
"they [had] been trained in all methods of assassination known to
us."[40] After lengthy logistical delays, Gabčík and Kubiš were finally dropped into Bohemia on the night of 28–29 December
1941. The code name for their mission was "Anthropoid." Their
target was the "Butcher of Prague," Himmler's SS deputy,
Reinhard Heydrich.

The son of a provincial music teacher, Heydrich had served in
the German navy in World War One and became an early recruit
to the SS before advancing swiftly in the Nazi ranks as a gifted
though ruthless administrator. With the outbreak of war, he masterminded the creation of the RSHA (Reich Security Head Office), which was intended to bring all German security and police

bodies under one roof. In September 1941, he was then appointed the "protector" of Bohemia and Moravia, where, as head of the occupation regime, he was to realize the territory's industrial potential to the benefit of Berlin and smash the Czech resistance.

Such was Heydrich's success in the latter objective that Gabčík and Kubiš were explicitly instructed not to make contact with the remains of the domestic Czech underground.[41] Though hampered in their mission by the comparative lack of local assistance, they were also aided by another result of Heydrich's success. Unlike his predecessor, their target evidently now felt safe enough to dispense with his SS escort (which he viewed as an affront to German prestige), and preferred to travel alone with a driver in an open-top Mercedes tourer. This fit of hubris gave Gabčík and Kubiš the opportunity they were looking for. They selected a quiet stretch of road in a Prague suburb, en route from Heydrich's residence to the city center, where traffic slowed to negotiate a hairpin bend. In addition, they noted that there were no police stations or SS garrisons in the vicinity, and a nearby tram stop would enable them to wait for their target without arousing suspicion. Gabčík would be stationed on the inside of the bend brandishing a Sten gun, while Kubiš would stand across the road armed with grenades. They planned to carry out their attack on the morning of 27 May 1942.

In the final weeks before the attack, a flood of correspondence ensued over the wisdom of the planned assassination. The local Czech resistance in Prague, which now had wind of the plan, was dismayed. Having barely survived one SS roundup, they were less than keen to invite another by such reckless action. In vain, they tried to persuade the assassins to disobey orders, stressing the calamitous reprisals that would surely follow for the innocent Czech population. They finally appealed directly to their superiors in London to call off the mission, claiming, "This assassination would not be of the least value to the Allies. . . . It would threaten not only hostages and political prisoners, but also thousands of other lives."[42]

The Czech exile government in London, however, was disinclined to agree to the request. Not only did President Beneš need a spectacular action to impress his more powerful allies, but he was also planning another high-profile assassination, this time of the propaganda minister of the occupation government, Emanuel Moravec. His response to the domestic resistance, therefore, was blunt. A demonstration of strength was required, he replied, "even if it had to be paid for with a great many sacrifices."[43]

Gabčík and Kubiš, meanwhile, prepared to carry out their mission. On the morning of 27 May, they traveled to their selected location in the suburb of Holešovice. Once there, they positioned themselves close to the bend in the road and posted a colleague farther up the hill to act as lookout. Weapons were silently assembled, and final preparations were made. Under the noses of numerous Czech commuters crowding into the waiting trams, the assassins waited for their target.

For almost two hours they waited. The rush hour crowds soon dispersed, and they were left loitering suspiciously on a street corner, worrying that their target had evaded them or that their mission had been betrayed to the Germans. Then, at 10:32, they received the signal that they were waiting for—Heydrich's car was approaching. As the Mercedes slowed to round the corner, Gabčík flung open his raincoat and aimed his Sten at Heydrich at almost point-blank range. But the gun jammed. Kubiš then stepped forward and threw a grenade, which missed and exploded against the rear wheel, hurling shrapnel in his own face, and showering a nearby tram with debris. As the Mercedes ground to a halt, Heydrich drew his pistol and prepared to give chase. However, after a brief exchange of fire with Gabčík, he collapsed in pain, and his attacker made good his escape.

As they fled the scene, Gabčík and Kubiš believed that they had failed. Their ambush had certainly been botched, and their last vision had been of Heydrich and his driver in hot pursuit. But, unknown to them, their target had, in fact, been mortally wounded. Heydrich had suffered a fractured rib and a ruptured spleen in the attack, but crucially, Kubiš's grenade had sent fragments of shrapnel and horsehair from the Mercedes's rear seat deep into his abdomen. Hurried to a local hospital, he was treated by the best Nazi surgeons, specially flown in by Himmler, but as infection set in there was little that could be done. In the early hours of 4 June, eight days after the attack, he finally succumbed to blood poisoning.

The grim reprisals foreseen by the opponents of the mission were quick to materialize. The nearby village of Lidice, which was wrongly suspected of sheltering the assassins, was razed to the ground, its two hundred menfolk murdered and its women and children sent to the concentration camps, where barely a handful survived. The village of Leźáky, where an SOE transmitter was discovered, was also destroyed, its fifty or so inhabitants simply massacred. The assassins themselves were finally tracked down in the crypt of a Prague church. There, during an intense SS assault, Kubiš was killed and Gabčík committed suicide. Their heads were later impaled on spikes by the Nazis to intimidate their fellow countrymen.

The Czech underground was also shattered. All those who had helped or sheltered the assassins were executed, along with their families. Reprisals continued throughout the summer, targeting the intelligentsia, nationalists, and ex-officers, and claiming nearly 1,500 additional lives. Farther afield, 3,000 Jews were deported from Theresienstadt for extermination, and another 150 Jews were murdered in Berlin. In all, Heydrich's death was avenged by the slaughter of over 5,000 individuals, the vast majority innocent civilians.

Officially, Operation Anthropoid was hailed as a tremendous success: a rejection of Nazi rule and a morale boost for the occupied nations of Europe. It demonstrated that no German was safe, however senior in rank and however far from the front line he might be. As the director of SOE noted, the killing was seen in London as "an act of justice."[44] The status of the Czechs within the Allied camp was also raised, just as President Beneš had planned. The shame of Munich was expunged, and now Lidice was commemorated across the world, becoming in the process a byword for Nazi brutality.[45]

In private, meanwhile, there was grave disquiet over the sheer scale of the reprisals. Though unrepentant about his assassination of Heydrich, Beneš shied away from targeting Heydrich's succes-sor, Karl Hermann Frank. Among British government circles, too, the general opposition to political assassination was rein-forced. Even SOE was shocked by the Nazi response. It viewed Heydrich's death very equivocally. On one level, it saw the oper-ation as a disaster: its nascent organization "in theater" had been smashed, and its agents had been murdered.[46] But it appreciated that Heydrich's position was such that his death had also effec-tively rendered the German secret intelligence agencies lame, if only temporarily. Thus it viewed Operation Anthropoid both as a lesson in what could be achieved by assassination and as a grave warning of the repercussions that could be expected. In future, plausible deniability would become a watchword for all missions, and other methods, such as kidnapping, would be attempted where possible. And if there really was no alternative to assassina-tion, then the target had to be well worth the reprisals.

In Germany, Heydrich was mourned like a favorite son. Himmler wept when he heard of his death, and Goebbels con-fided to his diary that Heydrich was "irreplaceable."[47] In an elab-orate state funeral, Hitler spoke of him as "a man with an iron heart."[48] His death, he said, meant more to him than the loss of a battle. In private he was less complimentary, denouncing Heydrich's "heroic gesture" of riding in an open, unarmored car as "damned stupidity, which serves the country not one whit."[49] In response to the killing, Hitler emphasized the need for redoubled vigilance and decreed that security regulations were henceforth to be heeded by all senior personnel. His own security was also to be tightened. After all, he stressed, *he* was obviously the enemy's real target, as only he was the guarantor of German victory.[50]

In the months after Heydrich's assassination, SOE continued much as before, outwardly undeterred but perhaps with a height-ened awareness of the potential backlash from high-profile oper-ations. The selection of targets, however, remained the exclusive preserve of the resistance organizations themselves. On Christ-mas Eve 1942, the murder of one of those targets, the com-mander in chief of Vichy French troops, Admiral Jean Darlan, spawned a controversy that has rumbled to this day. Though

Darlan's assassin was a French royalist student, he had been trained and armed at an SOE camp in the Algerian desert. And although explicit British involvement in the attack has been plausibly denied ever since, it is perhaps telling that many contemporaries—including Darlan himself on his deathbed—assumed it to have been an SOE mission.[51]

Whatever the truth of the Darlan case, by the summer of 1943, SOE had clearly overcome whatever qualms it may have had and was preparing to expand its policy of assassination. At a council meeting in late June, it was recommended that a "concerted execution campaign" should be instituted across occupied Europe.[52] This was the genesis of Operation Ratweek, a simultaneous, Europe-wide action targeting collaborators as well as SS, SD, and Gestapo staff. It was planned that an "execution month" would be declared, during which the European resistance movements would cause their German occupiers to live in fear. SOE would supply the Welrod silent execution pistol as well as lists of possible target "rats," if required.

Ratweek enjoyed only modest success, however. In Denmark and Holland it stalled completely, as the local resistance was often compromised or was simply wary of inviting the massive reprisals seen in the aftermath of Heydrich's death. In Belgium, too, the operation was dropped, largely due to the opposition of the Belgian exile government.[53] In the event, only occupied France saw any Ratweek operations. One resistance network, Armada, was especially active. Though it specialized in sabotage, one of its agents—a taxi driver code-named Khodja—found his métier in the grubby business of assassination. Operating in Lyon in the spring of 1944, Khodja succeeded in single-handedly eliminating eleven senior SD personnel.[54]

Thus, through the reluctance of many of its allies to carry out planned "wet operations," SOE was finally forced to devise alternatives for its assassination policy. In January 1944, it found a new target: General Friedrich-Wilhelm Müller, the commander of the German 22nd Infantry Division on Crete, who was responsible for a brutal campaign of repression against the local resistance. Yet rather than simply eliminate Müller, SOE conceived a daring plan to kidnap the general, spirit him to Cairo, and arraign him before a war crimes trial. An SOE team (led by the later author Patrick Leigh Fermor) parachuted into Crete and began studying the general's routines and security measures, but before they could act, Müller was replaced by the comparatively blameless Major-General Heinrich Kreipe. Undeterred, Leigh Fermor and his team opted to continue with their mission and succeeded in kidnapping Kreipe that April and, after hiding him for over two weeks in the Cretan mountains, sailing for Egypt.[55]

Given the concerns that were then rife in London, considerable thought was given to the problem of preserving the native population from the expected German reprisals. After their getaway, therefore, the SOE team left a number of items of British equipment in the general's car along with a letter:

Your Divisional Commander Kreipe was captured a short time ago by a British Raiding Force. . . . By the time you read this, he and we will be on our way to Cairo.
We would like to point out most emphatically that this operation has been carried out without the help of Cretans or Cretan partisans. . . . Any reprisals against the local population will be wholly unwarranted and unjust.[56]

When asked many years later why their target was not simply murdered, Leigh Fermor is said to have replied: "I'm surprised that you have put that question to a British officer."[57] Even Kreipe, though aggrieved by the loss of his Knight's Cross during a scuffle, nonetheless conceded that his captors had treated him throughout with "chivalry and courtesy."[58] When of a mind to do so, it seems, SOE was well capable of playing by the rules.

After the success of the Kreipe operation, kidnapping enjoyed a brief vogue among the British Special Forces. In January 1945, for example, two Italian double agents were kidnapped by SOE in northern Italy and brought to London for interrogation.[59] But the most audacious kidnap plot was hatched by the SAS soon after D-Day in the summer of 1944. At that time, Field Marshal Erwin Rommel, one of Hitler's most famous and decorated generals, was commanding Army Group B in Normandy and held the deputy command for the entire Western theater. A man of rare tactical talent, he was considered to hold the key to the German defense in the Normandy campaign, and thereby became a natural target for British clandestine agents.

Rommel had, of course, been targeted before. In the winter of 1941, British commandos had carried out an audacious long-range raid on Rommel's headquarters in the Libyan desert. And though they had achieved complete surprise, their quarry was not at home.[60] In mid-July 1944, another similar attempt was mounted. A team of five SAS men under the command of a French captain, Raymond Couraud, parachuted into the region of the Vexin, northwest of Paris, where Rommel had his residence at the château of La Roche Guyon. Their plan was to ambush the field marshal's car and take him to a nearby hilltop, from where the party and their prisoner would be exfiltrated by light aircraft.[61] However, while the kidnap team was preparing its move, Rommel was gravely injured on the evening of 17 July, when his car was driven off the road after a strafing attack by roving British fighter aircraft. He never returned to La Roche Guyon, and indeed never returned to active duty, committing suicide some three months later when implicated in the July Plot against Hitler. The SAS team, meanwhile, disrupted German supply and communication lines and then made their way to Paris to enjoy the imminent liberation. Their task had been ably, if unwittingly, achieved by the machine guns of an RAF Spitfire.

But all this is not to suggest that assassination had been abandoned by the British Special Forces and their allies. After all, the operational instruction to Rommel's would-be kidnappers stated that if they were unable to exfiltrate the field marshal, they were to kill him.[62] Assassination also remained the tactic of choice for eliminating low-level targets among the occupiers and their collaborators. In Denmark, for example, the resistance liquidated a succession of informants, in some cases using the Welrod silent pistol. In one instance, in the town of Aarhus in November 1944, a target was executed in a busy hospital ward without anyone noticing anything amiss.[63] In Norway, meanwhile, a number of collaborators were assassinated as the war neared its end: Ivar Grande, a senior Gestapo informant and spy, was gunned down in Ålesund in December 1944, and two months later, the head of the Norwegian police, Karl Marthinsen, was murdered in Oslo.[64]

As late as April 1945, SOE was still dropping assassins into Nazi-occupied Europe. One of the last of these was Wilhelm Borstelmann, a former POW, who had been persuaded to return to Hamburg, where he was to target U-boat commanders. Though the operation was a failure, it is perhaps instructive to note that the planning file spoke unashamedly of Borstelmann as "a first-class thug."[65] By 1945, it appears, the days of the gentleman spy were well and truly over.

The British attitude toward irregular warfare had shifted a great deal since Mason-Macfarlane had made his "unsportsmanlike" suggestion some six years earlier. Some, admittedly, preferred to cling to the old certainties and viewed the dark arts of assassination, kidnapping, and sabotage, if not as morally reprehensible, then at least as distasteful necessities that could be swiftly abandoned once victory was secured. But it is also obvious that a line had been crossed. SOE, especially, appeared to embrace the methods of the dirty war with alacrity, and even saw itself as the "fourth arm of modern warfare."[66] Its activities in the field—disrupting communications, fostering resistance, and tying down enemy troops—were of proven benefit to the Allied war effort. It brought the nefarious methods of the saboteur and the kidnapper out of the shadows and almost succeeded in making them respectable. In a few short years, it had established the political assassination, which was once viewed as utterly beyond the pale of decent human conduct, as a legitimate tool of subversive warfare. Its murder of Heydrich demonstrated that few Germans could consider themselves to be immune from its attentions. Hitler himself kept a wary eye on SOE, spending at least half an hour each day being briefed on its latest activities, both successes and failures.[67] He naturally saw himself as its primary target. There was a fair amount of conceit in this assumption, but he was not wholly mistaken. The British had, in fact, been wrestling with the idea of assassinating him almost from the outset of World War Two.

In September 1939, just as war erupted in Europe, the novel *Rogue Male* was published by Chatto and Windus in London. It was a fast-paced and crisply written thriller recounting the tribulations of a British gentleman-adventurer who, after a hunting trip in Poland, decides to cross the border and stalk an unnamed European dictator.

Traveling aimlessly, the protagonist finds himself being drawn to "the House" and becomes obsessed with "the idea of a sporting stalk." He discusses his motivations, suggesting that he had speculated on the methods of guarding "a great man" and on the ways in which they might be circumvented. Yet he concludes, "Like most Englishmen, I am not accustomed to enquire very deeply into motives," and admits that "I haven't any grievances myself. One can hardly count the upsetting of one's trivial private life and plans by European disturbances as a grievance."[68] But as he reaches the forests above "the House," he soon becomes wrapped up in the sense of adventure—the thrill of the chase.

> I arrived on the ground at dawn and spent the whole day in reconnaissance. It was an alarming day, for the whole forest surrounding the house was most efficiently patrolled. From tree to tree and gully to gully I prowled over most of the circuit, but only flat on the earth was I really safe. Often I hid my rifle and glasses, thinking that I was certain to be challenged and questioned. I never was. I might have been transparent.[69]

When he finally finds a likely vantage point with a clear shot to the house from around 500 yards, he observes his target as he comes out "to play with the dog or smell a rose or practise gestures on the gardener."[70] Then, after watching the security procedures in force and identifying an escape route, he settles down with his rifle:

At last the great man came out on to the terrace.... I had ten minutes to play with.... I made myself comfortable, and got the three pointers on the sight steady on the V of his waistcoat. He was facing me and winding up his watch. He would never have known what shattered him.[71]

Captured before he could get a shot off, the assassin is interrogated, tortured, and left for dead, spending the remainder of the narrative on the run from enemy agents determined to silence him. After eluding his pursuers, the protagonist then ends the novel by returning to the task that he had set himself at the outset. "My plans are far advanced," he concludes. "I shall not get away alive, but I shall not miss and that is all that really matters."[72]

Though the words *Germany* and *Hitler* are never mentioned in the book, it is patently obvious from the context and the detail given who the assassin's target was supposed to be. Indeed, subsequent editions and two later film versions dispensed with the pretense of anonymity altogether, the books often carrying a portrait of Hitler on the cover. The fact that Hitler should have been targeted in the novel is unsurprising. Concerns about the international situation were rife in Britain throughout 1939, and the suggestion that they could be eased if Hitler were "bumped off" would have been commonplace. What might be slightly surprising, however, is the novel's author. Geoffrey Household was an Oxford-educated former banker and banana merchant and an occasional writer of children's books. In the autumn of 1939, just after *Rogue Male* had been published, he was thirty-eight years old, with no military experience and a less than impressive curriculum vitae. Nonetheless, he was recruited to work for British military intelligence and later for SOE. As he recalled in his memoirs, the "sudden conjuring of Captain Household" was startling.[73]

As Household later conceded, his urge to join the British intelligence service had originated, at least in part, in a desire to "have a crack at Hitler."[74] After all, his feelings toward Nazi Germany, he admitted, had all the "savagery of a personal vendetta."[75] Yet, though his rise was swift, it would be wrong to conclude that he was immediately set to work on a real-life assassination plot. Indeed, so far as is known, he spent most of his intelligence career in the Middle Eastern section, serving in Palestine, Syria, and Iraq. British intelligence, for its part, recruited widely and eclectically and included many agents whose talents were less than immediately apparent. Thus it may be that Household's other skills were what attracted their attention. But it would also be absurd to suggest that the idea of assassinating Hitler had not been discussed. Perhaps one might conclude that the bold premise of Household's novel did not harm his application.

In due course, the first tentative plan for Hitler's assassination was formulated. As the diaries of the remarkable ornithologist–*cum*–intelligence officer, Richard Meinertzhagen, record, it originated in the spring of 1940 with Ze'ev Jabotinsky, a prominent and militant Zionist who was active in London at the time, trying to establish a Jewish army to combat Nazism alongside the Allies. Jabotinsky's plan was as simple as it was utterly impracticable. As a first step, he proposed the assassination of any prominent Nazi, who, it was thought, would then be the subject of a lavish funeral ceremony in Munich. At this point, British agents were somehow to switch the body for a little over 85 kilograms of high explosives, which could then be detonated during the requiem, thereby killing numerous senior Nazis.[76] Unsurprisingly, the proposal was turned down flat. Speculative in the extreme, it contained no details of how the initial target was to be assassinated, how the body was to be switched, or how the charges were to be detonated. Its primary failing was much more fundamental, however. The British, who were wrestling at the time with the ethics of assassination per se, were not yet prepared to contemplate indiscriminate slaughter, even if it was feasible in operational terms.

Ironically, the source for that story, Richard Meinertzhagen, had himself already been much better placed to carry out an assassination. As a senior member of the Anglo-German Association, he was occasionally summoned to meet Hitler in Berlin. The first such occasion gave rise to a memorable anecdote. On meeting Meinertzhagen, the Führer gave his trademark "German greeting," extending his right arm and shouting, "Heil Hitler." Meinertzhagen, thinking it strange that Hitler should salute himself, responded in kind, raising his own arm and proclaiming, "Heil Meinertzhagen." The remark was met with consternation and an uncomfortable silence.[77]

By the time of his last meeting with Hitler in June 1939, however, all traces of levity had long since vanished. Meinertzhagen, who had been an early enthusiast for Hitler, now referred to the Führer as a "rabid dog." Summoned to the Chancellery, he took the precaution of putting a loaded pistol in his pocket, as he recalled, to prove that he had "the opportunity to kill the man." After sitting through a forty-minute harangue from Hitler, with Ribbentrop interpreting, he made his excuses and left. He had not been searched and the pistol had not been detected. As he later confided to his diary:

> I had ample opportunity to kill both Hitler and Ribbentrop and am seriously troubled about it. If this war breaks out, as I feel sure it will, then I shall feel very much to blame for not killing these two.[78]

The fact that he had proved to himself that he had the opportunity appears to have been scant consolation for having failed to take it.

When the British finally got around to thinking seriously about targeting Hitler, the primary role was initially taken by the RAF rather than SOE. In early July 1940, barely two weeks after the French capitulation, Sholto Douglas, the deputy chief of the Air Staff, suggested a "special action" to coincide with the expected German victory parade in Paris, though adding that he considered it a "rather futile gesture" to bomb the parade itself. Three days later, however, Donald Stevenson, director of home operations in the Air Ministry, had already run with the idea, proposing what had been unthinkable only a year before. He wrote:

> We could try to kill the Führer. Doubtless the saluting base will be close to the Arche de Triomphe [sic] and no-one

can say what effect a few salvos of 40lb and 250lb bombs would be on an occasion of this kind... from our experience, provided we have good cloud cover, it is a practicable operation.[79]

Discussions continued for the next week or so, with all the military and strategic considerations of such a raid being aired, as well as the possible effects on French morale. However, the suggestion was finally dropped. As Stevenson himself admitted, the bombing of a military parade was considered inappropriate. Yet, curiously, the ethics of attempting to murder Hitler were not called into question.

Unbeknownst to the British, Hitler already had secretly visited Paris in the early morning of 28 June. Accompanied by his two court architects, Albert Speer and Hermann Giessler, and the sculptor Arno Breker, he led a three-hour whistle-stop tour of the Parisian sights, traveling in a convoy of three Mercedes. As he marveled at the Opéra, strolled by the Eiffel Tower, and mused at Napoleon's tomb, his motives were clearly artistic rather than political. There were no bodyguards, no security cordons, and no *Leibstandarte*. Parisian early risers reacted to him either with disdain or abject terror, but he remained unmolested. When the matter of the victory parade was raised, he declared that he had decided against it. He feared that the event might become the target of a British air raid.[80]

In time, and in comparison to some other schemes suggested, Stevenson's proposal would appear as a beacon of sanity, however. The following spring, word reached London that Hitler's personal pilot, Hans Baur, had become disillusioned with the war and was willing to defect and fly the Führer to Britain. The report came from the unlikely source of the British air attaché in Sofia, who had been approached by a Bulgarian named Kiroff, claiming to be Baur's father-in-law. When the tale reached Arthur Harris, the new deputy chief of the Air Staff, it was rightly judged to be a "fantastic story."

Despite the story's patent implausibility, instructions were nonetheless passed back to the source, just in case it was to turn out not to be "too fantastic for words." The intermediary was instructed that Baur was to approach the RAF's Lympne base on the Kent coast in a steep descent, firing red flares at thirty-second intervals. Upon landing, he was to taxi to a secure section of the airfield and stop his engines. His cargo was to be kept strictly confidential and would be described simply as a German "deserter."[81]

Within two weeks, a reply duly arrived from Sofia, giving more details. Baur, it said, usually flew at high altitude with an escort of three fighter planes. On approach, he would drop small yellow plaques bearing the initials *AB*. The communication requested that a beacon be lit at the airfield. A probable date for the defection was given as 25 March 1941, only three weeks away. The most likely time would be dawn or dusk.[82] In response, security measures at Lympne were stepped up: the garrison was reinforced, anti-aircraft batteries were installed, and a specially equipped Ford van was held in readiness, complete with a driver and two motorcycle outriders. The "prize," as Hitler was now described, was to be taken upon arrival directly to the Air Ministry in London.[83]

That spring was to see numerous momentous developments. British and German troops engaged in North Africa for the first time in late February, while the British scored a morale-boosting naval victory over the Italians in the Battle of Cape Matapan the following month. Across the Atlantic, meanwhile, the Lend-Lease Bill was passed by the U.S. Congress and became law, thus providing Britain with a vital matériel lifeline. Most significant, perhaps, Germany was forced to secure her Balkan flank by invading Yugoslavia and Greece in early April, and that campaign would fatally delay the planned summer invasion of the Soviet Union.

However, for those watching the skies over Kent, nothing happened. The target date came and went without incident. After a lengthy silence from the contact in Sofia, the special arrangements at Lympne were discontinued on 1 June. The Ford van and motorcycles were returned whence they came. The reinforcements were relocated without ever being aware of the curious story in which they had played a role. Their prize had flitted between Berlin, Munich, and Vienna that March, but plainly had not been induced to visit the Kent riviera.

In the absence of additional evidence, it is hard for the historian to conclude that the Baur story was anything other than a hoax. Baur certainly did not fit the role of a defector. A member of Hitler's inner circle and one of his oldest associates, he had, by 1941, already served as the Führer's pilot for nearly ten years, and he would remain scrupulously loyal until the very end. One of the last to leave the bunker in 1945, he lost a leg in the battle for Berlin and spent a further ten years in Soviet confinement. His memoirs, published after his release, still betrayed a distinct admiration for his former employer.[84]

The story's Bulgarian connection is harder to fathom. Baur's wife—far from being Bulgarian—was in fact born Maria Pohl in Danzig in 1907, and Hitler had even acted as best man at the couple's wedding in 1936. Yet Baur himself had a link to Bulgaria. He knew King Boris well, having flown with him many times. He had also received from the king a number of Bulgarian decorations, including the Order of St. Alexander, and a succession of gifts and trinkets.[85] It may be that the hoax was simply the result of jealousy in Sofia that a German pilot was being fêted in this way.

It is also telling that during the period that the hoax was being hatched, February and March 1941, Bulgaria was itself being drawn ever closer into the German sphere. In early February, for instance, high-level discussions had taken place in Sofia between Bulgarian generals and a delegation from the German General Staff. On 1 March, the Bulgarian government had then signed the Tripartite Pact, effectively allying itself with Berlin and allowing for the passage of German troops onto its territory. Four days after that, London had severed diplomatic relations with Sofia. Those unhappy with these developments might have viewed discrediting Baur as a good way to rock the boat, portraying him as a traitor to the Axis and a would-be defector.

Another tantalizing interpretation suggests that the Baur story was in some way connected with Rudolf Hess's ill-starred flight to Britain in the summer of 1941. Baur, for example, was

Men of the RSD, Hitler's most trusted bodyguard formation. Facing the camera is their commander, Johann Rattenhuber.

Hitler reviewing an honour guard of the SS *Leibstandarte*.

Maurice Bavaud   Georg Elser

The annual Nazi parade in Munich in 1938, which Bavaud hoped
to disrupt so spectacularly.

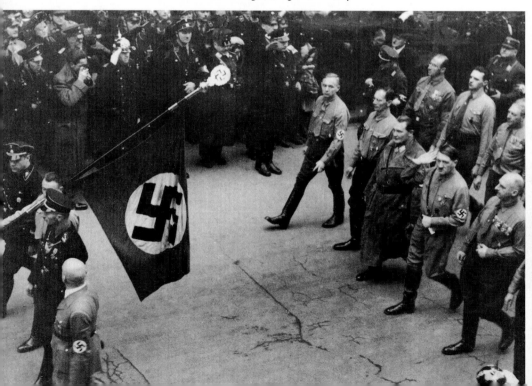

Hitler speaking at the Bürgerbräukeller in November 1939. Elser's bomb is hidden in the pillar covered by the swastika.

The aftermath of Elser's attempt – eight were killed and sixty-two injured, but Hitler had already left the hall.

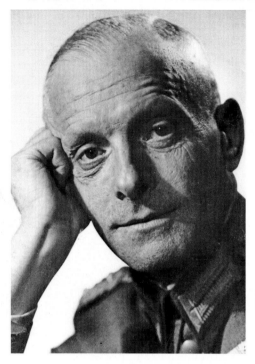

Hans Oster

Friedrich-Wilhelm Heinz

Erich Kordt

Wilhelm Canaris

Chamberlain's 'piece of paper', which robbed the *Abwehr* plotters of their trigger for action.

Hitler receiving the adulation of a Berlin crowd in 1938. The popular reaction to his diplomatic success at Munich further undermined the conspiracy.

Franciszek Niepokólczycki ('Theodore')

Stanislaw Lesikowski ('Forest')

Jan Szalewski ('Sable')

Slawa Mirowska

Hitler touring a defeated Warsaw in 1939.

Hitler's personal train *Amerika*: a target for Polish saboteurs.

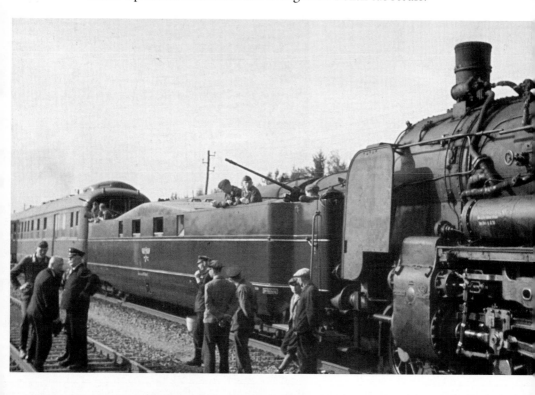

Hitler on the platform for his 50th-birthday parade in 1939: an 'easy rifle shot'.

Watching from the VIP stand:
Noel Mason-Macfarlane,
one of the earliest British
advocates of assassinating Hitler.

(*Above*) Geoffrey Household, whose writing may have inspired the British plot.

(*Above right*) James Joll: one of the architects of Operation Foxley.

Hitler walking on the Obersalzberg: at risk where he felt most secure.

Alexander Foote: 'innocent sports'.

Dmitri Medvedev, photographed
behind German lines in 1943.

Lev Knipper: an artful agent.

Hitler with Olga Tschechowa:
flirting with danger.

The Osteria Bavaria in Munich, scene of Moscow's first aborted plot.

Hitler's *Wehrwolf* HQ at Vinnitsa in the Ukraine: a target for the partisans and the NKVD.

Henning von Tresckow

Rudolf von Gersdorff

Georg von Boeselager

Axel von dem Bussche

Eberhard von Breitenbuch

Fabian von Schlabrendorff

Hitler visiting Army Group Centre at Smolensk in March 1943: another lucky escape.

Hitler speaking at the Berlin Armoury in 1944, where he would be targeted by history's first 'suicide bomber'.

Claus von Stauffenberg:
the most famous of Hitler's would-be
assassins, but in truth one of many.

Stauffenberg (*left*) meeting Hitler at
Rastenburg in July 1944, five days
before his attempt.

The destroyed map room at Rastenburg.

Göring visiting the scene.

Albert Speer:
an 'impulse of despair'.

In the last known picture of him, Hitler (*right*) inspects the damage to the
Reich Chancellery garden from the entrance to his bunker.

known to have flown with Hess on his early training flights and had supplied him with maps and flight plans. Moreover, his supposed flight to Britain preceded Hess's genuine flight by only two months. If one interprets Hess's flight, as some do, as a covert mission on the orders of the Führer, then it is not inconceivable that the Baur story also emanated from Hitler and that both schemes were part of a somewhat ham-fisted plan to destabilize Churchill's government (although it is hard to see how Baur's planned defection might have served that end).[86] In the absence of further archival disclosures and substantial research, all one can do is speculate.

By the middle of 1941, SOE was beginning to play its own part in targeting the German leader. That summer, it presented a "project for eliminating Hitler," which gained the approval of all relevant government departments before a change in circumstances caused the mysterious plan's cancellation.[87] Sadly, no records of this plan have survived, so the extent and influence of any lingering qualms about assassinating Adolf Hitler are impossible to ascertain. Nonetheless, it is clear that the subject was at least being discussed at the highest level and was being planned for.

Some weeks later, SOE's Mediterranean base at Cairo joined the fray. According to the memoirs of one of its officers, SOE Cairo was approached in the autumn of 1941 by a Macedonian "terrorist" by the name of Vilmar. It was informed that Vilmar, who was described as "a stout middle-aged man with an ugly leg wound," was suffering from terminal cancer and had offered his services to try to kill Hitler.[88] In return, the would-be assassin demanded only his living expenses and the promise of a posthumous decoration should he perish in the attempt.

Though SOE was profoundly unconvinced by him, Vilmar was supplied with the necessary papers to pose as a Bulgarian businessman and was infiltrated into Switzerland, from where he was to watch events in Germany and, if the opportunity arose, make his attempt. In due course, it was reported that Vilmar had traveled to Vienna shortly before Hitler was apparently scheduled to visit. Once there, he had approached the Bulgarian consulate

and had managed to secure access to a function at which the
Führer was to speak.

The night before the event, however, wine and women apparently proved Vilmar's undoing. After drinking too much in a
Viennese bar and boasting of his scars and his activities as an assassin, he was arrested by the Gestapo. While his forged papers
seem to have stood up to German scrutiny and he appears to have
kept his head under interrogation, he was nonetheless scheduled
for deportation. Returned to Bulgaria, he was never heard of again.

Though a diverting anecdote, the Vilmar story does not withstand closer scrutiny. The memoir from which it comes does not
give a date for the attempt, but it is clear from the context that it
took place between the late summer of 1941 and the summer of
1942. Yet, as a glance at Hitler's wartime itinerary confirms, Hitler
did not visit Vienna during this period. In fact, the very last time
he visited the city was in March 1941.[89] Whoever he was, and whatever he was doing, Vilmar was clearly *not* plotting to kill Hitler in
Vienna. Such duplicity should not be surprising. By the very nature of its work, SOE was often forced to rely on forgers, bur-
glars, safebreakers, and petty criminals. It was perhaps inevitable
that, once in a while, the crooks in turn took SOE for a ride.

While SOE deliberated, Hitler was steadily strengthening and
revising his security apparatus. The first major revision had appeared in 1940 in the aftermath of Georg Elser's attack. The
assassination of Reinhard Heydrich, two years later, prompted
another thoroughgoing reorganization.

A snapshot of the revised security measures can be seen with
Hitler's visit to Berlin on 30 May 1942, barely three days after
Heydrich had been ambushed. Where once crowds would have
gathered and a ceremonial procession might have been organized,
now the event was enveloped in a fog of secrecy. Hitler—who was
scheduled to speak at the Sports Palace before an audience of
cadets and invited guests—arrived direct from Wolfschanze. Outside the venue, approach roads, parks, and nearby houses were
placed under surveillance. Even sewers, tunnels, and public toilets
were patrolled. All local inhabitants were registered with the police, and all cars in the vicinity were subjected to spot checks. In-

side the Sports Palace, meanwhile, more than eighty Gestapo and police officers inspected and patrolled every inch of the building. No packages or bags were allowed in and no one was permitted to take photographs without written authorization.[90]

The contrast with the security regime of just a few years before is startling. In the summer of 1939, for example, public appearances were still relatively commonplace. They were minutely stage-managed, of course, but with the intention of showing a Führer at home with his *Volk*, patting children's heads or receiving bouquets from nearly hysterical women in traditional dress.

By 1942, however, the "man of the people" had become a virtual recluse. Public appearances had become increasingly rare. Though Hitler might still be glimpsed lunching in the Osteria Bavaria, he never toured the bombed-out cities and never visited the wounded in hospitals. Those public events that were authorized were still minutely stage-managed, but now with the intention of keeping Hitler from his people, preserving him from the uncomfortable realities of "total war." For the potential assassin, the almost boundless opportunities of a few years before had dwindled almost to nothing. Little surprise, then, that those who still sought to target Hitler were often left clutching at straws.

In the summer of 1944, SOE in Algiers was approached with another harebrained scheme to kill Hitler. Its initial reaction was one of caution, mindful perhaps of the Vilmar debacle, and the matter was referred to London for discussion. In time, it transpired that the "reliable source" behind the plan was a French colonel who claimed, somewhat bizarrely, that Hitler was hiding in a château near Perpignan in the south of France, and suggested that a combined air and ground assault be undertaken.[91] Though the scheme was rejected, it did force SOE and the British once again to consider the fundamental issue of whether they really wanted Hitler assassinated. To this end, at an SOE council meeting on 27 June, the "question of a deliberate and continuous effort to try and liquidate Hitler" was raised.[92] The following day, a second meeting was held, where the issue was discussed at length. Despite numerous objections, the director of SOE, General Colin Gubbins, set his organization the task of carrying out a detailed investigation of the feasibility of such an attack. It was to be christened "Operation Foxley."

In the months that followed, Operation Foxley concentrated on two broad areas: the possibilities of targeting Hitler at his residence at Berchtesgaden and on his private train. Its file grew into an astonishing collection of general information and sensitive intelligence, containing maps, photographs, and numerous hand-drawn sketches. It covered the topography and climate of the Obersalzberg region, Hitler's appearance, his security measures, his habits and routines, and a detailed examination of the procedures aboard his special train. Every aspect was covered, from the detail of the sentries' uniforms down to the various telephone extension numbers used in the Berghof complex.[93]

The resulting feasibility study appeared in November 1944. The identity of its author, code-named "LB/X," remains unclear. SOE files cite a mysterious Major H. B. Court as LB/X, but no personnel file for him survives and nothing more about him is known. It is most likely, however, that the study was the fruit of more than one hand, and it has been suggested that one of its contributors was the later historian James Joll, who was then an officer of SOE's German staff, Section X.[94] The file outlined the intelligence that had been gathered, and concluded by suggesting two possible courses of action. The first was that Hitler's train could be derailed or its water supply could be contaminated with poisons. The second was remarkably similar to the plot devised by Geoffrey Household five years earlier: that a sniper could be infiltrated into the area of the Berghof.

Of these two proposals, that centering on the Berghof was generally considered to have the best chance of success. The site, close to the Austrian-German border, had belonged to Hitler since 1933. Initially consisting only of a small country house, it had been expanded over the following decade with garages, bunkers, barracks blocks, and of course the residences of the senior Nazi potentates. Security at the complex was difficult to enforce, due to the wild, hilly landscape, but the entire site (encompassing over 7 square kilometers) was enclosed with barbed wire and patrolled by armed guards. Within that area, it was divided into a number of zones, each with its own fences, security, and access passes. Thus, though the almost constant presence of construction workers might have provided an opportunity, the best chances for a would-be assassin would be to target Hitler when he was outside the complex.

Tantalizingly, this was a regular occurrence. Hitler was accustomed to walking in the forests and meadows that surrounded the Berghof. Though security was tightened as the war progressed, he still insisted on an afternoon stroll to the nearby teahouse at the Mooslahnerkopf. For the duration of the walk, which was approximately 1,500 meters, mainly downhill, he would amble along alone or at the head of a small group of his visitors or intimates. Though the route was patrolled, Hitler disliked the obvious presence of guards, so lapses in security were not uncommon. On arrival at the teahouse, he would usually drink a cup of camomile tea and pick at a slice of apple cake. After that, he would invariably fall asleep, while the remainder of his party chatted on quietly. Then he would wake and ask to be driven back to the Berghof, often leaving his guests to walk.[95]

For an SOE sniper, therefore, Hitler's daily walks provided a clear opportunity, where his target was comparatively isolated, beyond the range of much of his security apparatus, and, crucially, out in the open. Given the likelihood that he would get only one shot, the sniper was to be supplied with explosive bullets. If he should fail, a second assassin might then attempt to ambush Hitler's car on the return journey from the teahouse, using a PIAT anti-tank weapon.[96] For all its pastoral innocence, the daily visit to the teahouse was perhaps the moment of Hitler's greatest vulnerability.

While its plans for Operation Foxley were being assessed and evaluated, Section X was warming to its task and turned its attention to other possible targets for its would-be assassins. In time, Himmler, Goebbels, Göring, and Bormann were all included on a list of "Little Foxleys" and were subjected to the same minute investigation. Of Goebbels, for example, it was ascertained (among many other details) that he took a morning nap at 10:30, carried a hip flask of brandy, and apparently owned a property in

Majorca.[97] He was, the report concluded, an "excellent candidate" for an assassination.[98] Most notably, however, the bizarre suggestion was made that Rudolf Hess might be persuaded (or even hypnotized) to return to Germany and play the role of an assassin.[99]

The Operation Foxley file is a remarkable collection of documents. It represents probably the best information then available about Hitler's movements, his habits, and his security arrangements. But one should not pretend that it was the finished article. It was certainly not a blueprint for an assassination. For example, it lacked contingency plans for the infiltration and exfiltration of the assassins. It even lacked assassins. Though a Captain Edmund Bennett was briefly considered for the job, described coyly as "a high-priority assassination task which would require his lying low in Germany,"[100] it does not appear that SOE was especially energetic in recruiting an agent.[101]

Foxley was still very much a planning document, a feasibility study, drawn up from behind a desk in London's Baker Street. The enormous gulf between planning and operation had yet to be bridged. True, much of that additional research and logistical work would have been carried out if Foxley had been placed into the operational phase. At that point, a sniper would have been recruited, supplementary training given, exfiltration arranged, and a provisional date for the action fixed. But, it must be stressed, none of that vital detail is included in the Operation Foxley file.

Foxley's primary shortcoming, however, was up-to-the-minute intelligence. It presented information on security at the Berghof that had been accurate, at the very latest, in the spring or early summer of 1944. Yet the Stauffenberg attack of 20 July 1944 (see Chapter 7) had brought about a fundamental rethink on security, and new procedures had been put into place. More seriously, Foxley concentrated its attention on sending a sniper to Berchtesgaden to assassinate Hitler at the Berghof, but in fact, Hitler left his residence there on 14 July 1944 and never returned. Even had an assassin succeeded in getting to his target area that autumn, he would have been left kicking his heels.

Whatever the relative merits or demerits of Operation Foxley, the fundamental issue of the advisability of assassinating Hitler had still not been resolved. While the report was being compiled, SOE, SIS, and the military were locked in an often heated debate about whether such a mission should be undertaken at all. Some, such as SOE's air advisor, Air Vice Marshal Ritchie, suggested that Hitler was the linchpin of the entire edifice of Nazism. "Remove Hitler," Ritchie wrote, "and there is nothing left."[102]

Others highlighted the dangers of making a martyr of the German leader. The head of Section X, Lieutenant Colonel Thornley, who was a persistent critic of Foxley, warned that the removal of Hitler "would almost inevitably canonise him and give birth to the myth that Germany would have been saved if he had lived."[103] Some of his staff concurred, adding that Hitler "should be permitted to live—until he dies of senile decay before the eyes of the people he has misled. Rob him of his halo! Make him a laughingstock!"[104]

Perhaps the most cogent argument, meanwhile, came from the chiefs of staff, who suggested that "from the strictly military point of view, it was almost an advantage that Hitler should remain in control of German strategy, having regard to the blunders that he has made."[105] Thornley agreed most emphatically, noting:

As a strategist, Hitler has been of the greatest possible assistance to the British war effort....his value to us has been equivalent to an almost unlimited number of first-class SOE agents strategically placed inside Germany.... [He] is still in a position to override completely the soundest of military appreciation and thereby help the Allied cause enormously.[106]

As he conceded, in November 1944 there was "a grave divergence of views" with regard to the "desirability and feasibility" of the proposed mission.[107] Needless to say, unless and until these wrangles could be satisfactorily resolved, Operation Foxley would never get the green light.

In the event, the whole issue was overtaken by the course of the war. In the winter of 1944, Germany was plainly heading for defeat. The Red Army was on the Vistula, and the British and Americans were on the Rhine. France had been liberated and fascist Italy had collapsed. With every Allied success on the battlefield, Foxley grew less and less urgent, less and less necessary. It was finally shelved indefinitely and consigned to the archives.

The furor surrounding Operation Foxley neatly encapsulated the prevailing British attitudes toward assassination as a weapon of war. Despite the numerous successes of SOE in the field, many senior military personnel had remained deeply skeptical of its unorthodox methods. And though they might have countenanced the liquidation of figures of lower status, they found it hard to agree to the murder of their enemy's head of state and commander in chief. This is not to suggest that the objections raised to Operation Foxley were in any way spurious or disingenuous. They were not. Rather, it is to recognize that elements of the British military and political élite were still not comfortable with covert operations of this magnitude. Killing Hitler was still, for some, beyond the pale. As Churchill himself had privately admitted: "That would be like anarchy."[108]

Indeed, Churchill's attitude toward resistance in general had cooled considerably once the Allied bridgeheads in Normandy had been established.[109] With that, it appeared, he considered the task of SOE and the native resistance movements to have drawn to a close. They had kept the flame of liberty alive and had prepared the way for the arrival of the professional soldiers. In a speech to the House of Commons, he even seemed to pour cold water on Operation Foxley itself. Referring to the failed German plot to kill Hitler in July 1944, he stated: "Decisive as [such attempts] may be one of these days, it is not in them that we should put our trust, but in our own strong arms and in the justice of our cause."[110]

While the British debates over Foxley raged, the Americans

were belatedly beginning to target Hitler themselves. The previous summer, a young German émigré, Egon Hanfstaengl, an
American Secret Service officer and the son of Hitler's former
foreign press chief, had volunteered to attempt to assassinate
Hitler. As Hitler's godson, Hanfstaengl had met the Führer many
times as a youth, and proposed to talk his way into the residence
at Berchtesgaden on the premise of acting as a messenger for his
exiled father. He was naively convinced that if he could get close
enough to Hitler to shake his hand, then he could kill him.[111]
Given the plan's somewhat unrealistic nature, it was rejected by
Roosevelt, who apparently preferred to avoid attempting to assassinate a fellow head of state.

The following year, however, the issue was raised once again
and in rather bizarre circumstances. A group of American Secret
Service (OSS) research operatives known as the "Choirboys" devised a plan that they thought would tip Hitler into insanity and
bring the war to a swift end. Mindful of their target's legendary
puritanism, they planned to expose him to a flood of pornogra-
phy, which could be dropped from the air around Hitler's headquarters near Berchtesgaden. After assembling an enormous
collection of suitable material, they called in an Air Force colonel
to discuss the number and type of aircraft that would be required
for the raid. However, the colonel was less than impressed, denouncing the Choirboys as maniacs and describing the plan as insane. With that, the operation was quietly dropped.[112]

Nonetheless, in June 1944, the prospect of targeting Hitler
was raised a third time. General Carl Spaatz, commander of U.S.
strategic air forces in Europe, requested a detailed photo reconnaissance of Hitler's residence at Berchtesgaden for an operation
he dubbed "Hellhound."[113] His intention had been the launching of an air raid on the area using P-38 fighter-bombers of the
15th Air Force in Italy. But, like the British, he soon became
mired in a discussion of the plan's merits and opted to cancel the
operation. Four months later, the U.S. Mediterranean Tactical
Air Force managed to overcome such concerns. On 4 November,
four P-47s of the 27th Fighter Group bombed a Milan hotel

where it was believed Hitler was staying.[114] Though a number of direct hits were scored, Hitler was staying at Wolfschanze in East Prussia at the time.

Not to be outdone, the RAF finally decided to raid Berchtesgaden. On the night of 25 April 1945, in one of the last aerial operations of the war, 359 Lancasters and 16 Mosquitoes targeted the complex of buildings that constituted Hitler's home. Two Lancasters were lost and four men from one crew were killed, but the target suffered substantial damage. As the Interpretation Report noted:

> A. Hitler's residence:
> A direct hit has destroyed the central part of the north side of the west wing. The east side of the main building has suffered slight damage from a glancing hit. Some outbuildings on the west side of the house have been destroyed and the side of the house is seriously damaged.[115]

As was probably surmised at the time, "A. Hitler" was in Berlin. And even if he had been present, he would doubtless have found refuge in the huge network of bunkers and tunnels that had been constructed at the site during the previous two years.[116]

So one has to wonder what military rationale would induce the RAF to target a few buildings in a remote area of southeast Germany with a force of 375 aircraft—a force comparable to the one that had devastated the city of Kiel ten days previously. Perhaps the RAF was genuinely attempting to kill the Führer. If that was the case, the archive file on the attack neglects to mention it as a priority. Perhaps it was attempting to disrupt the preparations for the putative "Alpine Redoubt," where the much-vaunted last stand of Nazism was supposed to take place. Rather, it may just be that the enormous raid on Berchtesgaden was merely the result of a fit of pique. It was, perhaps, a demonstration of what might have been done earlier had circumstances and tactical considerations—and scruples—allowed.

CHAPTER 7

Honor Redeemed:
The German Military

The assassination must be attempted at all costs.... What matters now is no longer the practical purpose of the coup, but to prove to the world and for the records of history that the men of the resistance movement dared to take the decisive step. Compared to this objective, nothing else is of consequence.

—HENNING VON TRESCKOW[1]

A T DAWN ON 5 OCTOBER 1942, A CONVOY OF TRUCKS RATTLED into the small eastern European town of Dubno. Inside were units of the local Ukrainian militia, a ragtag collection of extreme nationalists, anti-Semites, and petty criminals, who served as the enthusiastic auxiliaries of the SS. Their targets that morning were the remaining inhabitants of the Dubno ghetto.

Dubno itself was situated on the margins where Poland and the Russian Empire had once overlapped. Before 1939, it had spent a generation in the Polish Republic, but with Poland's demise that autumn the town had been annexed by the USSR and had found itself in "Western Ukraine." It was a quiet, unassuming place, nestling among gently rolling hills on the banks of the Ikva River. At its heart, along the narrow dusty streets, stood a large late-medieval palace—once the residence of the influential Ostrogski family—and an impressive Catholic church.

Of Dubno's fifteen thousand inhabitants, around half were Jewish, and the remainder was shared between the Polish and Ukrainian communities. They lived mainly as shopkeepers and merchants, with a few working in the new industrial concerns, a plow factory and a meat processing plant located just out of town.

The town's Jewish tradition was especially rich, stretching back to the Middle Ages and including a remarkable eighteenth-century scholar and preacher, Jacob Kranz (known as the Dubno Maggid), whose parables had become an integral part of Jewish religious and literary life. In the early decades of the twentieth century, Dubno's Jewish community could boast its own elementary schools, a hospital, and a good-sized synagogue.

By 1942, however, Jewish life in Dubno was approaching its end. Those of the town's Jews who managed to survive the early days of the German invasion had been confined to a hastily built ghetto, from which they would be escorted in work details to perform forced labor for their new German masters. Situated close to the town center, the Dubno ghetto was bounded on one side by the meandering waters of the river. Measuring approximately 400 square meters, it was enclosed with wooden boarding and barbed wire, except where three crudely constructed wooden gates controlled access. Beyond the ghetto walls, as one witness recalled, Dubno was "quite empty," but conditions within were predictably poor.[2] Hunger and disease were ever-present, although, perversely, overcrowding was eased by the high death rate. The first round of executions in Dubno had begun soon after the arrival of the German armies the previous summer. They had then restarted in the summer of 1942, when the ghetto was ordered liquidated. Truckloads of Jews were driven to the outskirts of the town, usually the nearby Shibennaya Hill, where they were forced to dig their own graves before being stripped and shot.

That cold October morning, the Ukrainian militia was ordered to finish the job of liquidating the Dubno ghetto. In a chaos of barked orders, screams, and truncheon blows, they began the task of herding the remaining inhabitants into the trucks and driving them to a disused airfield some distance out of town. There, the Jews—men, women, and children—were forced from the trucks and ordered by an SS officer to undress. Their personal effects were collected in separate piles: shoes, clothing, and underwear. Shivering in the autumnal chill, family groups embraced and said their last goodbyes. As one witness, a German civilian contractor, would later recall:

> I watched a family of about eight persons: a man and woman both about fifty years old, with their children of about one, eight, ten and two grown-up daughters of about twenty to twenty-four. An old woman with snow-white hair was holding the one-year-old child in her arms and singing to it and tickling it. The child was cooing with delight. . . . The father was holding the hand of a boy of about ten years old and speaking to him softly; the boy was fighting back his tears. The father pointed to the sky, stroked the boy's head and seemed to explain something to him.[3]

Just beyond, hidden from sight by a long mound of earth, three pits had been dug, each about 30 meters long and 3 meters deep. The SS men present were most likely members of *Einsatzgruppe C*, which had murdered its way through the Ukraine the previous summer. They had developed a grimly efficient method of mass murder, known as "sardine packing."[4] The massacre at Dubno would be a prime example of their "art." At the edge of each pit stood an execution squad of around twenty soldiers armed with rifles. Commanding them was an SS officer with a machine gun. On his order, a fresh batch of twenty Jews was counted off and herded behind the mound. Those who tried to escape were shot; the remainder were confronted by a huge mass grave containing hundreds of bodies. As a witness recalled:

> Tightly packed corpses were heaped so close together that only the heads showed. Most were wounded in the head and the blood flowed over their shoulders. Some still moved. Others raised their hands and turned their heads

to show that they were still alive.... The people, completely naked, went down some steps and clambered over
the heads of those lying there.... They lay down in front
of the dead or wounded; some caressed those who were
still alive, and spoke to them in a low voice. Then I heard
a series of shots.[5]

Surprised that he wasn't moved on by the SS guards, the witness
stood transfixed. He watched as the next batch was counted off
and ordered forward. An emaciated old woman was being carried
by two others; families went by, with sobbing, uncomprehending
children and bravely stoic parents. A young woman passed him.
She was slim and pretty with long, dark hair. Catching his eye, she
pointed to herself and said, "Twenty-three years old."[6]

The massacre at Dubno was no wild killing spree. It was cold,
calculated mass murder. Each batch of victims was forced to lie
on the dead from the previous batch; they were then shot in the
back of the head. This continued with deadly efficiency, layer
upon layer, until the pit was full. The corpses were then limed
to speed decomposition and the pit was covered with soil. At
Dubno that day, five thousand Jews are thought to have been
slaughtered.

For all its inhumanity, the massacre at Dubno was a small-
time affair. It represented the SS tidying up a few loose ends in a
provincial East European backwater. In terms of its scale it was insignificant. Its victims were but a fraction of the nearly 1.5 million
claimed by the *Einsatzgruppen*. Dubno is virtually unknown, unlike the most notorious killing sites, such as Babi Yar near Kiev
(33,000 victims), Ponary near Vilnius (about 80,000), Rumbula
near Riga (38,000), and the Ninth Fort in Kaunas (30,000). And
yet, two witnesses to the massacre were to ensure that Dubno
would earn profound importance.

The first was the German contractor quoted above. Hermann
Gräbe was chief engineer of a German construction company operating in the Ukraine, and one of his projects—the building of a
grain warehouse close to Dubno airfield—brought him to the site

on that fateful October morning. Though he could do nothing to stop the massacre, he was moved subsequently to protect those Jewish laborers in his charge, earning himself the later distinction of "Righteous amongst the Nations." His testimony at the Nuremberg trials, meanwhile, would give vital and damning first-hand evidence of the brutal methods of the *Einsatzgruppen*.

The second witness was a young Wehrmacht officer. Axel von dem Bussche-Streithorst, a twenty-two-year-old lieutenant in the élite 9th Infantry Regiment, was already a hardened frontline soldier. A veteran of the Polish campaign, the defeat of France, and the attack on the Soviet Union, he had sustained three serious wounds and had been awarded the Iron Cross during the battle for Mogilev. After being shot through the chest, he was recuperating in Dubno when his unit was ordered to participate in the "special operation" at the airfield. Though their participation was refused by a commanding officer, Bussche and his men were nonetheless present at the massacre. What he saw there shocked him to the core. As a Christian and heir to the finest chivalric traditions of the German army, he was horrified by the murder of so many helpless civilians. As he later recalled:

> There in the beautiful autumn sunshine, was a queue about a mile long of old men, women, children, babies—all naked.... It was the Jewish population, they were waiting to lie down in these enormous holes—graves that they themselves had been forced to dig—and be shot by the SS.[7]

One of the condemned, a young woman, fell to her knees before him, begging to be spared. In desperation, Bussche thought whether there was anything that he could do to halt the slaughter. In vain he urged his superior officer to act. He briefly considered the idea of stripping and joining the Jewish victims in the pit. He then thought, somewhat naively, of using his platoon to arrest the SS for their patent contravention of the German law code. There was also the option of simply gunning down the SS and their Ukrainian allies, but, faced with their overwhelming firepower, he thought better of it. In the end, fearing for his life whatever his course of action, he did nothing, and the young woman was ushered away to her death.[8]

Back in their barracks, Bussche and his comrades discussed what they had seen. Many were disgusted. The commanding officer, for example, considered that the Wehrmacht's honor had been impugned. Others felt that it was nothing to do with them and sought, as best they could, to banish the memory. As for Bussche, however, the memory of Dubno and of his impotence and disgust would stay with him. In its aftermath, he concluded that there were only three ways for an honorable soldier to react: "to die in battle, to desert, or to rebel."[9] He chose the last option. He was soon to join the ranks of the German resistance.

Of all the disparate resistance groups, the military opposition to Hitler was perhaps the most contradictory. At first sight, it is easy to assume that the German army was indissolubly wedded to the Nazi regime. As the most conservative and nationalist force in German society, the army was closest to the Nazi worldview and was the primary tool of Hitler's wars. Its cadres, restored, expanded, and bankrolled by the Nazis, had become one of the pillars of the regime, and its soldiers, whether wholly willingly or not, had become the executors of Hitler's campaign of territorial conquest. From the North Cape to the Sahara, they were the most visible symbol of Germany's expansion and Hitler's insatiable ambition. Yet, in spite of all this, it would be the German army that would supply Hitler with some of his bitterest opponents and which, in due course, would come closest to removing him altogether.

There are a number of factors that serve, at least in part, to explain this paradox. Firstly, the German army was largely immune to the penetration of Gestapo agents and party influence. In a throwback to its "apolitical" origins in the aftermath of World War One—a measure that was intended to protect against the contagion of communism—the army forbade active members of political parties from joining its ranks. Individuals conscripted or volunteering for service, therefore, were obliged to surrender their party membership, while Nazi functionaries who chose to sample the "glory" of life at the front rarely enjoyed the preferential treatment that they considered they deserved. This comparative insulation meant that the army could also serve as a haven for those compromised or even incriminated in the eyes of the authorities. One example was the writer Ernst Jünger, who went to ground in the ranks of the Wehrmacht to escape the politically charged atmosphere of civilian life.[10] Indeed, the army's autonomy, though largely symbolic, was jealously guarded to the very end. In the autumn of 1944, for instance, when it was decreed that the traditional military salute should be replaced by "Heil Hitler," many officers passed on the order and then concluded their announcement with the newly banned salute.[11]

More important, perhaps, the army was seen by many, not least among its own ranks, as the repository of all that was best in Germany. Though the sentiment had been somewhat diluted by the large expansion of the military in the late 1930s, many of the army's more established regiments still held to an older, more chivalric ethos than that propagated by Hitler. Those minority elements, while sharing the enthusiasm at Germany's rebirth and territorial expansion under Nazism, viewed the regime's excesses with undisguised distaste. When confronted with evidence of SS atrocities during the Polish campaign, for example, General List complained to his superiors of "illegal activities" and noted an "open ill-feeling" on the part of his men "towards anyone wearing an SS uniform."[12] Another officer, who would later find his way into the resistance, wrote during the Polish campaign that what he had seen there made him "ashamed to be German."[13]

This is not to suggest that the Wehrmacht was whiter than white, untouched by and immune to the barbarism of the SS. It was not. Though that myth was energetically propagated for some years after the war, it is untenable. The nature of the warfare on the Eastern Front and elsewhere led to an erosion of morality, which pervaded all strata of the military. Many of the atrocities—though arguably inspired by the SS—were actually carried out by regular troops and even reservists. In one well-documented case, a massacre in occupied Poland was found to be the work of a reserve police battalion from the solidly middle-class suburbs of Hamburg.[14] Clearly, the SS did not and could not operate alone, as if in a vacuum. Wehrmacht soldiers participated in the slaughter of the Holocaust at every level, from planning to execution. Their cooperation—or at least acquiescence—was arguably essential for the whole nefarious scheme to take place at all.[15]

Yet, though there are numerous examples of Wehrmacht soldiers closing their eyes to the mass murders or even participating in them, there are sufficient cases of the contrary to demonstrate that, among the officer corps at least, a sense of honor had not quite been extinguished. And it was this moral outrage that would drive many, like Bussche, to actively oppose the Nazi regime.

As a resistance center, the German military also had a number of distinct advantages over its rivals. As noted above, it was more or less immune to the attentions of the Nazi security organs. More important, it was perhaps the only body capable of removing the party leadership while simultaneously maintaining order, both at home and at the front, and providing a replacement administration. Most crucially, a few military figures, at staff level and above, had access to their target. They were also armed and, to put it bluntly, in the business of killing.

But the Wehrmacht also suffered a number of fundamental obstacles that hindered action. Firstly, the German military had a tradition of noninvolvement in politics. Though this tradition had been somewhat tarnished by the turmoil of the interwar years, it remained almost a mantra for many senior personnel and staff officers. For them, the German army was more than just the military arm of the state; it was the guarantor of the nation itself. In the opinion of one field marshal, who would repeatedly refuse to join the conspiracy, the use of force against the authorities was "totally contrary to the German military tradition."[16] Moreover, Hitler's government, though dictatorial, was legitimate, legal, and extremely successful. In such circumstances it was virtually impossible to contemplate that it might become the target of a military coup.

More significant, the German military was bound by its twin cultures of obedience and loyalty. These were no vague principles. They lay at the heart of the German soldier's self-image, his sense of duty, and his sense of honor. Obedience, as well as being crucial to the discipline of any army, was central to German political culture. Prussia itself had developed as an *Obrigkeitsstaat,* an authoritarian state, where every citizen knew his place, knew his duty, and obeyed his superiors. Loyalty, too, was of much deeper significance. Not only had Hitler required the German army to take an oath to him personally, he had also appointed himself supreme commander. Thereafter, any act of disloyalty or disobedience could be construed as a direct challenge to the state.

Quite apart from such apparently abstract concerns, a number of more immediate factors served to reinforce the soldier's natural sense of loyalty. First, it is generally considered fundamentally unpatriotic even to criticize one's government during wartime, never mind conspire to bring it down. Such reflexive loyalty was only strengthened in Nazi Germany by the continuing power of the "stab in the back" myth, in which the politicians were alleged to have betrayed the army at the end of World War I. Thus, during World War II, the prospects for the resistance were effectively undermined with each German victory. While he was seen to be winning, Hitler was untouchable. While the Wehrmacht was marching to success after success, the case put by the opposition was progressively weakened, and the chances of convincing the General Staff, or indeed the public, of the need for action diminished still further. As one conspirator noted grimly: "There is no point [in acting] while the people sing hosannas. It can only make sense when they scream for [Hitler's] crucifixion."[17]

By the time of Germany's first significant defeat, at Stalingrad in January 1943, voices were finally being raised in the military and beyond, criticizing Hitler's tactics and calling his decision making into question. Yet, just as Germany's Sixth Army was capitulating at Stalingrad, President Roosevelt was promulgating the policy of "unconditional surrender" at Casablanca. From then on, there was no alternative for every German soldier but to fight doggedly to save Germany from the specter of defeat, occupation, and Bolshevization. Before the conspirators could profit from any discontent, therefore, fate cut the ground from beneath their feet and they were left with little of substance to promise any would-be convert.

In these circumstances, the surprise is perhaps not that the majority of German soldiers felt unable to take action against the regime, but rather that so many were willing to do so. As knowledge spread within the military of the atrocities being committed in Germany's name, and as faith in Hitler as a military and political leader waned, so the conspiracy grew. For most, opposition to Hitler never went beyond a raised eyebrow or curses muttered under the breath. For others, opposition was openly expressed, but not acted upon for lack of opportunity, support, or personal valor. For a brave few, however, who combined motive, will, and opportunity, conspiracy against the Führer became *"eine Frage der Ehre,"* a question of honor.[18]

Yet, deciding to act was only a part of the answer. Some still clung to the naive idea that Hitler could simply be arrested and arraigned for trial. The majority, however, had long arrived at the conclusion that Hitler's hold on the German people was so strong that only his murder could bring the desired results. As one conspirator recalled:

> The general conviction [was] that German troops would never be willing to accept a different command as long as Hitler lived, but that news of his death would instantly bring about the collapse of the myth surrounding his name. Hence there was no way of gaining the support of large numbers of German troops without eliminating Hitler.[19]

Having decided on assassination, there was also the small matter of gaining access to the target. By 1941, Hitler had become a virtual recluse. By the time the war turned against him, after the debacle at Stalingrad, he eschewed almost all public appearances and was accessible only to his inner circle. When he did appear in public, his security apparatus was considerable. Wherever he went, he was constantly surrounded by SS and bodyguards, who were fiercely loyal and, by the outbreak of war, well drilled in their procedures.

In private, Hitler was scarcely more vulnerable. With the notable exception of Berchtesgaden, where he felt safest, he was still surrounded by a strict security cordon. And though his daily routine was known to the conspirators, it allowed few opportunities for action. Rising at 10 a.m., he held a daily situation conference at 11, which was followed by lunch and an afternoon nap. Dinner then began at 8 p.m. and would last until the early hours.[20] Realistically, therefore, any assassin would have to be either granted access to the morning conference or else invited to lunch or dine with the target. Once there, he would then have to consider his options. A pistol was unwise: both Hitler and his valets were routinely armed, and in the Führer's presence, all visiting officers were required to remove their belts and weapons. Furthermore, it was widely believed that Hitler not only wore a bulletproof vest but sported a service cap reinforced with steel[21] and had X-ray detectors installed at his headquarters.[22] In addition to all that, few members of the resistance felt that they had the nerve necessary to confront Hitler with a weapon.[23] Poisoning, too, was out of the question, as all Hitler's food was specially prepared by his own cooks and was tasted for him by his personal physician, Dr. Morrell.[24] The weapon of choice, therefore, was usually the time bomb.

Moreover, as innate conservatives, the military resistance was more concerned than most about the type of regime that might follow a successful assassination. Some, bizarrely, thought that Himmler might prove amenable and establish a moderate Nazi government.[25] The majority, however, preferred to target the entire leadership caste of the Nazi Party in one fell swoop. It made little sense, they would argue, to remove Hitler if in so doing power was handed to the unholy triumvirate of Goebbels, Himmler, and Bormann. Clearly, the domestic opposition faced complexities in their planning that simply did not apply to their counterparts in Moscow, London, or Warsaw.

The German military did not emerge as a genuine center of conspiracy until around 1941. With the exception of the Abwehr (see Chapter 3), few of its early plotters achieved anything of any consequence. In 1939, for example, the commander of Army Group A on the Lower Rhine, General Kurt von Hammerstein-Equord, had attempted unsuccessfully to induce Hitler to visit his headquarters in Cologne, with the idea of arresting him.[26] The following summer, a similar plot developed in occupied Paris with similar results. By the summer of 1941, however—paradoxically, when the German army appeared to be invincible—the first rumblings of a widespread military conspiracy began. Its nucleus would form in the unlikely location of the headquarters of one of Hitler's Army Groups.

It is not immediately obvious why Army Group Center should have developed into a "nest of intrigue and treason" against Hitler.[27] It contained, for example, Guderian's 2nd Panzer Group, and counted the SS Panzer Division *Das Reich* and the élite *Grossdeutschland* Regiment among its number. Its soldiers had made rapid initial gains in Operation Barbarossa, and, after tasting victory in the great encirclement battles of Minsk and Smolensk, had been ordered to march on Moscow. They had experienced the same elation, terror, and privation that were common across the Eastern Front. Some of them may have witnessed the atrocities committed to their rear by the SS and others. Many more would have heard the rumors. Army Group Center's commander, Field Marshal Fedor von Bock, certainly had. A career staff officer who had masterminded the annexation of Austria in 1938 and had led army groups in the Polish and French campaigns, Bock was already in his sixties. He was certainly no Nazi, but, although he had often expressed disquiet at SS activities, he contented himself with lodging a formal complaint with army headquarters in Berlin.[28] Though he sympathized with the conspirators, he was not prepared to act.

Bock's nephew, however, Colonel Henning von Tresckow,

was a man of a different stamp. A gifted soldier, Tresckow had fought in the First World War, where, as a seventeen-year-old lieutenant, he had been awarded the first of three Iron Crosses. A career as a staff officer beckoned, and in 1936 he left the Military Academy as the best cadet of his year. Despite initial enthusiasm for the Nazi regime, he quickly began to turn against Hitler. After the blatant illegality of the Röhm Purge in 1934, he was then shocked by the aggressive planning of the campaign against Czechoslovakia and disillusioned by the Blomberg and Fritsch crises (see pages 86–87) of 1938. Already by that time, he was beginning to think of high treason as the only answer to Germany's plight. "Hitler," he said to friends, "is a whirling dervish. He must be shot down."[29]

The outbreak of war in 1939 affected Tresckow deeply. In stark contrast to the vast majority of his countrymen, he saw the conquest of Poland—in which he participated as a major in an infantry division—as a psychological and moral defeat for the German people and for the nascent resistance, of which he was already a member. Hitler's methods, he feared, had been vindicated—those voicing opposition had been shouted down. His only hope at this point was that a military setback would create more favorable conditions for a coup.[30] Finally, in 1941, with the planning for the attack on the Soviet Union, Tresckow believed that setback to be close at hand. War against the USSR would end in German defeat, he thought, "just as surely as the Amen in church."[31] That defeat could then serve as the hour of Germany's rebirth and her liberation from Nazism.

Tresckow's plotting was given added impetus by the circulation of Hitler's draft directives for the Barbarossa campaign. Hitler had already warned that the war against the Soviet Union would be "very different from that in the west." He went on to outline the expanded role that the *Einsatzgruppen* were to play in the conflict. The brutal methods of racial warfare, which had already caused outrage among sectors of the German military during the Polish campaign, were now to be expanded. In the run-up to war, a series of directives was issued, giving responsibility to

Himmler's SS to take "executive measures vis-à-vis the civilian population." For those still in doubt as to what this all meant, a General Staff directive of May 1941 declared:

> Bolshevism is the deadly enemy of the National Socialist German people.... [The] struggle requires ruthless and energetic action against Bolshevik agitators, guerrillas, saboteurs, and Jews, and the total elimination of all active or passive resistance.[32]

On reading such orders, Tresckow was horrified. He saw the German army being dragged into the illegal, genocidal measures of the SS and Nazi Party. He saw Germany's honor being sacrificed on the altar of Hitler's megalomania. With uncanny prescience, he confided to a colleague:

> This will still have an effect in hundreds of years, and it will not only be Hitler who is blamed, but rather you and me, your wife and my wife, your children and my children, that woman crossing the street, and that lad there kicking a ball.[33]

Tresckow hurried to complain to his superiors. Halfhearted protests were raised, but to no avail. The orders stood.

Once the war against the Soviet Union was launched, Tresckow was well placed to keep himself informed of the atrocities being committed in the army's rear. As senior staff officer of Army Group Center, based in Byelorussia, he would have been aware of the brutal "pacification" campaigns then under way all around him. He would have seen the correspondence from the *Einsatzgruppen,* read the situation reports, and heard the rumors. Curiously, perhaps, he does not appear to have interceded to stop or limit the slaughter. He only acted, it appears, in one instance, and then only to secure the postponement of a planned massacre of "partisans and followers" until the agreement of the army high command had been given.[34]

It may be that he feared exposing himself as an opponent of

the regime or that he considered such actions to be futile. But Tresckow soon began to collect like-minded soldiers. He appointed trusted colleagues and friends to positions of influence in his headquarters. The first to arrive was his cousin Fabian von Schlabrendorff, a young reserve lieutenant and lawyer, whom he appointed as his aide-de-camp. Others would follow, including the later would-be assassins Rudolf-Christoph von Gersdorff, Eberhard von Breitenbuch, and Georg von Boeselager. Tresckow himself would become one of the most convinced and energetic advocates of opposition against Hitler, and his staff would serve as the nucleus of the conspiracy. He created a tightly knit and committed resistance cell, and located it on the general staff of one of Hitler's most prestigious army groups.

Tresckow's first tentative moves toward tyrannicide crystallized in the late summer of 1941. Based at the Army Group Center headquarters at Borisov in Byelorussia, he was soon made grimly aware of historical precedents. It had been there, in the winter of 1812, that Napoleon's exhausted army had crossed the Berezina River and finally ceded victory to the Russians. As if to ram the point home, the Germans retrieved a number of Napoleonic standards from the riverbed and sent them to Berlin for restoration. When SS units then massacred the Jewish population of the town, Tresckow was also made aware of the horrors of his own time.

He resolved to act, and, hatching a plan with Schlabrendorff, planned to kidnap Hitler during a forthcoming visit to Army Group Center. Once arrived at staff headquarters, he thought, Hitler's car could be commandeered and its occupants arrested. The Führer could then be put on trial and dealt with accordingly, perhaps by execution. The visit to Borisov was planned for 4 August. At dawn that morning, Hitler arrived at the local airstrip, was collected by a convoy of SS cars newly arrived the previous evening, and was driven the 4 kilometers to army group headquarters. Once there, he hurried into a meeting with Field Marshal von Bock and General Guderian. It is even suggested that he had time for a word with Tresckow himself, confiding to him his plans to turn postwar Moscow into an enormous lake.[35] That

afternoon, he was driven back to the airfield and flown to Rastenburg. According to one eyewitness, security for the visit had
been "incredible."[36]

For Tresckow, it was a grim realization. Unable to win Bock
over to the conspiracy, and unable to tackle the Führer's security
personnel head-on, he was effectively powerless. He also recognized the cruel dilemma of his position: by waiting for Hitler's
defeat, he was wasting the chance to save something from the
ruins of Nazism, but by acting precipitately, he risked abject failure and certain death. He needed contacts to the civilian resistance within Germany. Any arrest or assassination of Hitler, he
realized, had to be accompanied by a thoroughgoing coup to
seize political power and remove the Nazi Party.

That winter, while Schlabrendorff was sounding out possible
collaborators among the domestic opposition, Hitler's aura of in-
vincibility was finally and irreparably dented. In early December,
German forces faltered before Moscow, paralyzed by the freezing
weather and reeling from the determined counterattacks of fresh
Soviet troops. At one point, they had stood a mere 19 kilometers
outside the city's suburbs, but they were driven back, and the forward German salients were eliminated. Though they would succeed in stabilizing the front and even regaining the initiative, they
would never threaten Moscow again. It was their first defeat in
over two years of fighting.

That same month, as the Germans were freezing before the
Soviet capital, the Japanese were launching their surprise attack
on the U.S. base at Pearl Harbor. On 11 December, Hitler delivered a lengthy speech to the Reichstag attacking Roosevelt, praising the Japanese, and culminating in a declaration of war on the
United States. His closing words, announcing the commence-
ment of hostilities, were drowned out in a frenzy of cheering.[37]
Beyond the Reichstag, however, few viewed the prospect of
war with America with enthusiasm. Despite the best efforts of
Goebbels, public morale sank to a new low as the German people
prepared for indefinite warfare. The General Staff was alarmed at
the addition of a new enemy with almost limitless reserves. For
Tresckow, it marked the beginning of the end. He commented

sadly: "I wish I could show the German people a film, entitled 'Germany at the End of the War.' Perhaps then they would realize with horror, what we're heading for."[38]

One man who was slowly coming round to share this view was a brilliant young staff officer named Claus Schenk von Stauffenberg. Born into the Swabian nobility in 1907, Stauffenberg was an intellectual and a man of delicate health who had developed a profound, if mystical, sense of German nationalism. An early enthusiast for National Socialism, he had joined the cavalry in 1927 and progressed swiftly through the ranks, being elevated to the General Staff in 1939 and serving with distinction in the Polish and French campaigns. Stauffenberg was a comparatively late convert to the cause of the resistance. Indeed, when told of seditious plans by his colleagues in 1939, he told his wife that he knew such activities to be "tantamount to treason," but he had decided not to report them.[39] Clearly, he did not yet hold the view that Hitler had to be removed.

As with many of his colleagues, the decisive factor in Stauffenberg's conversion appears to have been the atrocities perpetrated by the SS against enemy civilians, and especially Jews. In the summer of 1941, for example, he seems to have had his first suspicions, and asked a colleague to "collect everything that implicated the SS."[40] At around that time, he also made the acquaintance of Henning von Tresckow, to whom he professed himself to be "no Nazi."[41] Though he would tentatively advocate a reckoning with what he called the "brown plague" of Nazism, he preferred to wait until the war was over. And crucially, right until the spring of 1942, he still believed that the war could be won, and preferred to temper outright criticism of Hitler as a military leader by suggesting that he might benefit from more capable advisors.

By that summer, however, Stauffenberg was openly advocating Hitler's removal. There were a number of factors that brought this shift about. The murderous treatment of Soviet prisoners and civilians, at a time when Stauffenberg was attempting to raise volunteer units among them, struck him as spectacularly wrongheaded.[42] Also, the thrust toward Stalingrad and the

Caucasus, begun that summer, was considered wildly optimistic. However, the decisive factor in Stauffenberg's conversion was the murderous policy of the SS on the Eastern Front. In May 1942, he received a graphic eyewitness account of the mass execution of Jews in a small Ukrainian town. His immediate reaction was that Hitler had to be overthrown.[43]

From that point on, with all the enthusiasm of a new convert, Stauffenberg repeatedly, and often incautiously, expressed his opinion on Hitler and the Nazi regime. The Führer, he said, was "foolish and criminal"; his war was "monstrous" and had been based on lies. He liked to quote the work of the mystical poet Stefan George, in whose circle Stauffenberg had participated as a young man. One of his favorites, entitled *The Antichrist*, appeared to him to be particularly apposite:

> *The high Prince of Vermin extends his domains;*
> *No pleasure eludes him, no treasure or gain.*
> *And down with the dregs of rebellion!*
>
> *You cheer, mesmerised by the demoniac sheen,*
> *Exhaust what remains of the honey of dawn,*
> *And only then sense the debacle.*
>
> *You then stretch your tongues to the now arid trough,*
> *Mill witless as kine through a pasture aflame,*
> *While fearfully brazens the trumpet.*[44]

For Stauffenberg, *The Antichrist* almost became a mantra. He would recite it with mystical fervor, "his great frame striding up and down the room and his . . . left hand gesticulating fiercely."[45] He also used it as an effective recruiting device. On one occasion, he merely quoted the poem and made no further comment, leaving the stark vision to do his persuading for him.[46]

In time, he came to advocate tyrannicide and even volunteered to carry out the attack himself.[47] Perhaps it is indicative of the currency of such opinions among the staff officers on the Eastern Front that Stauffenberg was never reported or cautioned

for his outspoken attacks on the regime. Rather, he was maneu-
vered into a field posting in North Africa, far away from the Soviet Union and far from the bloody brutality of the SS. In early
February 1943, he took up his post as senior staff officer in the
10th Panzer Division in Tunisia, but he would curb neither his
forthright opinions nor his conspiratorial activities.

It is, in fact, testament to the breadth of anti-Nazi feeling
within the Wehrmacht that the first conspiracy worthy of the
name originated from beyond the narrow circle of plotters
around Tresckow and Stauffenberg. In February 1943, General
Hubert Lanz, commander of an army group in eastern Ukraine,
had been directly ordered by Hitler to hold the city of Kharkhov.
On assessing his available forces, however—three SS-Panzer Divisions against fully three advancing Soviet armies[48]—he realized
that his orders amounted not only to a suicide mission but also to
the wanton sacrifice of élite fighting units. After conferring with
his chief of staff, Major-General Hans Speidel, and one of his
corps commanders, Colonel Hyazinth von Strachwitz, he concluded that Hitler had to be removed.

Lanz hatched a plan to kidnap Hitler during a forthcoming
visit to Army Group B headquarters at Poltava. Though an assassination was not initially planned, it was considered in the event
that the kidnap attempt met with resistance. Strachwitz assured
Lanz that his troops, men of the élite *Grossdeutschland* Division,
could be relied upon to provide the necessary muscle to overcome Hitler's security personnel. Hitler, it was naively assumed,
could then be handed over to the military authorities for trial as
a war criminal. When Lanz withdrew his forces from Kharkhov
on 15 February—in direct contravention of Hitler's orders—it
appeared that the time for action had come. Enraged, Hitler flew
to Army Group B two days later to manage the ensuing crisis. But
instead of visiting Poltava, he traveled instead to Zaporozhye to
confer with Lanz's superior, Field Marshal von Manstein. Lanz
was relieved of his command for disobeying orders and transferred to the reserve, and his plot unraveled as swiftly and silently
as it had developed. Unwittingly, Hitler had once again evaded
those who would do him harm.

Eight hundred kilometers to the north, meanwhile, a second plot was in an advanced stage of planning. This one was no half-hearted kidnapping; rather, it was very definitely and unashamedly an assassination. In the previous months, Tresckow's circle had been augmented by a number of new additions, who brought fresh energy and dynamism to the conspiracy. One of them was a young cavalry officer named Georg von Boeselager. Born in Kassel during World War I, Boeselager came from a traditional military family, and certainly would not have disappointed his forebears. Awarded the prestigious Knight's Cross during the French campaign, he then became only the fifty-third recipient of the Oak Leaves to the Knight's Cross during the advance on Moscow. In the following summer, his unit was absorbed into the cavalry regiment of Army Group Center. There, Boeselager the dashing young war hero met Tresckow the traitor.

In fact, Boeselager's flirtation with the resistance had begun some months before. Already in the summer of 1941, he had complained bitterly of Hitler's leadership and of the criminal nature of the Nazi regime. "When the war is over," he confided to colleagues, "it will be up to people like us to do something about it." He would soon learn that action was required with rather more urgency. In the summer of 1942, his brother Philipp, an officer on the staff of Field Marshal von Kluge, made a shocking discovery. In a meeting with SS General von dem Bach-Zelewski, he had queried the general's use of the phrase "special treatment" with regard to prisoners, Gypsies, and Jews. He was told bluntly that it meant death by shooting.[49] Few German soldiers on the Eastern Front would have been unaware of the brutal treatment meted out by the SS to the perceived enemies of the Reich, but here was confirmation from a very senior officer that mass murder was not only tolerated but was even official policy. It is inconceivable that Georg von Boeselager would have been long ignorant of his brother's stark realization.

Boeselager's arrival at Army Group Center headquarters, which had been engineered by his brother, began the process of transforming his principled but as yet unfocused criticism of the excesses of Nazism into something more immediately deadly.

Under Tresckow's tutelage, he underwent a "thoroughgoing re-orientation of his thinking" and emerged as a man in fundamental moral and religious opposition to Hitler, and who was moreover prepared to act.[50]

For Tresckow, meanwhile, Boeselager represented the reliable military force that he had so patently lacked at Borisov eighteen months previously. At this point, it appears that Tresckow was leaning toward the idea of shooting Hitler during one of the Führer's visits to the Eastern Front. When he learned of Hitler's visit to Army Group South in February 1943, for example, he hurried to Zaporozhye to demand why his fellow conspirators there had not seized their chance: "We have been waiting for an opportunity for months!" he raged:

> Waiting for it, longing for the day when we can kill this scoundrel who is destroying our Germany! The day never comes! Each time, it's no use! Each time, something goes wrong! And you here in Zaporozhye, who see things the way we do, you let the chance slip!"[51]

His new plan, therefore, envisaged Boeselager's cavalry troops providing the firepower to assassinate the Führer and take on the SS bodyguard. All he needed now was to provide the target. And in early March, he received news that the increasingly reclusive Hitler had agreed to visit Army Group Center headquarters at Smolensk.

From his previous experience, Tresckow was well aware of the complications and difficulties in executing such an operation. Given the chaos that could ensue, he felt he had to secure the co-operation, or at least acquiescence, of his superior officer, Field Marshal von Kluge. Kluge, however, though broadly sympathetic to the cause, could not align himself with it. He temporized and prevaricated, raising objection after objection. Despite Tresckow's persistent badgering, he simply could not bring himself to be party to the assassination of his commander in chief. Suspecting something was afoot, he turned on Tresckow on the morning of Hitler's visit, saying: "For heaven's sake, don't do anything today!"[52] Tresckow's reply is not recorded, but he clearly refused to listen.

In truth, Tresckow had begun to have second thoughts about using Boeselager and his troops. He may have feared a collective loss of nerve, or been unwilling to endanger the life of Kluge. So he had another plan up his sleeve. For some months, he and Schlabrendorff had been testing various explosives, mines, and fuses, with the intention of planting a bomb on Hitler's plane. As Schlabrendorff related:

> We finally decided on British explosives of the plastic type and British fuses. British planes had been dropping large amounts of such material over German-held territory, in an effort to equip Allied agents for acts of sabotage. Naturally, a good deal of this material fell into the hands of our own military.
>
> The British explosive had two great advantages. It was extremely powerful, but not bulky. A package no bigger than a thick book was capable of tearing apart everything within the space of a fair-sized room. . . . After we had concluded our experiments we went ahead with preparations for the assassination.[53]

Tresckow filled four clam mines with the plastic explosives and added a time-pencil fuse, which could be set to detonate after half an hour. He then fashioned the bomb into a parcel resembling two bottles of Cointreau. In this way, he thought, it could easily be infiltrated into Hitler's luggage for his return flight to Rastenburg.

On the morning of 13 March 1943, Tresckow himself drove to Smolensk airport to meet Hitler and his entourage. To his horror, he saw Hitler's party—consisting of cooks, bodyguards, adjutants, and a doctor—arrive in *two* identical aircraft.[54] If he was going to plant his bomb, he would have to make sure that he got the right one. Schlabrendorff, meanwhile, telephoned Berlin and advised his co-conspirators that Operation Flash was ready. He was informed that Berlin was prepared and that "the ignition can be switched on."[55] Returning to headquarters, Tresckow then participated in the official conference, chaired by Hitler, during which he appeared pale and distracted. After lunch, he sought out Schlabrendorff for moral support. "Should we really do it?" he asked.[56] Schlabrendorff was adamant. Soon after, Tresckow approached Colonel Brandt, a member of Hitler's staff, and coolly asked if he would be traveling back with Hitler. Brandt replied that he would, as he was due to make a presentation to the Führer during the flight. Tresckow then asked him if he might take two bottles of brandy back to High Command headquarters for his friend Colonel Stieff. Contrary to regulations, Brandt readily agreed. Operation Flash was under way.

After lunch, Tresckow then accompanied Hitler on his return journey to the airport. He bade his farewells and watched the Führer climb into one of the two specially equipped Focke-Wulf Condors. Schlabrendorff then surreptitiously set the fuse on the bomb and handed the parcel to Colonel Brandt, who also boarded the plane. A few minutes later the aircraft and their fighter escort disappeared into the clear skies above Byelorussia. Tresckow and Schlabrendorff then returned to headquarters. They knew the potential pitfalls, but, after months of planning and testing, they were confident of success. As Schlabrendorff wrote in his memoirs:

> We knew that Hitler's plane was equipped with special devices designed to increase its safety. Not only was it divided into several special cabins, but Hitler's own cabin was heavily armour plated, and his seat outfitted with a parachute. In spite of all this, Tresckow and I, judging from our experiments, were convinced that the amount of explosive in the bomb would be sufficient to tear the entire plane apart, or at least to make a fatal crash inevitable.[57]

With bated breath, the two assassins waited for news of the "accident." For two hours they waited. Then they received the crushing news that Hitler's plane had landed safely at Rastenburg. They had failed.

Their first priority, of course, was to alert their co-conspirators in Berlin that the attempt had not succeeded. That done, Tresckow calmly telephoned Colonel Brandt to inquire whether the parcel had been delivered to Colonel Stieff. When he was told that it had not, he apologized and explained that the wrong parcel had been sent by mistake and that another would be sent for exchange. The following day, Schlabrendorff hurried to Hitler's headquarters armed with two genuine bottles of brandy. He blanched when Brandt, clearly unaware of its contents, playfully juggled the bomb on handing it back to him.[58] Smiling weakly, he exchanged it for the brandy and made his excuses.

Once secure inside a railway carriage en route to Berlin, Schlabrendorff opened the package and cautiously examined the bomb. He identified the cause of their failure as a defective fuse, although others have suggested that the extreme cold in Hitler's plane (due to a malfunctioning heater) may have prevented the explosive from detonating.[59] Either way, Hitler had once again escaped injury. As one of the conspirators quipped, he appeared to have a "guardian devil."[60]

Nonetheless, despite the failure, the conspirators had not been discovered, and even the explosive had been successfully retrieved. Their colleagues in Berlin, though standing down, were ready for action. Once they recovered from their disappointment and their nerve-jangling experience at Smolensk, Tresckow and Schlabrendorff were free to resume their plotting. They wasted little time.

Some days later, Tresckow was informed that Hitler would be present at the annual Heroes' Day celebration in Berlin, where an exhibition of captured Soviet weaponry was also to be held. As most of the exhibits for the display had been collected by Army Group Center, he was told that his senior intelligence officer, Rudolf-Christoph von Gersdorff, had been detailed for duty at the ceremony. Gersdorff, who had often served as an unofficial emissary for Tresckow, was similarly convinced of the need to remove Hitler. And when asked if he would be prepared to undertake an assassination attempt, he readily agreed. Tresckow then proceeded to fill his colleague in on all the necessary details concerning the failed Smolensk attack, the resistance network in Germany, and the prospects for a new attempt. During a long walk along the banks of the Dnieper, he quipped to Gersdorff: "Isn't it dreadful? Here we are, two officers of the German General Staff, discussing how best to murder our commander in chief." He went on gravely: "It must be done. This is our only chance. . . . Hitler must be cut down like a rabid dog."[61] The following day, Gersdorff caught a flight to Berlin.

As he had been unable to plan his attempt in any detail, Gersdorff spent the day before the event surreptitiously reconnoitering the venue—the impressive Armory building on Unter den Linden—while being instructed on the procedures and protocol for the ceremony. He soon realized that security was such that it would prove impossible to plant a bomb under the dais, for example, or in the lectern. As he would later recall: "At this point it became clear to me that an attack was only possible if I were to carry the explosives about my person, and blow myself up as close to Hitler as was possible."[62] He was to be history's first suicide bomber.

That night, when Schlabrendorff arrived with the clam mines retrieved from Colonel Brandt, Gersdorff found that though the mines were small enough to be comfortably carried in his jacket pockets, the only detonator he had was an old ten-minute fuse that he had brought with him from Smolensk. Given that Hitler's tour of the exhibition was scheduled to last thirty minutes, he was reasonably confident of success. But nonetheless, feeling like a condemned man, he was unable to sleep.

The following day, as he loitered inconspicuously in the Berlin Armory, he watched a succession of party bigwigs and senior military personnel file into the hall. Göring, sporting a white uniform, red leather riding boots, and makeup, struck him as "grotesque." Himmler followed, along with Wilhelm Keitel, the head of the army, and Karl Dönitz, commander in chief of the German navy. If his attack was successful, Gersdorff realized, he could wipe out the entire leadership clique of Nazi Germany.

Around 1:00 that afternoon, the ceremony began. After a performance of the first movement of Bruckner's mournful

Seventh Symphony, Hitler ascended the podium to deliver a trademark speech full of optimism, defiance, and praise for Germany's fallen. As the speech drew to a close and applause echoed around the room, Gersdorff positioned himself at the entrance to the exhibition, preparing to welcome his guests. As introductions, greetings, and pleasantries were being exchanged with the paladins of the Reich, he reached into his jacket pocket and set the fuse. He had ten minutes.

He began gamely, providing information on the numerous items on display and attempting to engage Hitler's interest. As he pointed out the exhibits, he stayed as close as possible to Hitler's side, concerned that the explosives might detonate at any moment. However, he quickly realized that Hitler wasn't listening and was distracted. He tried once again to interest the Führer in one of the exhibits—one of the Napoleonic standards raised from the river Berezina at Borisov—but in vain. "Instead," he recalled, "[Hitler] went—or rather ran—out of the side door. . . . During [his] short tour around the exhibition, he had barely looked at anything and had not said a word."[63] The planned thirty-minute tour had lasted a mere two minutes.

Gersdorff was stunned, but as he could not follow Hitler without arousing the suspicion of the SS bodyguards, he had to accept that he had been thwarted. After hurrying to the lavatories to defuse his mines, he retired to a nearby club to compose himself. There, he was approached by an acquaintance who boasted that he "could have killed Adolf today." The man went on to explain that he had watched as Hitler "drove very slowly in an open-top car down [Unter den] Linden, right in front of my ground-floor room in the Hotel Bristol. It would have been child's play," he said, "to heave a hand grenade over the sidewalk and into his car."[64] Gersdorff said nothing.

In one week, Tresckow had made two attempts on Hitler's life. Both had failed, thwarted by circumstance and ill-fortune. One might have forgiven the plotters if they had abandoned their efforts, content that they had done their best and preferring to sit out the war and endeavor merely to survive. Such thoughts, especially after the unbearable strains of the past weeks, would certainly not have been far from their minds. But, remarkably, Tresckow took his failures as renewed inspiration. He refused to be disheartened and indefatigably drove his plans on. Fresh attempts, it appeared, would only be a matter of time.

In the early morning of 7 April 1943, Claus von Stauffenberg, the newly arrived staff officer of the 10th Panzer Army in North Africa, was directing a tactical withdrawal toward the Tunisian coast. Standing in his Horch jeep, issuing orders and directions, he was moving slowly along the column of vehicles and armor that had crammed into a mountain pass, when the convoy attracted the attention of American fighter-bombers patrolling overhead. Though he remained at his post for as long as possible, trying to manage the chaos developing around him, he soon became a target himself. As the planes approached on another strafing run, he finally threw himself from the vehicle and instinctively covered his head with his hands.

When the attack had subsided, Stauffenberg's jeep was peppered with holes. Though his driver was unhurt, a lieutenant traveling in the backseat had been killed. Stauffenberg had also been hit. He had lost his left eye, most of his right hand, and two fingers of his left. He was also riddled in the back and legs with shrapnel. Semiconscious and running a high fever, he was transferred to a nearby field hospital for emergency treatment. His doctors did not expect him to survive the day.[65]

After surgery, however, in which the remnants of his right hand and left eye were removed, his condition stabilized and he was eventually taken to a clinic in Munich. There, after a succession of follow-up operations, he slowly recovered. Sight in his remaining eye was restored, and he soon grew accustomed to the loss of his hand and fingers, even stubbornly insisting on dressing himself and tying his own shoelaces.[66] By early July, three months after his injury, he was discharged. Soon after, he was transferred to the staff of the Reserve Army, based in Berlin.

Stauffenberg refused to accept the easy life of a war invalid, however. Indeed, his experiences seem to have made him all the more determined. He confided to his uncle, Nikolaus von Üxküll, that he did not consider his survival to be mere good fortune; rather, he thought he had been spared for a purpose.[67] By late summer, he had made contact again with Tresckow. From then on, he would devote himself wholeheartedly to the preparations for a military coup.

As it turned out, from his position within the Reserve Army, Stauffenberg was superbly placed to become the linchpin of a new conspiracy. There he was responsible for updating the official emergency mobilization plans—code-named "Operation Valkyrie"—that were to be activated in the event of domestic unrest. It would be a simple task for him to revise the plans to suit his own purposes.

The original and official Operation Valkyrie had been drawn up early in 1943 to deal with possible internal disturbances such as a rising among foreign laborers within Germany, an SS revolt, or an enemy paratroop landing. Orders—approved by Hitler—had been distributed to the military districts, outlining how the disparate forces of the Home Army, training facilities, barracks, and reserve cadres were to unite and form into fighting units to secure key sites across the country. The plans were to be held in readiness, and, if required, were to be activated upon an agreed signal from the Supreme Army Command in Berlin. The unofficial Valkyrie, drawn up by Stauffenberg, differed from the original in one crucial respect. Its trigger was to be the assassination of Hitler, whereupon the loyal and dutiful troops of the Wehrmacht would seize control of the Reich in unwitting support of the resistance.

So far, so good. The conspiracy was taking concrete form: the assassination plot was accompanied by plans for a thoroughgoing coup d'état, a shadow government was waiting in the wings, and the military plotters were primed for action. However, as far as the conspirators were concerned, their plot still lacked two vital ingredients—the participation of senior army personnel and an assassin with access to Hitler.

Tresckow set about addressing the first of these problems. In the late summer of 1943, he sought to bring Field Marshal von

Manstein, then commanding Army Group South, into the conspiracy. Though he had already been promised the participation of Field Marshal von Kluge, the experience at Smolensk had convinced him that his superior could not be wholly relied upon in a crisis, especially a crisis of the sort that he hoped to engineer. Manstein, he thought, who had been a persistent critic of Hitler's tactics, might be trusted to take control of the army in the event of a successful coup.

Accordingly, Gersdorff was dispatched to Zaporozhye that August to sound out the field marshal. He began on what he knew to be safe ground: a criticism of Hitler's leadership style, his handling of the war, and the urgent necessity of changing course so as to avert catastrophe. Manstein agreed readily but argued that he was not the man to convince Hitler of anything. Gersdorff then replied tartly that perhaps the field marshals should all go to Hitler together and hold a pistol to his chest. Shocked, Manstein's response neatly summed up the attitude of the older generation of the military. "Prussian field marshals," he barked, "do not mutiny!"[68] This remark confirmed the view that Stauffenberg had expressed earlier in the year, when he commented: "Since the generals have so far done nothing, the colonels must now go into action."[69] Lieutenant Colonel von Stauffenberg was already preparing to put his superiors to shame.

Stauffenberg was to address the second problem: that of finding an officer who was both of sufficient rank to secure access to Hitler and determined and ruthless enough to play the role of assassin. In the autumn of 1943, Stauffenberg thought he had found his man in Colonel Helmuth Stieff, the diminutive head of the General Staff's organization branch. Stieff had initially been willing to take a bomb into one of Hitler's briefings, but by the time he received the necessary explosives in October, he had wavered. Stauffenberg, who had described Stieff as "nervy as a racing jockey," would have to look elsewhere.[70]

Soon after, Stauffenberg was approached by Axel von dem Bussche. In a long conversation he learned of the massacre at Dubno and of Bussche's resolve to act in the name of Germany. He was impressed by the young man's service record and his uninhibited attitude toward tyrannicide. If he could engineer him into a meeting with Hitler, he might have a good chance of success. He sent his would-be assassin to see Stieff at the high command headquarters in East Prussia, who had conceived of a plan to murder Hitler during a demonstration of new equipment.

Bussche, a tall, blond Aryan with a brilliant service record in one of Hitler's most prestigious divisions, was well suited for the role of a model Nazi. He was selected by Stauffenberg to wear the new greatcoat, designed for the Eastern Front, during Hitler's formal inspection.[71] Bussche set about planning his attack. Perhaps mindful of Tresckow's failure at Smolensk, he opted against a British chemical fuse and decided instead on a traditional 4½-second fuse culled from a German stick grenade. This he married to a kilo of explosives and then fashioned the bomb into a form that could fit into his coat pocket. His plan was to set the fuse as Hitler approached, cover its brief hiss by clearing his throat, and then leap on his victim, holding him in a deadly embrace. If he should fail, he planned to carry a stiletto blade tucked into his boot.[72] Thus prepared, he was ready for the "demonstration."

After several delays, Bussche returned to see Stieff at the end of November to make the final preparations. Two weeks later, he was informed that the demonstration had been scheduled to take place in the next few days. Then, on 16 December, he learned that the uniforms that he had been due to display had been destroyed in a British air raid. As replacements could not be sourced quickly, he was transferred back to active service on the Eastern Front, on the understanding that he would be recalled as soon as possible. A month later, however, he lost a leg at Nevel and, spending the remainder of the war in the hospital, was unable to play any further role in the conspiracy. Though a replacement "model" was found, the demonstration of new equipment never did take place and the attack was postponed indefinitely.

For the military conspirators, 1943 had brought little but frustration. Though they had been bolstered by the appearance of the energetic Stauffenberg, their first assassination attempts had been thwarted by bad luck and their target's unpredictability.

Understandably, they were growing disheartened. Many believed that their motive force and inner strength had been expended for precious little gain. Tresckow, especially, feared that they had missed their chance. And when he was promoted to the staff of the 2nd Army in November, his contacts to the opposition, which he had done so much to establish, were put under severe strain. Nonetheless, he sought, in vain, to secure access to Hitler himself to make one last attempt.[73] His star, it seemed, was waning.

Stauffenberg, too, was becoming impatient. Though he had repeatedly declared himself ready to act as assassin, and is even thought to have prepared an attempt that Christmas, his confederates considered him too important to the success of the coup as a whole to be risked.[74] After all, he had personally drawn up the plans for Operation Valkyrie, which would need to be activated in the event of a successful assassination. And few of the conspirators possessed his drive and charisma, not to mention his organizational skills. If Stauffenberg acted as the assassin, his allies believed, he could not be permitted to undertake a suicide mission. Moreover, given his extensive injuries, they doubted that he would be physically able to play the role. This was the impasse that the conspirators faced at the end of 1943. They could only have hoped that 1944 would bring more tangible results.

The opening months of the new year brought little good news, however. German troops were in retreat across Europe. In the east, the siege of Leningrad was finally lifted in January, after nearly nine hundred days, while farther south, Soviet forces were rapidly approaching the former Polish eastern frontier. In Italy, meanwhile, the battle for Monte Cassino was joined and the Anzio landings foreshadowed the capture of Rome. At home, the Royal Air Force and U.S. Army Air Forces continued to pound Germany's cities to rubble. For the resistance, therefore, the expected military collapse appeared to shuffle closer almost daily, while their own efforts had come to naught. In mid-February, they suffered another blow when the dismissal of Admiral Canaris suggested that the conspiracy itself might be compromised. Slowly, the Nazi security services were homing in.

So by March 1944, a degree of urgency had crept into the

opposition's planning. It was around this time that Eberhard von Breitenbuch sought out Tresckow. A cavalry captain and aide-de-camp to Field Marshal von Busch, the new commander of Army Group Center, Breitenbuch had long been an opponent of Nazism and had been in contact with the conspirators for some time. His own conversion to the cause was a gradual process, mirroring the gradual subordination and corruption of the Wehrmacht. The final break is thought to have come in 1942, when he was witness to a number of executions and brutal anti-partisan actions in the forest of Białowieża in eastern Poland. With that, he later recalled, the last remnants of his political faith and trust were destroyed. "What I had previously suspected," he wrote, "I now knew for sure."[75]

In early March 1944, Breitenbuch contacted Tresckow to tell him that he would be accompanying Field Marshal von Busch to brief Hitler at Berchtesgaden. After agreeing to attempt an assassination, he was swiftly supplied with explosives but demurred, distrusting their reliability and preferring to use a Browning pistol instead. It was impressed upon him by Tresckow that the chance "to end the war, with all its horrors, lay in his hands."[76]

On the morning of 11 March, Busch's party arrived at Salzburg airport and was whisked to Hitler's residence by car. By midday, they were waiting in an anteroom in the Berghof. As required, all of them had taken off their caps, belts, and sidearms. In addition, Breitenbuch had already removed his watch and wedding ring, to be sent to his wife, and had concealed his Browning pistol in a trouser pocket. His nerves were harder to conceal. As Göring regaled the visitors with the latest jokes, Breitenbuch was feeling the tension. "My heart was beating in my throat," he recalled, "as it was clear to me that, within half an hour, I would be dead."[77]

Presently, Keitel, Alfred von Jodl, and Goebbels arrived and Busch's party was finally ushered into the conference room by the SS bodyguard. Bringing up the rear of the group, Breitenbuch was suddenly stopped by a guard and curtly informed that junior aides were not to be admitted. Already nervous, he was then forced to endure his superior's vain and unwitting attempts to secure his entry, and was finally turned away, still with the pistol—cocked and loaded—in his pocket.

Another adjutant, similarly barred from the conference, accompanied Breitenbuch as he was escorted from the Berghof. While the two relaxed on the terrace outside, enjoying the view, they chatted. After a time, however, Breitenbuch fell silent. As his companion recalled:

> I noticed that [he] was no longer reacting when I spoke. His forehead was beaded with sweat and his hands were shaking. I asked him if he was ill and if we should order a car to take him to a hospital in Berchtesgaden, but he refused help and said he would be better soon.[78]

Only many years later would Breitenbuch reveal the reason for his sudden attack of nerves.

As 1944 wore on and Tresckow faded out of the reckoning, the resistance was left with little else to do but to hone its plans, reword its numerous declarations, and squabble over the makeup of the putative post-assassination government. Everything that they had tried had been thwarted, and now they had no one with access to Hitler. To make matters worse, events in the military sphere that summer appeared to herald the final collapse of Nazi Germany. On 5 June, Rome fell to the Americans, and the following day the Allied landings in Normandy opened the long-awaited second front. In the east, meanwhile, mid-June saw the start of a colossal Soviet offensive—code-named "Bagration"—against Army Group Center, which would cost Germany fully thirty divisions and over three hundred thousand men.[79]

At around that time, on 20 June, Stauffenberg achieved the breakthrough that his tenacity and determination had deserved. Promoted to full colonel, he was appointed chief of staff to the commander of the Home Army, General Fromm. In this capacity, he was required to supervise the raising, training, and supply of troop detachments across Germany for service at the front.[80] As befitted such an important post, he was also required to report to Hitler personally.

Stauffenberg first met Hitler on 7 June 1944. He had been summoned to a special briefing at Berchtesgaden, together with his superior officer General Fromm. Stauffenberg's reputation as a brilliant staff officer had evidently preceded him, and Hitler greeted him warmly, taking his one maimed hand in his. As was his way with new acquaintances, Hitler held eye contact with Stauffenberg in silence for a few moments, but Stauffenberg did not flinch.[81] The conference, when it began, was a small affair. Alongside Stauffenberg, Fromm, and Hitler, only Göring, Keitel, Himmler, and Speer were present. The items under discussion included arms production and a new type of mine intended to destroy minesweepers.[82] Stauffenberg's task was to outline the official preparations for Operation Valkyrie. Though drafts of the plan had been in existence for some two years by 1944, interest in them had been reawakened by the events of that summer.[83] Hitler listened attentively to Stauffenberg and approved the proposals.

Many who came into personal contact with Hitler came away profoundly moved, even hypnotized, by his magnetism and the force of his personality. Stauffenberg was not one of these. When asked by his wife whether Hitler's eyes had been impressive, he replied: "Not at all. Nothing! . . . as if veiled."[84] He went on to describe the atmosphere of the meeting as degenerate and fetid and claimed that he had found it hard to breathe. Of his fellow participants, he noted, only Albert Speer gave the impression of normality. The others, he said, were "patent psychopaths."[85]

A month later, on July 6, Stauffenberg was summoned back to Berchtesgaden to see Hitler again. Bringing explosives with him, in what Speer described as a "remarkably plump briefcase,"[86] he hoped to persuade Colonel Stieff to attempt an attack during another presentation of new uniforms to Hitler, scheduled for the following day at Schloss Klessheim near Salzburg.[87] Stieff's refusal, however, demonstrated to Stauffenberg that if he was to have any real chance of success, he would have to act alone.

Five days later, on the eleventh, he returned to Berchtesgaden for another meeting with Hitler. This time, he took the precaution of stationing a plane at Salzburg airport, ready to fly him to Berlin after the attack. Once again, he brought the bomb—concealed in his briefcase—into the conference room. But once again, he failed. Given Himmler's absence, he was persuaded by Stieff, much against his own instincts, to postpone the assassination until the entire leadership of the Reich could be targeted together.

That night, back in Berlin, Stauffenberg met Hans Gisevius, one of the conspirators from within the Abwehr. In a long and sometimes heated conversation, he allowed the strain of his unofficial activities to show. According to Gisevius, he was "rude" and "boorish," a "swashbuckler" who was playing the role of assassin and was attempting to "overcompensate for the inferiority feelings engendered by his mutilation."[88] Most historians are agreed that Gisevius was wide of the mark in his criticisms, prejudiced by his loyalty to Hans Oster and possessing an "unrivalled lack of tact."[89] But on one point his assessment was absolutely accurate. During his meeting with Stauffenberg, he recalled, he "had the impression that before [him] was a man who would go to the limit."[90] After all the near misses and frustrations of the preceding weeks, Stauffenberg was absolutely determined to act. As he confided to a colleague, it was too late for scruples:

> It is now time that something was done. But the man who has the courage to do something must do it in the knowledge that he will go down in German history as a traitor. If he does not do it, however, he will be a traitor to his own conscience.[91]

Four days later, Stauffenberg was again summoned to see Hitler, this time at his East Prussian headquarters, Wolfschanze, near Rastenburg. On arrival early that morning, he breakfasted and attended a briefing with Field Marshal Keitel. Soon after midday, he proceeded to Hitler's presentation room, where he participated in three short conferences, of no more than twenty minutes each. As before, he had the explosives with him, concealed beneath a spare shirt in his briefcase.

The bomb, which Stauffenberg had been ferrying between

Berlin, Berchtesgaden, and Rastenburg for two weeks, consisted of two 1-kilogram slabs of plastic explosives, British in origin, that had been captured from failed SOE circuits and had passed through the conspirators at the Abwehr. The fuse, known as a time-pencil, had come from the same source. In order for the bomb to be activated, the time-pencil would have to be pressed into the explosive and then set by squeezing the bronze casing with a pair of pliers. This crushed a glass vial and released acid, which ate through a piece of wire holding a spring-loaded detonator.[92] Naturally, the timing mechanism was far from exact and was easily influenced by external factors, such as temperature: slowing its action with the cold, and accelerating it with heat. Thus, in some circumstances, such as on a hot summer's day, it was possible that a thirty-minute time-pencil might detonate after only fourteen minutes.[93] Stauffenberg, therefore, had to hurry. He first had to ascertain that Hitler was indeed in the briefing room, and then had to excuse himself to set up his bomb. He would then have to return to the room, place his briefcase as close to his target as he could, and then leave the room again—all without arousing any suspicion. All of this only added to the tremendous stress under which he was already operating.

It is unclear exactly why Stauffenberg's attack of 15 July failed. Some suggest that Stieff scuppered the attempt by removing the briefcase from the room, as Göring and Himmler were once again absent.[94] Others maintain that Stauffenberg either wavered or was unexpectedly requested to make a presentation and was thus unable to excuse himself to set his fuse.[95] The most dramatic explanation claims that Stauffenberg left the room to confer with Berlin and prime his bomb, but when he returned Hitler had already left and the meeting was breaking up.[96] The truth may, of course, be more mundane: perhaps Stauffenberg—having traveled without his adjutant—had simply been physically unable to fuse his bomb, or he realized that he lacked the time necessary to leave the room, set the fuse, and then return. Whatever the cause of the failure—and it will probably never be known for certain—Stauffenberg had been frustrated again. However, spurred on by his repeated disappointments, he only grew more determined. Next time he would act, come what may. "There is no other choice," he said. "The Rubicon has been crossed."[97]

Back in Berlin, meanwhile, the resistance was facing a race against time. Their activities, it is claimed, were already known to the SS.[98] A week earlier, two of their most prominent civilian members, Adolf Reichwein and Julius Leber, had been arrested by the Gestapo. Both were implicated in the planning for Operation Valkyrie, and both were well aware of Stauffenberg's activities. It would surely only be a matter of time until they were "persuaded" to confess all they knew. Moreover, the conspirators had been so sure that the attempt of 15 July would go ahead that orders for the necessary troop movements in Berlin had been issued that morning, in anticipation of a successful attack. When the attack failed to materialize, the orders could be explained away as exercises or drill, but crucially, there could now be no more false alarms. If the troops were to be called out again, it would have to be in earnest.

Unsurprisingly, Stauffenberg was under tremendous strain at this time. Whereas a previous would-be assassin had claimed of his attempt that "you only do something like that once," Stauffenberg was already a veteran.[99] In little over a week he had arrived at three briefings with Hitler, carrying explosives. At two of those, he had come explicitly as an assassin. Each time he had had to risk betrayal, exposure, and certain death. Each time he had had to prepare himself psychologically for the greatest challenge of his life. And each time he had been thwarted. As a result—and as Gisevius discovered—he was tired, irritable, and preoccupied. One colleague spoke with masterly understatement of his nerves being "not in a good state."[100] Another summed up the situation by saying that Stauffenberg "had gone down that terrible road in vain."[101]

Yet Stauffenberg was determined that his efforts would not be in vain. On the morning of 20 July 1944, he flew to Rastenburg for the last time. Arriving with his adjutant, Lieutenant Werner von Haeften, he breakfasted in the sunshine beneath an oak tree before proceeding to a preliminary briefing and a meeting with Field Marshal Keitel at 11:30 a.m. There he learned that the conference with Hitler had been brought forward to 12:30 p.m., due to the expected visit of Mussolini that afternoon.

The venue for the conference was to be a briefing room in a long, single-story building located inside the inner perimeter of Wolfschanze. The block, often erroneously described as a wooden hut, was constructed of wood, fiberglass, and plaster with a roof of reinforced concrete resting on brick piers. The briefing room, located at its northeastern end, measured approximately 10 by 4 meters, with a number of windows opening out to the trees and grounds beyond. Inside, it was dominated by a heavy oak conference table, covered with maps, and surrounded by some twenty-five chairs to accommodate Hitler's numerous guests, adjutants, and stenographers.[102]

At 12:25 that afternoon, as Hitler's conference was due to begin, Stauffenberg asked Keitel's adjutant, Major von Freyend, if he might find somewhere to freshen up and change his shirt. He was ushered into Freyend's quarters, where he was joined by his own adjutant, Lieutenant von Haeften, who was naturally required to help the maimed man dress. There the two hastily constructed the bomb. They were hurriedly unwrapping the explosives and setting the fuse when a second adjutant interrupted them, saying that Stauffenberg was required for the briefing. Gruffly, the assassin replied that he was on his way, and left the room. Despite the extreme tension of the moment, most eyewitnesses recalled that he did not betray a trace of nerves.[103] He had, however, committed a grievous error. In his haste, he had had no time to set a fuse in the second slab of explosive. What is more, he had neglected to place the unfused explosive in his briefcase. His bomb, therefore, was only half the bomb that it should have been.

When he reached the conference room, the briefing was already under way: General Heusinger was making a situation report about the Eastern Front. Stauffenberg had requested a seat close to the Führer, as he claimed his hearing was still impaired following the injuries sustained in North Africa. Muttering his apologies, he pushed his way to his seat, with Heusinger and then Hitler to his left and Colonel Brandt, Tresckow's unwitting courier at Smolensk, to his right. His arrival was noticed by another participant, General Walter Warlimont, who would later recall that Stauffenberg appeared to him as

> the classic image of the warrior through all of history. I barely knew him, but as he stood there, one eye covered by a black patch, a maimed arm in an empty uniform sleeve, standing tall and straight, looking directly at Hitler... he was... a proud figure, the very image of the General Staff officer... of that time.[104]

Warlimont had no inkling that the "warrior" before him was about to try to kill his commander in chief.

Stauffenberg placed the briefcase on the floor in front of him, barely a meter from its intended target, and then, almost as soon as he had arrived, muttered something about a phone call and promptly left the room again. This was in itself unremarkable. The participants of Hitler's conferences were constantly coming and going; making telephone calls and fetching maps and documents. It is most unlikely, therefore, that Stauffenberg's sudden departure would have aroused any suspicion. General Heusinger, now twice interrupted, merely continued with his description of the perilous situation facing Army Group North in Russia.[105] It would not be long before he was interrupted again.

At around 12:42, Wolfschanze was shaken by an explosion. As one eyewitness recalled: "In a flash the map room became a scene of stampede and destruction... there was nothing but wounded men groaning, the acrid smell of burning and charred fragments of maps and papers fluttering in the wind."[106] Beyond the immediate vicinity of the map room, however, the explosion raised little more than a few eyebrows. In fact, the sound was not that unusual: weapons were constantly being fired in the area, and flak teams often practiced their drill.[107] One soldier even commented to Stauffenberg himself that it was probably an animal that had strayed into the minefield around the site.[108] This confusion enabled Stauffenberg to make good his escape. Convinced that Hitler had been killed, he bluffed his way past the sentries and hurried to Berlin with Lieutenant von Haeften to take charge of the resultant coup.

It did not take long, however, for word to circulate at Rastenburg that the explosion had not been an exercise or a distant mine. The briefing room had been all but destroyed, its windows and part of the wall blown out. Outside, the grass was littered with burned papers, splinters of wood, and rubble. As the wounded stumbled out, it soon became a makeshift field hospital. Inside the room, chaos reigned. As a cloud of smoke and dust cleared, the grisly scene slowly came into view. The floor had buckled under the force of the blast. The oak table, on which Hitler had been leaning, had been shattered. Everywhere wooden beams had collapsed into the room, bringing the plaster ceiling and partition walls crashing down. Injuries to the briefing participants were numerous. Almost all of them had suffered burst eardrums and concussion. Ten of them were more seriously injured, three of those gravely: General Heusinger's deputy, Colonel Brandt, had lost his left foot; Colonel Schmundt, one of Hitler's senior adjutants, had lost an eye and a leg; and General Korten—who had given Stauffenberg his seat—had been disemboweled. All three would succumb to their injuries. Amid the wounded, one man was already fading: the stenographer Heinrich Berger had lost both legs and lay in a spreading pool of his own blood. He would not last the afternoon.

Hitler found himself in the open doorway. Momentarily deafened and concussed, he was helped to his feet by Keitel and escorted to his bunker, where first aid was administered. He had suffered cuts to his forehead, burns to his right calf and left hand, and severe bruising to his lower right arm. In addition, over a hundred wooden splinters had to be removed from his legs.[109] He was shaken, agitated, and initially less than lucid—complaining that his new trousers had been ruined.[110] Within an hour, however, he had regained his composure. As one of his secretaries described:

> Curiosity drove us to the Führer bunker. I almost laughed
> at the sight of Hitler. He was standing in the little ante-

room, surrounded by several of his adjutants and servants. His hair was never particularly well cut, but now it was standing on end so that he looked like a hedgehog. His black trousers were hanging in strips from his belt, almost like a raffia skirt.... Smiling, he greeted us, "Well, ladies, everything turned out all right."[111]

Hitler's mood, in the aftermath of the attack, can only be described as euphoric. To a horrified Mussolini, he showed off his burns and his tattered clothes and hailed his survival as a "climax."[112] With others, he was less equivocal. One of his doctors recorded that Hitler repeated, over and over, "I am invulnerable, I am immortal."[113]

While Hitler exulted in his own survival, Stauffenberg was en route to Berlin to launch Operation Valkyrie. During the two-hour flight, however, he emerged as the prime suspect in the search for the assassin. As one contemporary recalled, it was not long before Stauffenberg's absence was noted. It was then realized that he had left the situation conference just before the explosion—on the pretense of making a phone call—and had then hurried off without waiting for a connection to be made.[114] Yet when he arrived in the capital that afternoon, shortly before 4:00, Stauffenberg was bemused to find neither friend nor foe there to meet him. Even his driver was absent, and he was forced to make his own way to Home Army Command on the Bendlerstrasse.

On arriving there, supposedly the nerve center of the coup, he was astonished to find only hesitation, inaction, and uncertainty. News from Rastenburg had been vague—a communications blackout had been imposed—and caution had been considered the best policy. Some orders *had* been issued, however. The conspirators had, for example, sent out the alert to implement the official Operation Valkyrie to all regional military commands. They had also attempted to bring loyal, or at least compliant, troops into the capital. But, in the flurry of rumor and counter-rumor, this had proved woefully insufficient. By the time that communications to

Hitler's headquarters were restored, at around 3 p.m., precious hours had already been lost. From then on, the Valkyrie orders of the conspirators would be followed everywhere by counterorders from the Führer and the high command:

Radio Message
The Führer is alive! In perfect health!
Reichsführer-SS C-in-C Replacement Army. Only his orders valid. Orders from General Fromm, Field Marshal von Witzleben and Colonel-General Hoepner not to be executed!
Maintain contact with *Gauleiter* and Senior SS and Police Commander![115]

Stauffenberg galvanized the plotters temporarily, issuing a flurry of instructions and harrying and cajoling by telephone. He also gave the first account of Hitler's death, claiming that he had seen the Führer's body being carried away and confessing that he himself had planted the bomb. "No one who was in that room," he asserted optimistically, "can still be alive."[116] Nonetheless, the mood among the conspirators in the Bendlerstrasse was worsening. Some, even several of those who were central to the plot, were already wavering, hedging their bets and seeking a way out of the impasse. By late afternoon, Stieff was informing on his erstwhile colleagues.[117] General Olbricht, too, was losing the stomach for the fight and was hesitating to draw soldiers into the insurrection that were not already compromised.[118]

Not far away, meanwhile, at Goebbels's Propaganda Ministry, a loyalist stronghold was forming. Though surrounded by troops obeying the Valkyrie order, Goebbels telephoned all and sundry to try to find out the truth about the attack at Rastenburg and to make sense of events in Berlin. At around 5 p.m., he finally made contact with Hitler, who informed him that a full-scale military putsch was under way. His first action was to summon Major Otto Remer, whose troops had surrounded the area under orders from the plotters in the Bendlerstrasse. Remer, a convinced National Socialist, had been told that Hitler was dead and that the SS was mounting a coup. His orders were to cordon off the government quarter and arrest a number of prominent Nazis, including Goebbels. The propaganda minister coolly countered that Hitler was alive—and, to prove the point, telephoned him at Rastenburg. When Remer took the receiver and heard Hitler's voice, he immediately and involuntarily snapped to attention. Hitler asked him if he recognized his voice. *"Jawohl, mein Führer"* came the reply. He went on: "I order you to seal off the government quarter and to crush any resistance with all means necessary. Every man who is not for me, is to be destroyed. Do you understand?" Remer replied once again: *"Jawohl, mein Führer."*[119] The tide was turning.

By 6:30 p.m., when Goebbels gave a radio broadcast confirming Hitler's survival, the putsch was already unraveling. As word spread that Hitler was alive, troops who had unwittingly served the conspiracy by moving into their Valkyrie positions in and around Berlin began to disperse. In the provinces, the official denial often arrived before the Valkyrie order, thereby sowing little but confusion and bemusement. In the few cities where the military had tentatively risen in sympathy with the coup—such as Paris and Vienna—order was restored with comparative ease. By midevening all that was left of the coup, in practical terms, was the Ministry on the Bendlerstrasse. Soon after nightfall, the building was ringed by SS troops and bathed in the stark glare of countless searchlights.[120]

Inside, the conspiracy had descended into acrimony. Field Marshal von Witzleben, foreseen by the rebels as the new commander in chief, had already left for home, declaring the coup to be "a fine mess."[121] Olbricht was also looking for a way out, asking Gisevius whether it wasn't too late for them to "call it all off."[122] As the evening wore on, some staff officers within the Bendlerstrasse who had not been privy to the plot decided to make a display of loyalty to Hitler. After confronting Olbricht, they armed themselves and demanded to see General Fromm, whom the conspirators had locked in his office earlier that day. In the ensuing melee, Stauffenberg was shot in the shoulder. With his conspiracy patently collapsing around him, he complained to a secretary, "They've all left me in the lurch."[123]

Some time later, Fromm was released from his confinement and returned to confront the conspirators. "Well, gentlemen," he began, "now I am going to do to you what you wanted to do to me this afternoon."[124] He declared them under arrest on a charge of high treason and demanded their weapons. General Beck asked to be allowed to keep his pistol "for his private use" and was brusquely urged to "do so at once."[125] The others were granted a few minutes to write their testimonies, statements, and last letters. Fromm then returned, declaring that a court-martial called "in the name of the Führer" had found them guilty as charged and condemned them to death. As the four conspirators were led out of the room, Beck made the first of his two botched attempts to shoot himself in the head. The aged general would later be dispatched by a sergeant.

Around midnight, in the courtyard of the Bendlerstrasse, the four men—Stauffenberg, Haeften, Olbricht, and Mertz von Quirnheim (Fromm's former chief of staff)—were led before a pile of building sand. There, illuminated by the headlights of the army motor pool, they faced a ten-man firing squad from the *Grossdeutschland* Guard Battalion. One by one, without ceremony, the four were shot. The only comment came when Stauffenberg was pushed in front of his executioners. As the shots rang out, he shouted, "Long live holy Germany!"[126]

In the aftermath, Hitler's Germany wrought its bloody revenge on Stauffenberg's Germany. It has been estimated that more than seven thousand arrests ensued, as those interrogated implicated a wider and wider circle of conspirators, plotters, and passive opponents of the regime. Even the families of those arrested were not spared, as their wives and children were consigned to the concentration camps for so-called *Sippenhaft,* or kin detention. Few of those directly implicated were spared. The vast majority of the remaining conspirators were hauled before the Nazi "People's

Court," headed by the screeching senior judge Roland Friesler. There they would be berated, abused, found guilty, and then invariably sentenced to death. Field Marshal von Witzleben, for instance, was hanged from a meat hook in Berlin's Plötzensee Prison, his death throes filmed for Hitler's viewing pleasure. Colonel Stieff suffered the same fate. Even General Fromm, whose actions had crushed the coup, was considered to have been complicit in it and was executed for cowardice in March 1945.

Tresckow, meanwhile, though somewhat remote from the epicenter of Stauffenberg's attack, was nonetheless well aware that his earlier efforts to mobilize the resistance and target Hitler were bound to come to light during the arrests and interrogations that followed. With his trademark resolve, he opted to take his own life. On the morning of 21 July, he met with his adjutant, Schlabrendorff, for the last time. He said:

> Now they will all fall upon us and cover us with abuse. But I am convinced, now as much as ever, that we have done the right thing. I believe Hitler to be the archenemy, not only of Germany, but indeed of the entire world. In a few hours' time, I shall stand before God and answer for both my actions and the things I neglected to do. I think I can, with a clear conscience, stand by all I have done in the battle against Hitler.[127]

With that, he asked his driver to take him to the front, where he wandered into no-man's-land. There, he simulated an exchange of fire with an unseen enemy, held a grenade to his head, and detonated it.[128] The official Wehrmacht report noted that "Major-General von Tresckow died a hero's death fighting in the front line."[129] Sadly, however, Tresckow's elaborate suicide did not save his family from persecution; his wife, Erika, endured seven weeks of Gestapo interrogation. Nor did it enable him to rest in peace. Though buried with full military honors, his body would be exhumed when his role in the conspiracy became known. It would be taken to Sachsenhausen concentration camp and incinerated.

Remarkably, one of the few conspirators to survive the frenzied bloodletting of that autumn was Tresckow's cousin and aide-de-camp, Fabian von Schlabrendorff. Despite interrogation and bestial torture—which even induced a heart attack—he stubbornly denied complicity and feigned ignorance of the activities of his fellow plotters.[130] Finally, at the limit of his endurance, he admitted to knowledge of Tresckow's plotting, but nothing more. Though tried before the People's Court, he was, surprisingly, acquitted on the technicality that his testimony had been extracted by the use of illegal torture methods. Nonetheless, still under suspicion and effectively under a death sentence, he was taken to the Flossenbürg concentration camp, where Oster and Canaris had been hanged some days before, then to Dachau, and then on an SS death march into Austria. Improbably, he survived it all and was liberated by American troops in early May 1945.

Schlabrendorff's resilience undoubtedly saved not only his own life but also those of a number of his former co-conspirators, including three of Hitler's would-be assassins. Axel von dem Bussche was in the infirmary at Hohenlychen in the summer of 1944, recuperating from the injuries received six months earlier on the Eastern Front. Bizarrely, he still had some parts of his bomb, kept in an old suitcase next to his hospital bed. When news of Stauffenberg's assassination attempt broke, he expected the worst and persuaded a colleague to dispose of them.[131] His role as a "model assassin" was not divulged, however, until after the war.

Rudolf-Christoph von Gersdorff, meanwhile, was serving in Normandy in the summer of 1944, as chief of staff to the 82nd Army Corps. That August, he was awarded the prestigious Knight's Cross for his actions in the Battle of the Falaise Gap. He, too, was never denounced as a would-be assassin, and his role in the Berlin Armory attempt emerged only with the postwar publication of his memoirs. Lastly, Eberhard von Breitenbuch, who had volunteered to shoot Hitler at Berchtesgaden, also escaped implication in July 1944. As a visitor to Hitler's bunker in the last weeks of the war, he would be a witness to the very death throes of Nazism that he had hoped to bring about a year earlier.[132]

All three—Bussche, Gersdorff, and Breitenbuch—would outlive their intended target by several decades.

One former assassin who was less fortunate was Georg von Boeselager. Though he avoided denunciation in the aftermath of Stauffenberg's attack, he could not avoid the attentions of the Red Army. In late August 1944, he was killed in a Soviet ambush while leading a cavalry brigade in defensive operations near the town of Łomza in northeastern Poland. Posthumously promoted to the rank of colonel, he was awarded the Oak Leaves and Swords to the Knight's Cross. He was twenty-eight.

Another whose plottings were not revealed was Hubert Lanz. Indeed, Lanz was to gain a quite different reputation. Despite falling into disgrace by disobeying Hitler at Kharkhov, he soon returned to the front, and in September 1943 was in command of the 22nd Army Mountain Corps in Greece. There, some of his troops were responsible for the massacre on the island of Cephalonia—made famous by the novel *Captain Corelli's Mandolin*—in which more than five thousand Italian soldiers were gunned down.[133] For his role as commanding officer, Lanz was convicted of crimes against humanity and sentenced to twelve years' imprisonment. Clearly the moral outrage he felt on being ordered to send his own troops to certain death in Kharkhov did not recur when he was ordered to massacre his erstwhile Italian allies.

The German military resistance existed in an extremely difficult environment. Not only was it plotting against the head of a well-organized police state, but it was doing so during a war in which the nation's very survival appeared to be at stake. Moreover, it was operating from within a culture that stressed honor, duty, and strict obedience to authority above all else. In this harsh terrain, it is perhaps surprising that its treacherous, if high-minded, notions took root at all.

There were further handicaps. Most of the plotters were far from revolutionary in their political outlook. Indeed, many of them had welcomed the early years of Hitler's rule, bringing as it did a German renaissance on the political stage and an expunging of the stigma of Versailles. Even Stauffenberg had been "enthusiastic" about Hitler's appointment in 1933 and had quite naturally and wholeheartedly supported the policies of rearmament and the expansion of the military.[134]

Perhaps because of this ambivalence, some elements of the resistance held a wildly unrealistic vision of what could be salvaged from the wreckage of Nazism. One extreme was demonstrated by Carl Goerdeler, one of the leading lights of the civilian resistance and the prospective post-coup chancellor. He envisaged a postwar Germany within the frontiers of 1914, with the addition of Austria, the Sudetenland, and a "modified" Polish Corridor.[135] Not only did he hope to turn the clock back to 1938–39, therefore, he even aspired to wish away the German defeat in World War I as well. Others, though more realistic, nonetheless shared some of Goerdeler's profound misconceptions. The socialist Julius Leber, for example, accepted the probable cession of East Prussia, the Sudetenland, and even his own native Alsace as inevitable. But he never abandoned hope of finding an honorable peace by which something of Germany could be saved.[136] Clearly, some among the resistance had not fully thought through the consequences of the Allied doctrine of unconditional surrender.

At heart, therefore, the plotters of the German resistance were conservative and patriotic, and though it had been these noble sentiments that had driven them to resist, those same sentiments had also to some extent clouded their worldview, and crucially had deterred them from striking unless order and continuity of government could be ensured. Thus, they were effectively seeking to achieve the nearly impossible. They wanted a surgical excision of Hitler as head of state without provoking a wider political and military collapse and while simultaneously preserving many of the benefits that their target had brought.

Inevitably, perhaps, they failed. The would-be assassins raised by Henning von Tresckow were foiled by a combination of Hitler's security measures, their target's capricious, unpredictable nature, and, crucially, their own bad luck. Stauffenberg's attack, meanwhile, in coming to fruition, allowed a number of other deeper failings to come to light. His first mistake, of course, was his failure to kill Hitler on that hot summer's day in Rastenburg. Many reasons have been put forward for this. It is often suggested that Stauffenberg's briefcase was inadvertently moved to the far side of the heavy oak table support, thereby shielding its target from its full force.[137] This was disputed, not least by Colonel Brandt, who was alleged to have moved it.[138] Others suggest that had the briefing taken place in one of Rastenburg's concrete bunkers, rather than a less substantial briefing room, then the blast would have had more concentrated, and lethal, effects.[139] While both these factors may well be important, Stauffenberg's most crucial mistake was surely his failure to fuse the second explosive charge, or at least to place it unfused in his briefcase. Numerous historians and experts have argued that, had that second charge been included, no one in the briefing room would have survived.[140] In that instance, the exact position of the bomb or the construction of the room would have mattered little.

Despite having failed to kill Hitler, the conspiracy as a whole was not necessarily doomed to failure. However, in reality, the entire Valkyrie plan was predicated upon Stauffenberg's mission being successful. There was no Plan B. This aspect explains, in part at least, the failings of the plotters in the Bendlerstrasse. While waiting for confirmation of Hitler's death, they wasted fully four precious hours that might otherwise have swung events in their favor. Their apparent timidity and lack of ruthlessness might also be seen as evidence that they already considered themselves to have failed. They hesitated to occupy the radio stations and only halfheartedly sought to neutralize their opponents. When Gisevius demanded some action and suggested the elimination of Goebbels, for example, he was given short shrift.[141] Schlabrendorff, though less of a hothead, would have agreed. In retrospect, he conceded: "Blood should have run. Instead the men of 20 July said to all and sundry: Have a seat."[142]

Some, in their critique of the conspirators, have gone further. One author dismissed the men around Stauffenberg as "dilettantes," outlining their failings as assassins despite their being "professional soldiers...[and] General Staff officers who had been trained in handling weapons...and knew the tools of the soldier's trade."[143] This is harsh, but there *is* something in it. Stauffenberg, for example, was an experienced soldier and (as all are agreed) a man of tremendous ability and intelligence. Yet, maimed as he was, he lacked the dexterity necessary for the task and, in the heat of the moment, failed to construct his bomb correctly. Moreover, he might have spared himself some stress and uncertainty if he had employed one of the more reliable fuses, such as the L-delay fuse, that were then available. Gersdorff, too, was forced to use an unsuitable fuse when the resistance was unable to supply him with anything more appropriate.[144] The bravery and moral integrity of these men are incontrovertible, but perhaps their abilities in the nefarious business of assassination were more questionable.

Predictably, perhaps, Goebbels's verdict on the plotters was also damning. He told Speer:

> If they hadn't been so clumsy! They had an enormous chance. What dolts! What childishness! When I think how I would have handled such a thing. Why didn't they occupy the radio station and spread the wildest lies? Here they put guards in front of my door. But they let me go right ahead and telephone the Führer, mobilize everything! They didn't even silence my telephone. To hold so many trump cards and botch it—what beginners![145]

If one is honest, it is hard to disagree with that assessment. It would appear to be a cruel paradox that the plotters' excessive reliance on obedience and legality was to be their downfall. One could say that they sought less to seize power than to inherit it by assassination.

It is, of course, an open question whether Stauffenberg's assassination of Hitler would, if successful, have resulted in the downfall of the Nazi regime at all. Some contemporaries were very positive and believed that the war would have come to an end. Hitler's secretary was one. She recalled her feelings in the aftermath of the bomb plot:

I don't know what would have happened if the assassination had succeeded. All I see is millions of soldiers now lying buried somewhere, gone forever, who might instead have come home again, their guns silent and the sky quieter once more. The war would have been over.[146]

This assumption has persisted into our own era. A recent television documentary, for example, calculated that over ten million soldiers and civilians died in Europe in the ten months from Stauffenberg's attempt in July 1944 to the final German surrender the following May.[147] The subtext is unspoken but nonetheless clear: these are lives that would have been saved had Stauffenberg succeeded.

However, a note of caution and indeed realism should be sounded. Even if the plotters had enjoyed better luck, had succeeded in murdering Hitler, *and* had prosecuted their coup with more vigor, it is far from clear that they would have achieved their wider aim. They enjoyed precious little popular support and even less international sympathy, and they still had to face down the massed ranks of the Gestapo and SS, as well as countless ordinary Germans who still felt bound by their oath of loyalty. One could conclude that even if their military collaborators had succeeded in rousing their troops for a showdown with Nazism, the best that the resistance might have expected was a bitter and bloody civil war. An early end to the battles then raging on the front lines was a pipe dream.

The fact that the resistance ultimately failed, however, should not blind us to the nobility of their cause. Without exception, they were motivated not by ambition, vainglory, or any craven fear of defeat. Rather they were inspired to act by their revulsion at the atrocities being committed in Germany's name. When they finally made their attack on 20 July, they did so not only to kill Hitler and strike a blow against Nazism but also, as Tresckow acknowledged, to demonstrate to the world that another, nobler Germany still existed. They were committing high treason for the sake of German honor.

In Stauffenberg, they found a leader of exemplary vigor,

dynamism, and moral force. Arguably, he drove the resistance to its bloody conclusion on 20 July after its previous efforts had come to naught. Without him, it has been suggested, it is unlikely that the attempt would have been made at all.[148] Understandably, therefore, that tall, elegant officer, with his eye patch, maimed arm, and penchant for poetry, has attracted all the plaudits and most of the attention. But, as we have seen, he did not and indeed could not act alone.

Space in the pantheon of the German resistance should therefore be made for the other assassins who, prior to Stauffenberg, sought to target Hitler. Gersdorff, Bussche, and Breitenbuch all ran the same risks as Stauffenberg and were driven by the same moral outrage, but they have been largely forgotten by history. Given that they did not enjoy the access to Hitler of their more illustrious colleague, their opportunities were more fleeting, but they were arguably no less significant. Crucially, they did not expect to leave the scene of their attack alive. As one of their number noted many years later and with some regret, "Our only fault is to have survived."[149]

Another of Stauffenberg's confederates who deserves special praise is Henning von Tresckow. Tresckow was the original *spiritus movens* of the German resistance. Despite being a graduate of the same conservative nationalist milieu that had nurtured Nazism, he recognized the criminal nature of the regime with absolute clarity. In 1938, for example, when Stauffenberg disapproved of the nascent resistance movement,[150] Tresckow was already advocating Hitler's removal, with violence if necessary.[151] He went on to organize three attempts on Hitler's life and formed his staff headquarters into a vital cell of the military resistance. To fellow conspirators he was calm and confident: an "extraordinarily strong personality," wrote one, "who combined military ability with an exceptional political spirit."[152] Most importantly, Tresckow had the gift of persuasion. As Eberhard von Breitenbuch wrote of him: "I have never met someone [like Tresckow], who was able, clearly and soberly, to convince his listeners of his opinion and to inspire them by his inner calm and his belief in his task."[153] In retrospect, it is hard to imagine

Stauffenberg operating as he did, and coming so close to achieving his goal, without the essential practical and psychological preparation that had been done by Tresckow.

The military resistance is often viewed, in the popular mind at least, as a Johnny-come-lately, stung into action by the fear of defeat when the war on the Eastern Front turned against Germany. However, the experiences that drove Tresckow and his confederates to resist show beyond all doubt that the road to Rastenburg did not begin at Stalingrad; it had begun at Dubno and a thousand other sites like it. The men of the resistance recognized Hitler's bestial racial war for the crime that it was, and were resolved to act—if not to end it, then at the very least to testify that not all Germans had lost their moral compass. Despite their failure, they personified all that was best of Germany.

CHAPTER 8

Revolt of the Acolyte: Albert Speer

I came to the decision to eliminate Hitler.... I, who had once wanted nothing more than to be Hitler's master-builder, ... was thinking how to obtain poison gas to destroy the man.

—ALBERT SPEER[1]

THE GERMAN CITY OF BRESLAU WAS ONCE DESCRIBED AS "the flower of Europe."[2] Straddling the river Oder in the eastern province of Silesia, it had grown rich on trade and religious patronage, and by the Middle Ages it was already one of the largest cities of northern Europe. Its wealth had manifested itself primarily in a frenzy of construction. In the city's spiritual heart, on the islands that broke the river's flow, a series of impressive brick Gothic churches were built, including the twin-spired Cathedral of St. John the Baptist, which dated from the mid-thirteenth century. The city's mercantile center, the main square or *Ring,* was adorned with a number of huge patrician houses and, most impressively, the enormous town hall, a riot of Gothic gables, gargoyles, and spires.

After centuries of urban growth and development, Breslau by the early twentieth century had a population of over six hundred thousand. The largest German city east of Berlin, it boasted all the accoutrements of the modern metropolis: parks, museums, theaters, cinemas, an opera, and a university. Its academic alumni boasted a number of Nobel laureates, including the chemist Fritz Haber and the historian Theodor Mommsen. It also served as the administrative and industrial hub for the surrounding province. In addition to all that, Breslau was home to a Jewish community of exceptional dynamism.

By early 1945, Breslau was still virtually untouched by the ravages of war. Located beyond the range of all but the most determined Allied aircraft, it had escaped serious material damage and had earned a reputation as "the Air-raid shelter of the Reich." Accordingly, it had attracted numerous additional industrial concerns and administrative offices, swelling its population beyond a million. And though its male contingent had been decimated by five years of fighting and its Jewish community had been exterminated or forced into exile, little else in the city betrayed the horrors then commonplace elsewhere in Europe.

In February of that year, however, all that was to change. When the Soviets launched their renewed offensive from the Vistula bridgeheads on 12 January, Breslau became the target of the 1st Ukrainian Front. As the Soviet vanguard raced across the still-frozen earth of Poland, the Germans fell back in disarray and town after town was liberated. Within a couple of weeks the Silesian frontier was reached. Soon after that, on St. Valentine's Day, Breslau found itself encircled.

The city had had some months to prepare for the expected siege. Despite lacking any natural or man-made fortifications, it had been declared a *Festung* or "fortress" late in 1944. Like its neighbors across eastern Germany, it was to be reinforced and defended to the last man. Cadres of *Volkssturm* militia were raised, the city garrison was reinforced, and concentric lines of defense were created on the outskirts. In late January, an improvised and hopelessly ambitious evacuation of the civilian population was attempted. Already on the fourteenth of that month, as news of the renewed Soviet advance reached the city, thousands of civilians had swamped the railheads. They were not permitted to leave until the morning of the twentieth and then only in prescribed groups. First came the women and children. In desperation, and in temperatures of -10°C, some sixty thousand left on foot. The following morning, four hundred bodies were recovered and buried in the city's parks. Countless more littered the roads to the south and west. Over the following days, the process was repeated again and again, as successive sections of the population were ordered to leave. It is estimated that in the initial evacuation a total of eighteen thousand individuals, mainly the very young and the infirm, fell victim to exposure.[3] In all, some ninety thousand civilians were to perish trying to leave Breslau.

Inside the city, meanwhile, the Nazi administration was showing its teeth. The two hundred thousand or so civilians who remained were terrorized and went in fear of the hated military police. Labor battalions, formed to build the barricades, were often subjected to military discipline. Deserters, shirkers, and those simply lacking the right documents were shot out of hand. On one day, a group of thirty-six foreign women, probably forced laborers, was executed.[4] Even the city's deputy mayor became a victim, shot on the main square for cowardice after he had taken his wife and children to the comparative safety of Berlin. As one memoirist recalled: "It was getting more and more dangerous in Breslau, not because of the Russians, but because of our own people."[5] Some sought refuge in suicide. Over one ten-day period in a single district, more than sixty cases were reported. In one example, a number of families were found huddled around the stoves in their apartment block. They had gassed themselves.[6]

The preparations for Breslau's defense demonstrated outright contempt for the fabric of the old city. Nothing was considered sacred. Church spires were transformed into machine-gun nests and the numerous bridges over the river were wired with explosive charges. Flak and artillery batteries were established in the parks and cemeteries, as well as in the botanical gardens and even in the grounds of the archbishop's palace. In the southern suburbs, where the Soviet attack was expected, entire residential blocks were razed to provide material for the barricades and to clear a field of fire for the defenders.[7] The task of clearing the condemned buildings was carried out by squads of pioneers, who brusquely informed the inhabitants of their forced eviction and then proceeded to hurl everything they could out of the windows before setting off dynamite in the basements.

As the Soviet noose tightened, the wanton destruction in the city plumbed new depths. In March, the elegant Kaiserstrasse in the northern suburbs was sacrificed to make way for an airstrip. The street, lined with expensive villas, administrative buildings, and three churches, was cleared and then systematically razed with explosives. In the aftermath, as teams of forced laborers were brought in to clear the rubble, thirteen hundred of them were killed by enemy artillery and strafing attacks.[8]

The architect of this insanity was Karl Hanke. A former teacher and early adherent of the Nazi cause, Hanke was very well connected, having served for many years as Goebbels's secretary and being close friends with Albert Speer. In 1941, after a spell as a frontline soldier, he had been promoted to the post of *Gauleiter* of Silesia, with his headquarters in Breslau. As the war neared its end in the spring of 1945, he emerged as one of Hitler's most loyal servants, sharing the delusions, parroting the latest slogans, and ruling his city with an iron hand. When visited by Speer just before the siege began, Hanke was merciless. Walking through his own residence—an elegant eighteenth-century palace—he said: "The Russians will never get their hands on this. . . . I'd rather burn it down."[9] When Speer protested and tried to talk him out of his vandalism, Hanke confessed that he "didn't give a damn" about the city. His propaganda line was similarly unequivocal. Breslau was to be defended to the last man and to the last bullet. "Those who fear an honorable death," he said, "will die in disgrace."[10] Yet, far from being viewed as a fanatic or a renegade, Hanke was officially lauded as a shining example to the rest of Germany. A Berlin radio broadcast on 14 April, for example, took a swipe at the "defeatists" and bemoaned the fact that "men like *Gauleiter* Hanke are lacking in the west."[11]

Under Hanke's leadership, Breslau stood firm against the Soviet onslaught. German forces defended doggedly as the fighting progressed from street to street, block to block, even room to room. They scored a number of minor successes, retaking some Soviet positions and tying down large numbers of tanks and infantry. Yet, though they could hold the front line, they were powerless to defend Breslau from air and artillery attack. As the siege progressed, the city was pounded into submission as wave after wave of fighter-bombers circled unhindered above and the distant artillery found its range. At its peak, over the Easter weekend, the bombardment made life aboveground all but impossible. The few civilians who were not already living in their cellars were soon forced underground. The German military commandant was even obliged to abandon his bunker.[12]

By the time Hanke fled and Breslau finally succumbed—four days *after* Berlin—the city had been transformed into a moonscape of ash, rubble, and shell holes. Almost all of its churches had suffered extensive damage; many were burned out. Countless university and municipal buildings had been destroyed, including the university library. Elsewhere, it was estimated that some twenty thousand houses had been razed, and more than 70 percent of the city as a whole had been destroyed.[13] As one man recorded, few districts escaped damage:

> I went over the piles of rubble toward the Kaiser Bridge. Everything destroyed. Garve Street to Stanetzski Street: ruins; Mauritz Square: ruins; Brother's Monastery: badly damaged; Brother's Street: largely burned out; Tauentzien Street, completely burnt out; my son's house ... burnt out down to the cellar. Not even a plank, just black walls.[14]

The human toll was no less shocking. Though exact figures will never be known, it is estimated that German military casualties approached thirty thousand, with around six thousand killed, while Soviet casualties reached sixty-five thousand.[15] Breslau's civilian deaths are thought to range between ten thousand and eighty thousand, with upward of three thousand suicides.[16]

The destruction of Breslau did, of course, have some military and political rationale. With his armies fighting on a much-reduced front, and with shortened lines of communication, Hitler could have had some genuine reasons for optimism in 1945, especially as he was facing an enemy that was now overstretched. His "fortress" order, therefore, foresaw the cities of the east as bulwarks against the Soviet tide. At best they would serve as the platforms for a German counterattack, and at worst they would be sacrificed to give Berlin breathing space to continue the fight. Moreover, the Germans and Soviets were locked in a bitter ideological struggle in which no quarter was expected and none would be given. German civilians in 1945 were reaping the whirlwind of destruction and brutality that their own soldiers had sown abroad. Now that they were defending their own towns, their own streets, and their own homes, they could scarcely be expected to surrender meekly.

And yet there was something more sinister to the exhortations to hold out and resist that emanated from Berlin. As one Breslau diarist noted with chilling accuracy: "They are not waging war against the enemy, they are waging war against their own people, against everything that is dear to them."[17] Had he known the truth, he scarcely would have believed it. On 19 March 1945, Hitler had issued his so-called Nero Order. Following a preamble stressing the exploitation of every means with which to combat the enemy, he ordered:

> All military transport, and communication facilities, industrial establishments and supply depots, as well as anything else of value within Reich territory, which could in any way be used by the enemy immediately or within the foreseeable future for the prosecution of the war, will be destroyed.[18]

Though it was couched in rational, military-strategic terms, the message of the Nero Order was brutally plain: nothing but scorched earth would be left for the invaders—or the survivors. As the inhabitants of Breslau would testify, Germany itself was to be destroyed.

· · ·

Hitler's will to destroy provides one of the most grimly fascinating episodes of the Second World War. It had first been foreshadowed late in 1941, when the Führer had prophesied:

> If one day the German nation is no longer sufficiently strong or sufficiently ready for sacrifice to stake its blood on its existence, then let it perish and be annihilated by some other stronger power...I shall shed no tears for the German nation.[19]

Considering that this statement was made at a time when German armies were still all-conquering and the specter of defeat had barely raised its head, it is tempting to dismiss it as mere bluster, uttered to shock or provoke a compliant entourage. However, by the late summer of 1944, when defeat was looming large for all those in Germany with eyes to see, Hitler's determination to usher in the disaster of total collapse was undiminished. His prophecy of 1941 was fast becoming a reality.

The first concrete demonstration of the scorched-earth policy came in July 1944, when the destruction was ordered of all war industries in France and the Low Countries. At a time when German armies were desperately trying to prevent the Allied breakout from Normandy, precious manpower was to be diverted to the sabotage and demolition of coal and mineral mines, power plants, and industrial premises. Though this decree was largely honored in the breach, it was soon extended elsewhere—to Italy, Hungary, the Balkans, and finally Germany proper. Later that year, Hitler boasted that "no city will be left in the enemy's hands until it is a heap of ruins."[20]

By the spring of 1945, the measures had been intensified. Though the failed Ardennes offensive had spent what remained of Germany's military reserves and defeat was only a matter of time, Hitler was still adamant that he would not capitulate. "Surrender is absolutely out of the question," he raged, warning: "We will leave nothing but a desert for the Americans, English and Russians."[21] Accordingly, all essential infrastructure—railway tracks, canals, telephone lines, and bridges—was slated for destruction. As Goebbels stated ominously: "If we go down, then the German people will go down with us."[22]

Hitler's armaments minister, Albert Speer, drew a stark image of what the scorched-earth edict could mean if it were followed to the letter:

> No German was to inhabit territory occupied by the enemy. Those wretches who did remain would find themselves in a desert devoid of all the amenities of civilisation. Not only the industrial plants and not only the gas, water, electrical works and telephone exchanges were to be completely smashed. Everything, simply everything essential to the maintenance of life would be destroyed: the ration card records, the files of marriage and resident registries, the records of bank accounts. In addition, food supplies were to be destroyed, farms burned down and cattle killed. Not even those works of art that bombs had spared were to be preserved. Monuments, palaces, castles and churches, theatres and opera houses were also to be levelled.[23]

The view of the aftermath presented by Hitler's own propaganda machine was scarcely more comforting. "Not a German stalk of wheat is to feed the enemy," one newspaper editorial warned, "not a German mouth to give him information, not a German hand to offer him help. He is to find every footbridge destroyed, every road blocked—nothing but death, annihilation and hatred will meet him."[24]

The roots of this destructive urge have been much discussed. On one level, perhaps, Hitler was still trying to expunge the memory of the ignominious end to the First World War. His fanatical resistance in 1945 was, in part at least, a replaying of the defeat of 1918. His exhortations to hold out might be seen as a stratagem to avoid the shame of another "stab in the back." As the historian Sebastian Haffner wrote:

[Hitler's] determination never again to allow a November 1918 to happen was the main impulse that drove him to become a politician. Now [in 1945], in a sense, Hitler had reached his original goal: another November 1918 was just around the corner, and Hitler this time was in a position to prevent it. He was determined to do just that.[25]

There is certainly something in this. But there are also other factors that contributed to Hitler's self-destructive mind-set in 1945. His nihilism was undoubtedly influential. But so, too, were his psychopathic and misanthropic tendencies, which, though always present, naturally came to the fore when disaster loomed. Mankind, he once stated, was nothing but a "ridiculous 'cosmic bacterium.' "[26] Man's suffering was nothing to him. He never visited the injured in hospitals, never toured the bombed-out cities, and never ventured into a concentration camp. His world consisted of enemies to be annihilated and allies to be exploited. There was precious little in between.

But these influences also fed into other, more complex belief systems. First, there was the "Valhalla mentality." According to Nordic mythology, the end of the world would come when the gods confronted their enemies, approaching from all quarters, and died a hero's death defying them. Thereafter, it was held that the sun would darken, the stars vanish, and the earth would sink into the sea. Though obscure, these myths had been popularized in Germany by the work of the composer Richard Wagner and had been successfully woven into the German nationalist psyche. They were frequently invoked by the Nazi élite: Göring, for example, recalled the related Germanic legend of deceit and slaughter by referring to Germany as "the Hall of the Nibelungs, built of fire and blood."[27] Hitler, too, was no less of an aficionado, being a regular visitor to the Wagner Festival at Bayreuth and an avid collector of original Wagner scores.[28] He clearly viewed the composer's opus almost as an ersatz religion.

But it appears that this interest went far beyond mere fashion or cultural curiosity. Some actually appeared to believe it. In the final days of the Reich, in April 1945, Gerda Bormann wrote to her husband in the Chancellery, describing how Germany's predicament reminded her of *Götterdämmerung*, the "twilight of the gods." "The Giants and the Dwarfs," she wrote,

> the wolf Fenris and the snake Mitgard, all the powers of evil . . . are storming over the bridge of the gods. . . . The citadel is tottering and all seems lost. But suddenly a new citadel rises, more beautiful than the one before, and Baldur lives again.[29]

Such was the mythological twaddle that sustained many of the leaders of the Third Reich in their final days.

Second, and perhaps most important, there was Social Darwinism. As is well known, Hitler viewed human existence as an exercise in the survival of the fittest. Naturally, he extended that concept to apply to nations as well. Thus, Germany was involved in a "fight for life," not only with its own internal "bacillus"—the Jews—but also with the other perceived lesser races of Europe. This struggle necessitated not only the thoroughgoing extermination of racial enemies but also the careful nurturing of the "best" of the German race, hence the bizarre reliance on pseudo-science, eugenics, and SS "breeding" programs.

The dark corollary to this racist claptrap was that the German race was constantly testing itself in warfare with its rivals. Hitler could encourage and cajole and, he thought, get the best out of them, but if they should fail, the laws of Social Darwinism were unequivocal—like their earlier victims, they would be scheduled for destruction. On this point, Hitler was merciless. "If the German people should lose the war," he once said, "then it would indicate that it did not possess the internal value that had been attributed to it, and [I] would have no sympathy with [it]."[30] On another occasion, his message was bleaker still:

> If the war is lost then the nation will be lost also. There is no need to show any consideration for the foundations which the German nation needs for its most primitive survival. On the contrary, it is better to destroy those things

ourselves. Because this nation has shown itself the weaker, and the future belongs exclusively to the stronger nation from the East. In any event, what remains after this struggle are only the inferior, for the good have died in battle.[31]

By 1945, therefore, Germany's "fight for life" had been lost, and—in Hitler's view at least—Germany did not deserve to survive.

Naturally, there were many—even among hardened Nazis—who disagreed with this worldview. Göring was said to have found it "disappointing,"[32] while Goebbels, usually Hitler's most rabid cheerleader, bemoaned the "totally mistaken assumptions" that had brought it about.[33] One of its more vociferous opponents, however, was the then minister for armaments, Albert Speer.

Speer had begun his career as an architect. As a student in Berlin in 1930, he had been inspired by hearing Hitler speak and had applied to join the Nazi Party. Within two years, he had made the acquaintance of Karl Hanke, then the party head of the Berlin West district, and had begun to get his first commissions. His organizational and architectural talents were soon noticed, and in 1933 he was given responsibility for the planning of Nazi events. Thereafter he moved swiftly into Hitler's inner circle, his path smoothed by Hitler's love of architecture and his own successful completion of numerous high-profile commissions, including the new Reich Chancellery in Berlin and the party rally grounds at Nuremberg.

Yet despite his closeness to the epicenter of power in the Third Reich, and his personal affection and admiration for Hitler, Speer denied that he had ever been a convinced National Socialist. By 1940, he claimed already to have identified the dark heart of Nazism, its "boastful arrogance, its greed and the excesses of the bad winner."[34] For this reason, he always sought to keep the party at arm's length and even refused an honorary rank in the SS. As court architect, he would stress, his role was a nonpolitical one. His was not the world of the concentration camps, the forced laborers, and the crude ideology of race—he was a manager, a technocrat, and an artist. If he did not personally take part in such abominations, he thought, he could escape implication in them. It was a façade that he would seek to maintain for many years.

In 1942, however, the halcyon days of the court architect came to an end. Thanks to his managerial skills—and the mysterious death of his predecessor—Speer was appointed minister for armaments, with the unenviable task of shifting German industry onto a total-war footing. Despite the disruption caused by Allied bombing and domestic labor shortages, he presided over an impressive rise in production, reaching a peak in 1944.

By that time, however—for all his successes—Speer had already passed the zenith of his career. His stark, unglossed view of Germany's predicament had ruffled feathers and he now found himself viewed with suspicion by the SS and out of favor with Hitler. He was intrigued against, sidelined by his rivals, and brusquely rebuked by the Führer; his memoranda were openly criticized and the presence of his deputy was often requested in his stead.[35] In time, the pressure took its toll. In January 1944, Speer was committed to a sanatorium suffering from exhaustion and nervous collapse. When he returned to work that spring, he noted his own growing disenchantment with the party, the SS, the conduct of the war, even Hitler himself. As Speer put it, "the veil had been lifted."[36] Part of that disillusionment was doubtless due to his appreciation that the war was already lost. He saw Germany's military potential being systematically degraded, and began to doubt that she could effectively defend herself. As he recalled in his memoirs:

> I could see omens of the war's end almost every day in the blue southern sky when, flying provocatively low, the bombers of the American Fifteenth Air Force crossed the Alps. . . . Not a German fighter plane anywhere in sight. No anti-aircraft fire . . . Total defencelessness.[37]

As a result, he contemplated resignation and then penned a number of memoranda to Hitler containing suggestions on how defeat might be postponed or at least ameliorated. But each of his proposals was scorned as Hitler blindly refused to hear anything of defeat. For the most part, the memoranda went unread. Their author, though he continued at his post, began to feel increasingly alienated.

When the scorched-earth policy then materialized, Speer was, by his own admission, "aghast." While he intended to salvage what was possible from the wreckage of the war for the benefit of its survivors, he saw his fellow ministers colluding in a program of unprecedented and, to him, unconscionable vandalism. He soon began to seek ways of circumventing and undermining the Nero Order. He forged numerous Wehrmacht orders, for example, demanding the preservation of a certain bridge or other item of infrastructure.[38]

But his most successful technique was what he called a "simple trick" to outwit Hitler.[39] In his memoranda and his face-to-face meetings with the Führer, he would use Hitler's own arguments and prejudices to get the outcome that he desired. He would argue that, given that the lost territories would inevitably be recovered by German forces, the ordered destruction of the infrastructure in those areas should be suspended so that order and military production could be restored by the returning German armies with a minimum of effort. Hitler, of course, was seduced by the prospect of his armies resuming the advance and reconquering lost territory, and readily agreed. Armed with the Führer's consent, Speer could then set about convincing the regional *Gauleiters* and occupation authorities to paralyze rather than destroy all affected installations. "Plans must be made," he wrote,

> so that if... industrial regions fall into enemy hands, the factories will only be crippled temporarily; this is to be achieved by removing various elements and taking them along on the retreat... without damaging the factories themselves.[40]

Speer worked tirelessly, devoting the same energy to undermining Hitler as he had earlier given to assisting him. Between February and April 1945, he made seventy visits around what remained of German-occupied territory, and hosted almost a hundred conferences.[41] In this way, he scored some notable successes, committing as many as sixty acts of high treason in the process.[42] He persuaded the German commander of Paris, von Choltitz, for example, to postpone all planned demolitions.[43] And he undoubtedly influenced the decision of the *Gauleiter* of Hamburg, Karl Kaufmann, not to allow the old city to be completely obliterated. In total, it is thought, his intervention resulted in the preservation of the mines and factories of Belgium and northern France, the canals of Holland, the nickel mines of Finland, the ore mines of the Balkans, and the oil fields of Hungary.[44] Yet by defying Hitler's direct orders, he was risking his life. His break with the regime had begun.

Throughout this period, Speer continued to petition Hitler with numerous memoranda, still hoping that sanity would prevail. Though he was actively defying Hitler, he clearly did not yet see the Führer himself as the root of the problem. That attitude was to change.

Speer's relationship to Hitler was a peculiar one. Speer himself was clear: "If Hitler had had friends," he once stated, "I would have been his friend."[45] One author has gone further, however, describing the relationship as a "dreadful love," and there does appear to be a curiously passionate element to it.[46] Hitler, it has been suggested, was quite taken with Speer, attracted by his Nordic looks and impressed by his quiet confidence and erudition.[47] Speer naturally reciprocated, intoxicated in part by his closeness to the epicenter of power, but also believing implicitly, and with all the enthusiasm of the acolyte, in Hitler and in Hitler's supposed genius.

Yet by the time of his return after illness in early 1944, Speer appears to have had little passion left. Though he and Hitler would patch up their relationship and return to some semblance of friendship and camaraderie, the spell had been broken. Speer even found that Hitler suddenly appeared physically repellent to him. "My God, how could I never have seen how ugly he is?" he recalled. "This broad nose, this sallow skin. Who is this man?"[48] Indeed, when a colleague commented that Hitler "could no longer be regarded as normal," Speer agreed without protest.[49] It is highly likely that he had already arrived at the same conclusion.

Then, in early February 1945, Speer was visited by a colleague from the electrical industry, Dr. Friedrich Lüschen. Lüschen asked him if he knew that certain passages of *Mein Kampf* were being widely quoted by the German people, and then handed him a slip of paper with Hitler's own words from two decades earlier:

> The object of diplomacy must not be to see that a nation goes down heroically but rather that it survives in a practical way. Hence every road that leads to this goal is opportune and the failure to take it must be looked upon as a criminal neglect of duty.[50]

In silence, Lüschen then handed Speer a second quote from the same source:

> The authority of the state can never be an end in itself; for, if that were so, any kind of tyranny would be inviolable and sacred. If a government uses the instruments of power in its hands for the purpose of leading a people to ruin, then rebellion is not only the right but also the duty of every individual citizen.[51]

Lüschen then departed without a word. Speer was left to contemplate the significance of the two passages, which, though dated, had been taken from a book lauded in Nazi Germany as the work of the modern-day prophet. He was stunned.

> Here was Hitler himself saying what I had been trying to get across during these past months. Only the conclusion remained to be drawn: Hitler himself—measured by the standards of his own political programme—was deliberately committing high treason against his own people. . . .

That night I came to the decision to eliminate Hitler.[52]

As Speer himself confessed, his plotting to murder Hitler had a "touch of the ridiculous" about it.[53] For one thing, he had somewhat ambitiously hoped to eliminate Bormann and Goebbels as well, considering them "more dangerous without Hitler than with him."[54] For another, he was no natural assassin. Born in 1905, he had been too young for service in World War One and had had nothing to do with the military thereafter. Indeed, coming from solidly middle-class stock, and being of a somewhat fragile constitution, it is doubtful whether he even had a schoolyard brawl to his name. Thus, having resolved to kill Hitler, he had very little idea of how he should proceed.

Though he still had access to his target, Speer decided against a frontal assault. Rather, he opted for a much safer, more remote method. While walking in the Reich Chancellery gardens that spring, he had noticed the ventilation shaft for Hitler's bunker. As he recalled in his memoirs, it was "camouflaged by a small shrub, level with the ground and covered by a thin grating."[55] There were no special security measures and no guards. It would not be difficult, he mused, to introduce poison gas into the bunker.

A few days later, as an air raid was pounding Berlin, Speer was in a shelter in the basement of the Armaments Ministry when he fell into conversation with one of his colleagues, Dieter Stahl, the head of munitions production. He knew Stahl well—and most important, trusted him—having already intervened to rescue him from the clutches of the Potsdam Gestapo after he had been reported for making defeatist comments. The two naturally discussed the coming collapse and the policies that, in their view, were hastening Germany's demise. Speer grew agitated, venting his frustration at the regime, saying: "I simply cannot stand it any longer and be witness to government by lunatics."[56] He went on to outline his plan to Stahl:

> I asked him whether he thought he could get hold of some of the poison gas tabun for me and when, not surprisingly, he looked at me questioningly, I told him that I wanted to try to introduce it into the Reich Chancellery bunker. He seemed neither surprised nor alarmed.[57]

Speer's choice of weapon was an interesting one. Tabun had first been developed before the war as an insecticide, but it had proved itself to be such a lethal nerve agent that its further development had been handled by the German military. A colorless, tasteless liquid, with a slightly fruity odor, tabun was effective by contact or inhalation of vapor, and worked by inhibiting the function of the enzyme cholinesterase, which is crucial to the transmission of nerve impulses to the muscles. Those affected lost all muscular control. The first symptom was the contraction of the pupils, which, in all but the brightest conditions, would induce near-blindness. Thereafter, increased saliva production would lead to frothing at the mouth. Increased nasal discharge and labored breathing would then be followed by vomiting and incontinence. Within an hour or so of exposure, most victims suffered violent convulsions and died, in effect, of asphyxiation.[58]

By 1942, tabun was being produced in a state-of-the-art plant in eastern Germany. It was synthesized on-site and loaded into aircraft bombs and shells in an underground facility manned by concentration camp inmates. The shells were then stored to await the order for deployment, an order that, perhaps because of Hitler's experience of gassing in World War One, never came. By 1945, however, Germany had a stockpile of some 12,000 tons of weaponized tabun.[59] Speer, as minister of armaments, would have been well aware of its existence and its potency.

When Stahl reported back to Speer some days later, however, his response was negative. After making inquiries, he had learned that liquid tabun was dispersed through the explosion of the shell and that it did not naturally evaporate or form smoke.[60] He concluded that tabun was not a suitable medium for Speer's plan, but promised instead to procure "one of the traditional types of gas."[61] In the meantime, while the two men investigated the possibilities, Speer was to be frustrated again: "Even if we could have obtained the gas," he wrote,

> those days would have passed fruitlessly. For when I invented some pretext at this time to inspect the ventilation shaft, I found a changed picture. Armed SS sentinels were

posted on the roofs of the entire complex, searchlights had been installed, and where the ventilation shaft had previously been at ground level, there now rose a chimney more than ten feet high, which put the air intake out of reach. I was stunned.[62]

Nonetheless, it would appear that it was not merely this purely technical hitch that deflected Speer from his task. It is said that he visited the Rhineland around this time, and one night sat incognito with a number of miners in an air-raid shelter. Listening to the conversations going on around him, he realized the extent to which these ordinary Germans still believed unreservedly in Hitler and his ability to save them from catastrophe. If he were to pursue his plan, he thought, he would be destroying their last vestige of hope, removing the one politician in whom they still had faith. With that realization, he abandoned his plot to assassinate Hitler.[63]

Given that so few of Speer's biographers make mention of this tale, one might assume that it is apocryphal. Speer was, after all, the poster boy of the Nazi regime and was unlikely to have passed incognito anywhere in the Reich. But the story might also be seen as a parable to explain Speer's own feelings toward Hitler at that time. Whatever its precise provenance, it is indicative of the mental and emotional turmoil with which Speer was wrestling.

This is a point that is confirmed by Speer's adjutant, Manfred von Poser. During a trip to Berlin that March, the two stopped on the *Autobahn* for a rest. Poser recalled:

[Speer] and I walked across some fields and climbed a hill. It was misty but sunny; we sat down, the earth around us smelling richly, and looked across the hills and that beautiful countryside. It was to be the only time I ever saw Speer give way to deep depression. "How can he do it?" he said, drawing a semi-circle with his arm. "How can he want to make a desert of all this?"[64]

So if one believes Speer's memoirs, the assassination plan was abandoned. Beset by fears of detection and its potential consequences for his family, Speer was relieved to be able to throw off the uncomfortable mantle of assassin. As he recalled: "The whole idea of assassination vanished from my considerations as quickly as it had come. I no longer considered it my mission to eliminate Hitler, but to frustrate his orders for destruction."[65]

Yet Speer did not, it appears, abandon his plotting completely. Under interrogation by the British late in 1945, Dieter Stahl revealed that there was more to the plot than later appeared in Speer's memoirs, or indeed in the vast majority of works related to his life. In the second half of March 1945, Stahl alleged, he had been called once more to see Minister Speer:

> [Speer] explained to me that he had now thought of a different plan. Himmler, Goebbels and Bormann, the three most dangerous and mischievous, gathered almost every evening in the Reich Chancery for the purpose of hatching their fiendish plans. . . . During night air raids all three drove in their cars . . . to the suburbs of Berlin and such a moment was to be used for an ambush.[66]

Speer went on to explain that he had found "a few brave men" to assist him, and added that he himself would "take on" one of the three cars. He asked Stahl to supply him with machine guns, pistols, ammunition, and a number of flares with which to blind his targets. Stahl duly delivered the required weaponry to Speer's office the following day, but as he had no further opportunity to speak to Speer alone, he could shed no more light on what, if anything, was undertaken.

Though Stahl is clear in his deposition that Speer was planning to murder his targets, it is possible that the plot mutated into a later conspiracy to kidnap Bormann, Himmler, and the Reich labor leader Robert Ley. In early April 1945, after Hitler had made it clear that he intended to meet his fate in Berlin, Speer apparently became disquieted that all the senior personnel

of the Nazi movement were planning suicide. He claimed that
they had a "moral duty to face trial by the enemy" and to answer
directly for their actions.[67] Moreover, their prosecution, he
thought, would "offer a chance to deflect the hate and anger
away from the German people [and] on to those who really deserved it."[68]

Accordingly, Speer hatched a conspiracy, in concert with the
Luftwaffe ace Adolf Galland, to kidnap the "terrible trio" and
thereby prevent them from committing suicide. As he recalled,
they would ambush their targets in the Berlin suburbs:

> Our plan was simple: When the enemy night bombers
> dropped white parachute flares, every car stopped and the
> passengers fled into the fields. Flares fired by signal pistols
> would undoubtedly produce similar reactions. Then a
> troop of soldiers armed with submachine guns would
> overpower the six-man escort squads....In the general
> confusion it would have been possible to bring the ar-
> rested men to a secure place.[69]

Though he decided against this course of action, Speer, it
seemed, was still plotting. And his plotting was not all entirely al-
truistic, for he was not above seeking to save his own skin. In the
dying days of the war, he devised a fanciful plan to escape to
Greenland, where, he thought, he could hide out until the dust
settled and write his memoirs. He and another Luftwaffe officer,
Werner Baumbach, commandeered a seaplane, loaded it with
provisions, skis, fishing tackle, kayaks, and of course "good
wines," and prepared their escape, but the plane was destroyed in
an Allied air raid. Speer himself was later dismissive of the plan,
describing it as "rank romanticism" and "fantasy, but fun while it
lasted."[70] In the event, he eschewed all such notions of escape
and meekly surrendered to arrest in mid-May 1945.

Unsurprisingly, perhaps, Speer's activities as a conspirator and
would-be assassin have attracted much attention, not all of it flattering. The root of this hostility is the conundrum of Speer himself. Most liberal commentators see Speer almost as one of their

own: a solidly middle-class intellectual, in stark contrast to the rabble of psychopaths, thugs, and careerists that made up the remainder of the Nazi hierarchy. Thus, they are appalled that he could operate in such company—"among murderers," as Speer himself put it in retrospect[71]—and place his genius at their disposal. In short, they would argue that he, of all the senior Nazis, should have known better. The damning verdict offered by the historian Hugh Trevor-Roper is perhaps typical. Speer, he concluded,

> is the real criminal of Nazi Germany; for he, more than any other, represented that fatal philosophy which has made havoc of Germany and nearly shipwrecked the world. For ten years he sat at the very centre of political power; his keen intelligence diagnosed the nature and observed the mutations of Nazi government and policy; he saw and despised the personalities around him, he heard their outrageous orders and understood their fantastic ambitions; but he did nothing.[72]

Following from this unease is a profound suspicion of Speer's motives in his apparently Damascene conversion at Nuremberg, where he was the only one of the Nazi hierarchy to express his contrition openly and confess his share of the collective responsibility for the crimes committed in Germany's name. Though he thereby avoided the death penalty and invoked Göring's wrath, he scarcely earned the respect of the Allies. Rather, he was viewed with intense skepticism. He was seen as a dissembler, a manipulator, and (in that curious English phrase) too clever by half. As Airey Neave warned his colleagues at Nuremberg, Speer was "more beguiling and dangerous than Hitler . . . we must not come under his spell."[73]

Naturally, these suspicions have also been extended to Speer's alleged assassination plot. When he first aired the plot at Nuremberg, Speer claimed somewhat disingenuously that he had intended "merely to mention [it] in order to show how dangerous Hitler's destructive intentions had seemed."[74] It soon became the centerpiece of his defense, however, and one of the highlights of the entire trial. He began modestly, suggesting that the matter was perhaps too technical or detailed to be of interest to the court. When pressed, he continued, apparently under duress, because "there is always something repellent about such matters."[75] He went on to outline his plan, citing the role played by Dieter Stahl—whose independent testimony gave him vital corroboration—and concluding that the changes to the ventilation system of the bunker had rendered the plan impossible.

The revelation of the plot caused some considerable excitement. Speer's fellow defendants were appalled. Jodl considered it "bad taste," and Rosenberg took the view that Speer should have kept his bombshell to himself. Göring was predictably outraged, audibly commenting that "if Speer was not hanged by this court then a kangaroo court would have him assassinated for treason."[76] The Allied prosecutors, meanwhile, merely wondered why Speer had chosen not to mention the matter when he gave his original statement.

Historians and commentators have been no less skeptical. Though his accomplice, Dieter Stahl, certainly thought Speer to be genuine and "never doubted his intentions," he is in the minority.[77] A former colleague, for example, described Speer's plot to kill Hitler as "a dream—for that was all it ever was."[78] One later biographer, meanwhile, described the idea of Speer the assassin as a "surrealistic absurdity."[79] Another dismissed the plot as "feeble," characterizing it as "bunker bunkum" and asking, with vicious sarcasm, if Nazi Germany had "run out of ladders" with which to scale the raised air intake to the bunker.[80] Some writers are more indulgent, usually relating the bare details given by Speer and Stahl without necessarily questioning their veracity. The German historian Joachim Fest, for instance, regards the plot as "romantic" and likens it to a game of "cops and robbers."[81]

So did Speer really want to kill Hitler? In assessing this issue, three charges are usually leveled. The first is that, given his apparently unrestricted access to his target, Speer's failure even to make an attempt is evidence of his lack of credibility. This argument seems at first sight to be persuasive, yet it fails to take account of

a number of important factors. It ignores, for example, the uncanny power that Hitler could exercise over those around him.
Speer himself wrote of Hitler's "hypnotic persuasiveness" and his
"personal magnetism,"[82] and confessed in his memoirs: "Quite
aside from any question of fear, I could never have confronted
Hitler pistol in hand. Face to face, his magnetic power over me
was too great."[83] His reluctance to risk a frontal assault, therefore, was as much due to fear of dissuasion and capture as pure
cowardice.

Furthermore, the extent of the access that Speer enjoyed,
though undoubtedly greater than that of the other would-be
assassins, is still questionable. It has been suggested that Speer
had numerous opportunities to shoot Hitler and that he was able
to come and go in the bunker, as he pleased, without being
searched.[84] However, in the aftermath of the 20 July plot, this
would appear more than a little implausible. Speer's meetings with
Hitler in the final months of the war were limited to the regular
situation conferences, which he attended along with many other
senior Nazis. The days of intimate soirees poring over building
plans alone in Hitler's quarters were by that stage long gone.

Moreover, this suggestion also contradicts a number of accounts that detail the security regime then in place. Major Frey-
tag von Loringhoven, for instance, one of the circle of adjutants
that were ever-present in the bunker, was unequivocal. "Nobody
was allowed into the bunker without being searched for
weapons," he stated, describing a "very carefully designed" security system in which coats and sidearms had to be surrendered
and briefcases searched before gaining access to Hitler's conference room via up to three SS pickets.[85]

This is a point that has been echoed by many others. Whereas
security procedures for Hitler's inner circle had formerly been
unevenly and inconsistently applied, after 20 July 1944 all staff
were subject to the same strict regime, regardless of their status.
Walter Warlimont, for example, who had been very close to
Hitler and had been injured in Stauffenberg's assassination attempt, recalled that "from [then] on, I was one of those officers
whose briefcase was searched by the SS guards before entering

the map room...my every movement was watched."[86] Speer clearly enjoyed an exalted position within the Nazi hierarchy, but in the dying days of the Third Reich, it is highly doubtful that he would have been able to engineer himself into a situation where he could assassinate Hitler.

Second, it has been suggested that Speer's apparent planning for the use of poison gas was a cunning deception. Speer himself, it appears, had authorized modifications to the ventilation system two years previously, intended to thwart just such an attempt. In designing the bunker in the spring of 1943, it is alleged, Speer was privy to a memorandum redrawing the ventilation fittings with a gravity trap, so that "war agents injected into them will run out again downwards."[87] This is indeed intriguing, but not necessarily damning. After all, one could counter that it was knowledge of this fact that led Speer to reject the liquid tabun as a suitable medium for the attack and seek a more traditional gas, which might escape the gravity trap.

Lastly, the plot is often portrayed as being part of a "charm offensive" cooked up with his defense attorney at Nuremberg to save him from the gallows. Though his performance in the dock probably *did* save his life, Speer later attempted to propagate the idea that he made no attempt to "play" Nuremberg to his own advantage.[88] He feigned embarrassment when divulging details of his plot, coyly sketching the story "with reluctance...for fear of seeming to boast about it."[89] His defense lawyer, meanwhile, would insist that his client was no longer in the business of self-preservation. With his insistence on admitting guilt, it was claimed, Speer knew he was courting the death penalty, but "he was adamant. He would shrug and say, 'So be it.'"[90]

This image of the penitent former Nazi minister offering up his secrets to his former enemies with no regard for his own fate is attractive but deeply unrealistic. Speer at Nuremberg was still very much in the business of self-preservation. He charmed his interrogators, stressed his good behavior, and highlighted the assistance that his specialist knowledge might still render the Allies.[91] In a three-page letter submitted to the American prosecutor, he claimed: "I myself have during this period not only given every possible information but further still calmly dispelled the objections of my former colleagues toward open information."[92] His subtext was clear. By reminding his jailers of his value both as a source of information and as a positive influence on his fellow inmates, he was hoping to avoid the death penalty.

Speer's revelation of the bunker plot, therefore, probably *was* intended as a ruse to soften the prosecution's view of him. In this purpose, he failed. The tribunal's judges were too astute to be impressed by what they recognized as a calculated attempt to win their sympathy.[93] In the event, however, it was not Speer's revelation of his plot to kill Hitler that saved him, it was his whole demeanor. Speer was informative and intelligent. He impressed the court with his apparent honesty and his calm and reasonable temperament. In addition, it was noted that he had been one of the "few men" with "the courage to tell Hitler that the war was lost."[94] These were the factors that won him the sympathy of the tribunal and, arguably, saved his life.

But one should not imagine that this renders the plot as a whole fraudulent. Speer certainly sought to exploit the story for his purposes at Nuremberg, but he did not invent it solely for that purpose. He was intelligent, even manipulative, but he was almost certainly not the Machiavellian schemer that many still perceive him to be. In short, those who ascribe to him the cunning and forethought to concoct a spurious plot in the last weeks of the Third Reich solely to ingratiate himself with his later prosecutors are reading far too much into the story.

So, what conclusions might one draw? Speer's plot is certainly a fascinating tale, all the more so because one cannot realistically expect to provide a definitive explanation for it. As Joachim Fest has noted, "many of the questions raised by Speer's life are unresolved to this day; some will never be cleared up."[95] Some might conclude that the plot to kill Hitler falls into that category. However, a sober reading of the available evidence suggests a quite simple conclusion.

For all his faults, Speer was not entirely deaf to the voice of his conscience. Indeed, the fact that the idea of assassination occurred to him at all is surely evidence not of his potential as a killer but rather of a belated and admittedly halfhearted moral renaissance. His plotting, therefore—tentative though it was—should perhaps be interpreted as a desperate eleventh-hour desire finally to do the right thing. His intention to kill Hitler was, as he confessed, "an impulse of despair."[96] But it was genuine enough, if only for that fleeting moment when he saw Germany peering into the abyss. It was genuine enough for him to risk his life by bringing in other conspirators, such as Stahl, and genuine enough for him to make less than discreet inquiries about the use of tabun.

Yet as Speer himself conceded, "from the intention to the deed, is a very long way."[97] And it is abundantly clear that he had barely begun to travel along that route. Beyond entertaining schoolboy fantasies about ambushes, flare guns, and poison gas, he never fleshed out his plans. He never set dates, assigned tasks, or addressed the grubby minutiae of planning a murder. He clearly never even thought through the consequences of his imagined actions, for if he had successfully introduced poison gas into the bunker, he would have had to reckon not only with the death of Hitler but also with those of all of the Führer's entourage: prominent Nazis and generals, but also secretaries, adjutants, and valets. He would have earned himself "not the fame of the classical tyrannicide, but the infamy of a mass murderer."[98]

For this reason, perhaps, Speer sits most uncomfortably in the presence of Hitler's genuine would-be assassins. He lacked the dynamism and inspiration of Stauffenberg, the quiet determination of Elser, and the principled resolve of Tresckow. For all his other talents, as an assassin he was an absolute beginner—a point he would later willingly concede, saying: "I would never really have done it. I couldn't have."[99]

Albert Speer was indeed a deeply ambiguous and contradictory character. He was cultured, highly educated, and urbane. He was praised by Stauffenberg as "a man that one could talk to," and even found himself allocated a seat in the post-Hitler cabinet, drawn up by the German resistance.[100] At Nuremberg, he was lauded by the American judge as "the most humane and decent of the defendants."[101] The British were no less effusive, describing him as "an impressive figure" and "a gifted and compelling man."[102]

But Speer was also a war criminal. Found guilty of war crimes and crimes against humanity, he was sentenced to twenty years' imprisonment for his role in the procurement and exploitation of slave laborers for German industry. The prison psychiatrist at Nuremberg tried to make sense of Speer by describing him as "a blinkered racehorse."[103] In retrospect, one can extend the metaphor a little more. Speer's blinkers had fallen away by the summer of 1944. From then on, he clearly saw the madness around him, but his residual loyalty to and even love for Hitler had effectively rendered him lame.

It was this cruel dilemma that tortured Speer in the last year of the war. Arguably, it would never leave him. He would later write: "I am obsessed by the thought of Hitler's two faces, and that for so long a time I did not see the second behind the first." In truth, he never really came to terms with Hitler. He described him as "an enigma, full of contradictions,"[104] cursed him as a megalomaniac, and bemoaned the failure of the various assassination attempts against him as a "tragedy."[105] But, despite all his criticisms, he protested that he would "not like to be numbered amongst those who malign him in order to exonerate themselves."[106] Speer plotted Hitler's death, then swore eternal fealty to his Führer and even risked his life to visit him one last time.[107]

In a sense, Speer never escaped Hitler's shadow. Imprisoned in Spandau after the war, he would confide to his diary that he was still "always listening to [Hitler's] voice, hearing him clear his throat, seeing his slightly stooped figure before [his] eyes."[108] He would even dream about him. "They are always the same," he said of his dreams. "About his knowing what I was doing against him, including my wanting to kill him."[109] Hitler's hold on him, he complained, was still too strong.[110] Therein, perhaps, lay the root cause of his inability to play the role of assassin.

Epilogue

Berlin: Monday, 30 April 1945, dawn

As a gray dawn lit the eastern skies over Berlin, the capital of Hitler's Reich was preparing for its final struggle. The morning was cool, with a damp breeze blowing down off the Baltic. It brought an unseasonable chill to the city's inhabitants—Germans and Soviets alike—huddled in the bombed-out buildings, squalid cellars, and makeshift shelters. The brightening skies revealed a chaos of rubble-strewn streets littered with corpses, burned-out vehicles, and the detritus of war. The stench of death and decay was everywhere. Smoke twisted and eddied, while dust and ash covered everything that failed to move. Smashed façades of houses stood like rotten teeth. The famed linden trees, now splintered and broken, were gamely struggling into leaf. There was no dawn chorus; sunrise was greeted only by the thunder of artillery, the sporadic crackle of gunfire, and the eerie scream of *Katyusha* rockets. All life that could escape the doomed city was long gone. Only soldiers and stranded civilians remained.

Elsewhere in the Reich, the scene was little better. Hitler held sway over two narrowing strips of territory, stretching from Rostock in the north to Salzburg in the south. Once the undisputed master of the continent, Hitler now controlled only two of Europe's capitals: Berlin and Prague. His once-victorious armies were in disarray and in retreat. In the west, mass surrenders of troops had become commonplace, and the invading armies were often met by white flags and scenes of liberation rather than conquest. Isolated pockets of resistance, particularly in the Ruhr, were encircled and contained as the front line moved inexorably eastward. As the fronts converged, the Soviet and American vanguards had met in celebration at Torgau on the Elbe, west of Berlin, five days previously. The remnant of Hitler's Germany had been bisected, its capital cut off from its Bavarian heartland. On 30 April, the British 2nd Army was approaching Hamburg, which would be taken three days later. Munich, the birthplace of Nazism, would fall to the Americans that very morning.

In the east, meanwhile, the conflict with the Soviets had lost none of its ferocity. The Balkans had been cleared, and Budapest and Vienna had fallen. From there the front line encircled Bohemia to the east, then ran northwest to the remains of Dresden, then north to Berlin, which had been encircled by the Soviet Army on 25 April. To the east of that line, the roads were clogged with German refugees trudging west, entirely at the mercy of their new Soviet masters. Active resistance behind the front had been all but snuffed out. Only the city of Breslau refused to submit. It was enduring its seventy-fourth day under siege. Now some 80 kilometers behind Soviet lines, all hope of relief had been abandoned, but the fanatics preached continued defiance. The siege, with all its attendant miseries, still had six days to run.

The morning of 30 April brought liberation to the Ravensbrück women's concentration camp 80 kilometers north of Berlin. It had been established in May 1939 to house some six thousand prisoners, but by October 1944, numbers had swelled to forty-two thousand. In mid-April 1945, a number of German inmates had been set free; others were handed over to the Red Cross and taken to Sweden. Some then had to endure a forced march west, leaving a remnant of around three thousand starving and sick individuals being cared for by fellow inmates. Their SS captors had fled.

As the Soviet Army arrived that morning, one survivor found herself in the nearby men's camp. The sights that greeted her there were "heartbreaking":

> 800 men are there, 400 of them dead or dying, lying on top of one another, and the remainder are not much better.... For eight days there has been no water, and the men are dying from hunger and thirst. It is just terrible. They don't even look like people, rather just distraught shadows of themselves. All that they have gone through has robbed them of their sanity. It is unbelievable and unimaginable.[1]

They were nonetheless among the lucky ones. Ravensbrück is thought to have claimed the lives of some sixty thousand inmates, among them the SOE agent Violette Szabo.

Berlin, meanwhile, had been cut off for five days. It had been subjected to one of the most intense assaults ever witnessed in human history. Some 2.5 million Soviet soldiers had massed east of the German capital. Divided between the rival Generals Zhukov and Konev, their primary objective was to enclose the city to prevent any German relief or, indeed, breakout. The two sides of the Soviet pincer had met at Ketzin, west of Potsdam, the previous week. They had established a formidable barrier—the German 9th Army, which had been caught in their jaws, had been all but destroyed—but it was not wholly impervious. The German 12th Army, under General Wenck, was still fighting to the southwest of Berlin, some 50 kilometers from the city center. Though supposedly battling their way in to relieve the capital,

Wenck's men were, in reality, only able to provide a brief exit route for some of the units shattered by the Soviet advance. Then they, too, joined the weary exodus to the west.

They were leaving a dying city. Supplies of electricity, gas, and water had practically ceased. The transportation network had ground to a halt. Key streets had been barricaded and bridges had been rigged with dynamite. The last plane had left Tempelhof airfield a week before, and the makeshift airstrip on the East-West Axis was repeatedly blocked by shellfire or crashed aircraft. Police and fire brigades had been stood down and ordered to join their nearest military unit. Public order was maintained by the lynch law of the SS and Gestapo.

Life for the many civilians left stranded in the capital was unutterably gruesome. Caught between the rock of German intransigence and the hard place of Soviet revenge, they had been reduced to a subterranean, nocturnal existence, huddling in cellars and rarely venturing out before dark. Nonetheless, hunger forced many out onto the streets to queue for what scarce provisions there were, or to participate in the looting of the city's commercial districts. Those who were caught looting could face a swift trial by a "flying court-martial." Execution was the usual sentence, and the corpses of the unfortunates would be hung from trees and lampposts or street barricades as a deterrent. It is thought that over a thousand Berliners met their end in this way.[2]

For those who remained at home, the perils were no less immediate. Men of military age lived in fear of discovery by the SS, which could result in forced conscription into a punishment battalion, or a summary execution. Discovery by the Soviets, meanwhile, could mean death or a lengthy sentence in the gulag. Those who sought to avoid the horrors by flying a white flag as the front line approached were ill advised. The gesture was not always recognized by the Soviets, and discovery by the Germans would invariably invite the death penalty.

Young women, meanwhile, lived in fear of rape. In self-preservation, they swathed themselves in head scarves, blackened their faces, and kept their legs covered. Some even contrived to feign an infectious disease—scarlet fever was a favorite—or to play at insanity. Those with blond hair were especially at risk, and families would often conspire to hide a young daughter, grand-daughter, or niece. The first echelon of Soviet soldiers were, in the main, impeccably behaved and more concerned with combat than anything else. But once they had passed, the next echelon wrought havoc. They usually came at night. Initially they de-manded watches and alcohol. Then they would return, often drunk, with the chilling refrain of *"Frau komm!"* Those Berliners that survived the ordeal would curse their misfortune in cheating death. In Berlin alone, there were thought to have been over a hundred thousand rapes committed during the siege.[3] Around ten thousand of those victims died, mostly by their own hand.

Considering the size of Berlin's population, there was a defi-nite shortage of shelters for civilians. Though there were a num-ber of purpose-built air-raid shelters dotted around the capital, many Berliners sought refuge in the tunnels of the underground system, where they were comparatively safe from the carnage aboveground. However, fears among the SS of a Soviet advance through the tunnels led to the decision to flood them by blowing a section of tunnel beneath the Landwehr Canal. Estimates of the extent of civilian casualties vary enormously, but the numbers drowned must run to several hundred.[4]

Another option was to seek shelter in one of the anti-aircraft complexes. One of the most famous of these was located close to the Berlin Zoo. Built in 1940–41 as part of a ring of flak installa-tions, the zoo tower was enormous. Standing more than 40 me-ters high, with walls of reinforced concrete nearly 2.5 meters thick, it resembled a medieval fortress—square in profile, with a turret at each corner. Beneath the roof, where four batteries of guns and flak crews were stationed, it consisted of a garrison, hos-pital, warehouse, and air-raid shelter capable of accommodating more than fifteen thousand civilians. It was well defended and well supplied, with its own independent water supply and electri-cal generators. It was known to the Berliners as "the safest coffin in the world."[5]

On 30 April, however, it resembled hell on earth. The entire complex shook with the constant thunder of incoming Soviet rounds and the reply of the anti-aircraft artillery—now lowered to target the ground forces approaching the Reichstag. Beneath its walls, Berlin's once-famous zoo was now a hades of freshly dug graves, screeching birds, and broken, dying animals. Inside the tower, the stench of disinfectant and cordite mingled with the sweat and urine of up to thirty thousand terrified Berliners. After a number of days, sanity was becoming a precious commodity. Suicides were so common that they were no longer counted. In the crush, they were often not even noticed until they began to decompose.[6]

The area of the capital controlled by Hitler's forces had shrunk rapidly since the city had been cut off. By the morning of 30 April, the central residential areas of Moabit, Lichtenberg, and Wilmersdorf had been lost. To the west, the old island fortress of Spandau would hold out for two more days. To the southwest, German troops on Wannsee Island were still resisting a determined Soviet assault. Beyond that, only the government district remained in German hands: a shrinking corridor running approximately from the Tiergarten in the west to Friedrichshain in the east, bounded to the south by the Landwehr Canal and to the north by the river Spree. That area was defended by a motley assortment of Axis forces, with élite paratroop and Waffen-SS units fighting side by side with the teenagers of the Hitler Youth and the old men of the *Volkssturm* militia. Numerous nationalities were also represented, with Belgians, Danes, and Dutch fighting alongside the Germans. One Waffen-SS unit, for example, whose final command post was just yards from Hitler's bunker, was a curious amalgam of French, Swedes, and Norwegians. It was commanded by candlelight from a wrecked underground train. Berlin was staging the last hurrah of the European extreme right.

Hitler's forces utilized similar strategies to those employed with some success in sieges elsewhere. Now largely bereft of heavy armor, which had either been pulverized or run out of fuel, they relied on creating fortified strongpoints, such as pillboxes and machine-gun nests, so as to slow the Soviet advance. In addition, small tank-killing units were formed, equipped with the disposable *Panzerfaust* bazooka. Such detachments would hunt down the massed Soviet T-34 tanks in the Berlin streets, seeking to nullify the Soviets' numerical advantage. Among their most effective exponents were the French soldiers of the *SS-Charlemagne* Division, who were said to have claimed over fifty kills in the central sector alone.[7]

The Soviets, meanwhile, naturally sought to exploit their dominance in men and machinery. Rather than launch a headlong attack en masse, however, they were divided into countless small, self-contained, assault groups, which would seek simultaneously to storm enemy positions from many directions with support from tanks.[8] When beaten back or facing stubborn resistance, they could call in an artillery strike or the withering fire of the *Katyusha* mobile rocket launchers. There was little that could resist their attentions for long.

By the morning of 30 April, the desperate defense of Berlin was reaching its denouement. The previous night, the 150th Rifle Division of the Soviet 3rd Shock Army had forced the Moltke Bridge and had taken up position close to the Reichstag. The former German parliament was seen by Stalin, somewhat bizarrely, as the symbol of Hitler's power. Its significance among his troops had been raised to the status of a trophy of war. It was "the lair of the Fascist beast," the "Bandit capital," and its capture—timed to coincide with the May Day parade in Moscow—was to be the ultimate demonstration of Soviet power.

That morning, the first waves of Soviet infantry had met stiff resistance. The damp air was filled with acrid smoke and a cacophony of small-arms fire, artillery, and rocket launchers. For the Soviets, progress toward their target was murderously slow. Heavy fire seemed to rain in on them from all quarters. In addition, their approach was littered with obstacles. As one war reporter noted: "If there had been no fighting, this distance could be crossed in a few minutes, but it now seemed impassable, covered with shell holes, railway sleepers, pieces of wire and trenches."[9] An awesome array of Soviet artillery was brought up in support, to subdue the German defenders. By midafternoon, the forward Soviet units had entered the ruins of the Reichstag. A further eight hours of bitter hand-to-hand fighting awaited them before the Soviet flag was finally raised from the roof.

Barely a kilometer away to the south, unbeknownst to the Soviet troops, lay the *Führerbunker*—the real lair of the "Fascist beast." Located beneath the garden of the Reich Chancellery, it was state of the art. Completed in 1943, it was entirely self-contained, with its own heating, lighting, ventilation, and water supply. A two-story complex, 8 meters belowground, it comprised Hitler's personal quarters, guest rooms, kitchens, map rooms, and a conference area. It was a concrete labyrinth, accessed by steps leading from the Chancellery and the Chancellery garden, with a spiral staircase connecting the two floors. The décor was spartan: bare concrete walls that sweated moisture, exposed wiring and plumbing. Only the Führer's own quarters made some concession to comfort, with simple furniture, carpets, and his favorite portrait of Frederick the Great.

By the end of April 1945, the bunker was home to around twenty-five people. As well as Hitler and Eva Braun, it was inhabited by Hitler's staff, including his bodyguards, two secretaries, his cook, his valet, his doctor, his SS adjutant, and Joseph Goebbels, together with his wife and six children. Beyond these, it was regularly visited by a host of generals, ministers, clerks, and adjutants, most of whom were quartered nearby. At any one time, therefore, it is likely to have contained around thirty people.

The atmosphere inside the bunker was a peculiar mixture of calm and desperation. Between bouts of frenzied activity, which usually coincided with Hitler's daily military conferences, a pregnant silence reigned, which was punctuated only by the echoing clatter of teleprinters, the drone of the generators, and the muffled thud of nearby shelling. The air was fetid and stale, deteriorating further at times when the ventilation system drew in smoke or cordite fumes. The lighting, which flickered incessantly, was never fully extinguished. The bunker personnel, therefore, inhabited a world of perpetual day, where all feeling of time was lost.

They slept little, napping where and when they could. Hitler, too, took to sleeping fully clothed, fearing that a direct hit or a surprise Soviet attack would catch him unprepared. The only thing he feared more than capture, it appeared, was capture in his underclothes.[10]

Yet, despite the all-pervading sense of death, a curious *joie de vivre* developed. This was perhaps aided by the incongruous presence of the Goebbels children, who played in the narrow bunker corridors, sang songs to "Uncle Adolf," and read fairy stories. Some of the younger staff followed their example and soon found release from the tension in wine and song. Indeed, a veritable bacchanal seems to have developed. While the Berliners aboveground starved, the inhabitants of the bunker drank champagne and ate caviar and sweets. One witness described the bunker as "a world peopled with zombies . . . whose only thought was to laugh and sing."[11] The carousing was kept from Hitler's earshot but was otherwise tolerated. Indeed, discipline became distinctly lax. Few of the staff bothered to get up when Hitler entered a room; many of them—including Eva Braun—even smoked in front of him, something that would have been unthinkable only a few weeks before.[12] Hitler's secretary recalled that in the last few days, one could talk to him about anything. She dared to ask why he was not fighting at the head of his troops.[13] He replied lamely that he did not want to fall into the hands of the Russians.

Physically, too, Hitler was fading. He had been in the bunker since the middle of January—three months, with only brief sorties to an outside world that he could no longer face. It may be, of course, that Hitler derived some curious enjoyment from bunker life. Claus von Stauffenberg, for instance, is said to have commented: "Hitler in the bunker—that's the real Hitler!"[14] Martin Bormann, too, would have concurred. He wrote to his wife in the autumn of 1944, contrasting Hitler's lifestyle with his own. "The Führer," he noted,

> lives down there in his bunker, and has only electric light and a rarefied atmosphere—the air pressure is always too high in his room because fresh air has to be pumped in

continuously. It is just as if he enjoys living in an unlit basement.[15]

Nonetheless, though Hitler himself may not have minded his self-imposed incarceration, it can have done little to reverse his physical decline. Hitler had been slowly poisoned by the cocktail of drugs prescribed by his physician, Dr. Theodor Morell. Narcotics, barbiturates, and sedatives, for example, were all administered on a regular basis for a variety of real and imagined complaints. In addition, every day, Hitler received up to five injections of the stimulant methamphetamine, used eyedrops consisting of a 10 percent solution of cocaine, and took up to sixteen "anti-gas pills" containing strychnine and belladonna.[16] Though the precise effect of these treatments is unknown, it is reasonable to conclude that Hitler not only suffered the toxic effects of strychnine poisoning but was also at the very least psychologically dependent on amphetamines—a condition that could explain many of his physical and psychological symptoms, such as mood swings, paranoia, cramps, and headaches. One eyewitness in the bunker recalled seeing the Führer in a "pitiful" state:

> His flabby left hand, in which he was clasping his steel-rimmed spectacles, was also clutching the table. His whole left arm, up to the shoulder, was trembling and, now and then, shuddering. This arm kept tapping the table rhythmically. To brace himself, he had wrapped both his left calf and foot around one leg of the table. The leg was throbbing, shaking. He could not control it.[17]

Though the diagnosis is disputed—and Hitler's own physicians considered his trembling to be hysterical in origin—it is possible that Hitler was also suffering from the advanced stages of Parkinson's disease.

In addition to all that, Hitler still bore the effects of the assassination attempt of the previous summer. Though he had not been seriously injured in the bomb attack, his health had nonetheless deteriorated markedly thereafter. As one of his former inti-

mates recalled, it was as though the shock of the Stauffenberg attempt had brought Hitler's "evil nature" into the open.

> He came into the map room bent and shuffling. His glassy
> eyes gave a sign of recognition only to those who stood
> closest to him. His chair would be pushed forward for him
> and he would slump down into it, bent almost double with
> his head sunk between his shoulders. As he pointed to
> something on the map his hand would tremble.[18]

Hitler was physically weak, his hearing was impaired, and he suffered from jaundice and bouts of depression. One visitor was profoundly shocked, seeing him as a broken-down old man with
festering sores. "I was really almost sorry for him," he recalled,
"because he looked horrible. . . . He was bloated. . . . His left eye
dropped a little to the left."[19] One of the bunker doctors concurred. Hitler, he remembered, "was a palsied, physical wreck, his
face puckered now like a mask, all yellow and grey."[20]

By the end of April, Hitler appeared emaciated, his complex-
ion was pallid, and his eyes were glazed. His once commanding
voice had weakened to a hoarse croak, and his once pristine uniform bore numerous food stains. On one of his last sorties from
the bunker on 20 April, he had received a delegation of Hitler
Youth boys in the Reich Chancellery garden. The newsreel im-
ages showed a man visibly diminished since the previous summer.
He stooped, trembled, and bore the jowly, toothless grin of a
man much older than his fifty-six years.

Mentally, too, he was at the end of his tether. One of his secretaries recalled: "We could see Hitler falling apart—he trembled,
he cried, he was constantly mumbling."[21] Another described his
growing apathy, his "pathological" craving for chocolate cake,
and the increasing monotony of his conversation. "In the last few
weeks," she remembered, he had "talked only about dogs and
dog training, food and nutrition and the stupidity and wickedness
of the world."[22]

With the collapse of his armies, his violent temper and inveterate paranoia had worsened still further. The forced inaction of

life in the bunker had done little to improve his temper. He paced the corridors, often clutching a tattered road map of Berlin, his mood swinging between resignation, impotent fury, and a curiously infectious and evangelical optimism. Pointless situation conferences were held, in which Hitler directed his nonexistent armies, raged about the failure of the expected relief force, and threw delusional tantrums about the betrayals that he saw all around him.

As far as can be ascertained, Hitler's logic in April 1945 was quite simple. He appeared to believe—influenced, perhaps, by Stalin's decision to stay in Moscow in 1941—that if he remained in his capital, then it would not, indeed *could not,* fall to the enemy.[23] It was this thinking that surfaced again and again in the situation conferences, exuding confidence in "wonder weapons," sure of the imminent collapse of the alliance ranged against him, and a fervent belief in ultimate victory. Yet, unlike Stalin in 1941, Hitler had no fresh troops and no debilitating winter snows with which to halt the enemy advance. His much-vaunted relief force was practically nonexistent and was too busy fighting for its own survival to the west of Berlin to mount any viable offensive operation.

In fact, in the very cockpit of his power, Hitler was effectively impotent. His control of the military had already slipped from his grasp. On 22 April, in a tumultuous situation conference, he had finally been told the unglossed truth about the failure of the expected relief force. With that, he had exploded into an uncontrollable rage, pacing the room, gesticulating wildly, and shouting himself hoarse about betrayal, corruption, and cowardice. Finally, he slumped back into his chair, pale-faced and shaking, his eyes fixed straight ahead. The war was lost, he said; the Third Reich was a failure, and all that was left for him now was to die.[24]

Though he soon regained his composure, his authority over his subordinates was crumbling. His own would-be brother-in-law, Hermann Fegelein, was arrested in civilian clothes in the Berlin suburbs, preparing to flee to Switzerland.[25] Degraded in rank and brought back to the bunker under armed guard, Fegelein would face a makeshift firing squad. When Hitler summoned General Karl Koller, his Luftwaffe chief of staff, to Berlin from Bavaria, he was rebuffed. Koller pleaded ill health and privately complained that the trip would be suicidal. And by the time he finally relented, passage to the capital had become impossible. Even within the environs of Berlin, Hitler's orders were being openly disobeyed. SS General Felix Steiner, for example, commander of one of the forces intended to relieve the capital, was formally removed from his command on 27 April after failing to make any headway whatsoever against the Soviets. Yet, rather than submit to his demotion, Steiner merely persuaded his intended replacement to allow him to remain in charge.[26] Elsewhere, the conscientious sought to preserve their troops from further risk in hopeless battles. Hitler's writ no longer ran uncontested.

Göring was the first of the inner circle to break ranks. On the twenty-third, he sent a telegram from Berchtesgaden in response to Hitler's decision to remain in Berlin. In it, he claimed that Hitler no longer enjoyed freedom of action and that he, as Hitler's anointed successor, was thus empowered to make contact with the Allies. His actions provoked rage in the *Führerbunker*. He was condemned by Hitler as "corrupt, and a drug-addict," and was to be placed under arrest for high treason.[27]

The following day, Speer arrived, driven by his own ego, or by some residual loyalty, to see Hitler one last time. Though he embellished the meeting in his published memoirs with confessions and tearful farewells, the truth was more prosaic. Hitler, he recalled, "showed no emotion at all . . . he was empty, burnt out, lifeless."[28] Speer, too, was strangely unmoved:

> While he spoke of his suicide and all that, I had the feeling I was speaking with someone who was already dead. And the truth is that nothing he said provoked any feelings in me, positive or negative . . . It was nothing. And that was the tragic end of it all.[29]

When they finally parted, later that night, the mood was scarcely better. Hitler, Speer recalled, was "prematurely aged" and "trembling" but "showed no emotion." "His words were as cold as his hand: 'So you're leaving? Good. *Auf Wiedersehen.*' No regards to my family, no wishes, no thanks, no farewell."[30] With that, Speer was dismissed and left Berlin.

Himmler was next. In the late afternoon of the twenty-eighth, word of Himmler's peace feelers to the Americans was received in Berlin. Like Göring, the *Reichsführer-SS* had proclaimed himself as Hitler's successor and had proposed negotiations with the Western Allies. Again, Hitler was incensed. Himmler would be arrested and expelled from the Nazi Party. Yet this was far more serious than Göring's defection. Hitler had utilized Göring's flair and aura of respectability, but had rarely seen the *Reichsmarschall* as anything more than a bloated dilettante. Himmler, however, was a man of a different stamp. He was a committed National Socialist and was viewed as the personification of loyalty. If *der treue Heinrich*—"faithful Heinrich"—had also succumbed to defeatism, then all really was lost. In his fury, Hitler finally made up his mind.

Hitler's resolve to commit suicide was not, however, a snap decision. It was not, as some commentators have suggested, a knee-jerk reaction to an unfavorable turn of events. Indeed, there is every reason to conclude that Hitler had made the decision already on 22 April, when he committed himself to remain in Berlin for the duration. Only the exact timing of the final act remained to be fixed.

To a large degree, that timing would be dictated by the inexorable advance of the Soviets. But, beyond that, Hitler was still determined to follow his own agenda. Even, or perhaps especially, in death, he wanted to remain in control. He ordered many of his papers to be burned on the twenty-second. Three days later, he instructed his valet on the disposal of his personal effects. Two days after that, on the twenty-seventh, he called a macabre meeting of the bunker staff, where his plans for suicide were discussed. Yet, in spite of all that, it may be that it was the high-level defections of Göring and Himmler, demonstrating that even the Nazi inner circle had lost the will to fight, that determined the exact timing of Hitler's death.

The night of the twenty-eighth, which followed the news of

Himmler's unilateral peace offensive, was one of feverish activity. Hitler was tying up the loose ends of both his personal and political lives. His first pressing task was to marry his long-standing mistress, Eva Braun. For this purpose a civic registrar was required, who was duly hauled, bewildered and bedraggled, from a nearby *Volkssturm* detachment to officiate. The ceremony took place in the map room of the bunker. Braun wore a black silk gown; Hitler was in uniform. It was a brief service: the bridal pair declared themselves to be of pure Aryan descent and free from hereditary diseases. Bormann and Goebbels stood as witnesses. The party then retired to Hitler's private suite, where they drank champagne and reminisced about happier times.

Hitler left the celebration to dictate his "political testament," a long-awaited justification for his actions, intended presumably to provide inspiration to those still fighting and give succor to those who were not.[31] During this period of reflection, it might have been appropriate for Hitler to cast a retrospective eye over his would-be assassins, if only to cover them once again with accusations of dishonor, treachery, and cowardice. He was aware of a few of them. Maurice Bavaud and Georg Elser were certainly well known to him, as was Claus von Stauffenberg, who had come closest to killing him. He may also have been made aware of Hans Oster's conspiracy, unearthed during the latter's interrogation and trial, concluded some weeks before.

However, there were many more assassins and enemy agents whose plottings had escaped Hitler's attention. The attempts mounted by the Poles, for example, were as yet largely unknown; so, too, were the plans hatched by the NKVD in the Soviet Union and by the SOE and RAF in Britain. Closer to home, Hitler was also ignorant of the plots of some of his own officers. Tresckow, for instance, had taken his secrets with him to the grave, while Schlabrandorff had resisted all attempts to persuade him to implicate his confederates Gersdorff, Boeselager, Breitenbuch, and Bussche. Speer, too, had been predictably tight-lipped about his halfhearted plotting during his final meeting with Hitler some days earlier.

In short, notwithstanding the frenzy of bloodletting of the

previous autumn—much of which had still not reached its conclusion—Hitler was unaware of the sheer number of plots that had been hatched against him and was unaware of the scale of the German resistance. He was also unaware of just how fortunate he had been to avoid assassination. His security regime had been formidable, but it had not been without its failings. His survival had not been due, as he believed, to the intervention of providence; rather, it had been due to the ill-fortune of his enemies, or even his own devilish good luck. Though he often did not know it, Hitler had flirted with death numerous times. Had his speech in the Bürgerbräukeller in Munich in 1939 lasted only fifteen minutes longer, for example, he would have been killed by Georg Elser's ingenious bomb. Had he dallied to take in the Armory exhibition in 1943, he would have fallen victim to the world's first suicide bomber. And had the fuse in Tresckow's "brandy bottles" not malfunctioned, Hitler would have been blown to oblivion in the skies above Byelorussia. It may be that this ignorance was bliss for the Führer, as it enabled him to pose, in his final act, as the beloved and respected leader of the "Aryan people" and to die, as he put it, "with a happy heart."

If Hitler did entertain any thoughts for his would-be assassins, he certainly did not consign them to paper. His political testament would disappoint all those who were seeking profundity or revelation. It consisted of little beyond a final bilious rant against the Jews, who, he believed, had plunged Germany into war and would have to atone for their guilt. Speaking without interruption, his eyes fixed on the middle distance, Hitler criticized the British for their "warmongering" and fired a Parthian shot at Göring and Himmler, attacking their "disloyalty" and the "immeasurable harm" that they had done to Germany by their treacherous dealings with the Allies. He concluded by announcing his intention to remain in Berlin:

> I cannot forsake the city which is the capital of the Reich. . . . I have decided therefore to remain in Berlin and there, of my own free will, to choose death at the moment

when I believe the position of the *Führer* and Chancellor can no longer be held.[32]

Contrary to his usual custom of endless revisions and alterations to dictated text, he accepted the first draft as final.[33] There was simply no time for stylistic flourishes.

The following day, the twenty-ninth, was the calm before the storm. One eyewitness's diary entry noted laconically: "29 April—We're trapped here, we just sit waiting."[34] Emissaries left the bunker to deliver Hitler's testament to the newly appointed chiefs of the party, military, and government. Others sought to escape by proposing to make contact with the relief force that was being annihilated to the west of the capital. Hitler now freely gave his consent, adding: "Tell [them] to hurry or it will be too late."[35] With Soviet troops now only 500 meters from the bunker, morale among those who remained sank to new depths. Talk of suicide was commonplace, and cyanide capsules were liberally distributed by the SS doctor. One member of the bunker entourage described himself as an "inhabitant of a morgue" where the corpses were stubbornly pretending to be alive.[36]

Death, however, was already casting its long shadow. That afternoon, news reached Berlin of the grisly fate of Mussolini, Hitler's fellow fascist and onetime ally. Captured by Italian partisans, he had been beaten and shot before being strung up by the ankles from a Milan gas station, to be vilified by a baying mob. The news strengthened Hitler's resolve to meet his end at a time of his own choosing. He reiterated the order that his body was to be burned, saying: "I will not fall into the hands of the enemy, dead or alive."[37] Soon after, Hitler's beloved Alsatian bitch, Blondi, was poisoned. Her five puppies were shot in the Chancellery garden. The six Goebbels children, meanwhile, were also being readied for death. That afternoon, they were told that they were to receive an injection to prepare them for a long journey. In due course, they would be sedated with morphine and given cyanide. Their mother believed that they could have no place in a world without Adolf Hitler.

That night, the commander of the Berlin garrison, General Weidling, attended his last situation conference in the *Führer-bunker*. He brought word of terminal ammunition shortages at the front and announced the impossibility of the situation. The Russians, he said, were making significant gains across Berlin and were currently only four blocks distant—less than 300 meters away. They would reach the Chancellery within twenty-four hours, he warned, while the capital itself would fall within two days at the outside. Hitler received the news in weary silence. Presently he gave his verdict: there was to be no breakout. The forces within the city were expected to fight to the last man.

The thirtieth of April 1945 was a day that had begun much like any other in the surreal world of the *Führerbunker*. Dawn had broken to the deafening cacophony of an intense Soviet artillery bombardment as the final advance on the Reichstag was begun. Hitler, who had retired to bed only shortly before dawn, rose un-usually early, at around 6 a.m., and wandered listlessly through his quarters, past the still-sleeping figures of his adjutants and sec-retaries. He spent the morning attempting to marshal the last—largely imaginary—German armies, though the telephone line out of the bunker was barely functioning. He received General Krebs and SS Brigadier Mohnke, the military commander of the Chancellery district, and listened in silence to their dire predic-tions. The time had come. He instructed his personal adjutant on the arrangements for his cremation—200 liters of precious fuel were to be requisitioned for the task. After that, he lunched, as usual, with his secretaries and his cook. His new bride—who was happily calling herself Eva Hitler—had declined to join them, and they ate in a curious atmosphere of forced levity, listening, ac-cording to one account, to Hitler giving forth about the correct procedures for mating dogs. As one of the secretaries recalled, it was "a banquet of death under the mask of cheerful calm and composure."[38]

After lunch, Hitler requested a final meeting with his en-tourage. He emerged from his private apartment in his trademark brown tunic and black trousers. He looked tired and drawn, and he stooped more than usual. His left hand tremored uncontrollably. Eva followed close behind, elegantly coiffured and wearing Hitler's favorite dress. The pair shook hands with each of the inner circle in turn. Few words were exchanged. Hitler mumbled, barely registering the former intimates before him. Eva smiled weakly and asked to be remembered to her beloved Bavaria. The pair then returned to their study and closed the heavy steel door behind them.

According to most accounts, there was now a lull of around twenty minutes, interrupted only by the vain last effort of Magda Goebbels to persuade Hitler to leave Berlin.[39] While the valets and adjutants waited outside the door, Hitler and Eva presumably composed themselves and said their own goodbyes. Eva was the first to die. Sitting demurely on the sofa, with her legs tucked beneath her, she opened the brass hull of a poison capsule, placed the glass vial of cyanide between her teeth, and bit down. The poison would have caused similar symptoms to a massive coronary. It was a quick death, but by no means the silent or dignified one she had desired. She would have suffered fits and convulsions and would have gasped for breath before losing consciousness. Hitler probably observed her death throes. He could not allow his new wife, by some quirk of fate, to survive him and be taken alive by the Soviets—the ultimate trophy of war. Once she was still—her body slumped over the arm of the sofa, her lips puckered and discolored—he sat down by her side, put his Walther pistol to his right temple, and squeezed the trigger.

Selected Bibliography

Archives

British Library Newspaper Archive, London
Bundesarchiv, Berlin
Bundesarchiv Militärarchiv, Freiburg
Fundacja Archiwum Muzeum Pomorskie Armii Krajowej, Toruń, Poland
National Archives, London
RTsKhIDNI (Russian Center for Historical Documents), Moscow
RGVA (Russian State Military Archive), Moscow
Studium Polski Podziemnej, London
TsAMO (Central Archive of the Ministry of Defense), Moscow
Wiener Library, London

Published Works

Christopher Andrew and Oleg Gordievsky, *KGB: The Inside Story of Its Foreign Operations from Lenin to Gorbachev* (London, 1990)

Christopher Andrew and Vasili Mitrokhin, *The Mitrokhin File* (London, 2000 edition)

John Armstrong (ed.), *Soviet Partisans in World War II* (Madison, 1964)

Michael Baigent and Richard Leigh, *Secret Germany—Claus von Stauffenberg and the Mystical Crusade Against Hitler* (London, 1994)

Correlli Barnett (ed.), *Hitler's Generals* (London, 1989)

Omer Bartov, *Hitler's Army* (Oxford, 1992)

Hans Baur, *Hitler's Pilot* (London, 1958)

Antony Beevor, *Berlin: The Downfall 1945* (London, 2002)

———, *Crete: The Battle and the Resistance* (London, 1991)

———, *The Mystery of Olga Chekhova* (London, 2004)

Nicolaus von Below, *At Hitler's Side* (London, 2001)

Richard Bessel (ed.), *Life in the Third Reich* (Oxford, 1987)

Tadeusz Bór-Komorowski, *The Secret Army* (London, 1950)

Włodzimierz Borodziej, *Terror und Politik* (Mainz, 1999)

Karl Dietrich Bracher, *The German Dictatorship* (London, 1971)

André Brissaud, *Canaris* (London, 1973)

Alan Bullock, *Hitler: A Study in Tyranny,* revised edition (London, 1962)

Michael Burleigh, *The Third Reich* (London, 2000)

Ewan Butler, *Mason-Mac* (London, 1972)

N. Cameron and R. H. Stevens (trans.), *Hitler's Table Talk 1941–1944* (London, 1953)

Ian Colvin, *Canaris: Chief of Intelligence* (London, 1951)

Norman Davies, *Rising '44* (London, 2003)

Sefton Delmer, *Trail Sinister: An Autobiography,* Vol. I (London, 1961)

Alexander Demandt (ed.), *Das Attentat in der Geschichte* (Cologne, 1996)

Harold Deutsch, *The Conspiracy Against Hitler in the Twilight War* (London, 1968)

Max Domarus, *Hitler: Speeches and Proclamations 1932–45*, 3 vols. (London, 1990–97)

John Erickson, *The Road to Berlin* (London, 1983)

———, *The Road to Stalingrad* (London, 1975)

Joachim Fest, *Inside Hitler's Bunker* (London, 2004)

———, *Plotting Hitler's Death* (London, 1997)

———, *Speer: The Final Verdict* (London, 2001)

———, *The Face of the Third Reich* (London, 1970)

M. R. D. Foot, *SOE: The Special Operations Executive, 1940–1946* (London, 1984)

Alexander Foote, *Handbook for Spies* (London, 1949)

Franklin L. Ford, *Political Murder: From Tyrannicide to Terrorism* (Cambridge, MA, and London, 1985)

Jozef Garlinski, *Poland, SOE and the Allies* (London, 1969)

Rudolf-Christoph von Gersdorff, *Soldat im Untergang* (Berlin, 1977)

Hans Gisevius, *To the Bitter End* (Cambridge, MA, 1947)

S. Grabner and H. Röder (eds.), *Henning von Tresckow: Ich bin der Ich war* (Berlin, 2001)

Hermann Graml, "Der Fall Oster," in *Vierteljahrshefte für Zeitgeschichte*, Vol. XIV, 1966

Helmuth Groscurth, *Tagebücher eines Abwehroffiziers 1938–1940* (Stuttgart, 1970)

Lothar Gruchmann (ed.), *Autobiographie eines Attentäters. Johann Georg Elser* (Stuttgart, 1970)

Lothar Gruchmann and Anton Hoch, *Georg Elser: Der Attentäter aus dem Volke* (Frankfurt am Main, 1980)

Richard Grunberger, *A Social History of the Third Reich* (London, 1971)

Hellmut Haasis, *Den Hitler jag' ich in die Luft* (Berlin, 1999)

Sebastian Haffner, *The Meaning of Hitler* (New York, 1979)

Theodore Hamerow, *On the Road to the Wolf's Lair* (Cambridge, MA, 1999)

Ted Harrison, "'Alter Kämpfer' im Widerstand: Graf Helldorf, die NS-Bewegung und die Opposition gegen Hitler," in *Vierteljahrshefte für Zeitgeschichte*, Vol. XXXXV, 1997

Hannes Heer and Klaus Naumann (eds.), *Vernichtungskrieg: Verbrechen der Wehrmacht 1941–44* (Hamburg, 1995)

L. Heston and R. Heston, *The Medical Casebook of Adolf Hitler* (New York, 1979)

Anton Hoch, "Das Attentat auf Hitler im Münchner Bürgerbräukeller 1939," in *Vierteljahrshefte für Zeitgeschichte*, Vol. XVII (1969)

Peter Hoffmann, *German Resistance to Hitler* (London, 1988)

——, *Hitler's Personal Security* (New York, 2000 edition)

——, *Stauffenberg* (London, 1995)

——, *The History of the German Resistance 1933–1945* (London, 1977)

——, "Maurice Bavaud's Attempt to Assassinate Hitler in 1938," in George Mosse (ed.), *Police Forces in History* (London, 1975)

Heinz Höhne, *Canaris* (London, 1976)

——, *The Order of the Death's Head* (London, 1969)

Alistair Horne (ed.), *Telling Lives* (London, 2000)

Geoffrey Household, *Against the Wind* (London, 1958)

——, *Rogue Male* (London, 1939)

Edward Hyams, *Killing No Murder* (London, 1969)

Anton Joachimsthaler, *The Last Days of Hitler* (London, 1996)

Antonius John, *Philipp von Boeselager* (Bonn, 1994)

K. Jonca and A. Konieczny (eds.), *Paul Peikert—Festung Breslau in den Berichten eines Pfarrers* (Wrocław, 1998)

Traudl Junge, *Until the Final Hour* (London, 2003)

Ian Kershaw, *Hitler*, 2 vols. (London, 2000)

Nikolai Khokhlov, *In the Name of Conscience* (London, 1960)

Klemens von Klemperer, *German Resistance Against Hitler: The Search for Allies Abroad* (Oxford, 1992)

Erich Kordt, *Nicht aus dem Akten* (Stuttgart, 1950)

E. Korpalski, J. Szynkowski, and G. Wünsche, *Das Führerhauptquartier im Bild und in Erinnerungen von Zeitzeugen* (Kętrzyn, 2004)

Helmut Krausnick, "Aus dem Personalakten von Canaris," in *Vierteljahrshefte für Zeitgeschichte,* Vol. X, 1962

W. G. Krivitsky, *In Stalin's Secret Service* (New York, 2000)

Christian Graf von Krockow, *Eine Frage der Ehre* (Berlin, 2002)

Wendy Lower, "'Anticipatory Obedience' and the Nazi Implementation of the Holocaust in the Ukraine: A Case Study of Central and Peripheral Forces in the Generalbezirk Zhytomyr, 1941–1944," in *Holocaust and Genocide Studies,* Vol. 16, No. 1, Spring 2002

Richard Lukas, *Forgotten Holocaust: The Poles Under German Occupation 1939–1944,* revised edition (New York, 2001)

Callum MacDonald, *The Killing of SS-Obergruppenführer Reinhard Heydrich* (London, 1990)

William Mackenzie, *The Secret History of SOE: The Special Operations Executive, 1940–45* (London, 2000)

Czesław Madajczyk, *Die Okkupationspolitik Nazideutschlands in Polen, 1939–1945* (Cologne, 1988)

Niklaus Meienberg, *Es ist kalt in Brandenburg* (Zürich, 1980)

Richard Meinertzhagen, *Middle East Diary 1917–1956* (London, 1959)

Susanne Meinl, *Nationalsozialisten gegen Hitler* (Berlin, 2000)

Susanne Meinl and Dieter Krüger, "Der politische Weg von Friedrich Wilhelm Heinz," in *Vierteljahrshefte für Zeitgeschichte,* Vol. XXXXII, 1994

Charles Messenger, *Hitler's Gladiator: The Life and Military Career of Sepp Dietrich* (London, 1988)

Russell Miller, *Behind the Lines* (London, 2002)

Simon Sebag Montefiore, *Stalin: The Court of the Red Tsar* (London, 2003)

W. Stanley Moss, *Ill Met by Moonlight* (London, 1950)

Marek Ney-Krwawicz, *The Polish Home Army 1939–1945* (London, 2001)

J. Noakes and G. Pridham (eds.), *Nazism 1919–45,* 3 vols. (Exeter, 1983–1988)

Operation Foxley: The British Plan to Kill Hitler (London, 1998)

Richard Overy, *Interrogations* (London, 2001)

————, *Russia's War* (London, 1998)

————, *The Dictators* (London, 2004)

Lauran Paine, *The Abwehr* (London, 1984)

Terry Parssinen, *The Oster Conspiracy of 1938* (New York, 2003)

Henry Picker, *Hitler's Tischgespräche im Führerhauptquartier 1941–42* (Bonn, 1951)

Gerhard Reitlinger, *The SS: Alibi of a Nation, 1922–1945* (New York, 1957)

Ralf Georg Reuth, *Goebbels* (New York, 1993)

Denis Rigden, *Kill the Führer: Section X and Operation Foxley* (London, 1999)

Hans Rothfels, *Die deutsche Opposition gegen Hitler* (Zürich, 1994)

Jürgen Runzheimer, "Der Überfall auf den Sender Gleiwitz im Jahre 1939," in *Vierteljahrshefte für Zeitgeschichte*, Vol. X (1962)

Walter Schellenberg, *Schellenberg* (London, 1969)

Ernst Günther Schenck, *Patient Hitler* (Augsburg, 2000)

Bodo Scheurig, *Henning von Tresckow* (Berlin, 2004 edition)

Fabian von Schlabrendorff, *The Secret War Against Hitler* (London, 1966)

Matthias Schmidt, *Albert Speer, The End of a Myth* (London, 1985)

Christa Schroeder, *Er war mein Chef* (Munich, 1985)

Gitta Sereny, *Albert Speer: His Battle with Truth* (London, 1995)

Robert Service, *Stalin: A Biography* (London, 2004)

Franz Siedler and Dieter Zeigert, *Hitler's Secret Headquarters* (London, 2004)

Albert Speer, *Alles, was ich weiß* (Munich, 2000)

————, *Inside the Third Reich* (London, 1970)

————, *Spandau—The Secret Diaries* (London, 1976)

Reinhard Spitzy, *How We Squandered the Reich* (Wilby, Norfolk, 1997)

David Stafford, *Churchill and the Secret Service* (New York, 1998)

————, *Britain and European Resistance, 1940–45* (London, 1980)

Alexander Stahlberg, *Bounden Duty—The Memoirs of a German Officer 1932–45* (London, 1990)

Johannes Steinhoff, Peter Pechel, and Dennis Showalter, *Voices from the Third Reich* (London, 1989)

Pavel Sudoplatov, *Special Tasks* (London, 1994)

C. G. Sweeting, *Hitler's Personal Pilot: The Life and Times of Hans Baur* (Washington, DC, 2000)

John Toland, *Hitler* (London, 1976)

Hugh Trevor-Roper (ed.), *Hitler's War Directives 1939–1945* (London, 1964)

———, *The Last Days of Hitler,* 7th edition (London, 2002)

Ann Tusa and John Tusa, *The Nuremberg Trial* (London, 1983)

Klaus Urner, *Der Schweizer Hitler-Attentäter* (Stuttgart, 1980)

Dan van der Vat, *The Good Nazi—The Life and Lies of Albert Speer* (London, 1997)

Walter Warlimont, *Inside Hitler's Headquarters* (London, 1964)

John Wheeler-Bennett, *The Nemesis of Power—The German Army in Politics, 1918–45* (London, 1961)

Notes

Introduction

[1] Benjamin Disraeli, Speech, House of Commons, 1 May 1865. Quoted in *The Oxford Dictionary of Quotations* (Oxford, 1949), p. 128.
[2] See Miles Hudson, Assassination (Stroud, 2000).
[3] See, for example, Willi Berthold, *Die 42 Attentate auf Hitler* (Munich, 1981).

Prologue

[1] Quoted in John Toland, *Hitler* (London, 1976), p. 156.
[2] Quoted in Konrad Heiden, *Der Führer* (London, 1967), p. 154.
[3] All statistics from Detlev Peukert, *The Weimar Republic* (London, 1991), p. 63.
[4] Karl-Alexander von Müller quoted in Harold J. Gordon, *Hitler and the Beer Hall Putsch* (Princeton, 1972), p. 288.
[5] The *Times* (London), 12 November 1923, p. 12.
[6] Quoted in Toland, op. cit., p. 167.
[7] See Ernst Günther Schenck, *Patient Hitler* (Augsburg, 2000), p. 300.

[8]Helene Hanfstaengl quoted in Toland, op. cit., p. 175.

[9]Gordon, op. cit., p. 465.

[10]The *Times* (London), 10 November 1923, p. 13.

[11]Quoted in Ian Kershaw, *Hitler: 1889–1936 Hubris* (London, 2000), p. 212.

[12]Quoted in Alan Bullock, *Hitler: A Study in Tyranny* (London, 1962 edition), pp. 119–20.

Chapter 1

[1]Quoted in Peter Hoffmann, *Hitler's Personal Security* (New York, 2000 edition), p. 24.

[2]Heinrich August Winkler, *Weimar 1918–1933* (Munich, 1998), p. 593.

[3]Max Domarus, *Hitler: Speeches and Proclamations 1932–45,* Vol. I (London, 1990), p. 228.

[4]Quoted in Ian Kershaw, *Hitler: 1889–1936 Hubris* (London, 2000), p. 423.

[5]See Bundesarchiv [hereafter BA], File R43II/990.

[6]BA, R43II/990-32, 138, 146.

[7]Quoted in Gerhard Reitlinger, *The SS: Alibi of a Nation, 1922–1945* (New York, 1957), p. 13.

[8]Heinz Höhne, *The Order of the Death's Head* (London, 1969), p. 21.

[9]Quoted in ibid., p. 24.

[10]Heinrich Himmler quoted in Peter Padfield, *Himmler: Reichsführer-SS* (London, 1990), p. 90.

[11]Himmler quoted in ibid., p. 99.

[12]Otto Kumm, later of the *Leibstandarte Adolf Hitler,* quoted in Johannes Steinhoff, Peter Pechel, and Dennis Showalter, *Voices from the Third Reich* (London, 1989), pp. 23–24.

[13]Höhne, op. cit., p. 64.

[14]Kurt Ludecke quoted in Charles Messenger, *Hitler's Gladiator: The Life and Military Career of Sepp Dietrich* (London, 1988), p. 45.

[15]Sefton Delmer, *Trail Sinister: An Autobiography,* Vol. I (London, 1961), p. 147.

[16]Ibid., p. 152.

[17]Hoffmann, *Security,* p. 21.

[18]Delmer, op. cit., pp. 111–13.

[19]Alan Bullock, *Hitler: A Study in Tyranny* (London, 1962 edition), p. 392.

[20]John Toland, *Hitler* (London, 1976), pp. 390, 402–3.

[21]Ibid., p. 394.

[22]Ibid., pp. 137–38.

[23]Hoffmann, *Security,* p. 19.

[24]Albert Speer, *Inside the Third Reich* (London, 1970), p. 55.

[25]Henry Picker, *Hitler's Tischgespräche im Führerhauptquartier 1941–42* (Bonn, 1951), p. 232.

[26]N. Cameron and R. H. Stevens (trans.), *Hitler's Table Talk, 1941–1944* (London, 1953), p. 176.

[27]Speer, op. cit., p. 177.

[28]Kershaw, op. cit., p. 343.

[29]Quoted in Hoffmann, *Security*, p. 264.

[30]See BA File R43II/990/F5.

[31]BA R43II/990/F5/192.

[32]Hoffmann, *Security*, p. 24.

[33]BA R58/724-16, 30–33.

[34]Hoffmann, *Security*, p. 178.

[35]Höhne, op. cit., p. 114.

[36]On Frankfurter, see Emil Ludwig, *The Davos Murder* (London, 1937).

[37]Quoted in Günter Grass, *Crabwalk* (London, 2003), p. 25.

[38]Though some claim that he survived the war and lived in Paris under an assumed name. See Ron Roisin, "Herschel Grynszpan: The Fate of a Forgotten Assassin," in *Holocaust and Genocide Studies,* Vol. 1, No. 2 (1986), pp. 217–28.

[39]Quoted in Hoffmann, *Security*, p. 31.

[40]The *Leibstandarte* was initially formed in March 1933 under another title. It then went through several name changes before being redesignated the *Leibstandarte SS Adolf Hitler* in 1934.

[41]Quoted in Höhne, op. cit., p. 148.

[42]Ulrich Frodien, *Bleib Übrig* (Munich, 2002), p. 136. Translated by the author.

[43]This contention is still controversial, but see, for example, *Operation Foxley: The British Plan to Kill Hitler* (London, 1998), p. 104; Ada Petrova and Peter Watson, *The Death of Hitler* (London, 1995), p. 90.

[44]Hoffmann, *Security*, p. 62.

[45]Quoted in Ewan Butler, *Mason-Mac* (London, 1972), p. 70.

[46]Hoffmann, *Security*, p. 32.

[47]Ibid., p. 48.

[48]Traudl Junge and Melissa Müller, *Bis zur letzten Stunde* (Munich, 2002), p. 37.

[49]Toland, op. cit., p. 779.

[50]Speer, op. cit., pp. 61–62.

[51]Hoffmann, *Security*, p. 265.

[52]Interview with Rochus Misch, *Der Spiegel,* 35/2004.

[53]Cameron and Stevens, op. cit., pp. 452–53.

[54]*Operation Foxley*, p. 104.

[55]Reinhard Spitzy, *How We Squandered the Reich* (Wilby, Norfolk, 1997), p. 86.

[56]Hoffmann, *Security*, p. 32.

[57]Hitler's favorites included the Kaiserhof in Berlin and the Osteria Bavaria and Café Heck in Munich.

[58]Klaus Urner, *Der Schweizer Hitler-Attentäter* (Stuttgart, 1980), pp. 209–10.

[59]See Stefan Keller, "Grüezi, Herr Reichskriminaldirektor!" in *Züricher Wochenzeitung,* 11 November 1998.

[60]Peter Hoffmann, "Maurice Bavaud's Attempt to Assassinate Hitler in 1938," in George Mosse (ed.), *Police Forces in History* (London, 1975), pp. 182–83.

[61]Urner, op. cit., p. 228.

[62]Hoffmann, in Mosse (ed.), op. cit., pp. 176–77.

[63]Quoted in ibid., p. 183.

[64]BA, R3017/110, Bavaud's *Anklageschrift,* 20 November 1939, p. 9.

[65]Ibid., pp. 20–21.

[66]Michael Burleigh, *The Third Reich* (London, 2000), p. 265.

[67]*Anklageschrift*, op. cit., p. 24.

[68]Ibid., p. 30.

[69]Ibid., p. 31.

[70]Ibid., p. 41.

[71]See interview with Emil Reuter in Peter Spinatsch, *Maurice Bavaud— Geschichte und Wirkungsgeschichte*, at http://www.maurice-bavaud.ch/ symp.htm.

[72]See H. W. Koch, *Volksgerichthof* (Munich, 1988), p. 219.

[73]Quoted by Hoffmann in Mosse (ed.), op. cit., p. 197.

[74]See *Ehrenbuch der Opfer von Berlin-Plötzensee* (Berlin, 1974).

[75]Quoted by Hoffmann in Mosse (ed.), op. cit., p. 182.

[76]Quoted in Niklaus Meienberg, *Es ist kalt in Brandenburg* (Zürich, 1980), pp. 133–34.

[77]Ibid., p. 46.

[78]Ibid., pp. 46–47.

[79]With thanks to Mr. Brian Baxter of the REME Museum, Berkshire, UK.

[80]Rolf Hochhuth, "Tell 38," in *Maurice Bavaud: Dokumentation zum 60. Todestag* (Berne, 2001), p. 48.

[81]Picker, op. cit., pp. 230, 247.

[82]Ibid., p. 231.

[83]BA R58/93-50.

[84]Hoffmann, *Security*, p. 105.

Chapter 2

[1]Bundesarchiv [hereafter BA], Elser Interrogation file, BA R3001/310/106.

[2]Joseph Goebbels, Vom Kaiserhof zur Reichskanzlei (Munich, 1934), p. 27.

[3]Quoted in John Toland, *Hitler* (London, 1976), p. 298.

[4]Rudolf Diels quoted in J. Noakes and G. Pridham (eds.), *Nazism 1919–45*, Vol. 1 (Exeter, 1983), p. 140.

[5]Richard Grunberger, *A Social History of the Third Reich* (London, 1971), p. 82.

[6]Ibid., p. 96.

[7]Edward Crankshaw, *Gestapo: Instrument of Tyranny* (London, 2002 edition), p. 91.

[8]Quoted in ibid., p. 89.

[9]Johannes Steinhoff, Peter Pechel, and Dennis Showalter, *Voices from the Third Reich* (London, 1989), pp. 50–51.

[10]Michael Burleigh, *The Third Reich* (London, 2000), p. 227.

[11]Grunberger, op. cit., p. 255.

[12]See the Web site of the Prora complex at www.museum-prora.de.

[13]Burleigh, op. cit., p. 250.

[14]Karl Dietrich Bracher, *The German Dictatorship* (London, 1971), p. 280.

[15]Steinhoff et al., op. cit., p. 48.

[16]Grunberger, op. cit., p. 350.

[17]See Guido Knopp, *Hitler's Children* (Stroud, 2002).

[18]Joachim Fest, *The Face of the Third Reich* (London, 1979), p. 130.

[19]Quoted in ibid., p. 147.

[20]Ibid., p. 141.

[21]Anthony Read, *The Devil's Disciples* (London, 2003), p. 198.

[22]Quoted in Ralf Georg Reuth, *Goebbels* (New York, 1993), p. 108.

[23]Quoted in Read, op. cit., p. 295.

[24]See Burleigh, op. cit., "Introduction."

[25]Quoted in Ulrich Herbert, "Good Times, Bad Times: Memories of the Third Reich," in Richard Bessel (ed.), *Life in the Third Reich* (Oxford, 1987), p. 97.

[26]On Elser see, for instance, Hellmut Haasis, *Den Hitler jag' ich in die Luft* (Berlin, 1999); Anton Hoch, "Das Attentat auf Hitler im Münchner Bürger-bräukeller 1939," in *Vierteljahrshefte für Zeitgeschichte*, Vol. XVII (1969), pp. 383–413; and Lothar Gruchmann (ed.), *Autobiographie eines Attentäters. Johann Georg Elser* (Stuttgart, 1970).

[27]Quoted in Haasis, op. cit., p. 164.

[28]Quoted in Lothar Gruchmann and Anton Hoch, *Georg Elser: Der Attentäter aus dem Volke* (Frankfurt am Main, 1980), p. 89.

[29]Ibid., p. 97.

[30]BA R3001/310/91.

[31]BA R3001/310/117.

[32]BA R3001/310/123.

[33]Hoch, op. cit., p. 400.

[34]BA R3001/310/193.

[35]BA R3001/310/150–53.

[36]BA R3001/310/178.

[37]BA R3001/310/184–85.

[38]Nicolaus von Below, *At Hitler's Side* (London, 2001), p. 42.

[39]Haasis, op. cit., p. 10.

[40]Max Domarus, *Hitler: Speeches and Proclamations 1932–45,* Vol. III (London, 1997), pp. 1865–75.

[41]Quoted in Haasis, op. cit., pp. 33–34.

[42]Quoted in ibid., p. 33.

[43]Quoted in Walter Schellenberg, *Schellenberg* (London, 1969), p. 41.

[44]Quoted in Haasis, op. cit., pp. 24–25.

[45]Toland, op. cit., p. 593.

[46]Quoted in Heinz Höhne, *The Order of the Death's Head* (London, 1969), p. 288.

[47]The British archival papers relating to the Venlo incident were released in 1995. They are held in FO371/23107/69 at the National Archives in London [hereafter NA].

[48]See Schellenberg, op. cit., pp. 30–44.

[49]See Sigismund Payne Best, *The Venlo Incident* (London, 1949).

[50]Hans Gisevius, *To the Bitter End* (Cambridge, MA, 1947), p. 405.

[51]*Völkischer Beobachter,* 10 November 1939. "Die wunderbare Errettung des Führers—Chamberlains frommer Wunsch ging nicht in Erfüllung."

[52]Ian Kershaw, *Hitler: 1936–1945 Nemesis* (London, 2000), p. 275.

[53]Burleigh, op. cit., p. 723.

[54]Denis Mack Smith, *Mussolini* (London, 1981), p. 281.

[55]BA file R43II/991.

[56]BA R43II/903/105. Poem by Martha Hilgenfeld of Berlin-Steglitz.

[57]NA GFM/33/1673/059585. Report from German legation in Berne, 10 November 1939.

[58]NA GFM/33/1673/059593. Report from German consulate in Zürich, 14 November 1939.

[59]NA GFM/33/804/2051. Report from German legation in Venezuela, 20 December 1939.

[60]NA GFM/33/2372/384400. Report from German embassy in Washington, DC, 11 June 1940.

[61]See BA file R43II/3465.

[62]BA R58/93/52, Heydrich to all senior SS, SD, Gestapo, and Kripo personnel.

[63]Hans Rothfels, *Die deutsche Opposition gegen Hitler* (Zürich, 1994), p. 111.

[64]Quoted in Toland, op. cit., p. 593.

[65]Gisevius, op. cit., p. 410.

[66]Quoted in Toland, op. cit., p. 594.

[67]Ibid., p. 591.

[68]BA R58/93/86, Heydrich Memorandum, 9 March 1940.

[69]See Peter Hoffmann, *Hitler's Personal Security* (New York, 2000 edition), pp. 111–17.

[70]Schellenberg, op. cit., p. 49.

[71]Gisevius, op. cit., p. 407.

[72]See, for example, Alan Bullock, *Hitler: A Study in Tyranny* (London, 1962 edition), pp. 566–67; Peter Padfield, *Himmler* (London, 1990), p. 283.

[73]Domarus, op. cit., pp. 1864–65.

[74]Hoch, op. cit., p. 384.

[75]Lothar Gruchmann and Anton Hoch.

[76]Peter Steinbach and Johannes Tuchel, "Der Widerstandskämpfer und das Attentat vom 8. November 1939—Deutungen und Diffamierungen," in *Frankfurter Rundschau,* 18 November 1999.

[77]Haasis, op. cit., p. 234.

[78]Peter Hoffmann, *The History of the German Resistance 1933–1945* (London, 1977), p. 258.

Chapter 3

[1]"Hans Oster" in *Neue Deutsche Biographie,* Vol. XIX (Berlin, 1998), p. 617.

[2]Quoted in William Carr, *A History of Germany 1815–1945,* 3rd edition (London, 1987), pp. 263–64.

[3]John Wheeler-Bennett, *The Nemesis of Power—The German Army in Politics, 1918–45* (London, 1961), p. 67.

[4]Quoted in John Wheeler-Bennett, *Hindenburg—The Wooden Titan* (London, 1967), p. 237.

[5]Ibid., p. 229.

[6]Adolf Hitler, *Mein Kampf* (London, 1969), p. 186.

[7]Wheeler-Bennett, *Nemesis,* p. 694.

[8]Marion Gräfin Dönhoff, *Preußen—Maß und Maßlosigkeit* (Berlin, 1998), p. 75.

[9]Grand-Admiral Erich Raeder quoted in Wheeler-Bennett, *Nemesis,* p. 291.

[10]Quoted in Heinz Höhne, *Canaris* (London, 1976), translated by John Brownjohn, p. 172.

[11]Quoted in Lauran Paine, *The Abwehr* (London, 1984), p. 33.

[12]Quoted in Höhne, op. cit., p. 174.

[13]Quoted in J. Noakes and G. Pridham (eds.), *Nazism 1919–45,* Vol. 1 (Exeter, 1983), p. 14.

[14]Max Domarus, *Hitler: Speeches and Proclamations, 1932–1945,* Vol. III (London, 1997), p. 1868.

[15]For a discussion of the significance of the Hossbach Memorandum, see Jonathan Wright and Paul Stafford, "A Blueprint for War? Hitler and the Hossbach Memorandum," in *History Today,* Vol. 38, No. 3, March 1988.

[16]Ian Kershaw, *Hitler: 1889–1936 Hubris* (London, 2000), p. 50.

[17]Quoted in Fabian von Schlabrendorff, *The Secret War Against Hitler* (London, 1966), p. 127.

[18]Ian Colvin, *Canaris: Chief of Intelligence* (London, 1951), p. 43.

[19]For a short biography of Blomberg, see Walter Görlitz, "Blomberg," in Corelli Barnett (ed.), *Hitler's Generals* (London, 1989), pp. 129–39.

[20]See Robert O'Neil, "Fritsch, Beck and the Führer," in Barnett, op. cit., p. 24.

[21]Quoted in Wheeler-Bennett, *Nemesis,* p. 372.

[22]Paul Leverkuehn, *German Military Intelligence* (London, 1954), p. 27.

[23]David Kahn, *Hitler's Spies—German Military Intelligence in World War II* (London, 1980), p. 218.

[24]Wheeler-Bennett, *Nemesis,* p. 341.

[25]Kahn, op. cit., pp. 314–17.

[26]Helmut Krausnick, "Aus dem Personalakten von Canaris," in *Vierteljahrshefte für Zeitgeschichte* (hereafter *VfZ*), Vol. X, 1962, p. 292.

[27]André Brissaud, *Canaris* (London, 1973), p. 5.

[28]Höhne, op. cit., p. 167.

[29]Ibid., p. 179.

[30]General Lahousen's description of Canaris quoted in Hans Gisevius, *To the Bitter End* (Cambridge, MA, 1947), p. 439.

[31]Peter Padfield, *Himmler—Reichsführer-SS* (London, 1990), p. 197.

[32]Höhne, op. cit., p. 471.

[33]Franz Maria Liedig quoted in Paine, op. cit., p. 29.

[34]Kahn, op. cit., p. 221.

[35]Colvin, op. cit., p. 43.

[36]Brissaud, op. cit., p. 106.

[37]Quoted in ibid., p. 102.

[38]Paine, op. cit., p. 33.

[39]Gisevius, op. cit., p. 282.

[40]Quoted in Hermann Graml, "Der Fall Oster," in *VfZ,* Vol. XIV, 1966, p. 27.

[41]*Neue Deutsche Biographie,* p. 616.

[42]Graml, op. cit., p. 31.

[43]Klemens von Klemperer, *German Resistance Against Hitler: The Search for Allies Abroad* (Oxford, 1992), p. 194.

[44]Terry Parssinen, *The Oster Conspiracy of 1938* (New York, 2003), p. 7.

[45]Liedig quoted in Höhne, op. cit., p. 262.

[46]Gisevius, op. cit., p. 421.

[47]Reinhard Spitzy, *How We Squandered the Reich* (Wilby, Norfolk, 1997), pp. 296, 300.

[48]Ted Harrison, "'Alter Kämpfer' im Widerstand: Graf Helldorf, die NS-Bewegung und die Opposition gegen Hitler," in *VfZ*, Vol. XXXXV, 1997, p. 412.

[49]Spitzy, op. cit., p. 293.

[50]Ibid., p. 296.

[51]Gisevius, op. cit., p. 424.

[52]Quoted in Ewan Butler, *Mason-Mac* (London, 1972), p. 70.

[53]Quoted in Ian Kershaw, *Hitler: 1936–1945 Nemesis* (London, 2000), p. 81.

[54]Domarus, op. cit., Vol. II, pp. 1056–57.

[55]Kershaw, *Nemesis,* p. 83.

[56]Joachim Fest, *Plotting Hitler's Death* (London, 1997), p. 77.

[57]Harrison, op. cit., pp. 385–423.

[58]Hjalmar Schacht, *76 Jahre meines Lebens* (Bad Wörishofen, 1953), pp. 487–88.

[59]See Susanne Meinl, *Nationalsozialisten gegen Hitler* (Berlin, 2000), p. 268.

[60]Susanne Meinl and Dieter Krüger, "Der politische Weg von Friedrich Wilhelm Heinz," in *VfZ*, Vol. XXXXII, 1994, pp. 39–69.

[61]William Shirer, *The Rise and Fall of the Third Reich* (London, 1964), p. 440.

[62]Domarus, op. cit., Vol. II, pp. 1150–61.

[63]Erich Kordt, *Nicht aus dem Akten* (Stuttgart, 1950), p. 258.

[64]Helmuth Groscurth, *Tagebücher eines Abwehroffiziers 1938–1940* (Stuttgart, 1970), p. 35.

[65]Quoted in Kershaw, *Nemesis,* p. 112.

[66]Alexandra Ritchie, *Faust's Metropolis* (London, 1999), p. 479.

[67]Gisevius, op. cit., p. 322.

[68]Quoted in Parssinen, op. cit., p. 133.

[69]Hans Rothfels, *Die deutsche Opposition gegen Hitler* (Zürich, 1994), p. 129.

[70]Quoted in Kershaw, *Nemesis,* p. 114.

[71]Quoted in ibid., p. 115.

[72]Kordt, op. cit., p. 262.

[73]Ibid.

[74]Quoted in Kershaw, *Nemesis,* p. 118.

[75]Alan Bullock, *Hitler: A Study in Tyranny* (London, 1962), p. 461.

[76]Domarus, op. cit., Vol. II, pp. 1183–93.

[77]Kordt, op. cit., p. 263.

[78]Ibid., p. 270.

[79]Parssinen, op. cit., p. 162.

[80]Gisevius, op. cit., p. 326.

[81] Kershaw, *Nemesis,* p. 120.

[82] Gisevius, op. cit., p. 330.

[83] Quoted in Martin Gilbert, *Churchill—A Life* (London, 1991), p. 600.

[84] Norman Davies, *Europe* (London, 1997), p. 990.

[85] Gisevius, op. cit., p. 326.

[86] Wheeler-Bennett, *Nemesis,* pp. 404–5.

[87] Groscurth quoted in Fest, op. cit., p. 124.

[88] Gisevius, op. cit., p. 359.

[89] Harold Deutsch, *The Conspiracy Against Hitler in the Twilight War* (London, 1968), p. 44.

[90] Kershaw, *Nemesis,* p. 270.

[91] Kordt, op. cit., p. 371.

[92] Ibid.

[93] Spitzy, op. cit., p. 305.

[94] Kordt, op. cit., p. 374.

[95] Klemperer, op. cit., p. 196.

[96] Deutsch, op. cit., p. 99.

[97] Spitzy, op. cit., p. 312.

[98] Peter Hoffmann, *German Resistance to Hitler* (London, 1988), p. 87.

[99] Fest, op. cit., p. 86.

[100] Lahousen quoted in Gisevius, op. cit., p. 439.

[101] Brissaud, op. cit., p. 112.

[102] Spitzy, op. cit., pp. 303–4.

[103] Parssinen, op. cit., p. 149.

[104] Wheeler-Bennett, *Nemesis,* p. 431.

[105] See Bullock, op. cit., p. 452.

[106] Kershaw, *Nemesis,* 123.

[107] Barry Leach, "Halder," in Barnett, op. cit., p. 105.

[108] Gisevius, op. cit., p. 326.

[109] Kordt, op. cit., p. 375.

[110] Deutsch, op. cit., p. 41.

[111] Theodore Hamerow, *On the Road to the Wolf's Lair* (Cambridge, MA, 1999), p. 239.

[112] Fest, op. cit., p. 98.

[113] Hoffmann, op. cit., p. 89.

[114] General Georg Thomas quoted in Hamerow, op. cit., p. 243.

[115] Spitzy, op. cit., p. 302.

[116] Witzleben quoted in Parssinen, op. cit., p. 167.

[117] Brissaud, op. cit., p. 89.

[118] Parssinen, op. cit., p. 100.

[119] Höhne, op. cit., p. 556.

[120] Christabel Bielenberg, *The Past Is Myself* (London, 1968), p. 79.

[121] Walter Schellenberg, *Schellenberg* (London, 1969), pp. 150–51.

[122] Ibid., p. 159.

[123] Ibid., pp. 160–61.

[124] Brissaud, op. cit., pp. 325–26.

[125] Ibid., p. 326.

[126] Höhne, op. cit., p. 583.

[127]Ibid., p. 595.
[128]Ibid.

Chapter 4

[1]Jan Szalewski quoted in Stanisław Majewski, "Zamach na Hitlera pod Starogardem," in *Litery* (Gdańsk, 1962), No. 3, p. 6.
[2]See, for instance, William Shirer, *The Rise and Fall of the Third Reich* (London, 1964), p. 653.
[3]Text quoted at http://www.mdr.de/viaeuropa/themen/377134.html.
[4]See Jürgen Runzheimer, "Der Überfall auf den Sender Gleiwitz im Jahre 1939," in *Vierteljahrshefte für Zeitgeschichte* (hereafter *VfZ*), Vol. X, 1962, pp. 408–26; see also Alfred Naujocks's deposition at Nuremberg, dated 20 November 1945.
[5]Henric Wuermeling, *August '39* (Berlin, 1989), p. 21.
[6]Jarosław Tuliszka, *Westerplatte 1926–1939. Dzieje wojskowej składnicy tranzytowej w Wolnym Mieście Gdańsku* (Toruń, 2002), p. 151.
[7]Max Domarus, *Hitler: Speeches and Proclamations 1932–1945*, Vol. III (London, 1997), p. 1754.
[8]Charles Sydnor, *Soldiers of Destruction* (Princeton, 1990 edition), p. 40.
[9]Quoted in Polish Ministry of Information, *The German Invasion of Poland: Polish Black Book* (London, 1940), p. 134.
[10]See Andrzej Suchcitz, "Poland's Defence Preparations in 1939," in Peter Stachura (ed.), *Poland Between the Wars 1918–1939* (Basingstoke, 1998), pp. 109–32.
[11]See, for instance, Wesley Adamczyk, *When God Looked the Other Way* (Chicago, 2004).
[12]From "Dabrowski's Mazurka," which became the Polish national anthem in 1926; quoted in Norman Davies and Roger Moorhouse, *Microcosm* (London, 2002), pp. 340–41.
[13]Norman Davies, *God's Playground: A History of Poland* (Oxford, 1981), pp. 36, 41.
[14]See Davies and Moorhouse, op. cit., p. 336.
[15]John Connelly, "Nazis and Slavs: From Racial Theory to Racist Practice," in *Central European History*, Vol. 32, No. 1, pp. 1–33.
[16]*The Goebbels Diaries, 1939–1941*, trans. F. Taylor (London, 1984), p. 16.
[17]Norman Davies, *Rising '44* (London, 2003), p. 90.
[18]Michał Grynberg (ed.), *Words to Outlive Us: Eyewitness Accounts from the Warsaw Ghetto* (London, 2003), p. 29.
[19]Richard Lukas, *Forgotten Holocaust: The Poles Under German Occupation 1939–1944*, revised edition (New York, 2001), p. 9.
[20]Quoted in ibid., p. 33.
[21]Roman Frister, *The Cap: The Price of a Life* (London, 1999), p. 9.
[22]Lukas, op. cit., p. 34.
[23]Tadeusz Bór-Komorowski, *The Secret Army* (London, 1950), p. 22.
[24]Lukas, op. cit., p. 35.
[25]Ibid., p. 36.

[26]Quoted in Joachim Fest, *The Face of the Third Reich* (London, 1970), p. 325.

[27]Quoted in Davies, *Rising*, p. 86.

[28]Bór-Komorowski, op. cit., p. 38.

[29]Włodzimierz Borodziej, *Terror und Politik* (Mainz, 1999), p. 174.

[30]See K. S. Rudnicki, *The Last of the War Horses* (London, 1974), p. 103. Also Wolfgang Jacobmeyer, "Henryk Dobrzański ["Hubal"]—Ein biographischer Beitrag zu den Anfängen der polnischen Résistance im Zweiten Weltkrieg," in *VfZ*, Vol. XX, 1972, pp. 65–74.

[31]Bór-Komorowski, op. cit., p. 22.

[32]Marek Ney-Krwawicz, *The Polish Home Army 1939–1945* (London, 2001), p. 2.

[33]Ibid., p. 27.

[34]See, for instance, Jan Karski, *Story of a Secret State* (Boston, 1944), or Stefan Korboński, *The Polish Underground State* (Boulder, 1978).

[35]See Appendix 35 in Davies, *Rising*.

[36]Bór-Komorowski, op. cit., p. 28.

[37]Jozef Garlinski, *Poland, SOE and the Allies* (London, 1969), p. 31.

[38]National Archives (London), T 160/1412, ref. C/8297, 10 December 1941, Menzies to Herbert Brittain (Treasury).

[39]See Martin Middlebrook, *The Peenemünde Raid* (London, 1982).

[40]Garlinski, op. cit., pp. 150–54.

[41]Ben Pimlott (ed.), *The Second World War Diary of Hugh Dalton* (London, 1985), p. 67.

[42]M. R. D. Foot, *SOE: The Special Operations Executive, 1940–1946* (London, 1984), p. 191.

[43]See, for instance, E. T. Wood, *Karski: How One Man Tried to Stop the Holocaust* (London, 1994).

[44]Ney-Krwawicz, op. cit., p. 36.

[45]Bohdan Kwiatkowski, *Sabotaz i Dywersja* (London, 1949), Vol. 1, p. 21.

[46]Lukas, op. cit., p. 49.

[47]Ney-Krwawicz, op. cit., p. 51.

[48]Peter Hoffmann, *Hitler's Personal Security* (New York, 2000 edition), pp. 150–51.

[49]Kwiatkowski, op. cit., p. 21.

[50]Ney-Krwawicz, op. cit., p. 48.

[51]Studium Polski Podziemnej Archive (hereafter SPP), ref: 3.6.3.3.13/1, 2, and 3.

[52]Bór-Komorowski, op. cit., pp. 115–16.

[53]Lukas, op. cit., p. 92.

[54]Ibid., p. 91.

[55]Bór-Komorowski, op. cit., p. 152.

[56]Borodziej, op. cit., p. 53.

[57]Kwiatkowski, op. cit., p. 21.

[58]See, for example, the file compiled for the failed attack on SS *Obergruppenführer* Friedrich-Wilhelm Krüger, SPP, ref: BI.9/71.

[59]Bór-Komorowski, op. cit., p. 155.

[60]Placard reproduced at http://wilk.wpk.p.lodz.pl/~whatfor/specjalna_operacja_bojowa_kutsch.htm.

[61]Halina Czarnocka (ed.), *Armia Krajowa w Dokumentach 1939–1945,* Vol. I (London, 1970), p. 220.

[62]On the Forster assassination attempt, see "Próba zamachu na kata Pomorze," in *Gdański Przekaz,* No. 5, 2000, pp. 9–10.

[63]Bór-Komorowski, op. cit., p. 114.

[64]Bundesarchiv, Berlin [hereafter BA], ref: NS19/2653.

[65]BA ref: NS19/2653, Europapress report, 10 May 1943.

[66]Stanisław Okecki, *Polish Resistance Movement in Poland and Abroad 1939–1945* (Warsaw, 1987), p. 95.

[67]Quoted in Lukaę, op. cit., p. 91.

[68]Bór-Komorowski, op. cit., p. 156.

[69]On the Kutschera attack, see Bór-Komorowski, op. cit., pp. 156–60, and Tomasz Strzembosz, *Akcje zbronje podziemnej Warszawy, 1939–44* (Warsaw, 1979), pp. 312–27.

[70]Quoted in Davies, *Rising,* p. 198.

[71]Quoted in Waclaw Długoborski, "Die deutsche Besatzungspolitik gegenüber Polen," in K. D. Bracher, M. Funke, and H-A. Jacobsen (eds.), *National-sozialistische Diktatur 1933–1945* (Bonn, 1983), p. 579.

[72]Hans Frank quoted in Norman Rich, *Hitler's War Aims,* Vol. II (London, 1974), p. 96.

[73]Czesław Madajczyk, *Die Okkupationspolitik Nazideutschlands in Polen, 1939–1945* (Cologne, 1988), p. 131. Goebbels's support for Frank is expressed in L. Lochner (trans. and ed.), *The Goebbels Diaries* (London, 1948), pp. 313–14, entry for 25 May 1943.

[74]Borodziej, op. cit., p. 75.

[75]See Hans Frank, *Das Diensttagebuch des deutschen Gouverneurs in Polen 1939–45* (Stuttgart, 1975).

[76]Lukas, op. cit., p. 92.

[77]The snake or viper was a common Nazi metaphor in describing resistance to German occupation. It featured in a number of campaign badges, such as the Warsaw Shield and the Anti-Partisan Badge.

[78]Hoffmann, op. cit., p. 197.

[79]Ibid., p. 135.

[80]Take, for example, the journey from Bad Polzin to Topolno on the Vistula and back to Plietnitz undertaken on 4 September 1939—a total of approximately 250 km.

[81]See the German *Wochenschau* newsreel covering the September Campaign held at the Imperial War Museum Film Archive, London.

[82]Hoffmann, op. cit., pp. 136–37.

[83]Ibid., p. 136.

[84]Ibid., p. 137.

[85]Interview with Ewa Klarner Huggins, granddaughter of Czesław Klarner, who was one of the hostages (5 December 2003).

[86]Jan Nowak, *Courier from Warsaw* (London, 1982), p. 60.

[87]Janina Karasiówna, "Pierwsze półrocze armii podziemnej SZP-ZWZ," in *Niepodległość,* Vol. 1, 1948; see also *Dziennik Polski,* 7 September 2003, p. 5.

[88]Nowak, op. cit., p. 60.

[89]Hoffmann, op. cit., p. 224.

[90]Albert Speer, *Inside the Third Reich* (London, 1970), p. 401n.

[91]F. Siedler and D. Zeigert, *Die Führerhauptquartiere. Anlagen und Planungen im Zweiten Weltkrieg* (Munich, 2001), p. 350.

[92]N. Cameron and R. H. Stevens (trans.), *Hitler's Table Talk 1941–1944* (London, 1953), p. 340.

[93]Christa Schroeder, *Er war mein Chef* (Munich, 1985), p. 112.

[94]See map 32c in Hoffmann, op. cit., pp. 222–23.

[95]E. Korpalski, J. Szynkowski, and G. Wünsche, *Das Führerhauptquartier im Bild und in Errinerungen von Zeitzeugen* (Ketrzyn, 2004), p. 28.

[96]Hoffmann, op. cit., p. 229.

[97]Bruno Dreyer quoted in Korpalski et al., op. cit., p. 183.

[98]Ibid., p. 29.

[99]Speer, op. cit., p. 526.

[100]See Ron Jeffrey, *Red Runs the Vistula* (Auckland, 1985).

[101]U. Neumärker, R. Conrad, and C. Woywodt, *Wolfschanze: Hitler's Machtzentrale im II Weltkrieg* (Berlin, 2000), p. 71.

[102]Hoffmann, op. cit., p. 67.

[103]Traudl Junge, *Bis zur letzten Stunde* (Munich, 2002), p. 59.

[104]Bór-Komorowski, op. cit., p. 153.

[105]Krzysztof Komorowski, *Konspiracja Pomorska 1939–1947—Leksykon* (Gdańsk, 1993), pp. 94–96.

[106]See Zygmunt August Sikorski, *Jan Kazimierz Szalewski—dzieje pomorskiego patrioty* (Gdańsk, 1996), pp. 61–67.

[107]Deposition of Jan Szalewski, ps. "Sobół-Sable," ref: M-14/623 POM in Fundacja Archiwum Muzeum Pomorskie Armii Krajowej oraz Wojskowej Służby Polek w Toruniu, Torun, Poland.

[108]See the account of Jan Szalewski, who led one of the units in the attack, as retold in Majewski, op. cit., p. 6.

[109]Jan Szalewski, "Zamach na Hitlera," in *Głos Nauczycielski,* No. 29, 1974.

[110]See Majewski, op. cit., p. 6.

[111]Sikorski, op. cit., p. 66.

[112]Konrad Ciechanowski, *Ruch oporu na Pomorzu Gdańskim 1939–1945* (Warsaw, 1972), p. 132.

[113]Letter from the Danzig Abwehr from 27 September 1944, reproduced in Sikorski, op. cit., p. 66.

[114]See, for example, Leon Lubecki, *Ruch oporu na Pomorzu Gdańskim w latach 1939–1945* (Gdańsk, 1961), p. 59.

[115]National Archive, London, HS6/624, Appendix 4.

[116]Hoffmann, op. cit., p. xxviii.

[117]Komorowski, op. cit., pp. 164–65.

[118]Ibid., p. 96.

[119]Piotr Stachiewicz, *Parasol* (Warsaw, 1981), p. 628.

[120]See Davies, *Rising,* Chapter VII.

[121]Komorowski, op. cit., pp. 164–65.

[122]See personnel file of Franciszek Niepokólczycki, ps. "Theodore," SPP ref: TP3/5920/2.

[123]Dariusz Baliszewski, "Polski Zamach na Hitlera," in *Newsweek Polska,* 04/2002.

Chapter 5

[1]National Archive (London) [hereafter NA], FO371/32878/N1688, British Embassy, Moscow, to Foreign Office, 30 March 1942.

[2]Statistics from Gerd Ueberschär, "Barbarossa," in I. C. B. Dear (ed.), *The Oxford Companion to the Second World War* (Oxford, 1995), pp. 109–13.

[3]Quoted in Max Domarus, *Hitler: Reden und Proklamationen,* Vol. II (Wiesbaden, 1973), p. 1732.

[4]Alexander Werth, *Russia at War: 1941–45* (London, 1964), p. 159.

[5]Von Hardesty, *Red Phoenix: The Rise of Soviet Air Power, 1941–45* (Washington, DC, 1982), p. 11.

[6]See John Erickson, *The Road to Stalingrad* (London, 1975), p. 87.

[7]Simon Sebag Montefiore, *Stalin: The Court of the Red Tsar* (London, 2003), p. 323.

[8]Werth, op. cit., p. 181.

[9]Montefiore, op. cit., pp. 330–31 and footnote.

[10]Quoted in Constantine Pleshakov, *Stalin's Folly* (London, 2005), p. 91.

[11]See, for instance, Viktor Suvorov, *Icebreaker: Who Started the Second World War?* (London, 1990).

[12]Quoted in Alan Bullock, *Hitler and Stalin: Parallel Lives* (London, 1991), p. 389.

[13]Quoted in Werth, op. cit., pp. 164–68.

[14]Montefiore, op. cit., p. 221.

[15]Anne Applebaum, *Gulag* (London, 2003), p. 123.

[16]Montefiore, op. cit., p. 219.

[17]Ibid., p. 222.

[18]Robert Conquest, *The Great Terror—A Reassessment* (London, 1990), p. 235.

[19]Montefiore, op. cit., p. 240.

[20]Mark Frankland, *Khrushchev* (London, 1966), p. 47.

[21]Montefiore, op. cit., p. 283.

[22]Michael Parrish, *The Lesser Terror* (Westport, CT, 1996), p. 57.

[23]See, for instance, Robert Conquest, "Playing Down the Gulag," in *The Times Literary Supplement,* 24 February 1995.

[24]Christopher Andrew and Vasili Mitrokhin, *The Mitrokhin File* (London, 2000 edition), p. 91.

[25]Ibid., p. 117.

[26]Christopher Andrew and Oleg Gordievsky, *KGB: The Inside Story of Its Foreign Operations from Lenin to Gorbachev* (London, 1990), pp. 128–29.

[27]Andrew and Mitrokhin, op. cit., p. 105.

[28]See W.G. Krivitsky, *In Stalin's Secret Service* (New York, 2000).

[29]Andrew and Gordievsky, op. cit., pp. 125–26.

[30]Quoted in Isaac Don Levine, *The Mind of an Assassin* (London, 1959), p. 125.

[31]Andrew and Mitrokhin, op. cit., p. 116.

[32]Ibid., p. 92.

[33]Some accounts maintain that Foote's plan was hatched in 1938; however, a

close reading of his memoirs makes it clear that it took place in 1939. See Alexander Foote, *Handbook for Spies* (London, 1949), pp. 30–35.

[34]Ibid., p. 26.

[35]Ibid., p. 32.

[36]Quoted in David Pryce-Jones, *Unity Mitford—A Quest* (London, 1995), p. 102.

[37]Traudl Junge, *Until the Final Hour* (London, 2003), p. 102.

[38]Foote, op. cit., p. 31.

[39]Ibid., pp. 31–32.

[40]Quoted in Neil Grant, *The German-Soviet Pact* (New York, 1975), p. 51.

[41]Foote, op. cit., pp. 32–33.

[42]See Anthony Read and David Fisher, *Operation Lucy* (London, 1980).

[43]Antony Beevor, *Stalingrad* (London, 1998), p. 108.

[44]Guy Sajer, *The Forgotten Soldier* (London, 1971), p. 382.

[45]Quoted in Werth, op. cit., p. 167.

[46]Parrish, op. cit., p. 121.

[47]Quoted in Werth, op. cit., p. 644.

[48]Richard Overy, *Russia's War* (London, 1998), p. 147.

[49]Heinz Höhne, *The Order of the Death's Head* (London, 1969), p. 372.

[50]See French MacLean, *The Cruel Hunters: SS-Sonderkommando Dirlewanger* (Atglen, PA, 1998).

[51]*SS-Gruppenführer* Hermann Fegelein quoted at http://www.wssob.com/008divfgy.html.

[52]Overy, op. cit., p. 146.

[53]Alan Clarke, *Barbarossa* (London, 1995 edition), pp. 154–55.

[54]Matthew Cooper, *The Nazi War Against Soviet Partisans 1941–1944* (New York, 1979), pp. 59–60.

[55]Kurt DeWitt, "The Partisans in Soviet Intelligence," in John Armstrong (ed.), *Soviet Partisans in World War II* (Madison, 1964), p. 339.

[56]Pavel Sudoplatov, *Special Tasks* (London, 1994), p. 129.

[57]Teodor Gladkov, *Legenda Sovetskoi Razvedki* (Moscow, 2001), p. 94.

[58]Pavel Sudoplatov, *Razvedka i Kreml* (Moscow, 1996), p. 155.

[59]See "Legendary Soviet Intelligence Officer Dies," in *Pravda*, 22 July 2003.

[60]Gladkov, *Legenda,* pp. 300–05.

[61]Dmitri Medvedev, *Otryad idet na Zapad* (Lvov, 1948), p. 27.

[62]Andrew and Gordievsky, op. cit., p. 252.

[63]Quoted in Medvedev, op. cit., p. 59.

[64]Vladislav Krasnov, *Soviet Defectors: The KGB Wanted List* (Stanford, 1986), p. 58.

[65]Nikolai Khokhlov, *In the Name of Conscience* (London, 1960), p. 16.

[66]Ibid., p. 54.

[67]Ibid., p. 60.

[68]*Ocherki istorii Sovetskoi Voennoi Razvedki,* Vol. 4 (Moscow, 1999), pp. 99–101.

[69]Khokhlov, op. cit., p. 75.

[70]Andrew and Gordievsky, op. cit., pp. 352–53.

[71]Sudoplatov, *Special Tasks,* p. 129.

[72]Peter Hoffmann, *Hitler's Personal Security* (New York, 2000 edition), p. 228.

[73]Franz Siedler and Dieter Zeigert, *Hitler's Secret Headquarters* (London, 2004), p. 111.

[74]Albert Speer, *Inside the Third Reich* (London, 1970), p. 330.

[75]Christa Schroeder, *Er war mein Chef* (Munich, 1985), p. 137.

[76]Nicolaus von Below, *At Hitler's Side* (London, 2001), p. 151.

[77]See, for example, Luiza Bilozerova, *Vervolf—rokovaia taina Gitlera?* (Vinnitsa, 1996).

[78]L. Heston and R. Heston, *The Medical Casebook of Adolf Hitler* (New York, 1979), p. 39.

[79]Wendy Lower, "'Anticipatory Obedience' and the Nazi Implementation of the Holocaust in the Ukraine: A Case Study of Central and Peripheral Forces in the Generalbezirk Zhytomyr, 1941–1944," in *Holocaust and Genocide Studies,* Vol. 16, No. 1, Spring 2002, p. 4.

[80]Ibid., p. 11.

[81]Siedler and Zeigert, op. cit., p. 116.

[82]Beevor, *Stalingrad,* p. 80.

[83]Richard Rhodes, *Masters of Death* (Oxford, 2002), p. 251.

[84]Speer, op. cit., p. 329.

[85]Walter Warlimont, *Inside Hitler's Headquarters* (London, 1964), p. 178.

[86]NA, FO371/32878/N1688, British Embassy, Moscow, to Foreign Office, 30 March 1942.

[87]Werth, op. cit., p. 711.

[88]Heinrich Himmler, *Der Dienstkalendar Heinrich Himmler 1941/42* (Hamburg, 1999), p. 717.

[89]Arkady Yarovoi, *Stavki Gitlera* (Moscow, 1992), p. 68.

[90]Ihor Kamenetsky, *Hitler's Occupation of the Ukraine 1941–44* (Milwaukee, 1956), p. 72.

[91]Teodor Gladkov, *Ostaius Chekistom!* (Moscow, 1989), p. 86.

[92]Ibid., p. 87.

[93]Sudoplatov, *Special Tasks,* p. 128.

[94]Gladkov, *Legenda,* p. 234.

[95]Hoffmann, op. cit., p. xxviii.

[96]Warlimont, op. cit., p. 550.

[97]C. G. Sweeting, *Hitler's Personal Pilot: The Life and Times of Hans Baur* (Washington, DC, 2000), pp. 183–84.

[98]Ibid., p. 181.

[99]Hoffmann, op. cit., p. 78.

[100]Hans Baur, *Hitler's Pilot* (London, 1958), p. 143.

[101]Ibid., p. 149.

[102]Hans Baur, *Mit Mächtigen zwischen Himmel und Erde* (Oldendorf, 1971), p. 231.

[103]NA, WO178/25, 30 Military Mission (USSR) to DMI, 8 October 1941.

[104]NA, HW1/206, C.S.S. Telegram.

[105]Barry Leach, "Halder," in Correlli Barnett (ed.), *Hitler's Generals* (London, 1989), p. 119.

[106]Christian Hartmann, *Halder: Generalstabschef Hitlers, 1938–1942* (Paderborn, 1991), p. 293.

[107]Werth, op. cit., p. 235–39.

[108]Ray Wagner (ed.), *The Soviet Air Force in World War II* (London, 1974), p. 66.

[109]Ibid., p. 120.

[110]NA, WO178/25, War Diary of 30 Military Mission (USSR), 7 December 1941.

[111]Franz Halder, *Kriegstagebuch* (Stuttgart, 1964), pp. 288–89, or *The Halder Diaries* (Boulder, 1976), Vol. II, pp. 1295–96.

[112]Bundesarchiv Militärarchiv, Freiburg [hereafter BA MA], *Fahrt mit Sonderzug Europa nach Orscha vom 11.-15.11.1941*, ref: N220/139.

[113]"Rege Lufttätigkeit," in BA MA, *Heeresgruppe Mitte Kriegstagebuch*, ref: RH19 II/378.

[114]Interview with T. K. Gladkov, Moscow, 16 April 2004.

[115]NA, FO371/32878/N1688, British Embassy, Moscow, to Foreign Office, 30 March 1942.

[116]NA, FO371/32878/N1685, Foreign Office to Embassy Moscow, 1 April 1942.

[117]NA, WO178/26, War Diary of 30 Military Mission (USSR), 17 June 1942.

[118]Sudoplatov, *Special Tasks*, p. 35.

[119]Franz von Papen, *Memoirs* (London, 1952), p. 486.

[120]NA, HW12/274/102378, Turkish Foreign Minister to Turkish Ambassador, Kuibyshev, 18 March 1942.

[121]NA, HW12/275/103640, Turkish Foreign Minister to Turkish Ambassador, Kuibyshev.

[122]Antony Beevor, *The Mystery of Olga Chekhova* (London, 2004), p. 176.

[123]Sudoplatov, *Special Tasks*, p. 134.

[124]A. Zoller (ed.), *Hitler Privat* (Düsseldorf, 1949), p. 160.

[125]Quoted in N. Cameron and R. H. Stevens (trans.), *Hitler's Table Talk 1941–1944* (London, 2000 edition), p. 5.

[126]Beevor, *Mystery*, p. 178.

[127]Quoted in Richard Grunberger, *A Social History of the Third Reich* (London, 1971), pp. 117–18.

[128]Beevor, *Mystery*, p. 159.

[129]Renate Helker and Claudia Lenssen, *Der Tschechow-Clan* (Berlin, 2001), p. 195.

[130]Sudoplatov, *Special Tasks*, p. 115.

[131]He went on to write two books of memoirs, *The Detachment Is Moving West* (1948) and *The Strong Spirited* (1964), and a novel about the Vinnitsa underground entitled *On the Shores of the Iuzhnyi Bug* (1957).

[132]Helker and Lenssen, op. cit., p. 198.

[133]Interview with former NKVD officer Igor Shchors, Moscow, 15 April 2004.

[134]Alan Bullock, *Hitler and Stalin: Parallel Lives* (London, 1991), p. 525.

[135]Montefiore, op. cit., p. 4.

[136]Milovan Djilas, *Conversations with Stalin* (London, 1962), p. 145.

[137]Daniel Rancour-Laferriere, *The Mind of Stalin: A Psychoanalytic Study* (Ann Arbor, 1988), p. 109.

Chapter 6

[1]Neville Henderson, quoted posthumously in the *New York Times,* December 31, 1942.

[2]Guido Knopp, *Hitler's Children* (Stroud, 2002), p. 9.

[3]Albert Speer, *Inside the Third Reich* (London, 1970), p. 218.

[4]Michael Bloch, *Ribbentrop* (London, 1992), p. 219.

[5]Chamberlain speech to the House of Commons, 31 March 1939, quoted in William Shirer, *The Rise and Fall of the Third Reich* (London, 1964), p. 554.

[6]Ewan Butler, "I Talked of Plan to Kill Hitler," in *The Times,* 6 August 1969, p. 1.

[7]E. T. Williams and H. Palmer (eds.), *The Dictionary of National Biography 1951–60* (Oxford, 1971), p. 712.

[8]Quoted in Ewan Butler, *Mason-Mac* (London, 1972), p. 74.

[9]E. L. Woodward and R. Butler, *Documents of British Foreign Policy* [hereafter DBFP], Series 3, Vol. IV, Appendix V, p. 623; Ogilvie-Forbes to Strang, 29 March 1939.

[10]See Heinrich Hoffmann, *Ein Volk ehrt seinen Führer* (Berlin, 1939), reproduced in Cowdery and Cowdery, *Masters of Ceremony* (Rapid City, SD, 1998), p. 119.

[11]Butler, *Mason-Mac,* p. 75.

[12]DBFP, 3, IV, Appx V, Mason-Macfarlane Memorandum, p. 626.

[13]Imperial War Museum Archive, Mason-Macfarlane papers, ref: MM40.

[14]See, for instance, Anthony Cave Brown, *The Secret Servant: The Life of Sir Stewart Menzies, Churchill's Spymaster* (London, 1987), p. 195.

[15]See Stephenson's entry in the *Oxford Dictionary of National Biography,* Vol. 52 (Oxford, 2004), pp. 513–14.

[16]See, for example, H. Montgomery Hyde, *The Quiet Canadian* (London, 1962), p. 8, and William Stephenson, *A Man Called Intrepid* (London, 1976), p. 38.

[17]Quoted in Cave Brown, op. cit., p. 195.

[18]Quoted in the *Times,* 6 August 1969, p. 9.

[19]Nigel West, *MI6 British Secret Intelligence Operations 1909–45* (London, 1983), p. 38.

[20]Christopher Andrew, *Secret Service* (London, 1987), p. 408.

[21]Quoted in Alan Judd, *The Quest for C* (London, 1999), p. 470.

[22]Christopher Andrew and Oleg Gordievsky, *KGB: The Inside Story of Its Foreign Operations from Lenin to Gorbachev* (London, 1990), p. 32.

[23]Andrew Cook, *On His Majesty's Secret Service: Sidney Reilly* (London, 2002), pp. 127, 131.

[24]Anthony Read and David Fisher, *Colonel Z—The Life and Times of a Master of Spies* (London, 1984), p. 12.

[25]Ibid., p. 276.

[26]Quoted in Roy Jenkins, *Churchill* (London, 2001), p. 567.

[27]George Orwell, "The Lion and the Unicorn," from *Orwell and Politics* (London, 2001), p. 104.

[28]Ben Pimlott (ed.), *The Second World War Diary of Hugh Dalton: 1940–45* (London, 1987), p. 67.

[29]Quoted in M. R. D. Foot, *SOE: The Special Operations Executive, 1940–46* (London, 1984), p. 19.

[30]David Stafford, *Churchill and the Secret Service* (New York, 1998), pp. 187–88.

[31]*Killing Hitler,* BBC Television, 2003.

[32]Stephen Dorril, *MI6: Fifty Years of Special Operations* (London, 2000), p. 377.

[33]Quoted in Russell Miller, *Behind the Lines* (London, 2002), p. 3.

[34]Ibid., p. 12.

[35]M. R. D. Foot, *SOE in France* (London, 2004), p. 79.

[36]*The Goebbels Diaries* (London, 1948), p. 65, 28 February 1942.

[37]Foot, *SOE in France,* p. 214.

[38]David Stafford, *Britain and European Resistance, 1940–45* (London, 1980), p. 35.

[39]Stafford, *Churchill,* p. 240.

[40]Ibid., p. 241.

[41]Callum MacDonald, *The Killing of SS-Obergruppenführer Reinhard Heydrich* (London, 1990), p. 121.

[42]Quoted in ibid., p. 156.

[43]Quoted in ibid., p. 160.

[44]Stafford, *Churchill,* p. 241.

[45]See Anthony Head, "The Tragedy of Lidice," in *History Today,* June 2002.

[46]William Mackenzie, *The Secret History of SOE: The Special Operations Executive, 1940–45* (London, 2000), p. 319.

[47]Ralf Reuth (ed.), *Joseph Goebbels Tagebücher 1924–1945,* Vol. IV (Munich, 1992), p. 1815.

[48]Quoted in John Toland, *Hitler* (London, 1976), p. 712.

[49]N. Cameron and R. H. Stevens (trans.), *Hitler's Table Talk 1941–1944* (London, 1953), p. 512.

[50]Peter Hoffmann, *Hitler's Personal Security,* 2nd edition (New York, 2000), p. 119.

[51]Anthony Verrier, *Assassination in Algiers* (London, 1990), p. 246.

[52]National Archive (London) [hereafter NA], HS8/199, Minutes of SOE council meeting, 22 June 1943.

[53]NA, HS6/272, File No. 240, correspondence from 5 August 1943 and 22 October 1943.

[54]Foot, *SOE in France,* p. 366.

[55]For more on the Kreipe kidnapping, see W. Stanley Moss, *Ill Met by Moonlight* (London, 1950), or Antony Beevor, *Crete: The Battle and the Resistance* (London, 1991).

[56]NA, HS5/728, report by Major Leigh Fermor.

[57]Quoted in Vera Rule, "An English Odysseus," in *The Independent on Sunday,* 9 November 2003.

[58]Moss, op. cit., p. 180.

[59]NA, HS6/823, HS8/886, HS8/887, Operation Boykin, planning, report, and interrogation.

[60]On Operation Flipper, see, for example, Michael Asher, *Get Rommel* (London, 2004).

[61]Interview with Professor M. R. D. Foot, formerly the SAS officer responsible for planning the kidnap mission, 25 February 2004.

[62]David Irving, *The Trail of the Fox: The Life of Field-Marshal Erwin Rommel* (London, 1977), p. 379.

[63]*Aarhus Stiftstidende,* 17.11.1944, with thanks to Anders Thygesen.

[64]Charles Cruickshank, *SOE in Scandinavia* (Oxford, 1986), pp. 18–19.

[65]NA, HS6/674, Operation Chalgrove correspondence, 27 January 1945.

[66]Quoted in Miller, op. cit., p. 23.

[67]See Foot, *SOE,* pp. 248–49.

[68]Geoffrey Household, *Rogue Male* (London, 1939), p. 15.

[69]Ibid., pp. 16–17.

[70]Ibid., p. 17.

[71]Ibid., p. 18.

[72]Ibid., p. 192.

[73]Geoffrey Household, *Against the Wind* (London, 1958), p. 98.

[74]*Dictionary of National Biography,* Vol. 28 (Oxford, 2004), p. 292.

[75]Household, *Wind,* p. 94.

[76]Richard Meinertzhagen, *Middle East Diary 1917–1956* (London, 1959), p. 179.

[77]Ibid., p. 149.

[78]Ibid., pp. 159–60.

[79]NA, AIR20/2081, Stevenson to Douglas, 13 July 1940.

[80]Albert Speer, op. cit., p. 246.

[81]NA, AIR16/619, Harris to Douglas, 21 February 1941.

[82]NA, AIR16/619, Harris to Douglas, 7 March 1941.

[83]NA, AIR16/619, Harris to Douglas, 18 March 1941.

[84]Hans Baur, *Ich flog Mächtige der Erde* (Kempten, 1956), translated by Edward Fitzgerald as *Hitler's Pilot* (London, 1958).

[85]C. G. Sweeting, *Hitler's Personal Pilot: The Life and Times of Hans Baur* (Washington, DC, 2000), p. 148.

[86]See, for instance, Peter Padfield, *Hess: The Führer's Disciple* (London, 1991).

[87]NA, HS6/623, Gubbins to Ismay, 20 June 1944.

[88]Julian Amery, *Approach March* (London, 1973), p. 240.

[89]Hoffmann, op. cit., pp. xx–xxxiii.

[90]Ibid., pp. 118–22.

[91]NA, HS6/623, p. 64.

[92]Quoted in Denis Rigden, *Kill the Führer: Section X and Operation Foxley* (London, 1999), p. 50.

[93]The file has been reproduced as *Operation Foxley: The British Plan to Kill Hitler* (London, 1998).

[94]Interview with Professor M. R. D. Foot, who knew Joll from his SOE days and claimed to have recognized his writing style in the Foxley file. A file in the National Archive in London (HS9/806/2) confirms that Joll was indeed seconded to Section X in the autumn of 1943.

[95]Traudl Junge, *Until the Final Hour* (London, 2003), p. 71.

[96]NA, HS6/624, pp. 72–74.

[97]Rigden, op. cit., pp. 72–73.

[98]NA, HS6/626, p. 2, Joll memorandum to Gubbins.

[99]NA, HS6/623, p. 33, memorandum of 18 December 1944.

[100]NA, HS6/623, p. 7, telegraphic communication, 16 March 1945.

[101]Rigden, op. cit., p. 88.

[102]Quoted in ibid., p. 55.

[103]Ibid., p. 52.

[104]NA, HS6/625, p. 15, memorandum of 12 October 1944.

[105]NA, HS6/623, p. 62, quoted in *Operation Foxley*, p. 15.

[106]Quoted in Rigden, op. cit., p. 52.

[107]Quoted in ibid., p. 58.

[108]Churchill to Major-General Ira Eaker, quoted in Hoffmann, op. cit., p. 194.

[109]Stafford, *Churchill*, p. 297.

[110]Martin Gilbert, *Winston S. Churchill*, Vol. VII (London, 1986), p. 868, House of Commons, 2 August 1944.

[111]Peter Conradi, *Hitler's Piano Player* (London, 2005), p. 291.

[112]Richard Harris Smith, *OSS: The Secret History of America's First Central Intelligence Agency* (London, 1972), p. 222.

[113]NA, AIR51/265, Operation Hellhound.

[114]K. Carter and R. Mueller, *The Army Air Forces of World War II* (Washington, DC, 1973), p. 488.

[115]NA, AIR51/220, Berchtesgaden.

[116]See Hoffmann, op. cit., p. 187, and Junge, op. cit., pp. 120–22.

Chapter 7

[1]Klemens von Klemperer, *German Resistance Against Hitler* (Oxford, 1992), p. 384.

[2]See Howard Reich, "Prisoner of Her Past," *Chicago Tribune*, 30 November 2003.

[3]Testimony of Hermann Gräbe at the Nuremberg Trial, *Trial of Major War Criminals Before the International Military Tribunal*, Vol. V (Nuremberg, 1947), pp. 696–99.

[4]See, for instance, Richard Rhodes, *Masters of Death* (Oxford, 2002), p. 114.

[5]Testimony of Hermann Gräbe, *Trial of Major War Criminals*.

[6]Gräebe's Nuremberg testimony, quoted in Gerald Reitlinger, *The SS: Alibi of a Nation, 1942–1945* (New York, 1957), p. 184.

[7]Alistair Horne, "Axel von dem Bussche," in Alistair Horne (ed.), *Telling Lives* (London, 2000), p. 218.

[8]*Stern*, "Die Radikalen sind fantasielos," Interview with Graf von der Groeben, 9 January 2003.

[9]Joachim Fest, *Plotting Hitler's Death* (London, 1997), p. 224.

[10]Peter Hoffmann, *German Resistance to Hitler* (London, 1988), p. 73.

[11]Richard Grunberger, *A Social History of the Third Reich* (London, 1971), p. 187.

[12]Helmut Krausnick, *Hitler's Einsatzgruppen* (Frankfurt/Main, 1985), p. 44.

[13]Major-General Helmuth Stieff quoted in Hans Rothfels, *Die deutsche Opposition gegen Hitler* (Zürich, 1994), p. 141.

[14]Christopher Browning, *Ordinary Men: Reserve Police Battalion 101 and the Final Solution in Poland* (London, 2001).

[15]See, for example, Omer Bartov, *Hitler's Army* (Oxford, 1992) or *Germany's War and the Holocaust* (London, 2003).

[16]Quoted in "Manstein" in Correlli Barnett (ed.), *Hitler's Generals* (London, 1989), p. 223.

[17]Quoted in Bodo Scheurig, *Henning von Tresckow* (Berlin, 2004 edition), p. 93.

[18]See, for instance, Christian Graf von Krockow, *Eine Frage der Ehre* (Berlin, 2002).

[19]Hans (Johnnie) von Herwarth, *Against Two Evils* (London, 1981), p. 254.

[20]Fabian von Schlabrendorff, *The Secret War Against Hitler* (London, 1966), pp. 267–68.

[21]Peter Hoffmann, *Hitler's Personal Security* (New York, 2000 edition), p. 123.

[22]Peter Hoffmann, *Stauffenberg* (London, 1995), p. 227.

[23]See Alexander Stahlberg, *Bounden Duty—The Memoirs of a German Officer 1932–45* (London, 1990), pp. 279–83.

[24]Schlabrendorff, op. cit., p. 234.

[25]Fest, op. cit., pp. 228–29.

[26]Peter Hoffmann, *The History of the German Resistance 1933–1945* (London, 1977), p. 114.

[27]Alan Clarke, *Barbarossa* (London, 1995 edition), p. 98.

[28]Fest, op. cit., p. 177.

[29]Quoted in Scheurig, op. cit., p. 71.

[30]Schlabrendorff, op. cit., p. 113.

[31]Quoted in Scheurig, op. cit., p. 110.

[32]J. Noakes and G. Pridham (eds.), *Nazism 1919–1945*, Vol. 3 (Exeter, 1988), p. 1090.

[33]Quoted in Scheurig, op. cit., p. 115.

[34]Christian Gerlach, "Männer des 20. Juli und der Krieg in der Sowjetunion," in Hannes Heer and Klaus Naumann (eds.), *Vernichtungskrieg: Verbrechen der Wehrmacht 1941–44* (Hamburg, 1995), p. 437.

[35]Schlabrendorff, op. cit., pp. 127–28.

[36]Ibid., p. 127.

[37]John Toland, *Hitler* (London, 1976), p. 696.

[38]Scheurig, op. cit., p. 136.

[39]Hoffmann, *Stauffenberg*, p. 117.

[40]Ibid., p. 133.

[41]Scheurig, op. cit., p. 127.

[42]Reinhard Gehlen, *The Gehlen Memoirs* (London, 1972), p. 101.

[43]Hoffmann, *Stauffenberg*, p. 151.

[44]Quoted in Michael Baigent and Richard Leigh, *Secret Germany—Claus von Stauffenberg and the Mystical Crusade Against Hitler* (London, 1994), pp. 127–28.

[45]John Wheeler-Bennett, *The Nemesis of Power* (London, 1961), p. 582.

[46]Joachim Kramarz, *Stauffenberg—The Life and Death of an Officer* (London, 1967), p. 134.

[47]Hoffmann, *Stauffenberg*, p. 154.

[48]See John Erickson, *The Road to Berlin* (London, 1983), pp. 47–48.

[49]Antonius John, *Philipp von Boeselager* (Bonn, 1994), p. 116.

[50]Ibid., p. 142.

[51]Stahlberg, op. cit., p. 281.

[52]Quoted in Fest, op. cit., p. 193.

[53]Schlabrendorff, op. cit., pp. 232–33.

[54]Rudolf-Christoph von Gersdorff, *Soldat im Untergang* (Berlin, 1977), pp. 127–28.

[55]Hans Gisevius, *To the Bitter End* (Cambridge, MA, 1947), p. 468.

[56]Scheurig, op. cit., p. 158.

[57]Schlabrendorff, op. cit., p. 236.

[58]Ibid., p. 237.

[59]See, for example, Fest, op. cit., p. 195.

[60]Gisevius, op. cit., p. 469.

[61]Gersdorff, op. cit., p. 129.

[62]Ibid., p. 130.

[63]Ibid., p. 132.

[64]Ibid., pp. 132–33. For English translation see Fest, op. cit., p. 196.

[65]Baigent and Leigh, op. cit., p. 6.

[66]Hoffmann, *Stauffenberg*, p. 181.

[67]Baigent and Leigh, op. cit., p. 7.

[68]Gersdorff, op. cit., p. 135.

[69]Quoted in Kramarz, op. cit., p. 104.

[70]Hoffmann, *Stauffenberg*, p. 227.

[71]Wheeler-Bennett, op. cit., p. 590.

[72]Hoffmann, *History*, p. 327.

[73]Schlabrendorff, op. cit., pp. 270–71.

[74]Fest, op. cit., p. 226.

[75]Frank Werner, "Eberhard von Breitenbuch," in *Gegen den Strom* (Bielefeld, 2005), p. 59.

[76]Scheurig, op. cit., p. 205.

[77]Werner, op. cit., p. 48.

[78]Stahlberg, op. cit., p. 298.

[79]Paul Adair, *Hitler's Greatest Defeat* (London, 1994), p. 171.

[80]Hugh Trevor-Roper (ed.), *Hitler's War Directives 1939–1945* (London, 1964), p. 222.

[81]Richard Overy, *The Dictators* (London, 2004), p. 20.

[82]Hoffmann, *Stauffenberg*, p. 239.

[83]Albert Speer, *Inside the Third Reich* (London, 1970), p. 509.

[84]Hoffmann, *History*, p. 380.

[85]Quoted in Kramarz, op. cit., p. 146.

[86]Speer, op. cit., p. 509.

[87]Fest, op. cit., p. 238.

[88]Gisevius, op. cit., pp. 507–12.

[89]Hoffmann, *Stauffenberg*, p. 256.

[90]Gisevius, op. cit., p. 510.

[91]Quoted in Hoffmann, *Stauffenberg*, op. cit., p. 243.

[92]M. R. D. Foot, *SOE: The Special Operations Executive 1940–1946* (London, 1984), pp. 72–73.

[93]Hoffmann, *Stauffenberg*, p. 258.

[94]Fest, op. cit., p. 247.

[95]Kramarz, op. cit., p. 155.

[96]Constantine Fitzgibbon, *The Shirt of Nessus* (London, 1956), p. 131.

[97]Quoted in Kramarz, op. cit., p. 157.

[98]Hoffmann, *History*, p. 379.

[99]Eberhard von Breitenbuch quoted in Fest, op. cit., p. 226.

[100]Hoffmann, *Stauffenberg*, p. 262.

[101]Fest, op. cit., p. 249.

[102]E. Korpalski, J. Szynkowski, and G. Wünsche, *Das Führerhauptquartier im Bild und in Erinnerungen von Zeitzeugen* (Kętrzyn, 2004), p. 110.

[103]See, for example, testimony of Kurt Salterberg in Guido Knopp, *Sie wollten Hitler töten* (Munich, 2004), p. 216.

[104]Walter Warlimont quoted in Hoffmann, *Stauffenberg*, p. 266.

[105]Kramarz, op. cit., p. 160.

[106]Walter Warlimont, *Inside Hitler's Headquarters* (London, 1964), p. 440.

[107]Traudl Junge, *Until the Final Hour* (London, 2003), p. 129.

[108]Fest, op. cit., p. 258.

[109]Ernst Günther Schenck, *Patient Hitler* (Augsburg, 2000), p. 301.

[110]Hoffmann, *History*, p. 404.

[111]Junge, op. cit., p. 130.

[112]Toland, op. cit., p. 801.

[113]Hoffmann, *Security*, p. 252.

[114]Nicolaus von Below, *At Hitler's Side* (London, 2001), p. 210.

[115]Hoffmann, *History*, p. 757.

[116]Schlabrendorff, op. cit., p. 287.

[117]Hoffmann, *Stauffenberg*, p. 270.

[118]Ibid., p. 269.

[119]Testimony of telephonist Alfons Schulz, quoted in Knopp, op. cit., p. 242.

[120]Speer, op. cit., p. 521.

[121]Quoted in Ian Kershaw, *Hitler: 1936–1945 Nemesis* (London, 2000), p. 677.

[122]Gisevius, op. cit., p. 554.

[123]Hoffmann, *Stauffenberg*, p. 276.

[124]Quoted in Gisevius, op. cit., p. 570.

[125]Ibid.

[126]Hoffmann, *Stauffenberg*, p. 277.

[127]Schlabrendorff, op. cit., pp. 294–95.

[128]Eberhard von Breitenbuch in S. Grabner and H. Röder (eds.), *Henning von Tresckow: Ich bin der Ich war* (Berlin, 2001), p. 60.

[129]Scheurig, op. cit., pp. 219–20.

[130]Schlabrendorff, op. cit., p. 313.

[131]Horne, op. cit., p. 218.

[132]Hoffmann, *History*, p. 332.

[133]Gerhard Schreiber, *Die italienischen Militärinternierten im deutschen Machtbereich 1943 bis 1945. Verraten—Verachtet—Vergessen* (Munich, 1990), p. 156.

[134]Hoffmann, *Stauffenberg*, p. 69.

[135]Klemperer, op. cit., p. 342, and Hoffmann, *Resistance*, p. 101.

[136]Klemperer, op. cit., pp. 382–83.

[137]See, for instance, Terence Prittie, *Germans Against Hitler* (London, 1964), p. 248.

[138]Hoffmann, *History*, p. 400.

[139]Gisevius, op. cit., p. 544.

[140]Fest, op. cit., p. 257.

[141]Gisevius, op. cit., p. 552.

[142]Prittie, op. cit., p. 248

[143]Hans Paar, *Dilettanten gegen Hitler* (Oldendorf, 1985), p. 172.

[144]Gersdorff, op. cit., pp. 130–31.

[145]Goebbels, quoted in Speer, op. cit., pp. 522–23.

[146]Junge, op. cit., p. 134.

[147]BBC Television, "Days That Shook the World" series, *Conspiracy to Kill: The Wolf's Lair,* broadcast 8 November 2004.

[148]Hoffmann, *History*, p. 380.

[149]Axel von dem Bussche quoted in Horne, op. cit., p. 219.

[150]Hoffmann, *Stauffenberg*, p. 104.

[151]Scheurig, op. cit., p. 74.

[152]Breitenbuch in Grabner and Röder, op. cit., p. 60.

[153]Ibid.

Chapter 8

[1]Albert Speer, *Inside the Third Reich* (London, 1970), pp. 574–75.

[2]See Norman Davies and Roger Moorhouse, *Microcosm* (London, 2002), p. 193.

[3]Sebastian Siebel-Achenbach, *Lower Silesia from Nazi Germany to Communist Poland 1942–49* (New York, 1994), p. 60.

[4]K. Jonca and A. Konieczny (eds.), *Paul Peikert—Festung Breslau in den Berichten eines Pfarrers* (Wrocław, 1998), p. 36.

[5]Ulrich Frodien, *Bleib Übrig* (Munich, 2002), p. 118.

[6]Jonca and Konieczny, op. cit., pp. 35–36.

[7]Ibid., p. 51.

[8]Ibid., p. 168.

[9]Speer, op. cit., p. 566.

[10]Quoted in Jonca and Konieczny, op. cit., p. 37.

[11]Quoted in Perry Biddiscombe, *The Last Nazis: SS Werewolf Guerrilla Resistance in Europe, 1944–1947* (Stroud, 2004), p. 38.

[12]Davies and Moorhouse, op. cit., p. 31.

[13]Ibid., p. 37.

[14]Horst Gleiss, *Breslauer Apokalypse 1945*, Vol. V (Wedel, 1986), p. 130.

[15]See Davies and Moorhouse, op. cit., p. 37.

[16]Gleiss, op. cit., p. 1094.

[17]Jonca and Konieczny, op. cit., p. 69.

[18]Hugh Trevor-Roper (ed.), *Hitler's War Directives 1939–1945* (London, 1964), pp. 293–94.

[19]Quoted in Sebastian Haffner, *The Meaning of Hitler* (New York, 1979), p. 160.

[20]Albert Speer, *Spandau—The Secret Diaries* (London, 1976), p. 200.

[21]Speer, *Inside*, p. 570.

[22]Joachim Fest, *Inside Hitler's Bunker* (London, 2004), p. 127.

[23]Speer, *Inside*, p. 541.

[24]Ibid.

[25]Haffner, op. cit., p. 153.

[26]Ian Kershaw, *Hitler: 1936–1945 Nemesis* (London, 2000), p. 500.

[27]Fest, *Bunker*, p. 77.

[28]N. Cameron and R. H. Stevens (trans.), *Hitler's Table Talk, 1941–1944* (London, 2000 edition), p. 147.

[29]Quoted in Fest, *Bunker*, p. 31.

[30]Quoted in Kershaw, op. cit., p. 780.

[31]Quoted in Haffner, op. cit., pp. 159–60.

[32]Speer, *Inside*, p. 571.

[33]Joseph Goebbels, *Tagebücher*, Vol. XV, p. 500 (14 March 1945).

[34]Joachim Fest, *The Face of the Third Reich* (London, 1970), p. 309.

[35]Joachim Fest, *Speer: The Final Verdict* (London, 2001), p. 193.

[36]Ibid., p. 204.

[37]Speer, *Inside*, p. 458.

[38]Richard Overy, *Interrogations* (London, 2001), p. 460.

[39]Speer, *Inside*, p. 538.

[40]Ibid., p. 539.

[41]Gitta Sereny, *Albert Speer: His Battle with Truth* (London, 1995), p. 482.

[42]Quoted in Overy, op. cit., p. 460.

[43]Fest, *Speer*, p. 232.

[44]Hugh Trevor-Roper, *The Last Days of Hitler*, 7th edition (London, 2002), p. 70.

[45]Quoted in Fest, *Face*, p. 307.

[46]Gitta Sereny, correspondence with the author, 4 November 2004.

[47]Sereny, *Speer*, p. 138.

[48]Quoted in ibid., p. 422.

[49]Quoted in Fest, *Speer*, p. 218.

[50]Adolf Hitler, *Mein Kampf* (London, 1939 edition), pp. 501–02.

[51]Ibid., p. 91.

[52]Speer, *Inside*, p. 574.

[53]Ibid.

[54]Quoted in Sereny, op. cit., p. 477.

[55]Speer, *Inside*, p. 575.

[56]National Archive (London) (hereafter NA), FO1078/236, Dieter Stahl Interrogation Report, 10 November 1945, p. 5.

[57]Quoted in Sereny, op. cit., p. 477.

[58]See Robert Harris and Jeremy Paxman, *A Higher Form of Killing* (London, 1982), pp. 53–57.

[59]Ibid., p. 62.

[60]NA, Stahl Interrogation, op. cit., p. 6.

[61]Speer, *Inside,* p. 576.

[62]Ibid., p. 577.

[63]Trevor-Roper, op. cit., p. 72.

[64]Quoted in Sereny, op. cit., p. 486.

[65]Speer, *Inside,* p. 577.

[66]NA, Stahl Interrogation, op. cit., p. 7.

[67]Speer, *Inside,* p. 622.

[68]Quoted in Sereny, op. cit., p. 507.

[69]Speer, *Inside,* pp. 622–23.

[70]Ibid., p. 659 and Sereny, op. cit., p. 511.

[71]Speer, *Inside,* p. 575.

[72]Trevor-Roper, op. cit., p. 215.

[73]Airey Neave, *Nuremberg* (London, 1978), pp. 138, 144.

[74]Speer, *Inside,* p. 689.

[75]*The Trial of the Major War Criminals Before the International Military Tribunal* (London, 1946), Vol. XVII, p. 32, testimony of Albert Speer, 20 June 1946.

[76]Ann Tusa and John Tusa, *The Nuremberg Trial* (London, 1983), p. 399.

[77]NA, Stahl Interrogation, op. cit., p. 6.

[78]Sereny, op. cit., p. 473.

[79]Matthias Schmidt, *Albert Speer, The End of a Myth* (London, 1985), p. 124.

[80]Dan van der Vat, *The Good Nazi—The Life and Lies of Albert Speer* (London, 1997), pp. 222–23.

[81]Fest, *Speer,* p. 246.

[82]See, for instance, Speer, *Inside,* p. 464.

[83]Ibid., p. 577.

[84]Peter Hoffmann, *Hitler's Personal Security* (New York, 2000 edition), p. 261.

[85]Anton Joachimsthaler, *The Last Days of Hitler* (London, 1996), p. 39.

[86]Walter Warlimont, *Inside Hitler's Headquarters* (London, 1964), p. 442.

[87]Van der Vat, op. cit., p. 157.

[88]Robert Conot, *Justice at Nuremberg* (London, 1983), pp. 496–97.

[89]Speer, *Inside,* p. 689.

[90]Sereny, op. cit., p. 570.

[91]Overy, op. cit., pp. 469–71.

[92]Quoted in ibid., p. 139.

[93]Tusa and Tusa, op. cit., p. 460.

[94]*Trial of the Major War Criminals,* op. cit., Vol. XXIII, p. 124, judgment regarding Albert Speer, 1 October 1946.

[95]Fest, *Speer,* p. 9.

[96]Sereny, op. cit., p. 478.

[97]Speer, *Inside,* p. 682.

[98]Schmidt, op. cit., p. 125.

[99]Quoted in Sereny, op. cit., p. 478.

[100]Peter Hoffmann, *The History of the German Resistance 1933–1945* (London, 1977), p. 368.

[101]Quoted in Tusa and Tusa, op. cit., p. 460.

[102]Neave, op. cit., p. 149.

[103]Speer, *Spandau,* p. 65.

[104]Albert Speer, *Alles, was ich weiß* (Munich, 2000), p. 50.

[105]Speer, *Spandau,* p. 399.

[106]Quoted in Trevor-Roper, op. cit., p. 74.

[107]Speer, *Inside,* pp. 635–41.

[108]Speer, *Spandau,* p. 215.

[109]Quoted in Gitta Sereny, *The German Trauma* (London, 2000), p. 284.

[110]Speer, *Spandau,* p. 211.

Epilogue

[1]Marie-Claude Vaillant-Couturier quoted in Sigrid Jacobeit (ed.), *Ich grüße Euch als freier Mensch* (Fürstenburg, 1995), p. 162.

[2]Joachim Fest, *Inside Hitler's Bunker* (London, 2004), p. 31.

[3]Antony Beevor, *Berlin: The Downfall 1945* (London, 2002), p. 410.

[4]Ibid., p. 371.

[5]Michael Foedrowitz, *The Flak Towers in Berlin, Hamburg and Vienna, 1940–1950* (Atglen, PA, 1998), p. 7.

[6]Cornelius Ryan, *The Last Battle* (London, 1966), pp. 381–82.

[7]Beevor, op. cit., p. 352.

[8]John Erickson, *The Road to Berlin* (London, 1983), p. 599.

[9]Quoted in Beevor, op. cit., p. 355.

[10]Peter Hoffmann, *Hitler's Personal Security* (New York, 2000 edition), p. 261.

[11]Nerin E. Gun, *Eva Braun* (London, 1968), p. 261.

[12]Traudl Junge, *Until the Final Hour* (London, 2003), p. 176.

[13]Ibid., p. 178.

[14]Quoted in Fest, op. cit., p. viii.

[15]Quoted in Franz Siedler and Dieter Zeigert, *Hitler's Secret Headquarters* (London, 2004), p. 177.

[16]See, for example, Ernst Günther Schenck, *Patient Hitler* (Augsburg, 2000), pp. 199–200, and L. Heston and R. Heston, *The Medical Casebook of Adolf Hitler* (New York, 1979), chapter 5.

[17]Ernst Günther Schenck quoted in James P. O'Donnell, *The Berlin Bunker* (London, 1979), pp. 139–40.

[18]Walter Warlimont, *Inside Hitler's Headquarters* (London, 1964), p. 462.

[19]National Archives (London), Liddell Diaries, KV4/195, p. 138, description by General Dietrich von Choltitz.

[20]Schenck quoted in O'Donnell, op. cit., pp. 136–37.

[21]Traudl Junge quoted in Gitta Sereny, *Albert Speer: His Battle with Truth* (London, 1995), p. 533.

[22]Quoted in Fest, op. cit., p. 23.

[23]Hugh Trevor-Roper, *The Last Days of Hitler,* 7th edition (London, 2002), p. 143.

[24]See, for example, ibid., pp. 105–6, or Joachim Fest, op. cit., pp. 62–64.

[25]Fegelein, SS liaison officer to the Reich Chancellery, had married Eva Braun's sister Gretl in 1944. He was executed on the night of Hitler's wedding.

[26]Fest, op. cit., p. 92.

[27]Trevor-Roper, op. cit., p. 124.

[28]Albert Speer, *Inside the Third Reich* (London, 1970), p. 639.

[29]Quoted in Sereny, op. cit., p. 530.

[30]Speer, op. cit., p. 647.

[31]See www.ess.uwe.ac.uk/documents/poltest/htm.

[32]Quoted in Alan Bullock, *Hitler: A Study in Tyranny,* revised edition (London, 1962), p. 794.

[33]Junge, op. cit., p. 184.

[34]Ibid., p. 186.

[35]Ian Kershaw, *Hitler: 1936–1945 Nemesis* (London, 2000), p. 825.

[36]Fest, op. cit., p. 107.

[37]John Toland, *Hitler* (London, 1997 edition), p. 886.

[38]Junge, op. cit., p. 186.

[39]See Anton Joachimsthaler, *The Last Days of Hitler* (London, 1996), pp. 153–54.

Index